Sonja E. Klocke, Jennifer R. Hosek (Ed.)
Christa Wolf

Companions to Contemporary German Culture

Edited by
Michael Eskin · Karen Leeder · Christopher Young

Volume 8

Christa Wolf

A Companion

Edited by
Sonja E. Klocke and Jennifer R. Hosek

DE GRUYTER

FSC
www.fsc.org

MIX
Papier aus verantwor-
tungsvollen Quellen
FSC® C016439

ISBN 978-3-11-049199-9
e-ISBN (PDF) 978-3-11-049600-0
e-ISBN (EPUB) 978-3-11-049345-0
ISSN 2193-9659

Library of Congress Cataloging-in-Publication Data
A CIP catalog record for this book has been applied for at the Library of Congress.

Bibliographic information published by the Deutsche Nationalbibliothek
The Deutsche Nationalbibliothek lists this publication in the Deutsche Nationalbibliografie;
detailed bibliographic data are available on the Internet at http://dnb.dnb.de.

© 2018 Walter de Gruyter GmbH, Berlin/Boston
Cover image: Christa Wolf. Demonstration on the Alexanderplatz, Berlin on 4 November 1989.
© akg-images / ddrbildarchiv.de / Manfred Uhlenhut
Printing and binding: Hubert & Co. GmbH & Co. KG, Göttingen
♾ Printed on acid-free paper
Printed in Germany

www.degruyter.com

Table of Contents

A Note on Translations

Quotations from Christa Wolf's work are given in German and English. In general, contributors' quotes in English refer to official English translations provided in the bibliography, unless no official translation existed, or if they needed to work with their own translation to make a particular linguistic or formal point. Each contributor acknowledges the translations used in their endnotes or highlights their own translations. All translations, whether official or undertaken by the contributors, follow the relevant German quotation in square brackets. The primary aim is to provide an accessible working translation.

To avoid unnecessary repetition, however, the titles of Christa Wolf's main works are given in German only. The titles of individual essays and poems are given both in German and in English throughout. For ease of reference, a list of translations of these main works is included here, and a more detailed Select Bibliography is given at the end of the volume.

Moskauer Novelle (1961)
[Moscow Novella]

Der geteilte Himmel (1963)
[*The Divided Heaven* (1965)]

Juninachmittag (1967)
['June Afternoon' in *What Remains and other Stories* (1993)]

Nachdenken über Christa T. (1968)
[The Quest for Christa T. (1970)]

Neue Lebensansichten eines Katers (1973)
['The New Life and Opinions of a Tomcat' in *What Remains and Other Stories* (1993)]

Kindheitsmuster (1976)
[*A Model Childhood*; *Patterns of Childhood* (1980)]

Kein Ort. Nirgends (1979)
[*No Place On Earth* (1982)]

Kassandra. Vier Vorlesungen – Eine Erzählung (1983)
[*Cassandra. A Novel and Four Essays* (1984)]

Störfall. Nachrichten eines Tages (1987)
[*Accident. A Day's News* (1989)]

Sommerstück (1989)
[Summer Play]

Was bleibt. Erzählung (1990)
['What Remains' in *What Remains and other Stories* (1993)]

Medea. Stimmen (1996)
[*Medea. A Modern Retelling* (1998)]

https://doi.org/10.1515/9783110496000-001

Leibhaftig (2002)
[*In the Flesh* (2005)]

Ein Tag im Jahr. 1960–2000 (2003)
[*One Day a Year. 1960–2000* (2007)]

Stadt der Engel oder The Overcoat of Dr. Freud (2010)
[*City of Angels. Or, The Overcoat of Dr. Freud* (2013)]

August (2012)
[*August* (2014)]

Ein Tag im Jahr im neuen Jahrhundert (2013)
[*27 September. One Day a Year* (2017)]

Sonja E. Klocke and Jennifer R. Hosek
Introduction: Reading Christa Wolf in the Twenty-First Century

Following a period of relative silence, Christa Wolf (1929–2011) was recognized for her oeuvre with several major prizes just before she passed away. Among these were the prestigious Thomas-Mann-Preis and the Uwe-Johnson-Preis (both 2010), as well as the Hörkules (2011) for her last novel, *Stadt der Engel* (2010) – an audience award that speaks particularly to the ongoing and even re-vived interest of a large Wolf fan base.[1] This influential figure was and is cele-brated not only nationally, but also internationally. The author of world-famous prose texts such as *Nachdenken über Christa T.* (1968), *Kindheitsmuster* (1976), *Kein Ort. Nirgends* (1979), *Kassandra* (1983) and *Medea. Stimmen* (1996) – all available in English translation – is considered by many to have been *the* pan-German writer. She not only occupied a central position in the literature of the GDR [the German Democratic Republic; East Germany], but also in public life and, until 1965, in GDR politics.

In order to appreciate Wolf's significance for the literature and culture of the socialist state, as well as for GDR citizens who had to deal with everyday life under socialism, it is vital to understand the political, social and cultural con-texts in which her writings developed – from the implications of World War II and the Nazi regime to the meanings of the fall of the Wall in 1989 and German unification just a year later. To this end, this introduction provides an overview of the most relevant political occurrences in the GDR as they pertain to develop-ments in cultural production, sketches the shape and influence of the GDR's 'cul-ture industry', including the East German film agency, the DEFA, and highlights the relationships of artists – and particularly Wolf's relationship – to the social-ist state. It traces Wolf's unique role in the socialist East and in post-unification

---

1 From 1961, when Wolf received the Kunstpreis der Stadt Halle and shortly afterwards the Hein-rich-Mann-Preis (1963) and the 'Nationalpreis 3. Klasse der DDR' (1964), the author grew accus-tomed to receiving literary awards fairly regularly. The 1970s and 1980s, in particular, also brought – in addition to further GDR prizes, among them the very prestigious Nationalpreis 1. Klasse der DDR (1987) – a great deal of recognition from both West Germany (the FRG; Federal Republic of Germany) and Austria, most notably the Georg-Büchner-Preis (1980) and the Öster-reichischer Staatspreis für Europäische Literatur (1985). Following German unification in Octo-ber 1990, interest in Wolf's literary work slowed down and only began to intensify again towards the end of the twentieth century, as evidenced in awards such as the Elisabeth-Langgässer-Lite-raturpreis, the Samuel-Bogumil-Linde-Preis and the Nelly-Sachs-Preis (all awarded in 1999).

https://doi.org/10.1515/9783110496000-002

Germany, particularly also in the so-called literary debate of the early 1990s, which ensnared her and proved significant for her reception post-1989. This introduction sets the stage for the investigations of this volume regarding the current and continuing relevance of Wolf's oeuvre within and outside of Germany, and within the context of world literature.

From the League of German Girls (BdM) to the Socialist Unity Party (SED)

Born in Landsberg/Warthe, what is today Gorzów Wielkopolski in Poland, on 18 March 1929, Christa Wolf left her hometown as a teenager, during the last days of World War II, for Mecklenburg-Vorpommern, a northeastern German state. Her efforts to be useful in society – she initially worked as a typist for the mayor of Gammelin and returned to school in Schwerin in 1946 – were impeded by a serious illness, for which she was admitted to a sanatorium for consumptives. It seems that in 1946, she developed a pattern that would shape her entire life: she would retreat into illness as a means of protection against psychological and physical strain. Aware of this paradigm, the author later employs it in her writing, in which most of her protagonists – from Rita in *Der geteilte Himmel* (1963) to the nameless narrator-protagonist in *Stadt der Engel oder The Overcoat of Dr. Freud* (2010) – react physically to stressful situations, particularly when these are brought about by political events.[2] Despite these physical challenges, Wolf graduated in 1949 from Gymnasium [high school] in Bad Frankenhausen am Kyffhäuser with an Abitur [the diploma necessary for university admission] and joined the SED [Sozialistische Einheitspartei Deutschlands; the Socialist Unity Party]. In the same year, she took up the study of German literature in Jena and Leipzig, finishing her degree in 1953.

How can we explain the early and rather swift decision of this former member of the Nazi youth organization BdM [Bund deutscher Mädel; the League of German Girls] in Hitler's Germany to join the socialist party in the GDR? Having

---

2 In an interview with Therese Hörnigk, Wolf admitted that it was characteristic for her 'eine solche Kluft zwischen Anspruch und Leistung nicht zu lange ertragen zu können' [not to be able to endure such a rift between demand and accomplishment for long], so that her 'Körper wehrt sich notfalls mit Krankheit' [body defends itself, in a pinch also with illness]. Christa Wolf, 'Unerledigte Widersprüche. Gespräch mit Therese Hörnigk' (1987/1988), in *Reden im Herbst* (Berlin/Weimar: Aufbau, 1990), pp. 24–68 (p. 32). Also see Sonja Klocke, *Inscription and Rebellion. Illness and the Symptomatic Body in East German Literature* (Rochester, NY: Camden House, 2015), pp. 34–113.

experienced the realities of war and its corollaries in a family that supported Hitler, Wolf trusted in the GDR's founding narrative. Positioned on the frontlines of the Cold War, both German states – the western FRG under American, British, and French influence, and the eastern GDR under Soviet rule – developed their own master narratives, complemented by a biased image of their respective counterpart, to support their individual claims to have drawn the right conclusions from the catastrophe of National Socialist rule. While Western propaganda, financed by the FRG government and the American defence department, collapsed Nazi terror and Communist dictatorship into a rhetoric of totalitarianism, the SED claimed that the GDR presented the only alternative to capitalism and National Socialism. Indeed, National Socialism was considered an outgrowth of the imperialist capitalist system.[3] The FRG's 'strong personal ties with the Third Reich' buttressed this understanding.[4] For instance, continuities in the staffing of leadership roles in government, the judiciary and business in the FRG influenced the GDR in declaring the capitalist West the exclusive successor of National Socialism, while they positioned themselves as the legitimate heir to the anti-fascist resistance to Nazi rule. In other words, the SED legitimated its claims to power through the discourse of anti-fascism.

Accordingly, Wolf came to regard socialism as the only feasible means of creating a better future after the catastrophe of the Nazi past – a premise she reiterated consistently, even after the fall of the Wall and well into the twenty-first century. She consistently placed herself and her work in the tradition of this founding narrative of the GDR as well. In *Stadt der Engel*, for example, the narrator – who strongly resembles the author – aligns herself with those anti-fascists who escaped Nazi Germany and found a home in California. Years after the socialist state had come to an end, Wolf's alter ego places herself in the tradition of the GDR's founding narrative when she affiliates with the descendants of German-Jewish and communist emigrants who were forced to flee Nazi Germany. Consistent with the political beliefs Wolf embraced during her post-World

---

[3] One powerful illustration of this position is Peter Weiss's *Die Ermittlung* [*The Investigation*], a documentary play that reconstructs the Frankfurt Auschwitz Trials using the court transcripts. Born in Germany, Peter Weiss fled the Nazis with his family and spent most of his life in Sweden. Peter Weiss, *Die Ermittlung. Oratorium in 11 Gesängen* (Frankfurt a. M.: Suhrkamp, 1965).

[4] Thomas Ahbe, 'Competing Master Narratives. Geschichtspolitik and Identity Discourse in Three German Societies', in *The GDR Remembered. Representations of the East German State Since 1989*, ed. by Nick Hodgin and Caroline Pearce (Rochester, NY: Camden House, 2011), pp. 221–249 (p. 222).

War II life, in the twenty-first century, she also positions herself as a GDR writer and anti-fascist.[5]

In a 1980s interview with Therese Hörnigk, Wolf explained that for her personally, and for her entire generation, socialism presented the only alternative to fascism. This specific GDR anti-fascism allowed them to engage with the reality that although they had been too young to actually participate in National Socialism, circumstances could have been different: in other words, they had narrowly escaped being directly culpable, and they should see this situation as a responsibility.

> Als wir fünfzehn, sechzehn waren, mußten wir uns [...] von denen abstoßen, die in diesen zwölf Jahren [des Faschismus] [...] schuldig geworden waren. Wir mussten diejenigen entdecken, die Opfer geworden waren, diejenigen, die Widerstand geleistet hatten. [...] Identifizieren konnten wir uns natürlich auch mit ihnen nicht, dazu hatten wir kein Recht. Das heißt, als wir sechzehn waren, konnten wir uns mit niemandem identifizieren. Dies ist eine wesentliche Aussage für meine Generation.[6]

> [When we were fifteen, sixteen, (...) we had to reject those who, in these twelve years [of fascism], had (...) become guilty (...) We had to discover those who had been victims, those who had resisted. (...) Naturally we couldn't identify with them either; we had no right to. That means, when we were sixteen, we could not identify with anyone. This is a crucial statement for my generation.]

Here, Wolf not only explains her own decision to dedicate her life and energy to the socialist project, but she shifts the emphasis from individual experience to her claim to speak for East Germans of her generation, often identified as '1929ers'[7] because they were all affected by the experience of fascism, and

---

5 On this aspect of Wolf's *Stadt der Engel*, see Elisabeth Herrmann, 'Weltbürgertum und nationale Verstrickung in Christa Wolf's *Stadt der Engel oder The Overcoat of Dr. Freud*', *Triangulum. Germanistisches Jahrbuch 2015 für Estland, Lettland und Litauen*, 21 (2016), 459–468; Sonja E. Klocke, 'Patientin unter Palmen. Symptomatische Körper, Leiden und Heilung in Christa Wolfs Stadt der Engel oder The Overcoat of Dr. Freud', *Triangulum. Germanistisches Jahrbuch 2015 für Estland, Lettland und Litauen*, 21 (2016), 469–480.
6 Wolf, 'Unerledigte Widersprüche', p. 29.
7 Mary Fulbrook, *Dissonant Lives. Generations and Violence Through the German Dictatorships* (Oxford: Oxford University Press, 2011). Fulbrook employs the term '1929ers' in her analysis of this generation's significance for the building of the GDR. She explains that her research on the 1929ers was initially provoked by a joke she heard repeatedly, 'to the effect that "Christa Wolf was born in 1929, like everyone else in the GDR"' (p. 252); see also Dorothee Wierling, 'How Do the 1929ers and the 1949ers Differ?', in *Power and Society in the GDR, 1961–1979. The 'Normalisation of Rule?'*, ed. by Mary Fulbrook (New York: Berghahn, 2009), pp. 204–219 (p. 205–208); Thomas Ahbe and Rainer Gries, 'Gesellschaftsgeschichte als Generationengeschichte. Theoretische und methodologische Überlegungen zum Beispiel DDR', in *Die DDR*

later of socialism. Vicarious culpability and separation from those in their parent generation, with whom Wolf and her peers could not identify due to their attitudes and actions during World War II, play a significant role. In Wolf's *Der geteilte Himmel* (1963), for example, Manfred, a representative of the 1929ers, articulates his desire to distance himself from his parents' generation. He explicitly asks Rita why this generation does not want to admit that Manfred's generation has, in a way, grown up without parents, for this 'perpetrator' generation has lost the authority to provide moral guidance (p. 17).

Finding Their Place in the GDR: Christa Wolf's Generation

Wolf and her GDR colleagues, who were born in the late 1920s (such as Günter de Bruyn, Günter Görlich, Hermann Kant, Erich Loest, Heiner Müller and Werner Heiduczek) and who emerged in the 1960s, also had to position themselves vis-à-vis another part of the 'parent generation' – the anti-fascists. These authors – often Jewish and/or communist survivors of Nazi concentrations camps or returning exiles, such as Johannes R. Becher, Bertolt Brecht, Willi Bredel, Eduard Claudius, Otto Gotsche, Stephan Hermlin, Anna Seghers and Stefan Heym – had been supported by the GDR government from the start, with the expectation that they imbue their literature with social and political meaning. Since they identified with the GDR and its ideology, their writings – which largely followed the requirements of socialist realism – reflected the favoured values and norms.[8] Considering themselves *Dichter im Dienst* [poets on duty], their fiction served as an effective means of educating the citizens and of convincing them of the legitimacy of the socialist state.[9] With their *Aufbauliteratur* [construction literature], they helped define GDR identity by developing modes of writing that praised workers in factories in a series of *Aufbauromane* [construction novels], which were published primarily between 1952 and 1956.

---

aus generationengeschichtlicher Perspektive. Eine Inventur, ed. by Annegret Schüle, Thomas Ahbe and Rainer Gries (Leipzig: Leipziger Universitätsverlag, 2006), pp. 475–571 (p. 481).

8 Socialist Realism as the required mode of writing in socialist societies was first formulated in the Soviet Union in the early 1930s and later advanced by Georg Lukács. Linking Hegel, the norms of the Weimar classic and (bourgeois) realism of the nineteenth century, Lukács emphasized an 'objective' portrayal of life and of types rather than specific characters. See Wolfgang Emmerich, *Kleine Literaturgeschichte der DDR. Erweiterte Neuausgabe*, reprint (Berlin: Aufbau, 2000), pp. 118–124 and pp. 174–175.

9 Günther Deicke, quoted in Emmerich, *Kleine Literaturgeschichte der DDR*, p. 404.

Moreover, these 'poets on duty' perpetuated the GDR's founding narrative of anti-fascism by celebrating the Communist martyrdom of anti-fascist resistance heroes and Red Army liberators. These early prose texts presented those who accepted the Soviet offer of redemption in the shape of socialist re-education with the opportunity to discursively associate with the resistance to and the victims of National Socialism. These foundational GDR texts and their way of describing social relations as family relations proved to be influential for the next generation of writers, who, like Wolf, had been teenagers in 1945. These fictional texts offered them a chance to replace their biological, sometimes Nazi-collaborator parents with the imaginary, anti-fascist parental figures of early GDR literature; in Wolf's case, the author Anna Seghers in particular played the role of a Jewish and Communist mother figure.[10]

Arriving in the Reality of GDR Socialism

Despite all efforts, *Aufbauliteratur* was in crisis by the end of the 1950s, not least because of the distance between most of its authors and the quotidian life of production workers. This target readership could not identify with the resultant works, and therefore this literature did not succeed in boosting worker morale or supporting ever-higher productivity quotas. At the Fifth Party Convention of the SED in July 1958, Walter Ulbricht, the first General Secretary of the Central Committee of the SED (1950–1971) and the head of state as chairman of the state council (1960–1973), demanded an overcoming of 'die Trennung zwischen Kunst und Leben, die Entfremdung zwischen Künstler und Volk, die in der bürgerlichen Gesellschaft so katastrophale Ausmaße erreicht haben' [the division between art and life, the alienation between artists and the people, which has reached catastrophic dimensions in bourgeois society].[11] As a result, one of the most significant publishers in the GDR, the Mitteldeutscher Verlag in Halle, called for the first Bitterfelder Konferenz to be held in the industrial town of Bitterfeld in April 1959. About 150 professional writers and approximately 300 writing workers met to discuss strategies for merging literature and (factory) life, mental and manual work, and material needs and ethical maxims.

---

10 Wolf, 'Unerledigte Widersprüche', p. 29. For an introduction to 'Aufbauliteratur', see Emmerich, *Kleine Literaturgeschichte der DDR*, pp. 113–173; for a detailed analysis of the function of 'Aufbauliteratur', see Julia Hell, *Post-Fascist Fantasies. Psychoanalysis, History, and the Literature of East Germany* (Durham, NC: Duke University Press, 1997).
11 *Dokumente zur Kunst-, Literatur- und Kulturpolitik der SED Vol. 1. 1946–1970*, ed. by Elimar Schubbe (Stuttgart: Seewald, 1972), p. 535.

They adhered to a double strategy. Following the motto 'Greif zur Feder, Kumpel, die sozialistische Nationalliteratur braucht dich!' [Seize the pen, pal, socialist national literature needs you!], they inspired workers to write. In their fiction, they were to document their struggles on the path to progress and to foreground the success of socialist production. This approach was also meant to support the socialist ideal of workers who were comfortable with 'high culture'. As a result, hundreds of *Zirkel schreibender Arbeiter* [Workers Writing Circles] developed. Here, blue- and white-collar workers alike collaborated in producing texts that were generated from their experiences and served their interests. The other strategy aimed at writers of fiction. Abiding by the call 'Schriftsteller in die Betriebe!' [Writers into the factories!], authors were encouraged to work with brigades in factories. It was hoped that, having gained firsthand knowledge about life and work in production facilities, writers could then adequately portray them in their fiction. Only rarely were experienced authors willing to exchange their pens for power tools in support of these efforts, among them Franz Fühmann, Brigitte Reimann and Christa Wolf.

Wolf turned her experiences in a brigade in the Waggonbauwerk Ammendorf [Ammendorf Railway Car Factory] – where she and her husband, Gerhard Wolf, also led a Workers Writing Circle – into her first literary success, *Der geteilte Himmel*. Connected with the tradition of the Bitterfeld conference, this novel simultaneously points to the next stages in the development of GDR literature and of Wolf's writing in particular. Similarly to Brigitte Reimann, who turned to the tradition of the *Bildungsroman* – a novel centring on the education and maturing of a protagonist – for her 1961 novel *Ankunft im Alltag* [*Arrival in Everyday Life*], Wolf places the development of a young woman at the centre of *Der geteilte Himmel*. Like Reimann's heroine, Wolf's Rita must endure an extended period of growth and learning before achieving arrival in an actualized 'everyday'. At this point, both authors believed in advancing the proposition that individuals could find their place in the existing reality of socialism through reasonable adaptation. Named after Reimann's novel, such *Ankunftsliteratur* [literature of arrival] transmits a sense of arrival in GDR society following the building of the Wall in August 1961. Typically, the heroes and heroines move beyond their dreams about socialism to a realistic assessment of the possibilities in the GDR, leading to a happy ending.

Der geteilte Himmel's characterization as *Ankunftsliteratur* remains debated, as Curtis Swope's and Anna Kuhn's contributions in this volume accentuate.[12] In

---

12 For a short introduction to 'Ankunftsliteratur', see Emmerich, *Kleine Literaturgeschichte der DDR*, p. 176. Contrary to the majority of scholars, Julia Hell and Renate Rechtien challenge the

this novel, Wolf bridges the gap between showing the officially desired, objective reality of work in a brigade and employing new writing strategies and messages that move beyond socialist realism. For instance, she forgoes linear narration and an omniscient narrator in favour of allowing her readers a more differentiated view of the protagonist's motivations. Although Wolf received the GDR's Heinrich Mann Prize for this novel in 1963, *Der geteilte Himmel* was controversial in East Germany – not least because, as Anna Kuhn's investigation points out, it broadened the parameters of what was acceptable in GDR literature.

The 'Clean-Sweep Plenum' of 1965

With *Der geteilte Himmel*, Wolf had clearly departed from the tradition of *Aufbauliteratur* and thus from her literary parent generation. As is typical of parent-child relationships, the rapport between these two generations was not entirely unclouded. Wolf characterized these constructed family relationships as unhealthy dependencies, since the authority of these parental figures and the GDR's political path could never be questioned.[13] Still, authors like Wolf, who had experienced National Socialism and World War II as children and adolescents, largely agreed with the first generation of GDR writers when it came to welcoming the construction of the Berlin Wall in 1961. After all, by diminishing the pressure of constant, direct confrontation with the West, the Wall's existence led to a more relaxed political atmosphere, held promise for a more tenable economic base and furthered societal modernization.[14]

Yet this period of relative openness was short-lived; a quiet, substantive conflict between the first and the second generation of writers as well as between artists and politicians emerged during the infamous Eleventh Plenum of the Central Committee of the ruling SED in 1965, also known as the *Kahlschlag-Plenum* [clean-sweep plenum]. At this party meeting, Erich Honecker, who later became the General Secretary of the Central Committee of the SED (1971–1989) and the

---

categorization of *Der geteilte Himmel* as 'Ankunftsliteratur', and the authors of the present Introduction agree. See Hell, *Post-Fascist Fantasies*, p. 165; Renate Rechtien, 'The Topography of the Self in Christa Wolf's *Der geteilte Himmel*', *German Life and Letters*, 63.4 (2010), 475–489 (pp. 477–478); Sonja Klocke, '(Anti-)faschistische Familien und (post-)faschistische Körper – Christa Wolfs *Der geteilte Himmel*', in *Christa Wolf im Strom der Erinnerung*, ed. by Carsten Gansel, with Sonja Klocke (Göttingen: V&R unipress, 2014), pp. 69–87.

13 Wolf, 'Unerledigte Widersprüche', pp. 29–30.

14 Mary Fulbrook, *The People's State. East German Society from Hitler to Honecker* (New Haven: Yale University Press, 2005), p. 37.

head of state as chairman of the state council (1976–1989), announced that scepticism and the development of socialism were mutually incompatible. His words officially put an end to any tendencies that he and his comrades associated with liberalism and the West. They may have functioned to divert attention away from increasing economic difficulties and were used to justify banning artistic works – perhaps most famously several films in the making and some that had already been produced, such as Kurt Maetzig's *Das Kaninchen bin ich* [*The Rabbit Is Me*].

Readers most familiar with box-office and advertisement-driven film industries should note that many nations publicly fund artistic production. This practice may seek to enable more variegated artistic expression than the market alone. It certainly recognizes the relationship between art and education, as alluded to in the above-described debates around *Ankunftsliteratur*, *Aufbauliteratur* and the *Bitterfelder Weg*. In the GDR as well, considerations other than profit drove cultural production; and, as a costly medium, film was particularly influenced by government stipulations.

Christa Wolf is best known as an author of literature, but she also adapted her fiction for cinema and wrote screenplays; her contributions to film were subject to state influence as well. Wolf and her husband wrote the screenplay for the film version of *Der geteilte Himmel*. Directed by Konrad Wolf, it premiered in 1964 and at first was deemed to support GDR ideology, despite its challenging aesthetics. The East German DEFA film expert Ralf Schenk describes the spirit in the studio during production as one of constructive critique of society and underscores that the 1963 GDR Youth Commission had made explicit its desire to involve the younger generation in social and political decision-making.[15] However, *Der geteilte Himmel's* distribution license was not renewed after it was criticized at the Eleventh Plenum for its depiction of undocumented emigration. Kurt Bartels's *Fräulein Schmetterling*, planned for 1966, for which Christa and Gerhard Wolf had also written the screenplay, was blocked entirely. Shortly after these disillusioning events, Christa Wolf went to work for the DEFA studios again, this time on Joachim Kunert's film adaptation of Anna Seghers's *Die Toten bleiben jung*, a novel thematizing the development of national socialism in Germany, which premiered in 1968. In the early 1970s, she became involved in *Till Eulenspiegel*, a film about a character understood as a proto-socialist hero of the Middle Ages; however, the film was only completed in 1975, by Rainer Simon, in a very different form from that which was originally intended. Peter Vogel's filming of Wolf's short story *Selbstversuch* was broadcast on GDR television in January 1990, and three months later on West German television's ZDF. The recent *Christa*

---

15 Ibid.

Wolf-Handbuch. Leben – Werk – Wirkung offers an extensive and definitive re-counting of Christa's Wolf's productions and reception.[16]

As this description of events suggests, the Eleventh Plenum was a momen-tous event in GDR socialism, one that lastingly influenced Wolf's relationship to the GDR, the SED and state socialism. The surprise sanctioning of *Fräulein Schmetterling* was both a sticking point and a case in point. From an aesthetic point of view, the international styles evident in the film were suddenly undesir-able and suspect. In his contribution to this volume, 'Modernity and the City in Christa Wolf's Oeuvre of the 1960s', Curtis Swope illuminates these influences – such as the montage techniques of modernist Italian cinema and especially the films of Federico Fellini, which served as inspiration. From a thematic viewpoint, Schenk interprets the film as a call for the youth to engage with society and question the increasing dogmatism of which the Party plenary was a symptom.[17] Especially when read in the context of the rapid changes in the urban environ-ment that preoccupied Wolf from the time of *Moskauer Novelle* (1959) to that of *Der geteilte Himmel* and the short story 'Unter den Linden' (1974), *Fräulein Schmetterling* expresses a transnational critique of modern housing projects sup-planting traditional neighbourhoods that was deemed critical of GDR building programmes.

Christa Wolf's work thus ran counter to Honecker's demands even early on. After all, he insisted that artists commit to a partisan approach to aesthetic and political evaluations of GDR reality – an approach that supported SED politics at all times. Wolf acquired a unique position in the GDR when she alone spoke out against Honecker's statement at the Eleventh Plenum. As a result of her engage-ment, Wolf's prospects of becoming a member of the Central Committee of the SED were upended, but instead she became the canonical GDR writer. She was nationally and internationally celebrated and was influential for decades, not least because her texts contravened Honecker's directives through their on-going struggle to negotiate notions of freedom and democratization in socialist society.[18]

---

16 Ralf Schenk, 'Informationsblatt zu Fräulein Schmetterling (Defa 1965/2005). Zur Erstauffüh-rung der dokumentierten Szenenfolge, Juni 2005' (Berlin: DEFA-Stiftung, 2005); Katrin Dautel, 'Rezeption in Film und Fernsehen, im Hörspiel und auf der Bühne', in *Christa Wolf-Handbuch. Leben – Werk – Wirkung*, ed. by Carola Hilmes and Ilse Nagelschmidt (Stuttgart: Metzler, 2016), pp. 370–376.
17 Schenk, 'Informationsblatt', p. 9.
18 *Kahlschlag. Das 11. Plenum des ZK der SED 1965*, ed. by Günter Agde (Berlin: Aufbau, 1991), p. 244. Here, Christa Wolf's 'Diskussionsbeitrag' (contribution to the discussion) and her 'Erin-nerungsbericht' (report from memory) are reprinted, on pp. 255–266, and pp. 344–354, respec-

Despite or perhaps because of the unique courage Christa Wolf demonstrated during the *Kahlschlag-Plenum*, she suffered tremendously from these events, fell into a deep depression that lasted for several months and required hospitalization in a psychiatric clinic.[19] In her entry for 1965 in *Ein Tag im Jahr 1960–2000* (2003), Wolf remembers: 'Das Plenum hat entschieden: Die Realität wird abgeschafft' [The general assembly has decided: reality will be eliminated].[20] She concludes this entry with the realization that Anna Seghers also

> sieht nicht, was sich mir aufdrängt. [...] Wegzugehen – nein, so weit bin ich auch in Gedanken noch nicht. [...] Aber ein Vorhang ist hinter mir gefallen. Ein Zurück in das Land vor diesem Vorhang, ein harmloses Land, gibt es nicht mehr.[21]

> [does not see what intrudes upon my mind. (...) To leave – no, I have not yet reached that point, even in my thoughts. (...) But a curtain has fallen behind me. A way back into the country lying before that curtain, a harmless country, no longer exists.]

In both denying and admitting that she has thought about leaving the GDR, she reveals the quandary dissenting intellectuals like herself faced after the Eleventh Plenum: because of the FRG elite's ties to the fascist German past, the West did not present a viable alternative for most of them, which meant they could only advocate reforms of the GDR from within.[22] Convinced of socialist ideals, and often with ties to administrative structures and institutions, these loyal dissidents were still considered oppositional by the government.[23] Christa Wolf was

---

tively. The English version of the 'Erinnerungsbericht', entitled 'Rummelplatz', appeared in Christa Wolf, *Parting from Phantoms. Selected Writings, 1990–1994*, trans. by Jan van Heurck (Chicago: University of Chicago Press, 1997), pp. 42–53. See also Jörg Magenau, *Christa Wolf. Eine Biographie* (Berlin: Kindler, 2002), pp. 172–191; Stefan Soldovieri, 'Censorship and the Law. The Case of *Das Kaninchen bin ich* (*I am the Rabbit*)', in *DEFA. East German Cinema, 1946–1992*, ed. by Sean Allan and John Sandfort (New York: Berghahn, 1999), pp. 146–163.
19 Ilse Nagelschmidt, 'Von der Zeitgenossenschaft zur Zeitzeugenschaft. Christa Wolf in Zeit- und Generationszusammenhängen', in Hilmes and Nagelschmidt, pp. 1–62 (p. 20).
20 Christa Wolf, *Ein Tag im Jahr. 1960–2000* (Munich: Luchterhand, 2003), p. 73.
21 Ibid., p. 81.
22 The so-called Brown Book was published in the GDR in 1965. It caused an international stir, as it documented 'the National Socialist past of some twelve hundred members of the elite who were now active in every professional sector in the FRG' (Ahbe, 'Competing Master Narratives', p. 222). Also see Monika Gibas, '"Bonner Ultras", "Kriegstreiber" und "Schlotbarone". Die Bundesrepublik als Feindbild der DDR in den fünfziger Jahren', in *Unsere Feinde. Konstruktion des Anderen im Sozialismus*, ed. by Silke Satjukow and Rainer Gries (Leipzig: Leipziger Universitätsverlag, 2005), pp. 75–106.
23 Jürgen Kuczynski employs the term 'loyal dissident' self-descriptively in his memoirs, '*Ein linientreuer Dissident*'. *Memoiren 1945–1989* (Berlin: Aufbau, 1992). In *Im Dialog*, Christa Wolf de-

among those writers who, in the wake of the Eleventh Plenum, decided to advocate for literature and art that refuses to affirm SED politics and instead focuses
on the subjective positions of individuals who strive to reconcile their socialist
ideals with life through quotidian socialism. As a result, the GDR secret service,
widely known as the Stasi, began surveilling Christa Wolf and her husband in
1965.[24] Intellectuals like the Wolfs were considered dangerous and consequently
were scrutinized until the socialist state came to an end. These intellectuals understood their prominent positions as carrying an obligation to highlight socialist values and to reflect on GDR society in the absence of a critical media presence.

Lesen und Schreiben and Subjective Authenticity

Wolf's volume *Lesen und Schreiben* (1968), one of the foundational texts of modern poetics in GDR literature, reveals the author's belief that literature has a responsibility to support social and political developments. It fulfils this duty by
developing prose that allows readers to imagine the possibilities of life in a socialist country – everyday life rather than the life of heroes, as demanded by socialist realism (pp. 47–48). These ideas first become visible in Wolf's story *Juninachmittag* (1967) and are then fully developed in one of the landmark texts in
her oeuvre, *Nachdenken über Christa T.* Published in 1968, this novel sparked
great public debate in the GDR. To a greater degree than in her previous fiction,
Wolf engaged in literature that negotiated societal controversies and cautiously
took up prevalent official and unofficial discourses. Moreover, readers in the
GDR, aware that books constituted the prime public space in which differences
of opinion were articulated, had developed expertise in uncovering such arguments.[25] They could expertly decipher the meaning of the rather gloomy, diegetic

---

scribes this position as 'Identifikation [...] im Widerspruch' [identification (...) in contradiction]
(Hamburg: Luchterhand, 1993), p. 75. Also see David Bathrick, 'Die Intellektuellen und die
Macht. Die Repräsentanz des Schriftstellers in der DDR', in *Schriftsteller als Intellektuelle. Politik
und Literatur im Kalten Krieg*, ed. by Sven Hanuschek, Therese Hörnigk and Christine Malende
(Tübingen: Max Niemeyer, 2000), pp. 235–248 (p. 240).
24 Stasi is the colloquial term for *DDR Staatssicherheit* (GDR State Security), which is short for
Ministerium für Staatssicherheit (Ministry for State Security), also abbreviated as *MfS*.
25 Jurek Becker, 'Die Wiedervereinigung der deutschen Literatur', *German Quarterly* 63.3/4
(1990), pp. 359–366 (p. 360); Holger Helbig, 'Wandel statt Wende. Wie man den Wenderoman
liest/schreibt, während man auf ihn wartet', in *Weiterschreiben. Zur DDR-Literatur nach dem
Ende der DDR*, ed. by Holger Helbig and others (Berlin: Akademie, 2007), pp. 75–88 (p. 84);
Frank Hörnigk, 'Die Literatur ist zuständig. Über das Verhältnis von Literatur und Politik in

atmosphere and Christa T.'s illnesses: following the *Kahlschlag-Plenum* of 1965, hope that the Wall's construction would lead to democratic socialism had waned. Accordingly, Wolf's fictional character suffers physically from the discrepancy between her personal desires and social expectations, although she resolves this struggle by developing a quasi-religious faith in the future of a humane socialism. Influenced by Ernst Bloch's *Das Prinzip Hoffnung* [*The Principle of Hope*] (1954), Wolf's novel is indebted to the utopian-Marxist belief in a humane socialism that – while it has not yet arrived – is sure to come.

Nachdenken über Christa T. also marked Wolf's breakthrough in her characteristic writing style: first, in her aesthetics of 'subjective authenticity', a new writing style she explained in a 1973 conversation with Hans Kaufmann ('Subjektive Authentizität'). Subjective authenticity, Wolf explained, aims to engage with objective reality in a productive manner that is meaningful to the subject while avoiding an unfettered subjectivism, which could obscure rather than illuminate reality (pp. 781–782). In this volume, Anna Kuhn exposes the gendering of both Wolf's concept of subjective authenticity and readers' responses to her texts, especially in the USA. Second, Wolf had developed a writing style involving a third person, which helped her to overcome the 'Schwierigkeit, "ich" zu sagen' [the difficulty of saying 'I'].[26] From this point onwards, we can observe this technique of employing a distancing third person in Wolf's oeuvre. She imagined such writing as a web and increasingly stressed the importance of this technique, which culminates in *Stadt der Engel*.[27]

Losing Hope: The Prague Spring of 1968

While 1968 marked the beginning of progressive action by groups such as the student, civil rights, and women's movements in the West, hopes for a better, hu-

---

der DDR', in *Geist und Macht. Writers and the State in the GDR*, ed. by Axel Goodbody and Dennis Tate (Amsterdam: Rodopi, 1992), pp. 23–34 (p. 26); Martina Langermann and Thomas Takerta, 'Von der versuchten Verfertigung einer Literaturgesellschaft. Kanon und Norm in der literarischen Kommunikation der DDR', in *LiteraturGesellschaft DDR. Kanonkämpfe und ihre Geschichte(n)*, ed. by Birgit Dahlke, Martina Langermann and Thomas Taterka (Stuttgart: Metzler 2000), pp. 1–32 (pp. 2 and 26); *Literatur ohne Land? Schreibstrategien einer DDR-Literatur im vereinten Deutschland*, ed. by Janine Ludwig and Mirijam Meuser (Freiburg: Fördergemeinschaft wissenschaftlicher Publikationen von Frauen, 2009), pp. 15, 34 and 45.

26 Christa Wolf, *Nachdenken über Christa T.*, 1968, reprint (Munich: dtv, 1993), p. 166.

27 Carsten Gansel and Christa Wolf, '"Zum Schreiben haben mich Konflikte getrieben". Ein Gespräch', in *Christa Wolf im Strom der Erinnerung*, ed. by Carsten Gansel, with Sonja Klocke (Göttingen: V&R unipress, 2014), pp. 353–366 (p. 354).

mane socialism diminished in the GDR and in other Eastern European countries after Warsaw Pact troops invaded Czechoslovakia and ended the Prague Spring revolt. For Wolf, who refused to sign a statement supporting the military and po-litical intervention against this grassroots call for political and social reform, the consequences were dire: only a 'self-criticism' declaration she composed with the help of her husband prevented her from being relieved of her duties on the steer-ing committee of the GDR association of writers, the Schriftstellerverband.[28] Mo-tivated by her desire to articulate her position publicly, she felt forced into this compromise, but she suffered physically and emotionally as a result. Several weeks in the hospital, as well as her writing, helped her to overcome her depres-sion in the face of the disturbing course of state socialist practice. Nevertheless, her entry for 1969 in *Ein Tag im Jahr* reveals her desolation, which was aggravat-ed by the increasing generational split between Wolf and Anna Seghers, which the younger woman could no longer overlook. Unlike Seghers – who, in a lead-ing article in the party organ *Neues Deutschland*, declares her conviction that one day people will remember the 'zauberhafte Verwandlungen [...] unserer Tage' [magical transformations (...) of our days] – Wolf admits that she has lost her be-lief in the success of real-existing state socialism: 'Das glaubt sie [Seghers], zu ihrem Glück. Ich nicht mehr [She believes that, fortunately for her. I do not any-more].[29]

Working Through the Past to Find Answers for the Present: *Kindheitsmuster*

Following the death of her mother in 1968, Wolf began work on one of her major projects, *Kindheitsmuster*. She had begun to perceive parallels between the GDR

---

28 The practice of 'self-criticism' was common in the GDR, as well as in most other countries under Soviet rule and in the Soviet Union itself. Party members who had strayed from the offi-cial party line and had hence fallen out of favour had to provide written and/or verbal state-ments admitting their ideological errors and affirming their renewed belief in the party line. Since such 'self-criticism' did not guarantee political rehabilitation, Wolf must have considered herself lucky to have been permitted to remain on the steering committee of the GDR writers' association.

29 Wolf, *Ein Tag im Jahr*, p. 128. Tensions between Seghers and Wolf gained strength over time, as another entry in *Ein Tag im Jahr* reveals (p. 189). See also Klocke, *Inscription and Rebellion*, p. 92. Real-existing socialism was a term coined by Erich Honecker in 1973. It pointed to the dis-crepancy between the utopian socialist promise and the often problematic conditions prevailing in the GDR.

and Nazi Germany, especially in the requirement to follow authoritarian demands, which motivated this endeavour. Traveling to her birthplace in Landsberg an der Warthe in 1971, which by then was Gorzów in Poland, Wolf found that the country offered a space for her to come to terms with her past and to understand her position in the present. Returning to a cultural space that was simultaneously familiar (in her memories) and foreign (in its present as a Polish town) emerged as a chance to think about the patterns children develop that later determine life and identity.

Kindheitsmuster is often characterized as the 'Buch ihrer Generation' [book of her generation], in which Wolf initiated a discussion of the deformation implied in growing up in Nazi Germany, particularly as a girl.[30] The 'Kälte, Lieblosigkeit, Verdrängung von Ängsten, Anpassung, Selbstbetrug sowie das Schaffen von Fremdbildern' [cold, unkindness, suppression of fears, adaptation, self-deception, as well as the construction of how others perceive you][31] – which was inherent in the Prussian parenting style prevalent in the 1960s, in the Nazi ideology learned in the Hitler Youth and, moreover, in a school system that propagated racism and chauvinism – affected all children and teenagers, and girls in particular, for the rest of their lives. In *Kindheitsmuster*, the protagonist, Nelly, develops an 'authoritarian personality' – a deep-seated desire to please the authorities instead of struggling for freedom. Since the novel points to the effects of the authoritarian character of the GDR, it was considered a provocation of hegemonic GDR historiography.[32]

For Wolf, writing the present alongside the past necessitated a new writing style – a challenge she repeatedly faced when writing prose texts, as she revealed in *Ein Tag im Jahr*: 'Wie die überlagernden Schichten, aus denen "Wirklichkeit" besteht, in die lineare Schreibweise hinüberretten?' [How to bring the stacked layers of which "reality" consists over into my linear writing style?].[33] It is this desire to reveal these 'stacked layers' which drives even her last novel, *Stadt der Engel*, as highlighted in the subtitle, *The Overcoat of Dr. Freud*. The particular voice Wolf had already fashioned in *Nachdenken über*

---

30 Ilse Nagelschmidt, 'Von der Zeitgenossenschaft zur Zeitzeugenschaft', p. 28.

31 Ibid.

32 Helen Bridge, *Women's Writing and Historiography in the GDR* (Oxford: Oxford University Press, 2002), p. 59. On the authoritarian personality, see Erich Fromm, 'Sozialpsychologischer Teil und Erhebungen', in *Studien über Autorität und Familie. Forschungsberichte aus dem Institut für Sozialforschung*, ed. by Max Horkheimer (Paris: Alcan, 1936), pp. 77–135; Caroline Schaumann, *Memory Matters. Generational Responses to Germany's Nazi Past in Recent Women's Literature* (Berlin: De Gruyter, 2008), pp. 78–80.

33 Wolf, *Ein Tag im Jahr*, p. 139.

Christa T. is further developed in the 1976 novel *Kindheitsmuster* – a change that also presented a challenge for translating Wolf's work, as Caroline Summers points out in this volume.

Biermann's Expatriation in 1976

Erich Honecker had raised faint hopes for a more democratic socialism in the GDR when, as the new head of state, he declared in September 1971: 'Wenn man von der festen Position des Sozialismus ausgeht, kann es meines Erachtens auf dem Gebiet von Kunst und Literatur keine Tabus geben' [As long as one proceeds from the firm position of socialism, there can be, in my view, no taboos in the areas of art and literature].[34] Yet the right to determine what suffices as 'the firm position of socialism' remained with the party and thus excluded all socialists and Marxists who were not willing to follow the party line blindly – such as Christa Wolf and, famously, the singer-songwriter and poet Wolf Biermann. Though the GDR was increasingly internationally recognized following the signing of the Basic Treaty between the GDR and the FRG in December 1972[35] and the Helsinki Declaration of the Conference on Security and Co-operation in Europe in August 1975, the East German regime felt the need to maintain pressure on artists and writers, who remained under close Stasi scrutiny. Biermann, a Jewish communist from Hamburg who had lost his father in a Nazi concentration camp and deliberately relocated to the GDR, remained a particular thorn in the flesh of party officials. Instead of imprisoning him and risking his becoming a symbolic martyr for oppositional groups, the government planned his expatriation while he was performing abroad.

Biermann had accepted the invitation of one of the largest West German unions, IG Metall [Industrial Union Metal], to do a concert tour in West Germany. Although the East German authorities had approved this tour, they used the singer's criticism of the GDR regime, which he voiced during a concert in Cologne on 17 November 1976, as reason for not allowing him to return to his East German home. Biermann's expatriation caused extreme anxiety among GDR intellectuals, who were appalled that a communist, whose communist Jewish father was

---

34 Quoted in Ilse Nagelschmidt, 'Von der Zeitgenossenschaft zur Zeitzeugenschaft', p. 24.
35 The Basic Treaty aimed to establish good, neighbourly relations between the two German states and granted de facto – albeit not de jure – legal recognition to the GDR. The FRG government stressed its intentions in a supplementary text that upheld the constitutionally anchored objective of unification. Permanent legations, rather than embassies, were opened in both German states to underscore the special nature of relations between the two.

murdered in a Nazi concentration camp, could be expatriated from the allegedly anti-fascist state. Led by the writer Stephan Hermlin, twelve artists – among them Christa and Gerhard Wolf – publicly protested against such despotism in an open letter to the SED regime, which was published in the West because the GDR newswire ADN refused to accept it.[36] The East German government re-acted with various measures that underlined the manner in which prominence tended to garner protection from harsh punishment, a practice that is at the centre of Anna Horakova's essay in this volume. In 'Learning from the Underground: Christa Wolf and the Fourth Generation of GDR Writers', she analyses Wolf's *Was bleibt* (drafted in 1979 and published in 1990) to demonstrate that young writers – such as Gabriele Stötzer, who, in Wolf's controversial novella, assumes the fic-tionalized form of the 'Girl' – had no safeguards vis-à-vis the regime. This Girl gives the protagonist a manuscript dealing with the prison sentence she had served after petitioning against Biermann's expatriation, while Wolf's protago-nist, an alter ego of the prominent writer, suffers under surveillance rather than a prison sentence. Privilege also has its ambivalences; while Wolf's protag-onist struggles to find a new literary language that would enable her to talk about this invasive shadowing in appropriate terms, the Girl has found precisely the kind of language for which Wolf's protagonist longs. In 1976, the writer Jürgen Fuchs – who, like Stötzer, was not protected by fame – was arrested and imprisoned, while the dissident Robert Havemann, who had already been removed from the party in 1963 for an interview he gave in a West German news-paper, was put under house arrest. More prominent authors – such as Jurek Becker, Gerhard Wolf and Sarah Kirsch – were removed from the party, and Ste-phan Hermlin and Christa Wolf received a *strenge Rüge* [severe reprimand]. While Christa Wolf remained a party member, she never attended a single party meet-ing after 1976.[37]

The Wolfs contemplated leaving the GDR following Biermann's expatriation, but they eventually decided to stay – encouraged not only by Christa Wolf's readers, but also by Erich Honecker himself. In an interview to which Honecker had summoned Christa Wolf, the author publicly insisted that 'jeder, der ausreis-

---

36 Stefan Heym, Heiner Müller, Volker Braun, Erich Arndt, Jurek Becker, Sarah Kirsch, Rolf Schneider, Franz Fühmann, Fritz Cremer and Günter Kunert were also among the first to sign the letter. Over the course of the subsequent months, several artists and intellectuals also signed the protest, but others wrote letters – published in GDR newspapers – supporting the SED re-gime's decision to expatriate Biermann. See Hannelore Scholz, 'Projektionsraum Romantik', in Hilmes and Nagelschmidt, pp. 143–163 (p. 144). See also Jana Simon, *Sei dennoch unverzagt. Gespräche mit meinen Großeltern Christa und Gerhard Wolf* (Berlin: Ullstein, 2013), p. 270.
37 Scholz, 'Projektionsraum Romantik', in Hilmes and Nagelschmidt, p. 145.

en will, soll ausreisen. Man muss die Voraussetzungen dafür schaffen, dass sie es nicht müssen' [everyone who wants to leave the country should be allowed to do so. One has to create a situation in which they do not have to leave].[38] For numerous intellectuals, Biermann's expatriation expressed the socialist country's inability to undertake reform, and many left – among others, Thomas Brasch, Sarah Kirsch and Hans Joachim Schädlich.[39] For Christa Wolf, however – who continued to believe in a humane, democratic socialism but turned away from the official party line entirely – West Germany did not present an alternative. There was, quite literally, no place on earth, as her eponymous novel *Kein Ort. Nirgends* states.

The Turn to Romanticism

Having lost her faith in the realization of socialist ideals in daily GDR life, Wolf – like many of her colleagues – sought refuge and space for the allegorical expression of social critique in the magic of Romanticism, in its legends, fairy tales and fragments. They recognized themselves in the tension that Romanticists such as Heinrich von Kleist or Karoline von Günderode had experienced vis-à-vis society. Based on such a congeniality of souls (*Seelenverwandtschaft*), GDR writers contemplated the affinity between these historical time periods (the turn of the eighteenth to the nineteenth century and their situation in the GDR of the 1960s and 1970s) as well as the shared desire for subjectivity and a new way of writing.[40] Wolf's preoccupation with the Romanticists began after the events

---

38 Simon, *Sei dennoch unverzagt*, p. 139.

39 See Andrea Jäger, *Schriftsteller aus der DDR. Ausbürgerungen und Übersiedlungen von 1961 bis 1989* (Frankfurt a. M.: Peter Lang, 1995), pp. 1–7. Jäger demonstrates that between the building and the fall of the Wall, approximately 100 writers left the GDR, the vast majority following Biermann's expatiation in 1976.

40 See, for example, Christa Wolf's essay 'Der Schatten eines Traumes. Karoline von Günderode – ein Entwurf' ['The Shadow of a Dream. A Sketch of Karoline von der Günderode']. Wolf draws parallels between the nineteenth and the twentieth centuries when she describes Germans as 'zerrissenes, politisch unreifes und schwer zu bewegendes, doch leicht verführbares Volk, dem technischen Fortschritt anhangend statt dem der Humanität' [inwardly divided, politically immature people, hard to activate but easy to seduce, devoted to the progress of technology instead of humanity] and expresses her affinity with the Romantics when she declares that she is 'fasziniert durch Verwandtschaft und Nähe, wenn auch der Zeiten und Ereignisse eingedenk, die zwischen uns und denen liegen' [fascinated by their kinship and closeness to us (although mindful, too, of the periods and events which separate us)]. Christa Wolf, 'Der Schatten eines

of 1968 and first became evident in her collection of stories entitled *Unter den Linden. Unwahrscheinliche Geschichten* (1974). The titular story, for example, opens with a Rahel Varnhagen quotation and justifies the reputation of the street Unter den Linden, famous for its location as the 'Ost-West-Achse' [East-West axis], with a dream: 'die Straße [ist mir] im Traum erschienen. Nun kann ich endlich darüber berichten. [...] Ich kann frei die Wahrheit sagen' [the street recently appeared to me in a dream. Now I can finally tell of it (...) I can freely tell the truth].[41] Thus the dream enables the exposure of truth, and Wolf combines such echoes of Romanticism with the realities of the contemporary world, as Swope demonstrates in his contribution to this volume. He reveals that the self in this story serves as a witness of actual social experiences and of the modern urban space, which are both shaped by the rifts in international politics.

Following Biermann's expatriation, Wolf's inner conflict between the ideals of socialism and the realities of the socialist state amplified and intensified her turn towards Romanticism. Just like her new heroines and heroes, whom Wolf described as 'Avantgarde ohne Hinterland' [avant-garde without a backcountry], the GDR author lacked any alternative space in the contemporary world.[42] Imagining a meeting between Karoline von Günderode and Heinrich von Kleist at the Merten residence in Winkel on the River Rhein on a June afternoon in 1804, Wolf conjures the existential problems that determine both the days of these Romanticists and her own conflicted times in *Kein Ort. Nirgends*. Opening up the historical dimension implies that there is and has been no place for her or for other intellectuals. Furthermore, the novella's final words, 'Wir wissen, was kommt' [We know what is coming],[43] allude to the characteristic fates of artists and intellectuals – such as the suicides of Karoline von Günderode and Heinrich von Kleist – that recur in societies determined by a blind belief in progress and economic expediency.

Traumes. Karoline von Günderode – ein Entwurf', in *Lesen und Schreiben. Neue Sammlung* (Darmstadt: Luchterhand, 1980), pp. 225–283 (p. 226).
41 Wolf, 'Unter den Linden', in *Unter den Linden. Unwahrscheinliche Geschichten*, p. 54.
42 Ibid., p. 112.
43 Wolf, *Kein Ort. Nirgends*, p. 150.

The 1980s: 'Today, Literature Has to Be Peace Research'

The desire to retreat from society and the criticism of utilitarian premises find expression in Wolf's next major works of fiction, *Kassandra*, *Störfall* (1987) and *Sommerstück* (1989). These works are deeply embedded in the political situation of the time. Both *Kassandra* and *Störfall* thematize the nuclear arms race between the USA and the Soviet Union, particularly the fact that both German states housed nuclear weapons. In her speech from 1980, 'Von Büchner sprechen' [Talking about Büchner], Wolf consequently stressed her belief in the significance of literature as 'Friedensforschung' [peace research].[44] Her Kassandra project, the eponymous novel and the lectures on poetics presented at the Goethe University of Frankfurt and published as *Voraussetzungen einer Erzählung. Kassandra* are more than an escape into legend. Rather, this turn towards myth from a feminist point of view allows Wolf to demystify notions of male heroism that have been passed down for centuries and to criticize the unquestioned belief in Western civilization and technology.

This criticism is already alluded to in *Nachdenken über Christa T.* and, as Deborah Janson highlights in her contribution, 'Unearthing a Post-Humanist Ecological Socialism in Christa Wolf's "Selbstversuch", *Kassandra* and *Störfall*', is more fully expressed in 'Selbstversuch'. Reading this short story, *Kassandra* and *Störfall* – Wolf's novella addressing the effects of the nuclear catastrophe in Chernobyl in April 1986 – together, Janson demonstrates that Wolf continuously decries the oppressive social structures associated with rationalism. In their stead, her work offers a vision of society that advances communication and mutual respect, pursues the development of life-sustaining technologies and emphasizes relationships rather than hierarchies, linking rather than ranking. Informed by recent thought in ecocriticism, Janson further reveals that Wolf's turn to the environment in *Störfall* is tied to her engagement with peace and her opposition to class society, which she considered influenced by patriarchy. Janson shows that Wolf developed a critique of the 'logic of domination' that justifies the exploitation of nature on the basis of (alleged) human superiority while overlooking the harm this outlook is doing to our planet and its inhabitants.

---

44 Christa Wolf, 'Von Büchner sprechen', in *Die Dimension des Autors. Essays und Aufsätze – Reden und Gespräche 1959–1985* (Darmstadt: Luchterhand, 1987), pp. 611–625 (p. 623).

Both Janson's and Sabine von Mering's contributions to this collection accentuate the relevance and cross-cultural applicability of Wolf's work, particularly in her response to the nuclear disaster of 1986, when her fears that a world fixated merely on progress would precipitate its own destruction seemed to be coming true. In 'Nature, Power and Literature: Rereading Christa Wolf's *Störfall. Nachrichten eines Tages* as "Ecological Force" in Times of Climate Crisis', von Mering highlights the significance of a juxtaposition in Wolf's text: while the narrator's brother is saved from a brain tumour by modern medicine, nuclear fission, which humans cannot control, destroys thousands of lives and causes incurable disease. Based on ecocritical theory – in particular, Hubert Zapf's notion of literature as 'ecological force' and Greg Garrad's idea of 'transformative discourses' – von Mering emphasizes that *Störfall* deals with the Janus-faced sciences, which Wolf considers the blind spot of contemporary civilization.

In 'Narrative Topographies in Christa Wolf's Oeuvre', Regina Criser points out another aspect of the novella that – perhaps due to *Störfall*'s emphasis on the nuclear catastrophe – has often been overlooked: like *Sommerstück, Störfall* is still influenced by Wolf's feeling of homelessness following Biermann's expatriation. In her analysis, Criser engages spatial aspects of Wolf's texts, focusing on their multiplicity of meanings. She draws upon Edward Soja's notion of thirdspace and Michel Foucault's ideas of heterotopia to illuminate how spaces in Wolf's novels, including *Der geteilte Himmel, Störfall* and *Sommerstück*, become alternative sites – for instance, between West and East. On one hand, these topographies resist binary structures – structures that, moreover, characterize the Cold War period. Criser shows, for instance, how the house constructed by Christa T. may be interpreted less as a failed attempt to find a place for herself in GDR society and more as an alternative home for her family. In several works, language also variously becomes a site of refuge and resistance. On the other hand, texts such as *Störfall* clearly reveal the probable impossibility of a long–lasting refuge outside of society. Criser shows how seepage from fraught German pasts contaminates present alternative sites. Moreover, she highlights how the houses in the countryside to which the protagonists in *Sommerstück* have withdrawn turn out to be not only contaminable, but impermanent. For Criser, Wolf's oeuvre ultimately emphasizes that sites of resistance, while they expand past national borders and geographical limits, are engendered within unique personalities.

In 'Literature and the Visual Art in Christa Wolf's *Sommerstück* (1989) and *Was bleibt* (1990)', Roswitha Skare emphasizes another aspect of *Sommerstück*, which she finds significant in the 1990 novella as well – namely, how the prose texts relate to the cover art and illustrations in their several editions. Deploying Gérard Genette's concepts of paratext and Roland Barthes's notions of anchorage and relay, Skare shows how these literary texts and their paratexts carry independent significances, multiply each other's possible interpretations and jointly synthesize new meanings. Skare's reading of *Sommerstück* and *Was bleibt* challenges Barthes's assertion that linguistic messaging anchors images by arguing that their paratextual images open up or close down interpretations of Wolf's linguistic texts – and vice versa. Paratexts shape how readers understand texts in the various circumstances in which these texts are interpreted.

1989/1990: A Turning Point in History

The second half of the 1980s was marked by signs of change all over Europe. In Poland, the first trade union that was not controlled by a Communist Party in a Warsaw Pact country was founded in 1980. Despite political oppression, *Solidarność* managed to engage with the government in roundtable talks that led to free elections in 1989. In the Soviet Union, the General Secretary of the Communist Party, Mikhail Gorbachev, set a course towards putative openness and restructuring – *glasnost* and *perestroika*, as expressed in the terms of the day – beginning in 1985. When Hungary tore down the Iron Curtain in the summer of 1989, the end of authoritarian, real-existing socialism seemed near. During those days, more and more East Germans took to the streets, particularly in Leipzig, to protest against their government for supporting the so-called Chinese solution – the Chinese government's ending of peaceful demonstrations in Tiananmen Square with tanks in June 1989. The increasing number of demonstrations all over East Germany eventually led to the fall of the Wall on 9 November 1989, and to German unification on 3 October 1990. This period of new orientation for East Germany is commonly referred to as the *Wende*, ironically a moniker first employed by the SED's last general secretary and head of state, Egon Krenz, in his inaugural address in October 1989. Krenz had served as Honecker's deputy since 1984 and hardly stood for real change, but the West German newsmagazine *Der Spiegel* nevertheless borrowed the term *Wende* – which was quickly adopted by the rest of the West German media – in their 16 October 1989 edition. This expression, coined by the last leader of the GDR regime, supplanted the term 'peaceful revolution', which was favoured by many East German citizens. The use of the label *Wende* was advantageous for both the GDR and the FRG regimes, since – as Christa Wolf pointed out – it obscured the nature of the events, instead conjuring up a metaphorical image of a captain tacking a ship.[45] Thus, *Wende* elides

---

45 Christa Wolf, *Stadt der Engel oder The Overcoat of Dr. Freud* (Berlin: Suhrkamp, 2010), p. 90;

the involvement of the activists who fought for their freedom and intended to reform the GDR and also denies East Germans agency more generally.

For Christa Wolf, 1989 and 1990 were busy years; many of her speeches from this time are compiled in the volume *Reden im Herbst* (1990). She actively fought for a socialism in which the very humanist ideals that had crumbled away in the GDR would be resurrected. Her ideas found their way into the pamphlet 'Aufruf für unser Land' [Appeal for our Country], which Wolf published together with thirty other authors in November 1989. In light of the deep crisis they observed, they called for an autonomous GDR, a socialist alternative to the FRG, characterized by solidarity, peace, social justice, freedom and environmental conservation, and they opposed what they deemed the selling out of their material and moral values.[46]

Unquestionably, Wolf's ideals stood in opposition to the End of History master narrative.[47] This accounting considers unification the telos of German history and the fall of the Wall the irrevocable delegitimation of the Marxist-Leninist master narrative, according to which human history inexorably advances towards a classless society. Wolf's public appearances, during which she repeatedly voiced her counternarrative, met with the disapproval of powerful West Germans in the media and politics alike. This disapprobation was acted out in the so-called *deutsch-deutscher Literaturstreit* [German-German debate on literature] beginning in 1990.[48] Triggered by West German media reactions to Wolf's 1990 novella *Was bleibt*, a menacing press campaign evolved, which was first directed against Wolf personally; as a woman, she seemed a particularly well-suited target.[49] Deliberately ignoring her enduring efforts to reform the socialist state from

---

Christa Wolf, 'Sprache der Wende. Rede auf dem Alexanderplatz' ['The Language of the Turning Point'], in *Auf dem Weg nach Tabou. Texte 1990–1994*, 1994, reprint (Munich: dtv, 1996), p. 11. See also Rainer Eppelmann and Robert Grünbaum, 'Sind wir die Fans von Egon Krenz? Die Revolution war keine *Wende*', *Deutschland Archiv*, 5 (2004), 864–869.

46 Christa Wolf, 'Für unser Land', in *Im Dialog. Aktuelle Texte* (Frankfurt a. M.: Luchterhand, 1990), pp. 170–171.

47 Francis Fukuyama, *The End of History and the Last Man* (New York: Free Press, 1992).

48 The so-called *deutsch-deutscher Literaturstreit* is documented in *Es geht nicht um Christa Wolf. Der Literaturstreit im vereinten Deutschland*, ed. by Thomas Anz (Frankfurt a. M.: Fischer, 1991); *Der deutsch-deutsche Literaturstreit oder 'Freunde, es spricht sich schlecht mit gebundener Zunge'*, ed. by Karl Deiritz and Hannes Krauss (Hamburg: Luchterhand, 1991).

49 On the gendered aspect of the campaign, see Anna Kuhn, '"Eine Königin köpfen ist effektiver als einen König köpfen". The Gender Politics of the Christa Wolf Controversy', in *Women and the Wende. Social Effects and Cultural Reflections of the German Unification Process*, ed. by Elizabeth Boa and Janet Wharton (Amsterdam: Rodopi, 1994), pp. 200–215 (esp. p. 208); Lennart Koch, *Ästhetik der Moral bei Christa Wolf und Monika Maron. Der Literaturstreit von der Wende bis zum Ende der neunziger Jahre* (Frankfurt a. M.: Peter Lang, 2000).

within, the media began to label Wolf a 'DDR-Staatsdichterin' [poet laureate of the GDR]. This practice persisted for the next twenty years, led by the literary critic Marcel Reich-Ranicki.[50] This insinuated affiliation with the GDR regime, together along with the misrepresentation of her link to the GDR's secret service, damaged her reputation for some time, yet her fans continued to celebrate her.[51] In its next phase, the *Literaturstreit* extended more generally to intellectuals who had allegedly stabilized the GDR regime. When the dispute expanded to include all politically engaged literature, including West German fiction and its putative *Gesinnungsästhetik* [aesthetics of political conviction], the debate's true motivation came to light: the campaign aimed to put an end to critical, political literature in unified Germany and to appropriate the authority to interpret (literary) history for the future – as Ulrich Greiner, one of the most influential literary critics in Germany and the head of the culture section of *Die Zeit* in 1990, eventually admitted.[52]

Thus the early 1990s ushered in traumatic events for Wolf: the demise of the GDR, and with it, of the hope for a realization of her socialist ideals; the so-called *Literaturstreit*, which reached its most vicious stage when the media inflated the author's fleeting cooperation with the Stasi between 1959 and 1962; and finally, the sense of betrayal she felt upon discovering that this state security force had kept the Wolf family under meticulous surveillance from 1968 until 1989. Their measures included a variety of IMs [*Inoffizielle Mitarbeiter*; unofficial informers to the Stasi], among whom were close friends of the Wolfs; additionally, their apartments were searched, their phone and mail were monitored fre-

---

50 See Anz, *Es geht nicht um Christa Wolf*, pp. 35–40.

51 Ibid., pp. 77–89.

52 Ulrich Greiner, 'Die deutsche Gesinnungsästhetik', in *Es geht nicht um Christa Wolf. Der Literaturstreit im vereinten Deutschland*, ed. by Thomas Anz (Frankfurt a. M.: Fischer, 1991), pp. 208–216 (p. 208). See also Stephen Brockmann, *Literature and German Reunification* (Cambridge: Cambridge University Press, 1999), p. 1; Keith Bullivant, *The Future of German Literature* (Oxford: Berg, 1994), pp. 70–71. In *Ein Tag im Jahr*, Christa Wolf recalls a Colloquium organized by the Bertelsmann group in 1990, where a Bertelsmann representative disclosed the impetus behind the campaign aimed at muzzling her: 'Natürlich handelt es sich um eine Kampagne gegen Sie. Natürlich geht es gar nicht um ihre Vergangenheit, sondern um Ihre Aktivitäten in der Gegenwart. Das stört. Und natürlich soll bei Ihnen alles, was einen Anhauch von links hat, zerschlagen werden. Die DDR muß unbedingt delegitimiert werden. [...] Sie kriegen bei uns in den Medien keinen Fuß mehr auf den Boden' [Naturally, it is a matter of a campaign against you. Of course it is not concerned at all with your past, but with your activities in the present. That is disturbing. And of course anything concerning you that has even a faint odour of the left must be smashed. The German Democratic Republic must unconditionally be rendered illegitimate. (...) You will no longer get a foot in the media's door here] (Wolf, *Ein Tag im Jahr*, p. 465).

quently, and their manuscripts were specifically censored. Still, when faced with attacks, Wolf, unlike many others, responded in a differentiated manner. Rejecting false accusations, she exposed the real, misguided motives behind the blanket condemnations brought forward in the so-called literary debate. Unlike any other public figure, she disclosed not only her victim files, but also the slim *Täterakte* [perpetrator files] the secret service had compiled on her. Although these so-called perpetrator files reveal that the Stasi quickly ended their cooperation with Wolf, who was an ineffective informant, the West German media's reports on her nevertheless refused to make room for nuances, opting instead for simplistic, harsh judgment.[53]

Coming to Terms with Hostility in Unified Germany

The public learned about Wolf's brief Stasi collaboration during the author's stay at the Getty Institute in Santa Monica, where she was a resident research fellow for nine months in 1992–1993. This 'Hexenjagd' [witch hunt], in Daniela Dahn's words, which reached Wolf even in the USA, was very stressful for the author.[54] Her readers only became privy to her resulting depression and death wish in 2010, when they read Wolf's last novel, *Stadt der Engel*. Here the protagonist – like Wolf, a resident research fellow at the Getty Institute in Santa Monica – reflects extensively on her potential guilt and on the possible reasons for suppressing memories of her brief collaboration with the Stasi. The protagonist finds new friends among the intellectuals at the Getty and the descendants of the predominantly Jewish émigrés who were forced to leave Nazi Germany. They support her identification with the anti-fascist resistance and with the GDR's founding narratives of anti-fascism, anti-racism and anti-capitalism. Wolf's alter ego finally comes to terms with her personal history in a socialist state, with the help of the temporal, spatial and ideological distance of the United States in the early 1990s.

It took Wolf more than fifteen years to write about the traumatic events of the 1990s in such clear terms. Her first major prose text composed after 1990, *Medea. Stimmen*, rewrites an antique myth, much like *Kassandra*. As John Pizer high-

---

53 Wolf published her Stasi files, both her victim and her perpetrator files, in *Akteneinsicht Christa Wolf. Zerrspiegel und Dialog*, ed. by Hermann Vinke (Hamburg: Luchterhand, 1993).
54 Daniela Dahn, in *Wohin sind wir unterwegs? Zum Gedenken an Christa Wolf* (Berlin: Suhrkamp, 2012), pp. 43–47 (p. 46).

lights in his contribution, 'From Pan-German Cosmopolitanism to Nostalgic National Insularity: A Comparative Study of Christa Wolf's *Kassandra* and *Medea*', the two books are linked by the protagonists' alienation: they feel connected to their communities despite the lack of empathy they receive. Yet there is more: although the two opposing factions in the Trojan War in *Kassandra* – similarly to the two German states in the 1980s – were threatened with annihilation, they are treated as unified in and through such martial bellicosity. Written in the wake of German unification, *Medea* instead showcases two geographical realms, Colchis and Corinth, which are separated by an unbridgeable divide. Thus, as Pizer demonstrates, we observe a transition from the Cold War novel to the post-unification novel – a shift from a fundamental advocacy of pan-German solidarity to a nostalgic embrace of a now-lost, discrete Colchis culture, clearly allegorizing the GDR. Medea, in particular, feels hurt, betrayed and exiled in her country, Corinth, which allegorizes post-1990 Germany. Not unlike Wolf following the so-called *Literaturstreit*, she has been turned into a scapegoat. A critique of patriarchy, war and the logics of possession, *Medea* is also an indirect reproach of the West German media that had projected an exceedingly unfavourable image of Wolf.

In *Leibhaftig*, published in 2002, Wolf seemingly returns to the GDR. Literary critics and scholars initially equated the protagonist with the author and hastily interpreted the book as Wolf's final farewell to the GDR and to illusions about the socialist model underlying the state.[55] The novel relates the medical history of a nameless female writer in a GDR hospital, which is – according to the medical personnel – a mirror image of depleted GDR society (p. 173). Without doubt, *Leibhaftig* presents a defining moment in Wolf's oeuvre, but can it be considered a goodbye? Particularly when read together with *Stadt der Engel*, *Leibhaftig* emerges as Wolf's first attempt to deal with the traumatic experiences of the early 1990s and the first stage of her healing process.[56] In *Leibhaftig*, which links the protagonist's bodily collapse to her sense of political crisis and epochal

---

55 On parallels between the protagonist and Wolf, who was hospitalized in Schwerin in 1988, see Martina Caspari, 'Im Kern die Krisis. Schuld, Trauer und Neuanfang in Christa Wolfs Erzählung "Leibhaftig"', *Weimarer Beiträge*, 49.1 (2003), 135–138 (p. 135); Christine Cosentino, '"Aus Teufels Küche". Gedanken zur Teufelsfigur in der Literatur nach 2000 – Christoph Heins *Willenbrock*, Christa Wolfs *Leibhaftig* und Monika Marons *Endmoränen*', *Germanic Notes and Reviews*, 35.2 (2004), 121–127 (p. 123); Charity Scribner, 'Von "Leibhaftig" aus zurückblicken. Verleugnung als Trope in Christa Wolfs Schreiben', *Weimarer Beiträge*, 50.2 (2004), 212–226 (p. 214). On Wolf's alleged farewell to socialism, see for example Carol Anne Costabile-Heming, 'Illness as Metaphor. Christa Wolf, the GDR, and Beyond', *Symposium*, 64.3 (2010), 202–219 (p. 203).
56 See Klocke, *Inscription and Rebellion*, pp. 72–113.

decline, one can also detect signs of what might be called a 'late style'. This topic is central to Catherine Smale's 'Towards a Late Style? Christa Wolf on Old Age, Death and Creativity in *Stadt der Engel oder The Overcoat of Dr. Freud*', in which she shows how, for Wolf, writing in the face of death is linked with an examination of her authorial role following the GDR's demise. The narrator of *Stadt der Engel* – also recalling the narrator of *Kindheitsmuster* – repeatedly comments on her experience of having outlived the state which engendered her creative output. Thus, as Smale shows, Wolf links the experience of old age with the task of private introspection and a more public engagement with the memory of the GDR and the writer's role in it.

Rather than focusing on the implications of Wolf's life phase for her writing, Beverly Weber's reading of *Stadt der Engel* is inspired by the significance of Wolf's critique of gender and 'civilization' in relationship to 'race'. Taking this last novel as a point of entry, Weber's 'Christa Wolf's Trouble with Race' reconsiders her oeuvre, particularly *Kindheitsmuster, Kassandra* and *Medea*, to show that race haunts Wolf's texts in the form of oblique but unsettling references to the racializations of whites, Jews, blacks and Native Americans. Wolf's trouble with race, Weber demonstrates, is in turn a troubling of race: a complex, incomplete revelation of the entanglements of race at the heart of that which is considered to be 'Western civilization'.

2011: The End

When Christa Wolf died in December 2011, the German media commemorated her in numerous, largely similar obituaries that echoed statements issued by politicians of the governing conservative party. These obituaries often reference allegations generated during the so-called *Literaturstreit*. Ambivalent, ironic or hostile, they downgrade or defuse Wolf's political stance, render the author and her politics futile or attempt to interpret her and her work through the ideologies dominating unified Germany. Resonating with the debates of the early 1990s, these newspaper publications are, once again, not about Christa Wolf. Rather, they reveal that Wolf appeared threatening at that time of economic crisis, since she embodied, in Ulla Berkéwicz's words, a 'Dichterin, der ihr Staat mißtraut hatte und die doch von den Feinden dieses Staats mit diesem Staat in eins gesetzt war, weil sie in ihr das sahen, was dieses Staates beste Chance gewesen wäre, seine Idee wirklich zu machen' [poet who was suspect to her state (the GDR) but who nevertheless was equated with this state by its enemies, because they recognized in her what the best chances for the realization of this state's founding ideals would have been].[57] Berkéwicz thus affirms the *Neue Zür-icher Zeitung*'s conclusion that Wolf stood for the humane traditions that the GDR claimed but never implemented; for socialist ideals that, particularly in times of economic crisis, when many were looking for alternatives to the capital-ist system, had to be devalued in order to legitimize contemporary pro-market politics in a time of global crisis.[58]

Despite such attempts to degrade Wolf and her significance as a writer, her posthumously published books – *Rede, daß ich dich sehe* (2012), *August* (2012), *Ein Tag im Jahr im neuen Jahrhundert* (2013), *Moskauer Tagebücher* (2014) and *Nachruf auf Lebende* (2014) – sold as well as her previous publications and have contributed to the latest Christa Wolf scholarship. The fact that several of these publications have been translated also points to the author's ongoing sig-nificance; after all, translations are deeply influenced by – and in turn influence – popularity. Translations also influence reception, and several of our contribu-tions engage in questions surrounding the relationships between the two. In 'Translating Subjective Authenticity from *Nachdenken über Christa T.* to *Stadt der Engel* and *August:* Re-presenting Christa Wolf's Subaltern Voice', Caroline Summers deploys Gayatri Spivak's notion of the subaltern to consider how An-glophone norms of translation tend to impact non-dominant language-culture writing. Summers elucidates the effects of these translation strategies on the ex-pression of Wolf's subjective authenticity, which, she demonstrates, is both a lin-guistic and a political practice. Through close readings of several renditions into English, Summers argues that, in the hegemonic world of Anglophone transla-tion and Western capitalism, Wolf's translated German, GDR voice takes on near-subaltern positionality, even as it resonates as world literature.

In 'The Protocol of Barriers to Thinking? Wolf's *Moskauer Tagebücher. Wer wir sind und wer wir waren* (2014)', Birgit Dahlke highlights another aspect of the link between Wolf and world literature. Through what might be called minor transnationalism in Christa Wolf's texts, cross-border reception expands in multiple directions.[59] The *Moscow Diaries* in particular articulate Wolf's poly-semous thoughts, generated by visits to the Soviet Union and other Eastern Euro-pean nations as well as Western countries, including the United States; Dahlke's essayistic tone gestures towards an homage to both Wolf's oblique and multilay-

---

57 Ulla Berkéwicz, in *Wohin sind wir unterwegs? Zum Gedenken an Christa Wolf* (Berlin: Suhr-kamp, 2012), pp. 35–38 (p. 38).
58 For a detailed analysis of these obituaries, see Sonja Klocke, 'The Triumph of the Obituary. Constructing Christa Wolf for the Berlin Republic', *German Studies Review*, 37.2 (2014), 317–336.
59 Françoise Lionnet and Shu-mei Shih, *Minor Transnationalism* (Durham, NC: Duke University Press, 2005).

ered prose style and the elusive subject itself. *Moskauer Tagebücher* is primarily a selection from Wolf's extensive and in part still unpublished diaries; Dahlke deploys them to explore the status of the East in Wolf's oeuvre and the hot-button question of Wolf's treatment of Stalinism, particularly after the purges orchestrated by this Soviet leader were officially denounced at the USSR's Twentieth Communist Party Congress in 1956. Wolf's engagement with National Socialism makes it all the more striking to Dahlke that the author did not develop an aesthetics capable of articulating Stalinism, despite a stated desire to do so in her diaries. Dahlke highlights the changing representations of Moscow and the Soviet Union, fluctuations that re-negotiate the meaning of the eastern Big Brother upon whom the GDR relied. Wolf's reception of the Soviet Union in the diaries moves from her conviction that it was possible to perfect the New Man in this crucible to her belief that the more westerly GDR was more promising. Dahlke thus deftly shows how Wolf's topographical moves between East and West are simultaneously topological moves, in which the meanings of East and West alter according to the particular, always relational, standpoint. Dahlke's exploration also responds to the topical, often disparaging assertion of Wolf's lack of engagement with Stalinism, the Eastern intellectual's critical stance towards many aspects of real-existing socialism and the National Socialist past notwithstanding.

The Reception of Christa Wolf's Work in a Transnational Context

Recent decades have increasingly demonstrated Christa Wolf's status as both a local and an international author. This volume contributes to such understandings by sketching some of the global influences of and in Christa Wolf's work – in China, Vietnam and the United States. By demonstrating the transnational influence of an author from the GDR, our project contributes to debunking the myth of the Eastern Bloc as isolated and provincial. It points to the international and transnational connections within and beyond the robustly active member states of the Council for Mutual Economic Assistance (COMECON).

In 'From Political-Realistic Reading to Multiperspectival Understanding: The Reception of Christa Wolf's *The Divided Heaven* in China', Fan Zhang and Yutian Chen describe and explain shifts in the reception and translation of Wolf's work, particularly *Der geteilte Himmel*, which has been translated three times and has enjoyed popularity since its introduction in 1982. The authors deploy Hans Robert Jauss's and Wolfgang Iser's reception aesthetics to investigate differing horizons of expectation among scholars and the public over several decades, incorporating the influence of enormous societal changes in their interpretations. Since the 1980s, China's move towards market liberalization has contributed to shifts in societal values, tending towards individualism and commodification. Zhang and Chen identify a corresponding increased tendency among scholars to highlight *Der geteilte Himmel*'s modernist aspects. Furthermore, they observe the continued popular interest in this tale about young people seeking orienting principles as related to disorienting changes in China, both then and now.

In 'Reading Christa Wolf in Socialist Vietnam', Huynh Mai Trinh uses Konstanz school reception theory in her study of Vietnamese translations of *Der geteilte Himmel* and Wolf's collections of essays and speeches, *Reden im Herbst* and *Im Dialog,* published as *Bầu trời chia cắt* and the essay collection *Sống hay là bị sống,* respectively. As a member of the Soviet-led COMECON that included China (until 1961), the GDR and other socialist nations around the globe, North Vietnam had a close relationship with the GDR, which continued after Vietnamese unification in 1975. Indeed, the fact that the essay collections were translated in Berlin in 2010 testifies to the Vietnamese community that established itself there during the Cold War.[60] While highlighting the distinctions between Germany and Vietnam, Huynh's work speculates on how Vietnamese readers may have found Wolf's themes of division and unification, the construction of socialist society, and migration particularly salient. Readers from this land marked by struggle continue to appreciate Wolf's long-term, critical engagement with her country. The work of Fan Zhang and Yutian Chen and of Huynh Mai Trinh, which consider the shifting but lasting importance of Christa Wolf in these para-socialist societies, are windows onto Wolf's significance as a global writer.

These contributions treating China and Vietnam also highlight the fact that Christa Wolf's work was received in distinct ways depending on context. Especially in circumstances marked by the events of World War II and the Cold War, different topics were of particular interest in particular national contexts. For instance, in Poland *Kindheitsmuster* was included in school reading lists for its critical engagement with German wartime acts and groundbreaking thematization of the expulsions of Germans from the areas of Hitler's Reich that became Poland after 1945.[61]

---

60 For more on GDR-Vietnam labour flows, see Christina Schwenkel, 'Rethinking Asian Mobilities. Socialist Migration and Post-Socialist Repatriation of Vietnamese Contract Workers in East Germany', *Critical Asian Studies*, 46.2 (2014), 235–258.
61 For example, see Margaret Elzbieta Maliszewska, 'Reise an den "Gedächtnisort" Polen in Romanen zeitgenössischer deutscher Autorinnen' (PhD diss., Queen's University, 2009). Our thanks

In this Eastern Bloc country with a long and complex history with neighbouring Germany, readers were (and are) quite interested in Wolf's work. More than six of her major texts, as well as short stories and selections, were translated, and treatments of them range from historical to political to aesthetic.[62] Monika Wolting points out that state cultural institutions influenced the timing of the translations and their paratextual glosses. Some themes were furthered and others suppressed. (For more on paratexts, see Skare in this volume.) Hubert Orlowski writes about this influence in his afterward to *Rozmyślania nad Christą T.* (1974), describing the six-year delay in this translation of *Nachdenken über Christa T.* (1968). Until 1989, Wolf's work was broadly and positively received by Polish Germanists and was seen as part of a young, progressive GDR literary movement.[63]

In contrast, between 1989 and 1992, as Wolting points out, Polish *feuilletons* picked up, translated and repeated the German *Literaturstreit*. Some of the very scholars who had previously praised her writings wrote harshly about Wolf, her work and the GDR. As mentioned above, the shift to more Western paradigms had taken place differently in Poland than it had in the GDR. Poland's *Solidarność* [Solidarity] movement struggled mightily throughout the 1980s and won arguably democratic elections in 1989, while the GDR was absorbed into the FRG system. Many in Poland found the reformist ideas of GDR intellectuals such as Wolf wrong-headed. Not until around 1992, and again with Wolf's death, did Wolf reception became more differentiated and variegated, focusing particularly on themes of (Polish) *Heimat*, gender and, again, the Nazi past.[64] The attack on

---

to Monika Wolting for her input. Email exchange with Jennifer Ruth Hosek, December 2017. Wolf was born in Landsberg, Germany – in what is today Gorzów Wielkopolski, Poland – and she and her family were expelled in 1945. The GDR did not thematize German forced migration because of its satellite relationship to the Soviets, whose forces had often treated fleeing Germans harshly. Progressives in the FRG also neglected the topic, at least until Chancellor Willy Brandt's normalization of the Polish-German border, in order to discourage claims by German expellees to land that was considered Polish after 1945.

62 Our thanks to Wolfgang Brylla for his input. Email exchange with Jennifer Ruth Hosek, December 2017. See also Wolfgang Brylla, 'Zur Christa-Wolf-Rezeption in Polen nach 1989', *Studia Niemcoznawcze*, 53 (2014), 379–395; *Deutschland- und Polenbilder in der Literatur nach 1989*, ed. by Carsten Gansel and Monika Wolting (Göttingen: V&R unipress, 2015).

63 Monika Wolting, '"Zukunft? Das ist das gründlich Andere". Zu Aspekten der Rezeptionsgeschichte von Christa Wolf in Polen', in *Zwischen Moskauer Novelle und Stadt der Engel. Neue Perspektiven auf das Lebenswerk von Christa Wolf*, ed. by Carsten Gansel and Therese Hörnigk (Berlin: vbb, 2015), pp. 151–170.

64 Ibid. See also Halina Ludorowska, 'Rezeption in Polen', in Hilmes and Nagelschmidt, pp. 360–363.

Wolf in Poland can be seen as a backlash against the state socialist systems in both countries.

Other contexts engendered different receptions, only some of which can be touched on here. For instance, the GDR and other state socialist countries had seen censorious slowdowns in the production of *Nachdenken über Christa T.* Interest in Christa T.'s engagement with her social environment was transnational, but was nevertheless generated by different motives and interpretations. In France, for example, the writer and critic André Wurmser argued that, while GDR readings saw the promotion of individualism, the novel actually advanced the development of personality.[65] Moreover, the publishing house of the French Communist Party had released *Der geteilte Himmel* as *Le Ciel partagé* by 1964, while the more independent leftist Le Seuil published *Christa T.* in 1972. In Italy, *Nachdenken über Christa T.*, which Anna Chiarloni sees as resonating with 1960s Italian New Subjectivity, was published in 1973 as *Reflessioni su Christa T.*[66] In contrast, *Der geteilte Himmel* did not come out until 1983 as *Il cielo diviso*. Reception of *Christa T.* in France and Italy, as well as in the United States, suggests both that the scholars there wanted to support the work against its devaluation in the GDR and that they saw it as an important expression of struggles for self-actualization in a communitarian vein. Interestingly, even in post-1990s, capitalist Poland, the individual protagonist in *Christa T.* is not emphasized. Additionally, unlike in Poland, *Kindheitsmuster* was not translated in Italy and France until 1992, suggesting that its themes were not as relevant for these nations, which had experienced World War II differently. The 1983 translations of *Kassandra*, on the other hand, found a large readership in many countries. Chiarloni suggests that themes such as patriarchy, pacifism and the increased danger of war on European soil due to the installation of short-range nuclear missiles there resonated very strongly in Italy, for instance. In contrast to reception in Poland and Germany, in Italy, France, and the US, as well as in China and Vietnam, the *Literaturstreit* controversy around Wolf's Stasi involvement and the publication of *Was bleibt* raised muted criticism and sometimes sympathy. Wolf was seen as a principled intellectual who sought to support and improve the GDR. Writing in *Libération*, Jean-Michel Palmier asserts, 'It is hard to grasp that one attacks such a person, a person who was actually brave.'[67]

In Western Bloc and Western countries post-Cold War – including France, Italy, and especially the United States – feminists commonly heralded (and con-

---

65 Alain Lance, 'Rezeption in Frankreich', in Hilmes and Nagelschmidt, pp. 354–360 (p. 355).
66 Anna Chiarloni, 'Rezeption in Italien', in Hilmes and Nagelschmidt, pp. 350–354.
67 Quoted in Alain Lance, 'Rezeption in Frankreich,' in Hilmes and Nagelschmidt, pp. 354–360 (p. 357).

tinue to herald) Wolf. While the writer did not call herself a feminist, an identification that state socialism deemed bourgeois, her work engaged woman-centred issues in transnationally relevant ways. Anna Kuhn's article in this volume, 'The Gendered Reception of Christa Wolf: From *Der geteilte Himmel* to *Kassandra*', draws upon and extends her own well-known scholarship to highlight and historicize US feminist reception. Kuhn shows the thematic and aesthetic shift in Wolf's writing from more straightforward, socialist realism to work that questions the seamlessness of relations between the socialist individual and socialist society and critiques patriarchy in both socialism and capitalism. Kuhn's gloss intriguingly and compellingly argues that those investigations that deploy Western feminist theory not only trenchantly unpack aspects of the East German writer's oeuvre, but presage the woman-centric themes that drive Wolf's later texts. Kuhn analyzes the decades-long reception of the author among scholars and the press in West and East Germany as well as in the United States to show how it is inflected by gender and geopolitics. Drawing on Sonja E. Klocke's assessment of Wolf's obituaries, Kuhn finds that the frequent excoriation of Wolf therein shows that the 'predominately male West German media's final discrediting of the GDR's most prominent woman writer was its ultimate Cold War political move. Twenty-two years after the collapse of East bloc communism, which ostensibly signalled the end of the Cold War, it again heralded the triumph of Western capitalism over Eastern socialism.'

In North America, the reception of Wolf often focused on general themes. For the general public, as Christine Zehl Romero explains, the distance between Europe and North America made the more general humanistic and aesthetic aspects of Wolf's oeuvre more salient than the political elements, although the English version of *Kindheitsmuster, Patterns of Childhood,* was read at least in part as an investigation of the Nazi regime. *Der geteilte Himmel* was available in 1965 as *The Divided Heaven* from the GDR's foreign language Seven Seas Press and was popular as a window into the German situation in Europe. In 2013, at the same time as the US translation of *Stadt der Engel* into *City of Angels. Or, The Overcoat of Dr. Freud* appeared, the Canadian University of Ottawa Press produced a new translation of *Der geteilte Himmel,* entitled *They Divided the Sky.* Wolf's very positive reception in the US may have positively influenced her status in Germany, particularly in the wake of the *Literaturstreit.* GDR literature and culture took on increasing importance in academic circles with the development of German Studies, and Christa Wolf's contributions, as well as the work of many female GDR authors, has received attention that continues today,[68] as this volume itself amply demonstrates.

68 Christiane Zehl Romero, 'Rezeption in den USA', in Hilmes and Nagelschmidt, pp. 363–369.

Curtis Swope

Modernity and the City in Christa Wolf's Oeuvre of the 1960s

The Marxist political scientist Marshall Berman sees modernity as a socio-economic process that disrupts inherited practices of social life and reshapes human minds.[1] Sometimes implicitly, sometimes explicitly, modernity played an important role in Christa Wolf's work long before science-minded novels such as *Störfall* (1987) and *Kassandra* (1983) and even before her 1973 'Neue Lebensansichten eines Katers', which satirized the popularity of cybernetics in East German discourse. In her work of the 1960s, from the *Moskauer Novelle* (1961), to the novel and film *Der geteilte Himmel* (1963, 1964), to the movie *Fräulein Schmetterling* (1965) and the short story 'Unter den Linden' (1974), the ruptures of modernity are most visible in Wolf's representation of cities.

In these texts, themes such as vital pedestrian life in the age of the automobile and old neighbourhoods threatened by the wrecking ball have two functions. The first is that they reveal the importance of the empirical social observation of modern realities in Wolf's oeuvre.[2] This is significant because research on the role of modernity in Wolf's texts has tended to treat modernity in idealist terms. In other words, scholars have focused more on the 'mental' component of Berman's definition of modernity than on the mundane, material side of it. For example, Julia Hell used classic tools such as the id and the ego to uncover mentalities and discourses rather than probe material realities.[3] Similarly, David

---

1 Marshall Berman, *All That Is Solid Melts into Air. The Experience of Modernity* (New York: Verso, 1983), pp. 15–19.
2 It should also be noted that scholars of East German literature and culture have recently downplayed the importance of modernity as a category for analyzing culture in the former East. Wolfgang Emmerich, for whom modernity was long a way to frame East German literature of the 1960s, has pronounced it no longer useful as an interpretive reference point. For Emmerich's assessment of modernity in East German literature see Wolfgang Emmerich, *Kleine Literaturgeschichte der DDR* (Berlin: Aufbau, 2000). For his recent rejection of modernity as a category see Wolfgang Emmerich, 'Zwischen Chronotopos und drittem Raum. Wie schreibt man die Geschichte des literarischen Feldes DDR', in *„Nach der Mauer der Abgrund'. (Wieder-)Annäherungen an die DDR-Literatur*, ed. by Norbert Otto Eke (Amsterdam: Rodopi, 2013), pp. 43–64.
3 Julia Hell, *Post-fascist Fantasies. Psychoanalysis, History, and the Literature of East Germany* (Durham: Duke University Press, 1997). The extremely varied and complex relationship between psychoanalysis and idealism obviously cannot be dealt with in the context of my study. For a clear but nuanced account of the ambiguous centrality of idealism to Freud's categories, see Joel Faflak, 'Schopenhauer's Telling Body of Philosophy', in *Idealism without Absolutes. Philos-*

https://doi.org/10.1515/9783110496000-003

Bathrick saw the Romantic heritage in Wolf as a discursive practice rather than a materialist social critique.[4] Myra N. Love revealed how Wolf's metaphors resisted intellectual and linguistic structures rather than social ones. For Andreas Huyssen, the reference point for Wolf's work was the Marxist philosopher Ernst Bloch, the most idealist of the Hegelian Marxists, who in the 1920s began espousing a less technocratic Marxism than the Leninism that predominated in the Soviet Union.[5]

However, modernity is not just a set of psychic or linguistic structures; it is also, as seen in Berman's definition, a physical imposition that operates on the mundane level of everyday life. Scholars have acknowledged the material side of modernity in the work of other East German writers, such as Heiner Müller, but have not analysed it in Wolf's. This could be because her oeuvre has been gendered in terms of 'subjective authenticity' and 'romanticism' or because of scholars' focus on how Wolf overcame a labour-based view of social experience.[6] Examining the city in Wolf's writings of the 1960s can redirect our attention to Wolf as a hard-nosed social observer willing to arrive at the subjective via an unvarnished account of the conditions of daily life.

The second function of urban space in Wolf's work is its close relationship to the increasingly experimental narrative forms of her texts. Wolf's modernism – that is, her literary experimentation in the 1960s – has been seen as a product of her quest for subjectivities opposed to the dictates of socialist reality.[7] That experimentation, however, is just as much a product of Wolf's socially attuned

---

ophy and Romantic Culture, ed. by Tilttama Rajan and Arkady Plotnitsky (Albany: SUNY Press, 2004), pp. 161–179.

4 David Bathrick, *The Powers of Speech. The Politics of Culture in the GDR* (Lincoln: University of Nebraska Press, 1995), p. 188.

5 Myra N. Love, '"To render the blind spot of this culture visible". Christa Wolf and the Citadel of Reason', in *Responses to Christa Wolf*, ed. by Marilyn Sibley Fries (Detroit: Wayne State Press, 1989), pp. 186–195; Andreas Huyssen, 'Traces of Ernst Bloch. Reflections on Christa Wolf', in Sibley Fries, pp. 233–247.

6 The popularity of the term 'subjective authenticity' as a category for analysis of Wolf's work is most likely attributable to Wolf's much-cited interview with Hans Kaufmann: 'Gespräch mit Christa Wolf', *Weimarer Beiträge*, 6 (1974), 90–112.

7 My work seeks to complement rather than revise this standard interpretation. For representative interpretations in this connection, see Therese Hörnigk, *Christa Wolf* (Göttingen: Steidl, 1989). I use the definition of modernism offered in Bathrick and Huyssen's *Modernity and the Text*. There, modernism is understood as the variety of self-consciously experimental ways in which twentieth-century writers tried to mediate modern experience; see Andreas Huyssen and David Bathrick, 'Modernism and the Experience of Modernity', in *Modernity and the Text. Revisions of German Modernism*, ed. by Bathrick and Huyssen (New York: Columbia University Press, 1989), pp. 1–16.

reckoning with modernity as she saw it unfolding in East Germany's city streets and public squares. In her work from the 1960s, temporal experimentation, shifting narrative perspectives, and metaphor stem as much from modern social realities as from idealistic preoccupations with subjectivity.

In addition, themes such as tenement demolition and techniques such as destabilizing narrative structures link Wolf's work to authors and film directors abroad who were active at the same time. For example, Italian film directors, including Federico Fellini, influenced Wolf's literary production.[8] Fellini and Wolf in turn both formed part of a pan-European phenomenon, criticizing modernity through treatment of one of its key aspects: urban space. In the post-War period, modern architecture's association with authoritarian planning regimes and the erasure of historic neighbourhoods gave rise to a broad, international discourse critical of modernist urbanism.[9] Wolf's work of the 1960s, far from being a parochialized relic of East German socialism or an individualized pursuit of authentic selfhood, was part of an international, modernist reckoning with daily realities of rapid change in the urban environment.

---

[8] Alexander Stephan noted this connection in his classic study of Wolf's work: Alexander Stephan, *Christa Wolf*, 4th edn (Munich: Beck'sche Reihe, 1991), 17. Henning Wrage and Marc Silberman have traced the availability of international films in East Germany; see Henning Wrage and Marc Silberman, introduction to *DEFA at the Crossroads of East German and International Film Culture. A Companion*, ed. by Wrage and Silberman (Berlin/Boston: De Gruyter, 2014), pp. 1–24 (pp. 7–9). Hunter Bivens argues that DEFA films and experimental films elsewhere in the 1950s and 1960s deal with modernity, but that the East German ones do so with different political agendas; see Hunter Bivens, 'Cinema and Socialist Modernity', in Wrage and Silberman, pp. 25–44. Klaus Wischnewski compiled self-assessments by Konrad Wolf, the director of the film version of *Der Geteile Himmel*, and included Wolf's account of his meeting Fellini in Italy in 1959; see Klaus Wischnewski, *Konrad Wolf. Selbstzeugnisse, Fotos, Dokumente* (Berlin: Henschel, 1985), p. 106. Barton Byg was the first scholar to systematically trace, generally with reference to the specific thematic content of films, the outlines of DEFA cinema's relationship to film noir and Italian Neo-Realism; see Barton Byg, 'DEFA and the Traditions of International Cinema', in *DEFA. East German Cinema, 1946–1992*, ed. by Seán Allan and John Sandford (New York: Berghahn Books, 1999), pp. 22–41. In this article, Byg called for further, intensive cultural studies work on the international connections of DEFA. The Wrage and Silberman volume cited above is a major contribution in this regard, but many more close critical readings – accompanied where possible by archival evidence – need to be done.

[9] William J.R. Curtis, *Modern Architecture since 1900*, 3rd edn (London: Phaidon, 1996), pp. 547–549.

The Modern City in *Moskauer Novelle*

In Wolf's *Moskauer Novelle*, Moscow's pedestrian culture and traditional neighbourhood life lend themselves to close, sociological observation. The main character, Vera, whose fraught reunion with a Russian soldier constitutes the novella's main plot, studies the city carefully. On one of her first nights in the Soviet capital, Vera decides that she must go to Red Square. She sets out on foot from her hotel, but is unable to find her way to the city's political centre. Instead, she wanders into 'Gassen, flankiert von kleinen, schiefen Holzhäusern, zwischen deren Pflaster Gras sproß' [alleys flanked by small, crooked wooden houses, where grass had sprung up between the paving stones].[10] In this neighbourhood, she discovers the 'old Moscow', a place where harmonica music rises up from behind wooden fences, where couples whisper in niches, and weak street lanterns create yellow rings in the darkness. Before reluctantly returning to her hotel, Vera continues her late-night Benjaminian *flanerie* to a busy nearby train station. In the juxtaposition between the unreached Red Square and the fascinations of close-knit neighbourhood life, the text evinces a close focus on the concrete way in which Moscow's socialist modernity, with its showpiece architecture, exists in opposition to but has not fully supplanted older forms of urban life.

Vera's sociological inquiry deepens as the novella progresses:

> Vera bekam nicht genug von dieser Stadt. Sie lief durch die Straßen, setzte sich in den Parks auf Bänke, fuhr unter und über der Erde kreuz und quer bis in die entlegensten Stadtteile. Am meisten erregten und fesselten sie die Menschen, zu jeder Stunde in Massen auf der Straße, und doch alles andere als Masse.

> [Vera could not get enough of this city. She walked through the streets, sat on benches in parks, rode under and above ground to the most distant quarters of town. The people excited and captured her most of all, at all hours on the street in masses, yet anything but a simple mass].[11]

On a trip with some of her German friends, she again eschews a standard tourist attraction, Mayakovsky Square, in favour of taking photographs of side streets in undiscovered neighbourhoods. The thrill of informal, everyday Moscow social life stands in opposition to state-shaped spaces such as Mayakovsky Square, site of the Peking Hotel, a significant work of Stalinist architecture. Such contrasts reveal the text's preoccupation with the power and limits of modern

---

10 Christa Wolf, *Moskauer Novelle*, in *Christa Wolf. Die Lust gekannt zu sein. Erzählungen, 1960–1980* (Frankfurt a. M.: Suhrkamp, 2008), p. 16. The translation is my own.
11 Wolf, *Moskauer Novelle*, 20–21.

state projects to dictate social life. It is for this reason that Vera recurrently views the city from above in her hotel and likens its streets and people to an organism.

The juxtaposition between Moscow's status as a vital urban organism and a site of modern state power become part of the work's literary experimentality as Vera's social observations of her time in Moscow interrupt the main plot about her relationship to Pawel. As a result of the passages about urban realities, then, the work takes on a more episodic quality that interferes with the forward progress of the narrative. In addition, vibrant street life as an antidote to modern tourism and state orchestration of space gives *Moskauer Novelle* international relevance. Jane Jacobs, in her *The Death and Life of Great American Cities* (1961), a book written at the same time as *Moskauer Novelle*, uses sociological analysis to lament state insensitivity to neighbourhood social patterns. Understood in the light of Jacobs's work, Wolf's novella emerges as part of an international discourse critical of the effects of modernity on the social space of the city.

Urban Bookends for *Der Geteilte Himmel*

In *Der Geteilte Himmel*, Wolf's breakthrough novel, close observation of urban life and modern social change also plays a significant role. The story centres on the characters Rita and Manfred and is told in retrospect, after Rita suffers an accident at work. In the two years leading up to the injury from which Rita is recovering, Manfred, a chemist, had helped her leave the village where she lived with her mother and grandmother. She joins her fiancé Manfred in Halle, as construction on the new city there is starting, to train to be a teacher and to work in a train-car factory. Manfred goes to a conference in West Berlin and refuses to return. Rita visits him there but ultimately returns to the East to continue her studies and contribute to socialist society.

In the novel's opening and closing bookends, more intensively than at other points in the novel, description of the city functions as a vehicle for reflecting on the material reality of urban life. The novel begins,

> Die Stadt, kurz vor Herbst noch in Glut getaucht nach dem kühlen Regensommer dieses Jahres, atmete heftiger als sonst. Ihr Atem fuhr als geballter Rauch aus hundert Fabrikschornsteinen in den reinen Himmel, aber dann verließ ihn die Kraft weiterzuziehen.

> [The city, on the threshold of autumn basked in the hot sun after long weeks of rain; its breath, coming faster than usual, puffed up through hundreds of factory chimneys into the clear sky, where it hung motionless].[12]

---

12 Christa Wolf, *Der geteilte Himmel*, 33rd edn (Munich: DTV, 1999), p. 5. The English for all quo-

The urban industrial environment even extends its reach to nature, producing bitter, 'verfluchte[s] Wasser, das nach Chemie stank' [accursed water that stank of chemistry].[13] Here, Wolf presents an urban milieu plagued by the ravages of a destructive industrial modernity and beset by the threat of atomic warfare.

Yet despite humanity's capacity to ruin its cities with polluting factories, urban space as a site of human reproduction and life – in the sense that Marx uses those terms in his early writings – plays a vital role: 'Ein Schatten war über die Stadt gefallen, nun war sie wieder heiß und lebendig, sie gebar und begrub, sie gab Leben und forderte Leben, täglich' [A shadow had fallen over the city; now it was warm and alive again, bearing and burying life, giving and taking it away].[14] The 'hot' and vital city is a site not just for destructive industry, but also – despite its modernity – for natural, bodily processes of death and regeneration. The evocation of the city as organism, an echo of *Moskauer Novelle*, resurfaces on the next page of the novel, as Rita awakens after her accident. The first thing she recalls as she awakens is the city. Her line of thought continues, 'Enger noch, die Fabrik, die Montagehalle' [the works and the workshop].[15] Wolf uses the moment of Rita's awakening to signal spatially the transition from the level of urban modernity to the particularities of the novel's plot. This micro level of the assembly shop – and, as the novel progresses, relationships and family – go on to structure the bulk of the novel. Right from the outset, however, Wolf delves into the specific physical realities of life in cities as it is reshaped by modern forces.

On the novel's last page, the city again holds out the promise of human creativity in concrete urban space. Rita's convalescence, like her relationship with Manfred, is over, and '[d]ie Dämmerung hängt tief in den Straßen. Die Leute kommen von der Arbeit nach Hause. In den dunklen Häuserwänden springen die Lichtvierecke auf' [the day [...] was drawing to a close. People were on their way home from work. Squares of light sprang up in the dark walls].[16] The twilight of early evening forms a mysterious backdrop to the rituals of daily life and signals the creative significance of quotidian activities, such as the walk home from work. Indeed, for Rita, the first act of what she calls her freedom is walking in the city:

---

tations from this novel is taken from Christa Wolf, *Divided Heaven*, trans. by Joan Becker (Berlin: Seven Seas Books, 1965).

13 Ibid., 5.
14 Ibid., 5.
15 Ibid., 6.
16 Ibid., 238.

Rita macht einen großen Umweg durch die Straßen und blickt in viele Fenster. Sie sieht, wie jeden Abend eine unendliche Menge an Freundlichkeit, die tagsüber verbraucht wurde, immer neu hervorgebracht wird.

[Rita went a long way out of her way, walking along many streets and glancing in at many windows. She saw how inexhaustible supplies of kindliness, used up during the day, were renewed each evening].[17]

The modern city, as much as it is a modern industrial beast, is also still a site for the reproduction of the rituals and emotions that sustain everyday human life across generations. It should be noted that Wolf locates the possibility for reclaiming those rituals and emotions in the socialist world; Manfred's life in his aunt's house in West Berlin seems by contrast an alienated existence, without hope for remediation.

Despite this strongly socialist aspect of the text, the passages about urban social life nevertheless give it a resonance that extends beyond East Germany.[18] The horrors of industrial modernity as experienced in the urban environment form the centrepiece of Michelangelo Antonioni's *Red Desert*, a 1964 film that was being made around the time that Wolf wrote her novel. Similarly, the fascination with the everyday relationship between work and home in the urban environment links Wolf's novel thematically to the second volume of Marxist sociologist and philosopher Henri Lefebvre's *Critique of Everyday Life* (1961), in which the spiritual privation and revolutionary potential of everyday social rituals is the primary focus. Through close engagement with changes in the urban environment in East Germany, Wolf developed critiques similar to those being developed by artists and intellectuals in other European countries.

Konrad Wolf's film based on the novel also pursued such internationally relevant lines of inquiry. In the celebrated but controversial film, the city plays an even more incisive role than in the novel as a material site in which modernity must be negotiated. The claustrophobic environment of Manfred's parents' apartment reveals the social pressures involved in the search for work and fulfilment in the urban environment. Visible in the background of such scenes are construction cranes that attest to the modern forces that are reshaping reality in the in-

---

17 Ibid., 238.
18 My analysis of the novel joins the now-substantial body of scholarship that has shown that *Der Geteilte Himmel* does not belong to the genre of *Ankunftsliteratur*. See Hell, *Postfascist Fantasies*, 165; Renate Rechtien, 'The Topography of the Self in Christa Wolf's *Der Geteilte Himmel*', *German Life and Letters*, 63.4 (2010), 477–478; Sonja Klocke, '(Anti-) faschistische Familien und (post-)faschistische Körper. Christa Wolfs Der geteilte Himmel', in *Christa Wolf. Erinnern und Erinnerung*, ed. by Carsten Gansel with Sonja Klocke (Berlin/Boston: De Gruyter, 2014), pp. 69–87.

dustrial city where the story is set. The film also makes use of the harsh dichotomy of human beings, often pictured alone in disturbing close-ups, and overscaled industrial and housing complexes. The modern urban environment once more appears as a threat to human existence.

As a result of the close observation of the urban environment, the film – like *Mokauer Novelle* and the novel *Der geteilte Himmel* – gains relevance beyond the temporal and geographic borders of East Germany. The dramatization of harsh urban realities recalls the Expressionist *mise-en-scène* of Murnau's *Der letzte Mann* [*The Last Laugh*, 1924]. The highly abstract compositions of on-location urban settings evoke the experimental urban films of the Weimar era, such as Walther Ruttmann's *Berlin Sinfonie einer Großstadt* [*Berlin. Symphony of a Metropolis*]. The representation of factories and modern housing complexes calls to mind Fellini's extensive use of modernist architecture in *La Dolce Vita* (1961) and Antonioni's critiques of modern architecture in *Eclipse* (1962).[19] The film version of *Der geteilte Himmel* and its international relevance form part of a broader critical discourse on modern urban life, in which Christa Wolf's work of the 1960s also participated. That discourse extended across borders to non-socialist countries. It also extended temporally, back to the experimental film and literature of the Weimar Republic, which was crucial to the development of the New Wave cinemas in France and Italy and played a significant but contested role in East German culture.[20]

---

19 While, as noted above, scholars have suggested affinities between Konrad Wolf's work and that of the French New Wave, little close analysis of film techniques and themes has been included in such comparisons. Wolf himself recounted a meeting with Fellini in 1959, during a week-long festival in Italy devoted to DEFA, in which the East German was keen to know how the Italian filmed his scenes on modern expressways and in crowded workers' districts. According to Konrad Wolf, Fellini answered him by simply leading him to the studio sets used for scenes that Wolf had assumed were filmed on location. This revelation was crucial for Wolf, who had long admired the gritty films of earlier Italian Neo-Realism but, through his meeting with Fellini, came to understand how realism contained the seeds of potentially more experimental aesthetic approaches. See Wischnewski, *Konrad Wolf*. For Fellini, as for Wolf, closer, seemingly more realist, empirical engagement with the urban environment was, paradoxically, part of a move away from the aesthetic dictates of realist narratives which could no longer account for the threatening and fragmented realities of modern urban life.
20 For the influence of 1920s German cinema on post-War film in France and Italy, see Barbara Mennel, *Cities and Cinema* (New York: Taylor and Francis, 2008), pp. 20–21. Debates about the role of 1920s avant-garde culture in East Germany have been extensive. Scholars have tended to focus on the legacy of Bertolt Brecht's epic theatre for 1960s East German literature. For an overview, see David Bathrick, 'Agitproptheater in der DDR. Auseinandersetzung mit einer Tradition', in *Dramatik der DDR*, ed. by Ulrich Profitlich (Frankfurt a. M.: Suhrkamp, 1987), pp. 128–149.

Order and Spontaneity in *Fräulein Schmetterling*

In the film *Fräulein Schmetterling*, which Christa Wolf herself had a key role in shaping, the sociological critique of urban life becomes even more intense. It also becomes more fraught in terms of its temporal connections back to the cinema of the Weimar era and to the urban films of the French and Italian New Waves. The film's many scenes of street life in contemporary Berlin and its mixture of documentary and narrative place it firmly within an international modernist tradition of filmmaking about the city that has resonance beyond the socialist world.

Incomplete at the time authorities shut down filming in December 1965, in the wake of the Eleventh Plenary of the Socialist Unity Party, *Fräulein Schmetterling* is a fragmentary *tour-de-force* through the social tapestry of an East Berlin undergoing rapid change. Teenage Helene and her six-year-old sister, Asta, try to make ends meet after their father dies. The girls learn that they cannot keep the family cigar store and that their old building, located near new highrise housing projects in Berlin, is slated for demolition. After failed turns as a fishmonger, clothing store clerk, and bus conductor, Helene receives a new apartment from the state. Unsatisfied, she returns to her old apartment, where she finds her little sister, who has been thrown out by the girls' aunt. This spare story is interspersed with scenes of Helene's fantasies about what her life should be – ranging from her desire to fly, to working as a glamorous flight attendant. A substantial portion of the surviving footage for the film consists of on-location, ambient scenes of streets, squares, alleys, and cafes in East Berlin, documentary scenes that are placed without commentary between the sequences in which the story moves forward. To an astounding extent, these documentary scenes resemble the subject matter and mood of documentary footage from Edgar Ulmer's, Billy Wilder's and Kurt and Robert Siodmack's film *Menschen am Sonntag* [*People on Sunday*, 1929/1930]. It is unclear, however, the extent to which this classic Berlin film was known in East Germany. The title appeared in social and film theorist Siegfried Kracauer's widely read study, *From Caligari to Hitler. A Psychological History of German Film* (1947).[21] The film scholar Noah Eisenberg has asserted, but not extensively documented, the film's influence on the French New Wave of the late 1950s and early 1960s, which was received in

---

21 Siegfried Kracauer, *From Caligari to Hitler. A Psychological History of German Film* (Princeton: Princeton University Press, 1947).

East Germany.[22] Although there is no hard proof for the line of influence from these German precedents to French and East German cultural production, it is clear – as with *Der geteilte Himmel* – that *Fräulein Schmetterling* constitutes a reckoning with international urban phenomena that was in tune with Western film themes and techniques.

The film is driven by close observation of urban milieus and by montages of new and old buildings in the urban environment.[23] Such scenes include narrow, trash-strewn alleys filled with children playing, subject matter that recalls Piel Jutzti's socialist film *Mutter Krausens Fahrt ins Glück* [*Mother Krause's Journey into Happiness*, 1929]. If in Jutzi's film, these alleys represented an urban milieu in desperate need of radical reform, in *Fräulein Schmetterling*, it is the radicality of reform – in the form of demolition of proletarian districts – that comes under social critique. Again, as with the connection to *Menschen am Sonntag*, there is not proof that Kurt Barthel or Christa Wolf knew Jutzi's films, but the visual similarities again suggest an awareness on the part of the film team of broader modern discourses about the city. The simultaneously joyous and threatening clamour of an old Berlin market hall similarly engages in rough-and-tumble social commentary about changes to the city in the post-War period. Such scenes –

---

22 Noah Isenberg, 'People on Sunday. Young People Like Us', essay for the Criterion Collection DVD of the film, 2011.

23 The focus on urban life must not be attributed solely to director Kurt Barthel's interest in the highly urban Neo-Realist films of Vittorio de Sica and the early Fellini; as has been shown, Wolf had been interested in urban spontaneity as an antidote to modern power projection and planning regimes since her debut work. Furthermore, as Barthel noted in a 2005 interview with the DEFA-Film-Stiftung, the script and the concept for the film were both Wolf's; see Ralf Schenk, 'Ein Gespräch mit dem Regisseur Kurt Barthel', in *'Fräulein Schmetterling', 1966–2005. Geschichte und Hintergründe* (Berlin: DEFA Stiftung and Bundesarchiv-Filmarchiv, 2005), pp. 19–27 (p. 19). Also, the many scenes in the film that deal with change in the urban environment express concerns found in other works of East German film and literature and in film abroad at this time. Such works are too numerous to list here. It is worth noting that some of the most famous examples, such as Heiner Carow's film *The Legend of Paul and Paula* (1973) and Günter de Bruyn's novel *Buridans Esel* (1968), postdate *Fräulein Schmetterling*. On the symbolic significance of tenement life in East German culture, see Irene Dölling, '"We All Love Paula but Paul is More Important to Us". Constructing a "Socialist Person" Using the "Femininity" of a Working Woman', *New German Critique*, 82 (Winter 2001), 77–90; Hunter Bivens, 'Neustadt. Affect and Architecture in Brigitte Reiman's East German Novel, *Franziska Linkerhand*', *Germanic Review*, 83.2 (2008), 139–166. While the juxtaposition of old and new buildings appears regularly in East German culture, it is far from being an East German peculiarity. In the United States, Samuel Fuller's social realist Los Angeles film *Crimson Kimono* (1959) contains stark, symbolic shots of old and new buildings in close proximity to one another. The Monsieur Hulot films of the French director Jacques Tati, most notably his *Mon Oncle* (1959), use changes in the urban environment and the contrast of new and old buildings to comic effect.

in addition to shots that mark the intense contrast between late nineteenth-century buildings and new, modernist apartments – place this GDR film within a larger international discourse on urban planning in cinema. It was not just in East Germany that buildings were being torn down at high rates and old market halls appeared as relics in fast-changing cities. Such thematic concerns in *Fräulein Schmetterling* reveal the embeddedness of the film in a broader, international response to urban change in the post-War period.

That broader resonance also operates at the level of the film's formal vocabulary, including its soundscape and urban montages, which reveal social fragmentation in the modern urban environment.[24] Some of these techniques are ones Wolf used in her written work. The ambient noise of the city, with snippets of conversation caught on the sidewalk, is characteristic of the French New Wave and appears in Wolf's short story, 'Unter den Linden'. The juxtaposition of image and reality, already present in *Moskauer Novelle* and *Der Geteilte Himmel*, plays a role in *Fräulein Schmetterling* when Helene's fantasy about what a new apartment might be like is contrasted to the harsh angularity of the cell-like habitation she actually receives. The film's abrupt transitions in subject and composition, a technique that undergirded Fellini's estranging montages of urban and interior space in *La Dolce Vita*, have affinities with Wolf's own play with narrative time in 'Unter den Linden'.[25] Thus, Wolf's keen, social observation of the way in which the economic and political forces of modernity reshape the city goes hand-in-hand – as it had for the Italian Neo-Realists and post-Neo-Realists – with her own filmic and literary turn to the experimental conventions of the avant-garde cinema of her time.

International relevance and the film's social observation of modernity are particularly closely linked in the film's final scene. Here, Helene and Asta join a circus clown in handing out flowers at random to the office and industrial workers thronging Alexanderplatz. The result is a romantic, urban spontaneity as passers-by redirect their routes along the sidewalk and react with various emotions to the unusual scene before them. The clown, Helene and Asta come upon a taxi stand where an unruly crowd is trying to push its way to the front of the line. In a seemingly spontaneous dance, the clown, with assistance from the girls, organizes the crowd and regulates the entry of passengers into

---

24 The relationship between Wolf's agenda and the film's formal vocabulary is necessarily difficult to reconstruct because we do not have full records of communication between Barthel, the master cinematographer Werner Bergmann, and Wolf.

25 On Fellini's treatment of urban modernity, see Alessia Ricciardi, 'The Spleen of Rome. Modernity in Fellini's *La Dolce Vita*', *Modernism/Modernity*, 7.2 (2000), 201–219.

the taxi seats.[26] In so doing, the group adds to its protest against alienated modernity (the handing-out of flowers) a correction of that modernity: the taxi stand comes to function better through their intervention. The reconciliation of planning and creativity happens here not as an idealist synthesis, but as a statement about the concrete use of urban space. The film's preoccupation with the use of space connects it to important Marxist theories of the city outside of East Germany. For example, the reclamation and humanization of spaces shaped by urban alienation was a central preoccupation of Henri Lefebvre's in his *The Urban Revolution* (1970). Wolf's *Fräulein Schmetterling*, in its theoretical implications about the status of the city at mid-century, stands as part of the international discourse on the way modernity was reshaping everyday life.

Urban Modernity in 'Unter den Linden'

In 'Unter den Linden', Wolf picks up thematically on *Moskauer Novelle*. There, Vera happily fails to find Red Square on her first night in Moscow and instead wanders through old neighbourhoods in stark contrast to the glittering official buildings of the city. In the 1968 short story, the narrator intends to go to the newly built quarters of Berlin but instead is drawn by a mysterious power back to the epicentre of the capital, the street of the story's title. An impressionistic sequence of urban encounters rather than a cohesive narrative, 'Unter den Linden' is the narrator's recollection of her time as a student at the Humboldt University. In a dream, she visits the Unter den Linden of the mid-1960s to investigate events related to her student past. Jarring juxtapositions between the current and the remembered boulevard structure the story. At its close, the narrator reaches an ambiguous self-realization when she meets a woman on the stately boulevard who is inexplicably happy – a woman who turns out to be the narrator herself.

The juxtaposition between the city as presented in official images and the street as a part of social experience is a key part of the story from the outset. The third paragraph begins,

---

26 This final moment of the film strongly resembles the French filmmaker Jacques Tati's 1959 film, *Mon Oncle*, which has Tati's courtly, naïve and charmingly bumbling Mr. Hulot reconfiguring and working against the grain of the highly modernist urban and interior spaces of France's new towns. Hulot, like the clown and the girls in *Fräulein Schmetterling*, uses a productive chaos to humanize, rather than obliterate, the effects of modernity in the urban environment.

Daß die Straße berühmt ist, hat mich nie gestört, im Wachen nicht und erst recht nicht im Traum. Ich begreife, daß sie dieses Mißgeschick ihrer Lage verdankt: Ost-West-Achse. Sie und die Straße, die mir im Traum erscheint, haben nichts miteinander zu tun. Die eine wird in meiner Abwesenheit durch Zeitungsbilder und Touristenfotos mißbraucht, die andere hält sich auch über lange Zeiträume für mich bereit

[It has never bothered me that the street is famous, not during my waking hours and most certainly not in my dreams. I am aware that it has suffered this misfortune on account of its location: East-West axis. The street and the one appearing in my dreams have nothing in common. The one is abused by newspaper pictures and tourists' photographs in my absence; the other stands at my disposal, undamaged, even over long periods of time].[27]

Like *Moskauer Novelle*, 'Unter den Linden' recovers the everyday experience in a modern city characterized by axial planning, the rifts of international politics, the propaganda of newspapers, and the trivialities of the tourist photo. The self here is not just a tool for expressing scepticism about official language, but is also a clear-eyed recorder of real social experience – in this case, of modern urban space.

The street that 'holds itself ready' is, of course, a highly personal street. However, the personal lens is used to underscore the difference between officialized state space and the lived experience of urban life. The story is, as such, not just a pursuit of subjective authenticity, but also a materialist critique of post-War urban planning's inveterate amnesia. Having followed a mysterious young girl through the library of the Humboldt University, the narrator emerges once again onto the street. There, she looks into the display window of a bookstore and sees the reflection of the newly built Lindenhof Hotel across the street. But,

[d]a ist in einem unbewachten Moment in der blitzenden Scheibe anstelle des Lindenhotels eine Trümmerlandschaft aufgetaucht, winddurchpfiffen, unkrautbewachsen, von einem Trampelpfad überquert

[then, when I let my guard down for a moment, a landscape of ruins appeared instead of the Linden Hotel in the polished glass, windswept, grown over with weeds, and traversed by a beat path].[28]

The modernist Lindenhof Hotel (which Wolf refers to here using a shortened name) was a showpiece of mid-1960s East German architecture, inspired by

---

27 Christa Wolf, 'Unter den Linden,' *Gesammelte Erzählungen* (Darmstadt and Neuwied: Luchterhand, 1974), p. 65. The translation for all quotations from the story is taken from Christa Wolf, 'Unter den Linden', trans. by Heike Schwarzbauer and Rick Takvorkian, in *What Remains and other Stories* (New York: Farrar, Straus and Giroux, 1993), pp. 69–120.
28 Ibid., 86.

the glamorous hotels of Morris Lapidus in Miami. The structure is juxtaposed in this quotation to the memory of the post-War ruins that preceded its construction. In making this juxtaposition, the text works against post-War planning regimes that sought the quickest possible erasure of a traumatic past. The material reality of the changing city is as important as the idealist endeavour of fashioning subjectivity.

Towards the close of the story, the narrator returns to the present to assess the boulevard one last time. Once again, the sociological analysis of urban space is central. In this case, modern bureaucrats are the focus:

> Die volle Stunde spült die Welle der Büroarbeiter aus den Verwaltungshäusern. Wohin fürchten sie nur, zu spät zu kommen? Welcher Zug wird ihnen abfahren, welcher Happen für sie immer weggeschnappt werden? Oder haben auch sie, die ihr Leben zu Millionen unter Wert verkaufen, die geheime Sehnsucht nach dem wirklichen Fleisch bewahrt, nach dem saftigen, roten Fleisch?

> [The stroke of the hour washes the wave of office workers out of the administration buildings. Where are they afraid of arriving at too late, anyway? What train will leave without them, what morsel will be snatched away forever? Or have those millions who sell their lives cheaply also retained the secret longing for the real meat, the juicy red, meat?].[29]

This passage, though elegiac in tone, nevertheless asks about the effects of bureaucratic modernity in a way that could be a platform for social research. Wolf's curiosity about the white-collar masses as a modern phenomenon resonates with Siegfried Kracauer's social research in his *Die Angestellten* [*The Salaried Masses. Duty and Distraction in Weimar Germany*, 1930]. Kracauer undertook the empirical study of office workers to understand their concrete role as an integral component of capitalist economic and social structures. Similarly, Wolf's story contains – as evident in the quotation here – materialist worries about the ramifications of mass culture for urban life. 'Administrative buildings' and 'meat', the intimacy of unalienated human social existence, are not simply idealist concepts to be synthesized in a Hegelian way. They also constitute real aspects of life as observed in the urban environment.

As with Wolf's other works of the 1960s, the engagement with the realities of urban modernity is both experimental and international in 'Unter den Linden'.[30] Its passages on urban modernity undermine traditional ideas about literary settings as ancillary to human action. In the quotations above, the city serves less as a backdrop to human action and more as a vehicle for ruminations on social

---

29 Ibid., 115.
30 While 'Unter den Linden' was published in 1974, Wolf worked on it from 1968 to 1969.

life that form a crucial part of the story's structural principle of impressionistic sequencing. Such ambiguous sequencing was a hallmark of the experimental representation of the city in French New Wave film. For example, Jean Luc Godard's *Masculin, Feminin* (1965) similarly injected characters' reflections on urban modernity into a meandering narrative focused on their relationships to one another. Wolf's work once more deserves attention as dealing with themes and ideas that were broader European concerns of the time, rather than only East German ones.

It has been the purpose of this to reveal that close social observation of modernity in the urban environment of the 1960s was a factor in the increasing experimentality of Christa Wolf's literary and filmic production during that time. The prominent place of modern urban life in Wolf's works and the role of the city in her innovative aesthetic schemes links her texts and films to a broader modernist treatment of the city that extends back to the 1920s in Germany and across the Iron Curtain to theorists and filmmakers in France and Italy. A key question, beyond the scope of this essay but possibly an avenue of further research, is to what degree the sociological, experimental, and international quality of the city in Wolf's production was specific to the early part of her career and to the context of 1960s urban shifts. Works like *Kindheitsmuster* (1976) and *Stadt der Engel oder The Overcoat of Dr. Freud* (2010) certainly have strong spatial dimensions that fit some of the aesthetic models that Wolf pursued in the 1960s. Evaluating the extent to which those models belong to multiple periods in Wolf's oeuvre could help clarify differences between her earlier and later literary production.

Regine Criser
Narrative Topographies in Christa Wolf's Oeuvre

Christa Wolf's life and work continue to escape convenient categorizations. Hailed as 'a writer critical of the East German Communist regime'[1] and acquiring the challenging status of 'state dissident writer'[2], the West German *feuilleton* transformed her into a '*Staatsdichterin*, or party hack'[3] in the aftermath of the GDR's collapse. Despite the lasting commercial success of her works even after unification, the GDR's most important 'historiographer'[4] 'never fully obtained a place untainted by ideology'.[5]

What scholarship has widely ignored is her equally important role as a careful 'geographer' of both divided and united Germany. This gap reflects the fact that 'little attention has hitherto been devoted to the significance of spatiality and place in GDR culture either before 1989 or since'.[6] Therefore, this chapter sets out to provide a topographical analysis of Wolf's oeuvre that excavates the distinct narrative topographies shaping the imagined space of her text. As my close readings highlight, in Wolf's writing

> representations of concrete space by no means merely have a referential function. Rather, they are in themselves meaningful, indeed self-reflexive. [...T]he descriptions of the way in which the protagonist [...] behaves in a given space, and often the effect this space has upon her, also illustrates that the meaning of a space is determined by the character who inhabits and passes through it.[7]

---

1 Anna K. Kuhn, 'World Literature Today', *World Literature Today*, 85.2 (2011), 69–70 (p. 69).
2 Anke Pinkert, 'Toward A Critical Reparative Practice in Post-1989 German Literature. Christa Wolf's *City of Angels or The Overcoat of Dr. Freud* (2010)', in *Memory and Postwar Memorials. Confronting the Violence of the Past*, ed. by Marc Silberman and Florence Vatan (New York: Palgrave Macmillan, 2013), pp. 177–196 (p. 178).
3 Kuhn, 'World Literature Today', p. 69.
4 Sonja E. Klocke, *Inscription and Rebellion. Illness and the Symptomatic Body in East German Literature* (Rochester: Camden House, 2015), p. 108.
5 Pinkert, 'Toward A Critical Reparative Practice', p. 179.
6 Renate Rechtien, 'Cityscapes of the German Democratic Republic. An Interdisciplinary Approach – Introduction', *German Life and Letters*, 63.4 (2010), 369–374 (p. 371).
7 Elizabeth Bronfen, *Dorothy Richards. Art of Memory. Space, Identity, Text*, trans. by Victoria Appelbe (Manchester: Manchester University Press, 1999), p. 11.

https://doi.org/10.1515/9783110496000-004

In *Nachdenken über Christa T.*, Wolf herself raised awareness of the importance of space, stating that 'so unwichtig sind die Orte nicht, an denen wir leben. Sie bleiben ja nicht nur Rahmen für unsere Auftritte, sie mischen sich ein, sie verändern die Szene' [But they're not so unimportant, the places we live in. They aren't only the framework for our actions, they involve themselves in the action, they change the scenery].[8] This contribution aims to analyse the specific, concrete places Wolf imagines for her protagonists as well as the narrative spaces that arise through their intersection, which ultimately 'involve themselves' in the telling of the stories. Doing so supplements analyses of Wolf's work focused on gender,[9] voice[10] and/or the body[11] with a spatial lens that expands our understanding of Wolf's conscious and careful staging of her texts.

Edward Soja's notions of thirdspace[12] as well as Michel Foucault's heterotopias[13] provide the theoretical framework for my analysis. Soja's insistence on the spatiality of every social process and his avoidance of spatial binaries mirror the pertinence of spatial webs and overlapping spaces in Wolf's writing. Furthermore, thirdspace as a lens and as the 'multiplicity of real-and-imagined place'[14] provides access to Wolf's narrative topography in all of its complexity that 'does not derive simply from additive combination of its binary antecedents [real vs. imagined] but rather from disordering, deconstruction, and tentative reconstruction of their presumed totalization producing an open alternative that is both similar and strikingly different'.[15] In a similar vein, Foucault's heterotopias

8 Christa Wolf, *Nachdenken über Christa T.* (Munich: Luchterhand, 2000), p. 153; Christa Wolf, *The Quest for Christa T.*, trans. by Christopher Middleton (London: Hutchinson, 1971). p. 136–137.
9 Among many others, see for example: Karin Eysel, 'History, Fiction, Gender. The Politics of Narrative Intervention in Christa Wolf's "Störfall"', *Monatshefte*, 84.3 (1992), 284–298; Sabine Wilke, 'Between Female Dialogics and Traces of Essentialism. Gender and Warfare in Christa Wolf's Major Writings', *Studies in 20th & 21st Century Literature*, 17.2 (1993), 243–262.
10 In addition to Julia Hell, *Post-Fascist Fantasies. Psychoanalysis, History, and the Literature of East Germany* (Durham, London: Duke University Press, 1997), see for example: Karen Jacobs, 'Speaking "Chrissandra". Christa Wolf, Bakhtin, and the Politics of the Polyvocal Text', *Narrative*, 9.3 (2001), 283–304.
11 In addition to Sonja E. Klocke, *Inscription and Rebellion. Illness and the Symptomatic Body in East German Literature* (Rochester: Camden House, 2015), see for example: Carol Anne Costabile-Heming, 'Illness as Metaphor. Christa Wolf, the GDR, and Beyond', *Symposium. A Quarterly Journal in Modern Literatures*, 64.3 (2010), 202–219.
12 Edward Soja, *Thirdspace. Journeys to Los Angeles and Other Real-and-Imagined Places* (Malden/Oxford: Blackwell, 1996).
13 Michel Foucault, 'Of Other Spaces. Utopias and Heterotopias', trans. by Jay Miskowiec, *Architecture/Mouvement/Continuité*, 5 (October 1984), 1–9.
14 Soja, *Thirdspace*, p. 6.
15 Ibid., p. 61.

are 'counter-sites [...] in which [...] all the other real sites that can be found within the culture are simultaneously represented, contested, and inverted'.[16] As my analysis will show, Wolf regularly employs these three modes of engagement in the narrative construction of her imagined spaces. Hence, like heterotopias, her texts 'display and inaugurate a difference and challenge the space in which we [and the protagonists] may feel at home'.[17] The protagonists of Wolf's texts strive to position themselves in GDR society but continuously fail to do so, which initially triggers their withdrawal from politicized urban spaces to rural settings. Ultimately, however, these protagonists seek geographically transient and linguistically anchored forms of belonging, leaving divided and united national spaces behind.

Arrival

The process of arrival can be understood as coming to, engaging with and getting to know a new place. With regard to Christa Wolf's oeuvre, the act of arrival is predominantly reflected in her earlier texts. I will focus here on *Der geteilte Himmel* (1963) and *Nachdenken über Christa T.* (1968) as texts that exemplify the protagonists' arrival in GDR socialism through the search for a physically tangible home.

In *Der geteilte Himmel*, Rita's search for such a home remains unsuccessful; the spatial realities of the text reflect the fragmented spatial realities of a Germany divided by the Berlin Wall and ultimately 'construct a reality that is significantly at odds'[18] with 'a sincere contribution to GDR Ankunftsliteratur'.[19] Rita's inability to secure a physical place of belonging might arise from the gendered division of space that Julia Hell has detected:

> Wolf thus opposes the maternal realm to the order of the father(s) in terms of margin vs. center, old vs. new, past vs. present. Accordingly, her protagonist moves from the margin to the center, from the past to the present, from the realm of the mother to that of the (substitute) father: Rita thus lives in the city with Manfred, works in the factory where she meets Meternagel, and studies at the institute where she is taught by Schwarzenbach, with the

---

16 Foucault, 'Of Other Spaces', p. 3.

17 Peter Johnson, 'Unravelling Foucault's "Different Spaces"', *History of the Human Sciences*, 19.4 (2006), 75–90 (p.84).

18 Renate Rechtien, 'The Topography of the Self in Christa Wolf's *Der geteilte Himmel*', *German Life and Letters*, 63.4 (2010), 475–489 (p. 488).

19 Ibid., p. 477.

two mentor figures assuming paternal roles in different domains, productions and politics.[20]

Despite the novel's detailed descriptions of these mentors' well-meaning support, the places they embody ultimately remain insecure, instable, even inhospitable. The factory, for example, 'war ein kreischendes, schmutziges Durcheinander' [was one huge, dirty, screeching confusion][21] and is dominated by the 'kochende Unruhe der Fabrikhalle' [eruptive confusion of the works].[22] Even though, over time, Rita manages to navigate this 'confusion', her arrival does not transform into a sustained sense of belonging. Similarly, the descriptions of Manfred's parents' house, which she perceives through his eyes as the conglomerate of various caskets ('Wohnsarg, Eßsarg, Schlafsarg' [living coffin, sleeping coffin, eating coffin]),[23] highlight notions of discomfort and alienation. Even though Rita initially feels at home in their shared, small room in the attic, 'Manfred's departure to the West removes the only place where Rita could at least temporarily feel anchored'.[24] This persistent if subconscious experience of displacement is underscored in the epilogue of the novel, when Rita, peeking into the windows of strangers' apartment during a walk, encounters everyday life under GDR socialism, from which she nonetheless remains removed. As Julia Hell argues, the voice of the prologue and the epilogue alike 'belongs to a collectivity which does not include her'.[25] Given that this walk occurs after the erection of the Berlin Wall, rather than manifesting Rita's arrival in GDR socialism, the text establishes doubts that such an arrival is even possible.

Nachdenken über Christa T. (1968) engages these doubts further as well as more intentionally and once again represents, contests and inverts their resolution through the symbol of the country house that Christa T. designs and has built against all odds in the GDR's shortage economy. The decision to create a home for herself and her family seems noteworthy for a person whom the narrator perceives as perpetually displaced: 'Immer schien es, als habe sie auf sich genommen, überall zu Hause und überall fremd zu sein, zu Hause und fremd in der gleichen Sekunde' [It always seemed that she'd taken it upon herself to be at home everywhere and a stranger everywhere, at home and a stranger in the

---

20 Julia Hell, *Post-Fascist Fantasies*, p. 175.
21 Christa Wolf, *Der geteilte Himmel* (Munich: Luchterhand, 2000), p. 45; Christa Wolf, *Divided Heaven*, trans. by Joan Becker, (New York: Adler's Foreign Books, 1983), p. 28.
22 Ibid., p. 47; p. 30.
23 Ibid., p. 216; p. 165.
24 Rechtien, 'The Topography of the Self', p. 482.
25 Hell, *Post-Fascist Fantasies*, p. 170.

same instant].[26] Hence, building a house appears as an attempt to get rid of the lingering strangeness that prevents Christa T.'s full arrival in the socialist society of the GDR.

The house is situated away from an urban centre, in the countryside, and is significantly removed from the closest village. While the countryside appears as a logical choice due to Christa T.'s husband's profession as a veterinarian and their shared feeling of belonging to this space,[27] the deliberately chosen distance from the village is indicative of a wished-for disassociation from society in general, making the house as much a place of resistance as of integration. The narrator focuses her interpretation on the aspect of integration and describes Christa T.'s house as a conscious act of putting down roots, arguing that

> dieses ganze Haus nichts weiter war als eine Art Instrument, das sie [Christa T.] benutzen wollte, um sich inniger mit dem Leben zu verbinden, ein Ort, der ihr von Grund auf vertraut war, weil sie ihn selbst hervorgebracht hatte, und von dessen Boden aus sie sich allem Fremden stellen konnte.

> [this house should be nothing but a sort of instrument that she meant to use to link herself more intimately with life, a place with which she is profoundly familiar because she had created it herself and on whose territory she could take her stand against anything alien].[28]

In addition to the life-affirming, rooting aspects of the house, this interpretation of the house's purpose supports the impression that Christa T. is socially displaced. The 'alien' which Christa T. has to face can be read as a descriptor for the socialist society of the GDR as well as a metaphor for the cancer growing inside of her. Furthermore, her desire for a place that is 'profoundly familiar because she had created it herself' insinuates that the same cannot be said of GDR society. Since Christa T. only spends a few nights in the completed home before succumbing to her cancer,[29] the narrator's reading of the house as an instrument by which she attaches herself more closely to life appears too narrow. More than just rooting herself in the GDR, the construction of the country house ensures a home for Christa T.'s family. Even though the struggles of building the

---

26 Christa Wolf, *Christa T.*, p. 22; *Quest for Christa T.*, p. 13.
27 '[E]s war gerade nicht die schönste Ecke, die da vor ihnen lag, eher eines der dürftigen Stücke, nur daß es unter der Beleuchtung dieses Tages sich verschönte – auf einmal merkten beide, daß sie hier nicht mehr weg wollten'; Wolf, *Christa T.*, p. 161; 'it wasn't exactly the most beautiful scene they were facing, in fact it was drab, except that it looked better in the light of this particular day – they both suddenly noticed they didn't want to leave the place'; *Quest for Christa T.*, p.145.
28 Wolf, *Christa T.*, p. 170; *Quest for Christa T.*, p. 161.
29 Ibid., p. 169.

house are a critical commentary on her 'unvollkommenen sozialistischen Heimat' [imperfect socialist homeland],[30] the house is also a legacy for her family, for whom it secures a place of belonging inscribed with personal significance and familial meaning, and hence ultimately with the 'hope for an ideal socialist state'.[31] Klocke argues that, rather than equating 'Christa T.'s retreat to the countryside and her eventual death with a rejection of the GDR',[32] her move to the countryside can be understood as an attempt 'at overcoming the tensions between compliance with established norms and health on the one hand and resistance and illness on the other hand by embarking on a process of creative writing'.[33] I suggest that the notion of resistance expresses the creative act of designing the house as well as Christa T.'s attempts at creative writing; both the house and writing offer aspirational alternatives to the binary of West and East.

Remaining in the GDR, both Rita and Christa T. struggle to establish a sense of belonging connected to the ideologically charged space of the GDR. Both protagonists extensively reflect on this struggle, and it appears that it is this critical engagement with GDR society and their lived experience – as well as their sharing of this experience with selected friends – that creates a space of belonging. A sense of home is therefore located neither inside nor outside of the GDR, but rather in a thirdspace arising from within this binary. The struggle of belonging and positioning oneself successfully within GDR society, as explored in these texts, already foreshadows the act of withdrawal that the next set of texts engage in more detail.

Withdrawal

The wariness about real-existing socialism that was already apparent in the protagonists' difficulties in developing a sense of belonging in the GDR in works such as *Christa T.* moved further into the foreground of Wolf's oeuvre after the expulsion of Wolf Biermann from the GDR in 1976.[34] *Störfall* (1986), and *Sommerstück* (1989) both grapple with the need to withdraw oneself from the political sphere and seem to arrive at similar spatial conclusions. Such parallels between the texts reflect the far-reaching impact of Biermann's expatriation on

---

30 Wolf, *Christa T.*, commentary 214, translation my own.
31 Klocke, *Symptomatic Body*, p. 56.
32 Ibid., p. 38.
33 Ibid., p. 49.
34 Resch, *Understanding Christa Wolf*, p. 138.

intellectuals in the GDR as well as the simultaneity of the texts' production.[35] Their narrative topographies are closely connected, and their focus on the act of social and spatial withdrawal can be read as a reaction to Biermann's expulsion as well as a commentary on the final decade of the GDR's existence. With that in mind, the protagonists' self-selected retreat from GDR society seems indicative of a larger disillusionment with the realities of GDR socialism. As Wolf noted in her preparatory sketches to *Sommerstück*, 'alle, die sich hier zusammengefunden haben, sind vor irgendetwas auf der Flucht' [everyone who has come together here is fleeing from something].[36]

This notion of flight as a veiled criticism of GDR socialism is a recurring motif in *Sommerstück* and *Störfall*. With the plot of both texts anchored in a contemporary rural space, the intellectuals and artists in these texts seek alternative forms of belonging outside or at least on the margins of (GDR) society. However, the failure of this project is inscribed into the texts from the start, since their attempts to distance themselves from the political and social conflicts of their time remain futile: 'Und was die Konflikte anging: die holten uns ein; sie waren das Thema in den Freundeskreisen, die sich auf dem Lande zusammenfanden' [And regarding the conflicts: they caught up with us; they were the topic in the circle of friends who come together in the countryside].[37] In *Störfall*, the first-person narrator faces the tensions arising in the aftermath of the nuclear disaster at Chernobyl, pondering the Janus-faced character of technological advances. On the one hand, they have caused man-made destruction of nature and immense environmental pollution. On the other hand, technological progress enables doctors to perform brain surgery on her brother. The elements of the text's spatial triad (countryside – hospital – spaces of technological progress) bleed into each other, despite their significant geographical distance. Even though the narrator withdrew to her country home 'um ruhig zu schlafen' [in search of peaceful slumber],[38] she is constantly reminded that she cannot escape the events taking place elsewhere. The nuclear accident and the subsequent fear over atomic particles seeping into the soil and the air emphasize the permeability of national borders and the inability to escape from nuclear fallout, even behind the seemingly insurmountable Berlin Wall. Furthermore, another product of technological

---

35 Ibid., p. 139.

36 Akademie der Künste, Berlin, Christa-Wolf-Archiv, Nr. 2256; all translations of archival material are my own.

37 *Nuancen in Grün*, ed. by Angela Drescher (Berlin: Aufbau, 2002), p. 155, Translations are my own.

38 Christa Wolf, *Störfall. Nachrichten eines Tages*, p. 81; *Christa Wolf, Accident. A Day's News*, trans. by Heike Schwarzbauer and Rick Takvorian (New York: Noonday, 1991), p. 76.

advancement, the telephone, repeatedly interrupts the narrator's desired soli-
tude and renders her withdrawal from the world a fantasy.

Even more than these technologically driven interferences in the countryside, it is the seeping in of Germany's fascist past and of memories of the Second
World War that severely endanger the narrator's refuge. In the text, the invasion
of the supressed past is embodied by a man who claims 'er habe damals fün-
fundvierzig, mit seiner Mutter und seinen Geschwistern als Flüchtling in
einem Zimmer dieses Hauses gewohnt' [that he had lived in a room of this
house with his mother and brothers and sisters as a refuge back in '45].[39] The
man's attempt to revisit the spatial remnants of his immediate post-War past confronts the narrator with the ideologically charged past of her country retreat.
Similarly, the encounter between the narrator and the visitor reveals that this
traumatic past remains unresolved, even 40 years after the War's end. This spatial stronghold of history and trauma is intensified by the visitor's claim that 'auf
diesem Grundstück damals seine kleine Schwester begraben worden sei, als sie
an Typhus gestorben war' [his little sister had been buried on this land back
then, after dying of typhoid fever].[40] By mentioning his sister's death, the
man's presence and his memories overwrite the narrator's regenerative space
as a burial site. Hence, despite repudiating the visitor's recollection, the narrator
finds her country home fundamentally changed after their encounter: 'Ich habe
mich umgedreht und im Gegenlicht, weil die Sonne schon hinter das Dach ger-
utscht war, das Haus liegen sehen, und sein Gesicht, das mir bis dahin fast
immer freundlich erschienen war, hatte sich zur Fratze verzerrt' [I turned around
and saw the house against the light, as the sun had already slipped behind the
roof, and its face, which always seemed friendly to me up till then, was twisted in
an ugly grimace].[41] The unwanted exposure to the spectres of Germany's fascist
past causes the narrator's momentary estrangement from her country home and
underscores the space's interconnectedness with historical and present conflicts.

Similarly to previous texts, such as Der geteilte Himmel and Kindheitsmuster,
Störfall addresses the persistence of the fascist past, which does not seem to be
successfully absorbed and negotiated in the encompassing, deceptively equaliz-
ing and state-orchestrated category of victims of fascism. In this text, Wolf also
touches upon the subject of German war refugees, a group to which Wolf and
several of her protagonists belong and also an issue suppressed by the historical

---

39 Ibid., p. 80; p. 75.
40 Ibid.
41 Ibid., p. 82; p. 77.

narrative of the GDR.[42] Broaching this subject in a text reflecting on the aftermath of Chernobyl links the long-lasting contaminating effects of both historic disasters. And even though the brother's surgery is completed successfully and the narrator is able to re-establish a sense of comfort in her country home,[43] the text itself has already exposed her hope of a lasting retreat and refuge in nature as a deception that leaves her without a space of belonging.

From the beginning, *Sommerstück* echoes this notion of spatial impermanence: 'Jetzt, da Luisa abgereist, Bella uns für immer verlassen hat, Steffi tot ist, die Häuser zerstört sind, herrscht über das Leben wieder die Erinnerung. Es sollte nicht sein' [Now that Luisa has departed, Bella has left us forever, Steffi has passed away, the houses are destroyed, life is governed once more by memory. It wasn't to be].[44] Once again, the search for belonging is imagined through the symbol of the house. While Christa T.'s house provided temporary belonging and especially hope that the next generation would be able to create a place for themselves in the GDR, in *Sommerstück*, the characters' houses are destroyed, taking the spatial alienation described in *Störfall* to another extreme. Given the crucial position of the houses in the narrative topography of *Sommerstück*, their destruction signals a further progression in the characters' displacement and disillusionment with GDR socialism in Wolf's oeuvre. In *Sommerstück*, the houses are at once a gathering place and a physical manifestation of the desire to belong, as well as independent agents in the plot. The narrator observes:

> Häuser können stärker sein als die Menschen, die in ihnen leben und sie halten, jedenfalls für eine gewisse Zeit. Häuser können schwächer werden als ihre Bewohner und von ihnen Fürsorge und Zuwendung brauchen, eine andauernde Aufmerksamkeit. Bedrohlich wird es, wenn die schwachen Zeiten von beiden zusammenfallen.[45]

> [Houses can be stronger than the people who live in them and hold them, at least for a certain amount of time. Houses can become weaker than their inhabitants and need their care and affection, an enduring attentiveness. It becomes threatening when the weak times of both coincide.]

---

42 For further details, see Manfred Wille, Johannes Hoffmann and Wolfgang Meinicke, *Sie hatten alles verloren. Flüchtlinge und Vertriebene in der sowjetischen Besatzungszone Deutschlands* (Wiesbaden: Harrassowitz, 1993).

43 'Und ich habe mich wohl gefühlt in meinem Sessel, in diesem Raum und in dem alten Haus'; Wolf, *Störfall*, p. 104 f; 'and I felt good in my chair, in this room and in the old house'; *Accident*, p. 101.

44 Wolf, *Sommerstück/Was bleibt* (Munich: Luchterhand, 2001). p. 11; unless otherwise indicated, all translations from *Sommerstück* are my own.

45 Ibid., p. 195.

The novel details each of these phases in the relationship between houses and inhabitants. Hence, the opening sentence of the text recalling the final destruction of the houses seems to imply that the final, 'threatening' stage of the relationship has been reached. In light of the houses' destruction, the inhabitants themselves appear to be experiencing 'weak times', which once more exposes the hope for retreat and recuperation in nature and in the countryside as a mere fantasy.

Even though the destruction of the rural idyll is inscribed in the text from the beginning, the novel explores in depth the characters' hopes and desires to create a new home away from the 'Neubauviertel einer brandneuen Stadt' [newly constructed district of a brand new city][46] and from the city 'wo ihr [the protagonist, Ellen] beinahe nichts mehr recht war' [where almost nothing was still right for her].[47] The experiences of a life surrounded and governed by nature reawaken in the characters the hope that a true, simple life might still be possible, even within the regulated and politically overdetermined GDR society: 'Gab es das also doch, wonach wir instinktiv gesucht hatten, als die falschen Wahlmöglichkeiten uns in die Zwickmühle trieben: ein dritte Sache? Zwischen Schwarz und Weiß, Recht und Unrecht, Freund und Feind – einfach leben?'[48] [What we had searched for instinctively, when the false alternatives had driven us into a corner, does that exist after all – a third thing? Between black and white, right and wrong, friend and foe – simple life?][49] Here, the narrator's description of the countryside echoes Soja's notion of thirdspace as 'an open alternative that is both similar and strikingly different'[50] from the binary oppositions, a 'third thing'.

However, similarly to the shadows cast over the narrator's rural refuge in *Störfall*, the protagonists in *Sommerstück* have to recognize that even this space cannot be unhinged from the problems of its time. The impacts of Germany's fascist past once more bleed into the space through the concentration camp memories of one of the friends, who survived his internment.[51] More importantly, the friends' attempts to preserve the houses and the purity of the countryside are countered and overwritten by acts of destruction against abandoned rural property executed by a group of juveniles from the area. Similar to the visitor's Second World War memories in *Störfall*, the youngster's violence against things and

---

46 Ibid., p. 62.
47 Ibid., p. 17.
48 Ibid., p. 77.
49 Translation from Resch, *Understanding Christa Wolf*, p. 141.
50 Soja, *Thirdspace*, p. 6.
51 Wolf, *Sommerstück*, p. 154.

animals alike shifts the protagonists' perception of their rural surroundings. All of a sudden these appear 'fremd, düster, bedrohlich und gefährlich' [foreign, gloomy, threatening, and dangerous],[52] transforming into the 'utterly transitory or fleeting constructions [...] on the outskirts of cities'[53] that recall Foucault's notion of heterotopias.

This encounter late in the novel is foreshadowed; the text already bears linguistic traces of this disillusionment with the recuperative potential of the countryside early on. As Resch points out, nature is often described in the language of warfare throughout the book, and '[e]verything associated with life in the country is unfamiliar and surprising to people conditioned by the environment of the city'.[54] Hence, the inhabitants are estranged from city life and the political sphere it signifies as well as disillusioned with the therapeutic promise of the countryside. As in *Störfall*, the text simultaneously constructs and deconstructs the rural sphere as a space for withdrawal and retreat. Stranded between two equally alienating spaces, the protagonists are left without any spatial options to recover – with no place on earth. Therefore, as I will discuss in the final section below, they turn to transient, imaginary spaces of belonging.

Removal

Wolf's earlier texts had already started to experiment with shifting belonging to imagined spaces, specifically to the act of writing. This narrative move becomes more prominent in the later texts of Wolf's oeuvre, particularly in *Was bleibt* (1990) and *Stadt der Engel* (2010). The collapse of the GDR and its subsequent erasure from Germany's contemporary geography noticeably intensified the motif of imagined belonging; however, it is noteworthy that it spans the historical caesura of 1989, as this implies a disillusionment with the GDR and the FRG alike. The topography of *Was bleibt* is anchored in the urban, politically charged sphere of Berlin and divided into the inside of the narrator's private apartment and the outside – the city. However, both spatial realms continuously overlap and intersect through the act of state surveillance. Despite being subjected to the least aggressive kind of observation, every aspect of the narrator's life is impacted by the state's distrust, which manifests itself in the ominous presence of

---

52 Ibid., p. 108.
53 Johnson, 'Unravelling Foucault', p. 79.
54 Resch, *Understanding Christa Wolf*, p. 141. As she points out, the text uses words such as penetrate, occupy, conquered, seized and challenge to describe the impact of nature on the protagonists.

the state security, the Stasi. Altering her apartment to impede her observer's gaze and even modifying her behaviour in the apartment to undermine the success of the surveillance, the narrator realizes 'daß ich mich seit dem vorigen Sommer [the start of the surveillance] in meiner eigenen Wohnung nicht mehr zu Hause fühlte' [that I had not felt at home in my own apartment since last summer].[55] Under the influence of state-supported monitoring, the unit of home and apartment is torn apart causing the narrator's fundamental alienation from her private sphere. Combined with her alienation from the cityscape, from Berlin as a 'Nicht-Ort [...] ohne Geschichte, ohne Vision, ohne Zauber, verdorben durch Gier, Macht und Gewalt' [a non-place (...) without history, without vision, without magic, spoiled by greed, power, and violence],[56] the narrator is once again faced with a lack of places that can inspire a feeling of belonging. Rather than resolving this issue through the creation of an alternative home in the countryside, the narrator addresses this spatial and ideological challenge through reflections on an 'anderen Sprache' [other language][57] that will allow her someday to describe her experience truthfully. In the imagination of the narrator, this new, free language would 'das Sichtbare dem Unsichtbaren opfern, würde aufhören die Gegenstände durch ihr Aussehen zu beschreiben [...] und würde, mehr und mehr, das unsichtbare Wesentliche aufscheinen lassen' [casually sacrifice the visible to the invisible; would stop describing objects by their appearance [...] and would increasingly allow their invisible essence to emerge].[58] In the light of the overarching effects of state control, this new language endows the narrator with hope that, at some point in the future, she will be able to recall and describe her life under state surveillance. Hence, thinking about this language projects the narrator's search of belonging not only into the future, but also into a non-geographic and linguistic sphere.

This notion of linguistically anchored belonging is explored in more detail in *Stadt der Engel*, which functions as an intertext to several of Wolf's previous novels.[59]

---

55 Wolf, *Sommerstück/Was bleibt* (Munich: Luchterhand, 2001).p. 237; *Christa Wolf, What Remains and Other Stories*, trans. by Heike Schwarzbauer and Rick Takvorian (New York: Farrar, Straus and Giroux, 1993), p. 244.

56 Ibid., p. 241; p. 248.

57 Ibid., p. 223; p. 231.

58 Ibid., p. 228; p. 236.

59 This claim is also put forward by Pinkert, 'A Critical Reparative Practice', p. 179; as well as Kaleen Gallagher, 'The Problem of Shame in Christa Wolf's *Stadt der Engel Oder The Overcoat of Dr. Freud*', *German Life and Letters*, 65.3 (2012), 378–397 (p. 380).

While these parallels also imply similar narrative topographies within these works, *Stadt der Engel* is the first to effectively position the narrator in 'a self-imposed Californian exile',[60] and hence in a contemporaneous space outside of the GDR and the Eastern Bloc. This notion of exile corresponds to the narrator's journey to the homes of German – often Jewish – immigrants who fled the Third Reich during the 1930s. Even though the narrator has to accept that their traces have mainly been erased from the cityscape – 'Nichts davon war geblieben' [None of it was left][61] – her connection to these intellectuals, many of whom were threatened by fascism and later became supporters of the GDR, is a prerequisite for her coming to terms with her dual perpetrator roles: as a follower of the Nazis and as a brief collaborator with the State Security of the GDR. The geographical distance and the self-selected flight to a city whose history is nonetheless inscribed with a German intellectual history untainted by fascism and state surveillance appear as narrative strategies to navigate the narrator's profound personal crisis. Furthermore, her exposure to past and present German immigrants in Los Angeles challenges nationally anchored perceptions of belonging, since they remain simultaneously bound to the German nation and scarred by the fascist German past.

Thus the protagonist has a similar experience of being inseparably connected to a place that is wounding her. While daily faxes inform her about the latest developments in her defamation by West German journalists, her American audiences readily equate her with the new, unified Germany: '[d]ie Menschen vor mir nahmen mich ganz selbstverständlich als Vertreterin des heutigen Deutschland, sie verhörten mich über den Zustand dieses Landes, West oder Ost spielte für sie keine Rolle' [The people here took me, totally understandably, as representative of today's Germany. They asked me about the situation in 'Germany' – West vs. East meant nothing to them].[62] The geographical and ideological division that has defined the narrator's life up to this point is erased in the perception of her audience. Nonetheless, her own encounters with Los Angeles are still very much shaped by the Cold War, as 'the systemic violence and moral bankruptcy of capitalism' that the narrator expects 'is confirmed, when the reader

---

60 Gallagher, 'The Problem of Shame', p. 378. This idea of Los Angeles as an exile can also be found in Pinkert, 'Critical Reparative Practice', p. 182; and in Elizabeth Boa, 'Labyrinths, Mazes, and Mosaics. Fiction by Christa Wolf, Ingo Schulze, Antje Ravic Strubel, and Jens Sparschuh', in *Debating German Cultural Identity Since 1989*, ed. by Anne Fuchs, Kathleen James-Chakraborty and Linda Short (Rochester: Camden House, 2011), pp. 131–155.

61 Wolf, *Stadt der Engel* (Berlin: Suhrkamp, 2011), p. 340; *Christa Wolf, City of Angel or The Overcoat of Dr. Freud*, trans. by Damion Searls (New York: Farrar, Straus and Giroux, 2013), p. 259.

62 Ibid., p. 280; p. 211.

is taken through the poor inner city neighborhoods of Los Angeles and later to the casino in Las Vegas'.[63] Thus, *Stadt der Engel*, similarly to the texts discussed above, features a displaced narrator who cannot fully arrive (in Los Angeles) and feels utterly alienated from the unifying Germany. In an attempt to counter this displacement – reviving the motif of linguistic belonging from *Was bleibt* – the narrator proclaims: 'Meine Person war an die Sprache gebunden, die Sprache sei meine eigentliche Heimat' [My personhood was tied to language, language was my real homeland].[64] The use of *Heimat* seems momentous here, since the concept is lifted out of the geographically defined limits of the nation-state and transposed to the linguistic sphere, with its emphasis on sharing, exchange and community. In replacing the dominant nation-state with a belonging in language, the narrator effectively counters her displacement by embracing her transience and the accompanying mode of searching and traveling.

The journey is an under-recognized spatial mode that spans Wolf's oeuvre and captures the attempts of various protagonists to counter and cure their (ideological) homelessness. The spatial web of these texts expands beyond the borders of the GDR, probing their limits and limitations. The varied reflections on creating alternative spaces of belonging concurrently situated inside and outside of these borders evoke a thirdspace and heterotopia that functions simultaneously as a space of resistance to state surveillance and GDR socialism and as a space of hope for the socialist ideal. In moving this space from urban centres, to rural idylls, to domestic spaces and to the transient space of language, the narrative topographies of Wolf's oeuvre map various models of resistance, ultimately emphasizing that the most functional spaces of belonging are engendered from ourselves and in the creative sphere, stretching beyond geographic limits and national borders.

---

63 Pinkert, 'Critical Reparative Practice', p. 189.
64 Wolf, *Stadt der Engel*, p. 354; *City of Angels*, p. 269.

Anna K. Kuhn
The Gendered Reception of Christa Wolf

Until the fall of Communism, indeed even after its demise, the reception of GDR literature was largely determined by the politics of the Cold War. This was especially true in the divided Germanies. In the East, censors and party-line critics were responsible for ensuring that East German writers adhered to Communist orthodoxy and socialist realist literary norms. Critics in the West strove to ferret out criticisms of 'real-existing socialism'[1] in GDR texts in order to legitimize Western capitalist political systems. Christa Wolf was critically acclaimed in both East and West Germany, but her reputation was not limited to German-speaking countries. She was an internationally celebrated writer, whose works were translated into thirty European and non-European languages. Although she had a large female readership, most of her critics were men. As we know from reader response theory, men and women read differently, because they bring different experiences and expectations to bear on a text.[2] I argue that the reception of Wolf's texts in Germany and the United States differed according to the gender of the reader. Male critics tended to read Wolf politically – as a GDR writer whose texts reflected issues confronting all the members of her society (the *Der geteilte Himmel* model) – while women tended to read her as an East German woman writer who addressed issues of politics and gender (the *Christa T.* model).

With the notable exception of Christa Wolf and Heiner Müller, GDR literature was virtually unknown in the United States.[3] Unlike those of her compatriots,

---

My readings of Wolf's texts are based on my study: *Christa Wolf's Utopian Vision. From Marxism to Feminism*, 2nd edn (Cambridge/New York: Cambridge University Press, 2008).

1 This term, coined by Erich Honecker in 1973, pointed to the discrepancy between the theory and praxis of GDR socialism, between actual conditions prevailing in the East German state and its initial, utopian socialist promise.

2 See *Reception Study. From Literary Theory to Cultural Studies*, ed. by James Machor and Philip Goldstein (New York: Routledge, 2001); Judith Fetterley, *The Resisting Reader. A Feminist Approach to American Fiction* (Bloomington: Indiana University Press, 1978); and Ruth Klüger, 'Frauen lesen anders' ['Women Read Differently'], in Klüger, *Frauen lesen anders. Essays* (Munich: dtv, 1996), pp. 83–104.

3 In a paper published shortly after the fall of the Wall, David Bathrick argued that, '[s]een from the broadest perspective of literary life in this country, as defined by what books appear on best-seller lists, what works are reviewed and discussed in the leading literary periodicals (such as the *New York Review of Books*, *New York Times Book Review*, etc.), what writers have had signifi-

https://doi.org/10.1515/9783110496000-005

Wolf's texts – beginning with *Nachdenken über Christa T.* (1968) – were readily accessible, in generally excellent English translations,[4] through the prestigious publishing house of Farrar, Straus and Giroux. This chapter traces the development of Wolf reception in East and West Germany and the United States, discussing her disparate treatment by male and female critics. Initially, Christa Wolf's following in the US was largely among scholars of German studies. By the mid-1970s, GDR studies was a recognized area of teaching and research at some US colleges and universities.[5] Conversant with the work of their East and West German academic counterparts, American GDR scholars also followed the West German literary establishment's reception of Wolf. Wolf's early texts, *Moskauer Novelle* (1961) and *Der geteilte Himmel* (1963), followed social realist precepts, in keeping with the Socialist Unity Party's mandate that literary production serve the development of the socialist state. Wolf was therefore subsumed into the canon of GDR literature, and her texts were narrowly read through the lens of East German politics. *Moskauer Novelle*, which Wolf later criticized for its ideological and psychological naiveté and simplistic formal structure,[6] is imbued with the telos of socialism's inevitable triumph. Consonant with the Party's mandate that communal needs be given precedence over those of the individual, it presents readers with the straightforward linear narrative of an exemplary heroine willing to renounce personal happiness for the good of the socialist cause.[7]

---

cant creative influence on American writers, there is practically no reception of GDR literature in the United States'. Bathrick mentions two notable exceptions to this rule: the 'experimental' writers Heiner Müller and Christa Wolf. Bathrick, 'Productive Mis-Reading. GDR Literature in the USA', *GDR Bulletin*, 16.2 (Fall 1990), 1–6 (pp. 1–2).

4 *Christa T.* was translated by the poet Christopher Middelton, and many of her later works were sensitively translated by Jan van Heurek.

5 Although the GDR was founded in 1949, it was not officially recognized until 1974, at which time diplomatic relations between the two Germanies were established, and the GDR became a subject of interest to scholars in the West.

6 'The Sense and Nonsense of Being Naïve', in *Christa Wolf. The Author's Dimension – Selected Essays*, ed. by Alexander Stephan, trans. by Jan van Heurek (New York: Farrar, Straus and Giroux, 1993), pp. 49–57.

7 Despite its dogmatism, Wolf's debut novella provides valuable insights into early GDR *Aufbauliteratur* [literature of socialist development], which is predicated on the foundational myth of the GDR as the anti-fascist counterpart to the Federal Republic. Many communists who had been persecuted and forced into exile during the Third Reich returned to Germany after the War and helped build up the East German state. They propagated the notion that socialism was the only antidote to fascism – a notion to which Christa Wolf, among others, subscribed. For a discussion of early GDR writing, see Julia Hell, *Post-Fascist Fantasies. Psychoanalysis, History and the Writing of East Germany* (Durham: Duke University Press, 1997).

At first glance, *Der geteilte Himmel* appears to follow the same narrative trajectory. Wolf again employs the classical conflict between duty and inclination to chart what has been called 'the socialist education of Rita Seidel'.[8] As a direct outgrowth of the *Bitterfelder Weg*, the Party's call for writers to enter factories and write about the world of production, *Der geteilte Himmel* is based on Wolf's experiences as a member of a railway car brigade. It charts the development of Rita Seidel from country innocent to committed socialist, with the help of three socialist role models. Rita's lover, Manfred Herrfurth, impervious to socialism's utopian promise of non-alienated social relations, functions as a foil for this positive triumvirate. When he flees to West Berlin, Rita decides to stay in the GDR and work to build up the East German state – a decision that is rendered irrevocable when the Wall is erected on 13 August 1961. Although conventional when measured against her later oeuvre, *Der geteilte Himmel*'s more experimental form was unprecedented for its time. It reflects Wolf's uneasiness with socialist realism's schematic narrative models and can be read as a transitional text.

Unlike *Moskauer Novelle*'s linear structure, *Der geteilte Himmel* employs flashbacks and multiple, shifting, overlapping narrative perspectives as Rita, confined to a sanatorium in the wake of an ostensible accident at the factory, reflects on the events that brought her there. It further deviates from socialist realist norms by calling on readers to actively engage in the construction of the text. Although Wolf never directly mentions the Wall, we learn much later in the text that the 'accident' occurred on 13 August 1961, and that it was a suicide attempt.[9] Critics in both East and West Germany seized upon Wolf's broaching of such taboo subjects as suicide and *Republikflucht* [flight from the republic]. They were also quick to point out that *Der geteilte Himmel*'s politically correct characters remain flat, whereas the problematic, psychologically complex Manfred is

---

8 Willkie K. Cirker, 'The Socialist Education of Rita Seidel. The Dialectics of Humanism and Authoritarianism in Christa Wolf's *Der geteilte Himmel*', *University of Dayton Review*, 13.2 (Winter 1978), 105–111.

9 Most critics read Rita Seidel's accident as a suicide attempt prompted by the Wall's construction. A notable exception is Sonja Klocke, who argues for a more nuanced reading. In her view, Rita places herself in danger not out of despair for the loss of her lover, whom she had already renounced, but out of despair at love's transitoriness and because she faults herself for not having succeeded in winning Manfred over to the socialist cause. See Klocke, '(Anti-)faschistische Familien, (post)faschistische Körper und die Frage nach der Ankunftsliteratur. Christa Wolfs 'Der geteilte Himmel' [(Anti-)fascist Families, (Post)fascist Bodies and the Question of the Literature of Arrival. Christa Wolf's *Der geteilte Himmel*], in *Christa Wolf. Erinnern und Erinnerung*, ed. by Garsten Gansel and Sonja Klocke (Göttingen: Vandenhoeck and Ruprecht, 2014), pp. 69–87. Both readings are anathema to the prevailing socialist aesthetic norms of the time, which demanded positive heroes and uplifting themes.

fleshed out in greater detail and is therefore more likely to engage readers' interest. Moreover, while clearly a product of Bitterfeld, *Der geteilte Himmel* focuses less on details of the work world and more on interpersonal relationships, thereby adumbrating what would become a distinctive feature of Wolf's oeuvre. In contrast to the lacklustre reception of *Moskauer Novelle*, *Der geteilte Himmel* was widely discussed in the West German press and, while controversial, was also a success in the GDR, where its violation of socialist realist taboos and more complex representation of socialism prompted a literary debate about the role of literature in socialist society.[10] When Wolf received the GDR's Heinrich Mann Prize for *Der geteilte Himmel* in 1963, it cemented her position as an East German writer, while broadening the parameters of what was acceptable in GDR literature.

Nachdenken über Christa T., a work of mourning in which a nameless narrator struggles to come to terms with the premature death of her friend, marks a radical break with socialist realism, heralding the breakthrough to Christa Wolf's aesthetics of 'subjective authenticity' – the interjection of a subjective authorial voice into her narrative – that would become the hallmark of her writing. Abandoning a linear, mimetic narrative, Wolf melds author and narrator and draws on such modernist writing strategies as montage, ambiguity, contradiction, reflections on the act of writing, and textual lacunae to explode socialist realist expectations. The dialogic voice of the narrator addresses herself, Christa T., as well as readers, and calls on them to actively engage in the constitution of her self-reflective, multitemporal, multivalent, open-ended text. In writing her friend's life, Wolf eschews socialist realism's claim to 'objectivity'. She augments the narrator/author's memories with diary entries, letters and writing fragments from the budding writer Christa T. To round out her story, she also 'invents truthfully, based on her own experience'.

By centring her narrative on a nonconformist figure – who, measured by the standards of her society, is a failure – Wolf flies in the face of socialist realism's demand for exemplary heroic characters. In the figure of Christa T., Wolf presents readers with a committed socialist who, like Wolf herself, is unable to reconcile her humanistic vision of socialism – as the coming-into-being of the fully rounded individual within the socialist collective – with the technocratic, instrumentalist society that characterized the GDR of the 1950s and 1960s. Unwilling to compromise her principles and conform to the cynicism of the status quo, the outsider Christa T. founders in the public sphere. Despairing at her inability to

---

10 See *Der geteilte Himmel und seine Kritiker. Dokumentation* [Divided Heaven and Its Critics; Documentation], ed. by Martin Reso (Halle: Mitteldeutscher Verlag, 1965).

contribute to the development of the socialist society to which she is morally committed, she retreats into domesticity, falls ill and ultimately dies. In the words of the West German critic Marcel Reich-Ranicki, 'Christa T. dies of leukae-mia, but her real sickness is the GDR'.[11]

Der geteilte Himmel initiated a productive literary debate in the GDR; the publication of *Christa T.*, which was read as an anti-GDR book, resulted in a back-lash against its author. Early attempts to suppress the book by delaying its ap-pearance and releasing a limited edition[12] were followed by an overwhelmingly negative critical reception. Reading the text against socialist realist aesthetic norms, critics rejected both its form and its content. Wolf was accused of formal-ism, solipsism and Western decadence. The book was enormously popular with Wolf's largely female readership, however. Extant copies of the scarce book were passed around like contraband. Wolf's public readings were packed and prompt-ed intense discussions about the dialectic of the individual and society. Clearly, Christa T.'s dis-ease resonated with women in East Germany.

It resonated with West German women as well, gaining Wolf a loyal reader-ship that identified with Christa T.'s quest for self-actualization, despite their dif-ferent socio-political situations. *Nachdenken über Christa T.* was also well re-ceived by the largely male West German literary establishment and marked the beginning of its acclamation of a critical GDR writer whose commitment to a Marxist utopian socialist project would increasingly bring her into conflict with the state. While acknowledging its more personal tone, most critics contin-ued to read *Christa T.* within a narrow political context, with some seeking to cast her as a dissident.[13] Over the years, as Wolf became increasingly critical of the

---

11 'Christa Wolfs unruhige Elegie', *Die Zeit*, 25 May 1969. My translation.

12 According to Roland Wiegenstein, 5,000 copies of *Christa T.* were printed in the GDR in 1968, of which 800 were delivered in 1969. Following the critical rejection of the book, the publisher sold the remaining 4,200 copies to the West German publishing house Luchterhand. Given that many of the original 800 copies were disseminated among critics, libraries and Party function-aries, the number available to the general public was actually lower. Quoted in Heinrich Mohr, 'Produktive Sehnsucht. Struktur, Thematik und politische Relevanz von Christa Wolfs *Nachdenk-en über Christa T.*', *Basis. Jahrbuch für deutsche Gegenwartsliteratur*, vol. 2, ed. by Reinhold Grimm and Jost Hermand (Frankfurt a. M.: Athenäum, 1971), pp. 191–233 (pp. 216–217 fn 20). See also *Dokumentation zu Christa Wolfs 'Nachdenken über Christa T.'*, ed. by Angela Drescher (Hamburg/Zurich: Luchterhand, 1991) for access to more recent documents that only became available after unification.

13 To read Wolf as a dissident is to misunderstand her complex relationship to socialism and the GDR state. Wolf embraced socialism following the collapse of the Third Reich, viewing it as the only viable alternative to capitalism, which she, following communist ideology, linked to fas-cism. While she became increasingly disenchanted with and critical of the actual existing social-ism of the GDR, she viewed her criticisms of the state as inducements for reform. Wolf remained

GDR, her standing in the West would help protect her against capricious political retaliation on the part of the East German state.

In the United States, the predominantly male, left-leaning scholars of GDR literature tended to echo the West German assessment of *Christa T.* Wolf continued to be viewed first and foremost as a socialist writer struggling against the aesthetic and political strictures of a repressive regime, a writer whose criticisms of GDR society were universal – that is, applicable to both men and women. Alexander Stephan was particularly adamant in his insistence on a gender-neutral reading of her texts, claiming that Christa T. could just as easily be Christian T. As late as 1979, Stephan argued that Wolf was 'not a woman writer, at all events not in the sense in which women writers are conceived of by many of the more militant feminists'. Her books, he maintained, 'are concerned primarily not with women's problems, with a specifically female appropriation of reality or a specifically female aesthetics [...] nor are they written especially for women'.[14]

Stephan's resistance to gender-specific readings of Wolf's texts was doubtless reinforced by Wolf's categorical rejection of the term 'feminism', a movement she perceived as arising out of and reflecting conditions in the capitalist west. Like other GDR women writers, Wolf at that time subscribed to the orthodox Marxist doctrine that the 'woman question' would be resolved once women were fully integrated into the world of production and socialism had been fully achieved in the GDR – a view that she would later call into question.[15]

The 1975 formation of the Coalition of Women in German (WiG), an organization of feminist German studies scholars seeking a venue for research not sufficiently recognized in traditional German departments,[16] was decisive in generating the American feminist reception of Christa Wolf. Wolf's aesthetics of subjective authenticity captured the imagination of these scholars, who opened

---

committed to the utopian socialist project as envisioned in the early writings of Karl Marx for her entire life.

14 Stephan, 'The Emancipation of Man. Christa Wolf as a Woman Writer', *GDR Monitor*, 2 (1979/1980), pp. 23–31 (p. 25). Not all male critics were so resistant to feminist readings of Wolf's texts, but in general, their interpretations were gender-blind and focused on literary and/or political issues. See Katharina von Hammerstein's repudiation of Stephan's argument: 'Warum nicht Christian T? Christa Wolf zur Frauenfrage untersucht an einem frühen Beispiel: *Nachdenken über Christa T.*', *New German Review*, 3 (1987), 17–29.

15 See Anna K. Kuhn, 'Christa Wolf. Literature as an Aesthetic of Resistance', in *Literature and the Development of Feminist Theory*, ed. by Robin Goodman (New York: Cambridge University Press, 2015), pp. 155–171.

16 See Angela Bammer, 'The American Feminist Reception of GDR Literature (With a Glance at West Germany)', *GDR Bulletin*, 16.2 (Fall 1990), 18–24, for an excellent overview of Women in German and the feminist reception of GDR literature in the US.

up new avenues of inquiry into her work, producing sophisticated interpretations of *Christa T.* that directly challenged Stephan's myopic assessment. Leftist feminists were intrigued by Wolf's historically and materially grounded construction of '"I"– a gendered "I" – embedded in the "we" of historical community'.[17] In Wolf's writings, many saw the possibilities of a feminist socialism that could overcome the limitations of Marxism's exclusive focus on the communal and of bourgeois feminism's emphasis on the individual – a way of conjoining the personal and the political.[18]

Other scholars drew on deconstructive and feminist approaches to produce innovative readings of *Christa T.* that were grounded in contemporary critical theory. In 'Christa Wolf and Feminism. Breaking the Patriarchal Connection', for example, Myra Love, seeking to understand Wolf's appeal for a US readership, argues that American women's 'experience of patriarchy in their own lives', rather than a burning interest in GDR socialism, accounted for the popularity of Wolf's text. Love's experiential and conceptual point of departure is the notion that 'the identification of subjectivity and dominance lies at the heart of patriarchy'.[19] In her view, *Christa T.* resonates with women in the West because the text subverts the system of dichotomous oppositions that informs the patriarchal model of perception and discourse. She follows theorists such as Roland Barthes and Jacques Derrida to maintain that male domination is rooted in Western logocentric and phallocentric structures of thought and discourse. Logocentrism's asymmetrical privileging of a central term, against which its opposite or negation is posited (e.g., subject/object, speech/silence, presence/absence), coupled with patriarchal phallocentricity, consigns woman to the abjected position of the Other. Unlike patriarchal writing, which seeks to assert mastery over its object of narration and which, according to Barthes, constitutes a 'closed' system,[20] Wolf's aesthetic of subjective authenticity embeds the writer in her text, allowing her to establish a dialogic relationship with her characters and readers. In *Christa T.*, Wolf's use of 'self-interrupting and non-linear methods of commu-

---

17 Ibid., p. 21.

18 Ibid.

19 Myra Love, 'Christa Wolf and Feminism. Breaking the Patriarchal Connection', *New German Critique*, 16 (Winter 1979), 31–53 (pp. 31–32).

20 As Barthes notes: 'All modes of writing have in common the fact of being "closed" and thus different from spoken language. Writing is in no way an instrument for communication, it is not an open route through which there passes only the intention to speak [...]. Writing is an anti-communication, it is intimidating'; Roland Barthes, *Writing Degree Zero*, trans. by A. Lavers and C. Smith (New York: Hill and Wang, 1953), pp. 119–120. Quoted in Love, 'Christa Wolf and Feminism', p. 33.

nication which characterize conversation', according to Love, 'fosters communication and allows her to break down the opposition between writing and speech'.[21] Moreover, Wolf's dialogic style establishes a reciprocity between the narrator and Christa T. In reflecting on/recreating her friend's life and her own, the narrator becomes receptive to Christa T.'s iconoclastic way of being and comes to reassess her own life. As the narrator seeks to make her absent (dead) friend present in the text through reflection, Love claims, the presence of 'Wolf in the text which constitutes itself in relation [not in opposition] to the absence which is Christa T.' signifies a 'process of self-constitution in intersubjective relationship' and represents the 'coming into being of subjectivity free of domination'.[22] In Love's view, by treating Christa T. not as an object (of narration), but as a subject, Wolf breaks with the patriarchal paradigm.

Similarly, in 'The Difficulty of Saying "I" as Theme and Narrative Technique in the Works of Christa Wolf', Jeanette Clausen, building on Love's study, seeks to understand *Christa T.* within the context of patriarchal society. The 'difficulty of saying "I"' is a motif sounded by the aspiring writer Christa T. and a recurrent theme in Christa Wolf's writings. Dieter Sevin reads this theme as GDR-specific – as the problematic of a writer struggling against socialist realist proscriptions in an effort to write in a new, subjective way.[23] Clausen, drawing on the work of Mary Daly and Monique Wittig, presents a gender-specific perspective on this motif and its attendant scepticism towards language. Clausen points to the fraught situation of saying 'I' for women who, under patriarchy, must use an androcentric, phallocentric language to express the self. Probing the degree to which women are able to articulate a specifically feminine experience of reality in patriarchal language, she reprises Wittig's observation that for women, the use of the genderless pronoun 'I' masks the sexual identity of the speaker and may allow them to feel deceptively at home in a male-dominated language. According to Wittig, 'the female saying "I" is alien at every moment to her own speaking and writing. She is broken by the fact that she must enter this language in order to speak or write.[24] By having both Christa T. and the narrator thematize

---

21 Ibid.
22 Ibid., p. 34.
23 Sevin, *Christa Wolf, 'Der geteilte Himmel'; 'Nachdenken über Christa T.'* (Munich: R. Oldenbourg, 1982), pp. 105–107.
24 Jeanette Clausen, 'The Difficulty of Saying "I" as Theme and Narrative Technique in the Works of Christa Wolf', in *Gestaltet und Gestaltend. Frauen in der deutschen Literatur*, ed. by Marianne Burkhard, *Amsterdamer Beiträge zur neueren Germanistik*, v. 10 (Amsterdam: Rodopi, 1980), pp. 319–333 (319).

the difficulty of speaking in the first person, Wolf emphatically draws attention to this conundrum.

Among the more striking features of Wolf's text are its blurring of the identity between the narrator and Christa T. and its play with pronominal reference. This partial melding of the separate identities of the two female protagonists, in Clausen's view, 'allows their common experience and solidarity as women to become visible'. Together with the innovative use of pronouns, this blurring helps to circumvent the linguistic impasse confronting women in patriarchal society.[25] Christa T. uses the third person singular feminine pronoun *sie* [she], rather than the first person *ich* [I], when writing about her life. The narrator, who also struggles with the difficulty of saying 'I', at times uses the first person, but employs third person narration when writing about her friend.[26] Using the third person, linguistically gendered pronoun *sie* [she], Clausen argues, enables Wolf to establish the 'sexual identity of the speaker so that it does not remain buried in the [genderless] *ich*'. It thus allows the narrator and Christa T. to avoid being subsumed into the more universal 'I' that may not conform to their own sense of self.[27] While *Christa T.*'s narrative 'I' may be broken into first and third person, 'the juxtaposition and partial blurring or fusing of *sie* and *ich* can, Clausen claims, also be seen as a means of healing the split and of 'feminizing' the first person pronoun'.[28]

It is unlikely that Wolf was familiar with Clausen's and Love's readings of *Christa T.*,[29] and we have no way of knowing how she would have responded had she indeed read them. When she wrote *Christa T.*, Wolf was not consciously critiquing patriarchy and androcentricity.[30] By the time she wrote the introductory essay 'Berührung' [Touching] for *Guten Morgen, Du Schöne* [Good Morning, You Beauty] (1977) – interviews with East German women that illuminate the disparity between the theory and praxis of socialism in the GDR – however, the situation had fundamentally changed. Wolf had come to understand that despite the equity afforded women under socialism, deforming patriarchal structures that silenced marginalized groups, including women, were still operative in GDR society. Distinguishing between gender equity and emancipation, Wolf

---

25 Ibid., p. 324.
26 The narrator also uses the second person familiar *du* [you] and the impersonal pronoun *man* [one] when addressing herself and Christa T.
27 Clausen, 'The Difficulty of Saying "I"', p. 324.
28 Ibid.
29 Wolf's knowledge of English was still quite limited in the early 1980s.
30 Wolf contributed to the historically grounded materialist feminism that only emerged in the GDR in the mid-1970s.

notes that: 'Economically and legally we are equal to men [...] and now we experience to what degree the history of a class society, the *patriarchy* [my emphasis], has deformed its objects and how much time it will take until men and women become subjects of history'.[31]

Thus Clausen's and Love's analyses proved prescient, foreshadowing an evolution in Wolf's feminist consciousness that would find its ultimate expression in her ambitious 1983 Cassandra project. Presented as the prestigious Frankfurt Poetics Lectures (1982),[32] the four lectures that comprise Wolf's 'Voraussetzungen einer Erzählung. Kassandra' ['Conditions of a Narrative. Cassandra'] document the genesis and coming-into-being of the narrative *Kassandra*, which constitutes the fifth lecture.[33] The catalyst for *Kassandra* was the reheating of the Cold War in the early 1980s, when Ronald Reagan entertained waging a 'limited nuclear war' on European soil and NATO and the Warsaw Pact nations were engaged in a new nuclear arms race. Wolf traces the origins of human self-destructiveness and the 'delusional thinking' that brought us to the brink of annihilation back to the cradle of Western civilization – to the exclusion of women, the rise of patriarchal values and the hierarchical thinking that informed Greek society. She rewrites the history of the Trojan War from the perspective of the marginal figure of Cassandra, embedding it within a critique of the Western patriarchal literary and aesthetic tradition. Prefacing her lectures on poetics with a repudiation of classical normative poetics as developed by Aristotle and Horace, among others, she goes on to reject the *Iliad* for its glorification of war and its veneration of the hero. Reading as a woman, Wolf dismisses Homer's text as alien and alienating. She rejects this foundational text of Western literature, with its focus on male figures and masculinist values and its marginalization and instrumentalization of women, for its inscription and valorization of patriarchal ideals.

'Voraussetzungen einer Erzählung' discusses the plight of the woman writer, a topic Wolf had previously explored in her Büchner Prize speech, *Kein Ort, Nirgends* and her essays on the German Romantic writers Karoline von Günderrode and Bettine von Arnim. In her third lecture on poetics, she explores the notion of women's writing, arguing that it is grounded in women's different experience of

---

31 Wolf, Christa, *Werkausgabe in 12 Bänden*, ed. by Sonja Hilzinger (Munich: Luchterhand, 1999–2001), vol. 8: *Essays, Gespräche, Reden, Briefe 1975–1986* (2000), p. 122 (my translation).
32 An article on Christa Wolf by Sara Lennox, a leading member of the Women in German Coalition, was among the items on display at the University of Frankfurt exhibit that accompanied Wolf's Lectures on Poetics.
33 The English translation inverts Wolf's intended order, presenting the narrative first, followed by the *Conditions of a Narrative*. It thereby puts American readers at a disadvantage, since the earlier lectures are vital for an informed reading of the narrative.

reality, their marginalization and objectification in patriarchy, their embrace of gender difference, their refusal 'to integrate themselves into the prevailing delusional systems' and their striving for autonomy.[34] Pondering the pitfalls of logocentrism – to which she, as a Western writer, subscribes – Wolf links the precarious political situation of the 1980s to the patriarchy's dualistic, hierarchical world view, its valorization of instrumental rationality and its exclusion of women.

In her *Kassandra* narrative, Wolf rewrites the history of the Trojan War from the perspective of the losers, using an extended interior monologue by the hitherto peripheral figure of Cassandra. Conceived as a 'model for a kind of utopia', *Kassandra* records Troy's transition to a patriarchal society at a time in which traces of earlier, more egalitarian communal structures are still discernible. Cassandra, princess of Troy, bears witness to King Priam's exclusion of Queen Hecuba from the governing council, his acquiescence in the creation of facile images of the enemy and his use of his daughter as bait to lure the enemy. It can be read as an anti-*Bildungsroman* in which the privileged daughter disavows her father and the palace, choosing autonomy over integration into a society that has lost its moral compass by emulating the patriarchal values of its foe, the Greeks.

Kassandra marked a milestone in the US reception of Christa Wolf, its overtly feminist message making it her most popular text in that country. Reviews in both the *New York Times Book Review* and in *The Women's Review of Literature* testify to Wolf's stature in American letters and point to a growing general readership. The negative review by the classicist Mary Lefkowitz in the *Times*[35] was convincingly rebuffed by Marilyn French's astute essay in *The Women's Review of Literature*. Situating Wolf's *Kassandra* within a feminist literary recuperative project, French lauds precisely what Lefkowitz condemns: tackling the androcentric history that has been handed down and instead imagining a different, more humane, egalitarian world.[36]

Notwithstanding Wolf's positive reception by a larger American general public, it was feminist scholars and teachers in German studies, versed in German literary and political history, who would continue to produce the most nuanced

---

34 Christa Wolf, *Cassandra. A Novel and Four Essays*, trans. by Jan van Heurck (New York: Farrar, Straus and Giroux, 1984), p. 259.

35 Mary Lefkowitz, 'Can't Fool Her', *New York Times Book Review*, 9 September 1984. Lefkowitz faults Wolf for deviating from the ancient mythological tradition. In her insistence on upholding the androcentric Western literary canon and criticizing Wolf for interjecting her views of the modern world into the text, Lefkowitz misreads Wolf's project and disavows the power of literature to imagine alternative realities.

36 Marilyn French, 'Trojan Woman', *The Women's Review of Books*, 2.3 (December 1984), 13–14.

analyses of Wolf's complex texts. Over the following decades, these scholars were among Wolf's most loyal readers and critics. Unlike many of their male counterparts – especially those West German critics who attacked her in the 'German-German literary debate', discussed below, and who denounced her following revelations of her involvement with the *Staatssicherheit* (Stasi), the East German secret police – these feminist scholars defended Wolf against the unfair campaigns waged against her,[37] predating by some twenty years Günter Grass's stinging denunciation of the West German press at her memorial service for its relentless persecution and 'public execution' of Wolf.[38]

In 1990, a year after the fall of the Wall, Christa Wolf published *Was bleibt*. Written in 1979 and reworked in 1989, the narrative records the psychic toll a two-year surveillance by the Stasi has taken on the narrator. Wolf's text, which appeared just when the corruption and brutality of the East German state and the pervasiveness of the Stasi were coming to light, unleashed a storm of criticism. The West German media, which had been instrumental in creating the image of Wolf as a writer of conscience – someone who spoke truth to power, be it in the socialist East or the capitalist West –turned on her with a vengeance. Conflating the text's first-person narrator with Christa Wolf and faulting her for not having published the story earlier, articles in leading *feuilletons* accused her of capitalizing on the recent Stasi revelations to claim victim status for herself. Calling attention to her privileged status, her ability to travel freely to the West and to buy Western consumer goods, the media systematically deconstructed the image of Christa Wolf which they had helped create, branding her a state poet (*Staatsdichterin*). Overnight, Wolf was transformed from a moral institution into a party hack. As a discourse of totalitarianism gained currency in the Federal Republic and a Stalinist GDR was equated with the Nazi dictatorship, Wolf's decision to remain in the GDR instead of emigrating to the West was condemned for legitimizing an outlaw state (*Unrechtsstaat*).

In 1993, Wolf's revelation that for three years, from 1959 to 1962, she had been an IM (*inoffizieller Mitarbeiter*), an unofficial informer for the Stasi – an association she claimed to have forgotten/repressed – fanned the fires of the *Was bleibt* polemic. Wolf was certainly not the only GDR intellectual to have had connections to the secret police. Newspapers at the time were rife with revelations about prominent writers who had been in its employ, including the playwright

---

37 The Coalition of Women in German sent a private letter of support to Christa Wolf during the *What Remains* controversy. WiG members also defended her publicly; see for example: Anna K. Kuhn, 'Rewriting GDR History. The Christa Wolf Controversy', *GDR Bulletin*, 17.1 (1991), 7–11; see also footnote 46.

38 Grass, 'Was bleibt. Trauerrede von Günter Grass', *Frankfurter Rundschau*, 14 December 2011.

Heiner Müller and the poet Sascha Anderson. Wolf's early, relatively brief, inconsequential Stasi involvement, at a time in which she still believed that the GDR could fulfill socialism's utopian promise, stands in contrast to Müller's ten-year connection, which was active well into the 1980s. Yet the press was far more lenient towards Müller.[39] Even though it soon became known that Wolf had proved to be such a failure as an informer that the Stasi broke off ties with her, and that she herself had been the object of their observation for decades,[40] the West German media continued its relentless defamatory attacks on her.

The publication of the Stasi files was fraught with problems. The facile division of the files into 'victim' and 'perpetrator' categories created a false dichotomy, since many GDR citizens, including Christa Wolf, had been informers but had also been under Stasi surveillance. Moreover, while initially only 'victims' were granted access to their files,[41] many 'perpetrator' files were leaked to the press and became fodder for a sensationalistic media. Alison Lewis, among others, has pointed out the pernicious political uses to which the Stasi files were put, questioning who gets to decide which files are made public and to whom.[42]

The Christa Wolf controversy quickly devolved into the acrimonious 'German-German literature debate',[43] in which the legitimacy of all GDR literature was at stake. Claiming that it had always granted East German writers an advantage, the West German literary establishment now demoted the politically engag-

---

39 Asymmetry in the press's treatment of the two writers was one of the main points in a letter of solidarity with Christa Wolf written by American academics, printed in the *Feuilleton* section of *Die Zeit* on 18 June 1993.
40 Wolf published her forty-two 'victim' Stasi files and her slim 'perpetrator' file, together with letters and other pertinent documents, in *Akteneinsicht Christa Wolf. Zerrspiegel und Dialog – Eine Dokumentation*, ed. by Hermann Vincke (Darmstadt/Neuwied: Luchterhand, 1993).
41 Thus Wolf only learned about her 'perpetrator' file illegally, through the intervention of an official working at the so-called *Gauck-Behörde*, the administrative office where the files were housed.
42 Lewis, 'Reading and Writing the Stasi File. On the Use and Abuses of the File as (Auto)Biography', *German Life and Letters*, 54.4 (2004), 377–397; see also Anke Pinkert, 'Toward a Critical Reparative Practice in Post-1989 German Literature. Christa Wolf's *City of Angels or The Overcoat of Dr. Freud*', in *Memory and Postwar Memorials. Confronting the Violence of the Past*, ed. by Marc Silberman and Florence Vatan (New York: Palgrave Mcmillan, 2013), pp. 177–196.
43 The 'German-German literature debate' is a misnomer. It was not a debate at all – certainly not a debate between East and West writers and critics about the function of literature. Rather, it was series of unilateral attacks by the West German media that can be divided into three phases. The first phase was a condemnation of Wolf following the publication of *What Remains*; the second a repudiation of all GDR literature, which had supposedly only been read for its political content; the third was a rejection of all politically engaged literature in East and West and a call for a depoliticized literature for the newly unified German republic.

ed literature of the GDR to *Gesinnungsästhetik* [ideology-driven aesthetics] and reasserted a commitment to an autonomous *l'art pour l'art* aesthetics.

Throughout the debate, there was widespread international support for both Christa Wolf and GDR literature.[44] Among Wolf scholars, the controversy again sparked a discussion about gender – a discussion that itself often broke down according to gender lines. Thus for example, the British Germanist Peter Graves, like most male scholars, argued that gender was insignificant in the attacks on Wolf.[45] American and German feminist scholars, on the other hand, pointed out that a close examination of the misogynist language, condescending tone and disdain for Wolf's treatment of the quotidian activities of women's lives manifest in the West German attacks on her writing and person left little doubt that gender factored into the disparate treatment of Wolf.[46]

Günter Grass, one of Wolf's staunchest defenders, was among the first Western intellectuals to situate the attack on Wolf within the context of German unification. Grass shared Wolf's view that the hasty German unification under the auspices of Helmut Kohl's conservative Christian Democrat government was tantamount to a colonization of the GDR. He read the attack on Wolf – who, as late as 4 November 1989, had called upon her compatriots to stay in the East and work to create a democratic socialist state – as an effort to relegate the GDR to the dustbin of history by delegitimizing its most prominent writer.[47] Christiane Schoefer's insightful article in the *Nation* elaborates on Grass's position: 'The literary campaign reveals the hidden agenda of the conservative model of German unification, which is intent not only on doing away with the Communist East but on erasing the history of the GDR and the very idea of socialism itself. Wolf is a sacrificial lamb in a larger project: the ideological shaping of unified Germany'.[48]

---

44 The terms of the debate, however, had been set in the attacks, and those supporting Wolf and GDR literature were forced to engage in the debate on those terms, leaving them in a defensive and weakened position.

45 Peter Graves, 'The Treachery of St. Joan. Christa Wolf and the *Stasi*', *German Monitor*, 30 (1994), 1–12.

46 See for example: Anna K. Kuhn, '"*Eine Königin köpfen ist effektiver als einen König köpfen*". The Gender Politics of the Christa Wolf Controversy', *German Monitor*, 31 (1994), 200–215; Christiane Zehl Romero, 'Was war? Was bleibt? Was wird? Christa Wolf Then and Now', *Michigan Germanic Studies*, 21.1/2 (1995), 103–138; and Claudia Mayer-Iswandy, 'Between Resistance and Affirmation. Christa Wolf and the German Unification', *Canadian Review of Comparative Literature*, 22 (1995), 815–835.

47 '*Nötige Kritik oder Hinrichtung? SPIEGEL-Gespräch mit Günter Grass über die Debatte um Christa Wolf und die DDR-Literatur*', *Der Spiegel*, 29 (1990), 130–143.

48 Schoefer, 'The Attack on Christa Wolf', *The Nation*, 251 (October 1990), 448. Schoefer leaves open the gender implications of the attack, saying that it was unclear whether they played a

While the attacks on Christa Wolf may have traumatized her and diminished her reputation, they did not silence her. In speeches, essays[49] and diary entries[50] as well as in her final work of fiction, *Stadt der Engel oder The Overcoat of Dr. Freud*, she continued to uncompromisingly scrutinize her own behavior as she worked through her relationship to the East German state. Wolf remained steadfast in her allegiance to the socialist project, continuing her outspoken critique of capitalism and criticizing the new Berlin Republic.[51] It is therefore perhaps not so surprising, although nonetheless shocking, that the German media would use the occasion of her death in 2011 to vilify her once again. As Sonja Klocke's perceptive analysis of Christa Wolf's obituaries shows, many if not most of the obituaries published in the Federal Republic resurrected the discourse of the 1990/1991 literary campaigns. Equating Wolf with the totalitarian GDR state and misrepresenting her Stasi connection, these obituaries, Klocke argues, are not merely personal attacks on her oeuvre and person. Rather, they once again aim at 'eradicating the GDR and, more importantly, the legitimacy of socialist thought per se'.[52] As Klocke notes, the discourse that emerges in many of Wolf's obituaries 'tries to capitalize on her death by reiterating the irreversible "death of socialism" [...] – conveniently timed during one of the greatest crises global capitalism has faced in history'.[53] Thus the predominately male West German media's

---

role. The rewriting of post-War history by the West German press would prove even more far-reaching and pernicious. On 2 November 1990, Ulrich Greiner, who had helped spearhead the attack on Wolf, rejected the Leftist politically engaged literature of the Federal Republic that had served as a powerful vehicle of *Vergangenheitsbewältigung* [coming to terms with the Nazi past] as well. His repudiation of all politically engaged literature as *Gesinnungsästhetik* allowed the broader neoconservative political agenda of the literature debate to become apparent. Unification was seen as marking the end of socially critical post-War German literature. The literature of the new Germany was once again to assume its proper function – as an art form devoid of social agendas. See Ulrich Greiner, 'Die deutsche Gesinnungsästhetik', *Die Zeit*, 45, 2 November 1990, p. 63.

49 See, for example, Wolf, *Auf dem Weg nach Tabou. Texte 1990–1994* [On the Way to Tabou. Writings 1990–1994] (Cologne: Kiepenheuer and Witsch, 1994), and *Rede, dass ich dich sehe* [Speak So That I Can See You] (Berlin: Luchterhand, 2012).

50 Christa Wolf, *One Day a Year. 1960–2000*, trans. by Lowell Bangerter (New York: Europa Editions, 2007), and *Ein Tag im Jahr im neuen Jahrhundert. 2001–2011* [One Day a Year in the New Century. 2001–2011], ed. by Gerhard Wolf (Berlin: Suhrkamp, 2013).

51 For a discussion of Wolf's literary and political engagement after German unification, see also Sonja Klocke, 'The Triumph of the Obituary. Constructing Christa Wolf for the Berlin Republic', *German Studies Review*, 37.2 (2014), 317–336, esp. 325–331.

52 Ibid., 328.

53 Ibid. Klocke is referring to the global recession that ensued in the wake of the US housing market crash of 2007.

final discrediting of the GDR's most prominent woman writer was its ultimate Cold War political move. Twenty-two years after the collapse of Eastern Bloc communism, which ostensibly signalled the end of the Cold War, it again heralded the triumph of Western capitalism over Eastern socialism.

Deborah Janson
Unearthing a Post-Humanist Ecological Socialism in Christa Wolf's 'Selbstversuch', *Kassandra* and *Störfall*

Due to her overarching focus on individual self-realization within socialist society and her long-standing desire to achieve democratic socialism in the GDR, Christa Wolf can be viewed as an adherent of socialist humanism. Other than concentrating on practical action to reach socialist goals, this branch of humanism resembles traditional humanist philosophy in many ways. Both emphasize the potential value and goodness of human beings and the importance of addressing human needs and problems solely by rational means. Instead of a religion that relies on a transcendental deity and miracles, humanists use science and its method of critical inquiry – logical reasoning, empirical evidence and sceptical evaluation – to obtain reliable knowledge that can be used to benefit humankind. As a humanist, Wolf was primarily concerned with human welfare and, in this regard, with the desire to create a socialist utopia that would foster the full development of its citizens. She even maintains some of humanism's biases towards non-human animals, who garner less of her attention and concern than human beings, in part because she (like other humanists) perceives them to lack speech.[1] Nonetheless, Wolf differs from traditional humanists in numerous ways. She is highly critical of behaviour associated with Western rationalism, especially as exercised by members of the male-dominated science and medical professions. For example, she objects to their belief in the mind-body split and their view that it is acceptable to exploit and abuse nature for human gain. Instead, she regards human beings as part of nature and recognizes that our survival is linked to that of the earth. From the publication of her short story 'Selbstversuch', to her rewriting of the Greek myth in her novel and essays about *Kassandra*, to her rendering of the ecological disaster in Chernobyl in *Störfall. Nachrichten eines Tages*,[2] Wolf decries oppressive social structures associated with patriarchy and rationalism and emphasizes an appreciation of the every-

---

1 See Christa Wolf, *Störfall. Nachrichten eines Tages* (Berlin: Aufbau, 1987), pp. 89–90.
2 Christa Wolf, 'Selbstversuch', in *Gesammelte Erzählungen* (Darmstadt: Luchterhand, 1981), pp. 158–185; Christa Wolf, *Kassandra. Erzählung* (Darmstadt: Luchterhand, 1983); Christa Wolf, *Voraussetzungen einer Erzählung. Kassandra – Frankfurter Poetik-Vorlesungen* (Darmstadt: Luchterhand, 1983). Wolf first published 'Selbstversuch' in academic journals in 1973, both in the GDR (*Sinn und Form*, 25.2 [1973], 301–323) and in the FRG (*Merkur*, 27 [1973], 1136–1155).

https://doi.org/10.1515/9783110496000-006

day aspects of life that allow us to value and respect our planet. As this essay demonstrates, Wolf's interest in overcoming hierarchical dualisms that prevent us from valuing difference and treasuring the earth closely align her with adherents of ecocriticism. Like other ecocritical feminists, Wolf ventures into a post-humanist world by expanding the circle of moral concern beyond what is strictly human and by highlighting changes that human beings need to make to achieve a partnership with the earth that will result in our collective flourishing.

Theoretical Background

Several strands of ecocriticism had gained prominence in North America by the early 1990s.[3] At that time, ecofeminists concentrated on examinations of the relationship between women and nature, sometimes from an essentialist perspective, but primarily out of an awareness that the traditional association between women and the non-human has resulted in the exploitation of both. Besides ecofeminists, other ecocritics in the 1990s – including Patrick Murphy, Greta Gaard, and Karen Warren – examined the relationships between literature and the physical environment and between narration and science, bringing an earth-centred stance to literary studies.[4] As Cheryl Glotfelty notes in her introduction to *The Ecocriticism Reader* (1996), ecocritics often emphasize the importance of place and the depiction of nature in literary texts and promote an awareness of the interconnectedness between human life and the more-than-human world, with the notion of the 'world' expanded to include the entire ecosphere.[5]

In general, German and European literary scholars did not develop an interest in ecocriticism until several decades after their North American counterparts. Until then, they focused primarily on the value of human culture and the agency of human beings, giving little attention to the interconnections between the human and the non-human. Many scholars of German literature from both Europe and the United States were also reluctant to embrace ecocriticism because of its alleged opposition to theory. While North American ecocritics writing in the

---

3 The French feminist Françoise d'Eaubonne is often credited with introducing the term 'ecofeminism' in her book *Le Féminisme ou la mort*, which appeared in 1974.
4 *Ecofeminist Literary Criticism. Theory, Interpretation, Pedagogy*, ed. by Greta Gaard and Patrick D. Murphy (Urbana/Chicago: University of Illinois Press, 1998); *Ecological Feminist Philosophies*, ed. by Karen J. Warren (Bloomington: Indiana University Press, 1996).
5 Cheryl Glotfelty, 'Introduction. Literary Studies in an Age of Environmental Crisis', in *The Ecocriticism Reader. Landmarks in Literary Ecology*, ed. by Cheryl Glotfelty and Harold Fromm (Athens: University of Georgia Press, 1996), pp. xv–xxxvii (p. xix).

1990s acknowledged a certain reluctance to embrace theory, this was due to their perception that the dominant literary theories of the day, including poststructuralism and postmodernism, offered nothing of value to ecocritical analysis. For example, Jonathan Bate criticized linguistic constructivism in *Romantic Ecology* (1991), maintaining that it was 'profoundly unhelpful to say "There is no nature" at a time when our most urgent need is to address and redress the consequences of human civilization's insatiable desire to consume the products of the earth'.[6] Even as late as 2015, American ecocritics such as Elizabeth Ammons criticized 'postmodern fundamentalism' for allowing scholars to 'retreat into abstraction'.[7] Instead, they share with Glotfelty the awareness that we need to move away from the theoretical status quo so that we can focus on the important role that literature plays in inspiring readers to act on nature's behalf.[8] Stacy Alaimo also sees 'a troubling parallel between the immateriality of contemporary social theory and a widespread, popular disregard for nonhuman nature', proposing instead a theory of trans-corporeality that examines 'the many interfaces between human bodies and the larger environment'.[9] These American ecocritics are joined by international scholars of German and European literature, including Kate Rigby and Axel Goodbody, who recognize that 'ecocritical antipathy to theory is on the wane' because relevant theories are being developed.[10] Foremost among these is material ecocriticism, a recent theoretical trend that seeks to engage with the materiality and agency of the physical world through the study of literature. Material ecocritics, such as Serenella Iovino and Serpil Oppermann, recognize that 'meaning and matter are inextricably entangled' – a view shared by Rigby and Goodbody, who suggest that the material world tells a story that must be listened to if we want to help save both ourselves and our 'earth others'.[11]

---

6 Quoted in 'Introduction' by Kate Rigby and Axel Goodbody, in *Ecocritical Theory. New European Approaches*, ed. by Axel Goodbody and Kate Rigby (Charlottesville: University of Virginia Press, 2011), pp. 1–14 (p. 2); Jonathan Bate, *Romantic Ecology. Wordsworth and the Environmental Tradition* (London/New York: Routledge, 1991).

7 *Sharing the Earth. An International Environmental Justice Reader*, ed. by Elizabeth Ammons and Modhumita Roy (Athens: University of Georgia Press, 2012), p. xii.

8 Glotfelty, 'Introduction', p. xvi.

9 Stacy Alaimo, *Bodily Natures. Science, Environment, and the Material Self* (Bloomington: Indiana UP, 2010), pp. 2, 4.

10 Rigby and Goodbody, 'Introduction', p. 1.

11 Serenella Iovino and Serpil Oppermann, 'Introduction. Stories Come to Matter', in *Material Ecocriticism*, ed. by Serenella Iovino and Serpil Oppermann (Bloomington: Indiana University Press, 2014), pp. 1–17 (p. 5); Kate Rigby, 'Gernot Böhme's Ecological Aesthetics of Atmosphere', in Goodbody and Rigby, pp. 139–152 (p. 141).

Of central importance to Wolf and other creative writers and literary scholars concerned with the environment is a critique of behaviour associated with Western rationalism. Inspired by the ideas of the seventeenth-century philosopher René Descartes, rationalists during the Enlightenment and beyond viewed reason as the chief source of knowledge and regarded physical evidence and sense experience as unnecessary in determining the truth about many issues, including the identification of material objects. Descartes's famous dictum, 'I think therefore I am', reflects the rationalist view that the mind (spirit/intellect) is separate from and superior to the physical body.[12] This hierarchical juxtaposition of mind over matter has been associated with value dualisms such as man over woman, (human) culture over nature and human beings over non-human animals, with the result that any groups associated with the nature side of the ranking are viewed as inferior, making their exploitation for the benefit of 'mankind' justified. This 'logic of domination', which separates and elevates human beings above the rest of nature, has resulted in the degradation of the planet and all those living on it.[13]

Gender and Science in 'Selbstversuch'

Wolf's short story 'Selbstversuch' (1973) offers an example of her opposition to the pseudo-objectivity characteristic of rationalism as well as a feminist critique of Western science – two areas of interest she shares with ecocritics.[14] Set in 1992, the futuristic story features a female scientist who willingly participates in a sex-change experiment. She volunteers to take injections of a transformative substance called 'Petersein Masculinum 199' [Bepeter Masculinum 199, p. 206] because she has learned that to prove herself as a woman, she has to show her readiness to become a man.[15] Her personal (female) perspective is provided in the form of a 'Traktat' [treatise], which she writes once she has aborted the experiment and which serves as a supplement to the factually accurate yet emotionally empty report s/he has been obliged to compile. Because she has been

---

12 From René Descartes's *Discourse on the Method* (1637).
13 For an ecofeminist critique of the logic of domination, see: Karen Warren, 'The Power and Promise of Ecological Feminism', *Environmental Ethics*, 12.2 (1990), 125–160.
14 Both areas of criticism are also undertaken by feminist ecocritics and posthumanists. See, for example, Karen Warren and Jim Cheney, 'Ecological Feminism and Ecosystem Ecology', in Warren, pp. 244–262; Donna Haraway, 'Situated Knowledges. The Science Question in Feminism and the Privilege of Partial Perspective', *Feminist Studies*, 14 (1988), 575–599.
15 Wolf, 'Selbstversuch', p. 166.

sworn to secrecy, the female scientist addresses her treatise only to the professor who heads the experiment, explaining to him that her participation was motivated in part by the desire to learn his secret – to understand how he, a prominent and highly respected male scientist, manages to remain emotionally detached from his work.[16] She not only learns the answer to this question, but also finds out why men view themselves as superior to women, and why they think women should not be scientists. The experiment can thus be viewed as a critique of the logic of domination – of men's attempt to colonize or suppress women – an interpretation that is supported by the name the professor gives the protagonist after s/he has transformed into a man. He calls her 'Anders', which in English means 'Other' and can be associated with the European colonizers of foreign lands who suppressed or annihilated the native culture, replacing it with their own, which they regarded as superior. In her 'post-colonial' treatise, the protagonist recalls that after her transformation, she could still distinctly feel that the woman she once had been 'wie eine Katze zusammengerollt in mir schlief' [slept curled up like a cat inside of me],[17] again suggesting the suppression of the female. Her treatise also reveals that while s/he was a man, s/he learned just how biased scientific discourse is – that it does not value difference, but rather promotes indifference towards others and disdain for women who try to pursue both career and family.[18] She reports that, as a man, s/he learned to focus exclusively on work and to let women be in charge of emotions, family, poetry and the soul[19] – realms that men feel they have no time for, since they must carry the burden of the world on their shoulders and devote themselves unwaveringly to a reality consisting of only three things: 'Wirtschaft, Wissenschaft, Weltpolitik' [economics, science, and world politics].[20] The experiment thus allows the protagonist to gain insight into the limits that traditional Western science – and Western society more generally – place on both sexes and to challenge the ruse of the male having superior capabilities in intellectual matters and representing the objective norm in the conception and execution of scientific experiments.[21]

---

16 Ibid., pp. 159–163.
17 Ibid., p. 164.
18 Ibid., pp. 180, 168–169.
19 Ibid., pp. 181–182.
20 Ibid., p. 182.
21 Wolf confirms this intent in her 1974 interview with Hans Kaufmann, in which she reflects on gender issues addressed in 'Selbstversuch', stating that it is important to acknowledge that the sexes have different needs, and that men and women – not just men – are the models for human beings. See Christa Wolf, 'Die Dimension des Autors. Gespräch mit Hans Kaufmann', in *Lesen und Schreiben. Neue Sammlung* (Darmstadt: Luchterhand, 1980), pp. 68–99 (pp. 93–94).

In her insightful reading of 'Selbstversuch', Friederike Eigler discusses the relevance Wolf's ideas hold for a critical reflection on the relationship between gender and science. Eigler supports her reading with a discussion of the ideas of three contemporary feminist science critics and/or post-humanist feminists: Donna Haraway, Evelyn Fox Keller and Sandra Harding. Eigler points out, for example, that the protagonist's experiment allows her to become 'a bio-technologically engineered transsexual', akin to Haraway's concept of the cyborg as a hybrid figure that undercuts the male-female dualism by challenging 'not only the distinction between organisms and machines, the physical and the non-physical, but the entire Western tradition of dualistic thinking that underlies these binaries and perpetuates the domination and marginalization of all "others"'.[22] Like Haraway, Fox Keller also questions the male-female binary, exposing the androcentric bias common in the formulation of scientific hypotheses and the choice of research problems as well as the scientific practice of regarding the male subject as the norm for all human beings. Similarly, Harding challenges the presumed objectivity in the sciences and the excessive focus on ranking gender differences when conducting research – a practice that reflects the 'masculine investment in the evolved distinctiveness of men's achievements and the unevolved naturalness of women's activities'.[23] These ideas are illustrated in Wolf's story, which shows that male success does not depend on biology, but on gendered constructions of what male (and female) human beings are supposed to be and do. Since all research has certain biases and interests, both Wolf and Harding emphasize the importance of acknowledging them. Doing so would challenge claims to objectivity that uphold the male-female binary and would allow more diverse groups to be involved in research projects that recognize 'the situatedness of the subjects of knowledge'.[24] Wolf illustrates this goal, Eigler suggests, when she has her female scientist end her treatise by proposing an experiment that has both social and scientific implications: 'der Versuch zu lieben. Der übrigens auch zu phantastischen Erfindungen führt: zur Erfindung dessen, den man lieben kann' [the attempt to love. Which, by the way, also leads to fantastic discoveries: the invention of the one who can be loved].[25] Eigler writes:

---

22 Friederike Eigler, 'Rereading Christa Wolf's "Selbstversuch". Cyborgs and Feminist Critiques of Scientific Discourse', *The German Quarterly*, 73.4 (2000), 401–415 (p. 407).
23 Quoted in Eigler, 'Rereading Christa Wolf', p. 405; Sandra Harding, *The Science Question in Feminism* (Ithaca: Cornell University Press, 1986), p. 100.
24 Eigler, 'Rereading Christa Wolf', p. 410.
25 Wolf, 'Selbstversuch', p. 185.

The narrator's proposed project of improving human relations is not at odds with her involvement in the sciences. Rather, if one reads the narrator's final proposition as a call for women's participation in the sciences and for a situated approach to the sciences, the new experiment becomes an integral part of the larger project of promoting social change.[26]

To create someone who is loveable and who can love would require shedding gender biases and the pseudo-objective stance that posits researchers as 'invisible and disembodied', making it possible for scientists to see differences without ranking them, to overcome alienation and to end the marginalization of female scientists and the suppression of women more generally. Though this story does not discuss human beings' relationship to nature, it does contain a post-humanist/feminist critique of Western science as well as an ecofeminist critique of patriarchy's logic of domination that can be used not only when defending the rights of women, but also when opposing the domination of nature.

Partnership: An Alternative to Patriarchy in *Kassandra*

Wolf's ecofeminist critique of patriarchy, especially the role it plays in the militarization of society, is strongly evident in *Kassandra*, a novel and four essays published ten years after 'Selbstversuch', during the height of nuclear tensions between the Soviet Union, the United States and their respective allies. Some of the ecofeminist themes Wolf discusses in this work correspond to those addressed by North American ecofeminists, such as Susan Griffin, Riane Eisler, and Starhawk. These include the role that denial, secrets and deception play in patriarchal governments that are highly militarized; connections between the public and private realms; and the need for an alternative, peaceful, environmentally concerned society based on partnership that is inspired by pre-patriarchal matriarchies and an immanent rather than a transcendent spirituality.

Wolf turned to the Greek myth about Kassandra when searching for the roots of civilization's self-destructive tendencies. In studying the ancient myths, she discovered similarities in the mentality that led to the Trojan War and the mindset that caused the nuclear arms build-up during the Cold War. In both instances, military conflict resulted either from misunderstandings and misguided ideals or from egotistical, delusional thinking on the part of political leaders who

---

26 Eigler, 'Rereading Christa Wolf', p. 411.

callously used false pretences to retain or gain political power. As in the Greek myth, Wolf's Kassandra had been granted the gift of prophecy by Apollo – who, because she rejected him as a lover, turns the gift into a curse by ensuring that no one will believe her pronouncements about the future. Yet there is a twist to how Wolf explains Kassandra's inability to convince others of what she knows to be true. It is not due to Apollo's divine powers, but to her psychologically motivated denial about what her father, the Trojan King Priam, and members of his court are planning. For example, a visionary trance reveals to her that her brother, Paris, has not abducted Helena, the wife of the Spartan king Menelaos, even though that is what the people have been told and what provides the premise on which the war is to be fought. When she confronts her father with this truth, he acknowledges it but demands her loyalty and silence. To Kassandra's great shame, she obliges. Wolf's Kassandra thus censors herself to protect the court with whom she was once aligned and in whom she still, to an ever-lessening degree, believes. Having encountered her own self-censor many times, Wolf uses Kassandra to depict the harm it can cause. She suggests that we could prevent wars if we did not let ourselves be deceived by our leaders or blinded by our ideals, and if we did not remain silent out of complacency or a desire to fit in.[27]

War is of ecocritical concern because it results not only in the death of many human and non-human animals, but also the destruction of the environment. Furthermore, the development of weaponry causes the solidification of patriarchy because the deliberations needed to build and deploy the weapons are carried out primarily by men and in secret. This situation is apparent in Wolf's *Kassandra:* whereas Troy had once been characterized by gender equality – and some women, including Kassandra, had served on the king's council – as war plans developed, their contributions gradually came to be viewed as undesirable, and they were removed from their positions. The more the women were shut out, the less principled the male leaders' behaviour became, as they allowed themselves to mistreat women and lie to the public about their intentions.

In response to their exclusion from political affairs and the escalation of tensions between the Trojans and the Greeks, the women from both societies founded an alternative community that was open to all social classes from both cultures, including men wounded in battle. Members of this community lived in caves outside of Troy, on the banks of the Scamander River. Many of them wor-

---

27 Wolf's *Kassandra* and Griffin's *A Chorus of Stones* contain numerous similarities. Both authors address the interconnections between the past and the present and the public and the private, and both also see the Trojan conflict as a starting point for the debilitating role that secrecy and denial play in waging war. See Susan Griffin, *A Chorus of Stones. The Private Life of War* (New York: Doubleday, 1992).

shipped the earth goddess Cybele, and all were devoted to healing and supporting each other, hoping to create the 'alternative of living' when otherwise confronted only with the choice between killing and dying that defined the larger
patriarchal society surrounding them.[28] Wolf thus posits a community of like-
minded women who knew their utopian experiment would soon come to an
end at the hands of the invading Greeks, but who nonetheless felt that their
time together was worthwhile, especially if their future counterparts would discover the evidence of their existence and be inspired by it.

The alternative community that Wolf depicts in *Kassandra* resulted from the
research she undertook when preparing to write the novel. In her second essay,
she discusses the Minoan culture that, as she notes, appealed to feminists looking for an alternative to the disappointments associated with patriarchy. Meeting
up with two American scholars of German literature on the island of Crete in
1980, Wolf shares their enthusiasm for ancient Minoa as a model for a feminist
utopia: 'es *gab* es doch einmal, das Land, in dem die Frauen frei und den Män-
nern gleichgestellt waren. In dem sie die Göttinnen stellten' [once upon a time
there really *was* a country where women were free and equal to men. Where
women produced the goddesses].[29] Though Wolf seems to recognize that these
'sanfte Vorstellungen' [sweet apprehensions] may be 'Irrtümer' [misapprehen-
sions] by the time she writes her novel,[30] the appeal such a society held for
her is reflected in the alternative community she depicts in her fictional account.
Furthermore, it strongly resembles the concept of a partnership-based society
that North American ecofeminists advocated in the late 1980s and early
1990s.[31] These authors were inspired by the possible existence of pre-patriarchal
societies that were peaceful, did not subordinate women to men and did not see
the earth as an object for exploitation and domination. They assumed these early
communities were instead egalitarian, worshipped an immanent nature goddess
rather than a transcendental god and recognized our planet as a living system
designed to maintain life. Even though Wolf, as a socialist humanist, did not herself practice a goddess-centred religion, she nonetheless rejects the notion that a
male god rules the earth, and she criticizes patriarchal religions that exclude

---

28 Wolf, *Kassandra*, p. 134; Wolf, *Cassandra*, p. 118.
29 Wolf, *Voraussetzungen*, p. 61.
30 Ibid.
31 See Riane Eisler, *The Chalice and the Blade. Our History, our Future* (San Francisco: Harper,
1988); Marija Gimbutas, *The Language of the Goddess. Unearthing the Hidden Symbols of Western
Civilization* (New York: Harper and Row, 1989); Starhawk, *The Fifth Sacred Thing* (New York: Bantam Books, 1993). See also: *Reweaving the World. The Emergence of Eco-feminism*, ed. by Irene
Diamond and Gloria Feman Orenstein (San Francisco: Sierra Club, 1990).

women and nature from the spiritual realm. In her second essay, Wolf maintains that the new gods, propelled by masculine thinking, created a bias that become the law of the land – a law 'das die Mutter Natur nicht lieben, sondern durchschauen will, um sie zu beherrschen und das erstaunliche Gebäude einer naturfernen Geisteswelt zu errichten, aus der Frauen von nun an ausgeschlossen sind' [that does not seek to love Mother Nature but to fathom her secrets in order to dominate her, and to erect the astounding structure of a world of mind remote from nature, from which women are henceforth excluded].[32] Wolf also criticizes the rationalist worldview that denies the existence of anything it cannot account for and that therefore is unable to perceive what Wolf calls 'das Dritte: das lächelnde Lebendige, das imstande ist, sich immer wieder aus sich selbst hervorzubringen, das Ungetrennte, Geist im Leben, Leben im Geist' [the third alternative: the smiling vital force that is able to generate itself from itself over and over: the undivided, spirit in life, life in spirit].[33] Based on the ideas Wolf expresses in her *Kassandra* novel and essays, she clearly shared with other ecocritics a vision of society that would care for the planet and all those living on it and emphasize relationships rather than hierarchies, linking rather than ranking.

Several other important themes that Wolf explores in her *Kassandra* essays include her appreciation for the everyday aspects of life that make up the private realm and her awareness of the effect that public affairs have on private life – for example, the effect of war on the personal lives of its victims. Some of the everyday feelings, activities and objects that she is thankful for are labelled in her third essay as 'Tagesgenüsse' [daily pleasures]. They include the morning light, fresh eggs for breakfast, coffee, the sea breeze, the good soup at lunchtime, happiness about purchasing the electric hot plate that will free her from dependence on propane gas, good cheese and red wine in the evenings and the drowsiness one experiences just before falling asleep.[34] Wolf enjoys all of these everyday pleasures, despite her fear – caused by a news report – that Europe will face nuclear annihilation within four years if it does not drastically change its policies. The threat makes her wonder about the meaning of these pleasures, and of life itself, if it is all to end soon: 'Wozu die Kochplatte? Wenn es keinen Strom, nichts zu kochen, keinen Menschen geben sollte, der ißt' [What is the point of the hot plate if there should be no electric current, nothing to eat, no one to eat it?].[35] Wolf's concern over the end of life as we know it should nuclear conflict ensue illustrates the connection between the public and private realms

---

32 Wolf, *Voraussetzungen*, p. 75.
33 Wolf, *Kassandra*, pp. 121–123.
34 Wolf, *Voraussetzungen*, pp. 109–110.
35 Ibid., p. 110.

that politicians and scientists – two groups who dominate the public realm – try to keep separate. Scientists, who pride themselves on maintaining emotional detachment, have developed weapons of mass destruction that political leaders will deploy if they can find no other way to defend themselves or the ideals their countries hold dear (such as 'freedom' in the West or 'socialism' in the East).[36] This would in turn result in the obliteration of life, with all of its 'private' concerns, in both the East and the West, as well as in the contamination of the beautiful planet that is our life source.

Nature Matters in *Störfall*

In her *Kassandra* texts, especially the third essay, Wolf addresses the threat nuclear science poses to all forms of life on the planet. She thus uses her literary talents to investigate the very real danger that the proliferation of nuclear weapons presented in the early 1980s and to forewarn us of the risk that nuclear waste and other environmental hazards present to the planet's survival. The world was confronted with a formidable manifestation of this threat only three years after *Kassandra*'s publication, when the Chernobyl Nuclear Power Plant suffered its catastrophic nuclear reactor accident on 25–26 April 1986. In response, Wolf wrote *Störfall. Nachrichten eines Tages* to illuminate once again the dangers of nuclear technology via a work of fiction. More than any other work by Wolf, this novel serves as a cautionary tale about actual and potential environmental destruction, encouraging readers to interpret the plot and its themes both 'intratextually and extratextually' – that is, as a work of fiction whose focus is not only 'on what has happened but on what can happen'.[37]

Material ecocriticism provides a fruitful approach to understanding the ecocritical aspects of *Störfall*, a story that highlights the interconnections between mind and matter and the agency of material things. The novel conveys the thoughts, emotions and reactions of a first-person female narrator who, while spending the day at her family home in the East German countryside, is consumed with worry over two disparate yet simultaneously occurring events: her brother's brain surgery and the effects of the fallout from a recent nuclear reactor meltdown in a neighbouring country. The story thus revisits Wolf's ambivalent

---

36 Ibid., p. 108.
37 Patrick Murphy, 'Dialoguing with Bakhtin over Our Ethical Responsibility to Anothers', in *Ecocritical Theory. New European Approaches*, ed. by Axel Goodbody and Kate Rigby (Charlottesville: University of Virginia Press, 2011), pp. 155–167 (p. 164). Murphy discusses cautionary tales as chronotopes that are set in a specific 'time-place', but also provide warnings about the future.

interest in science and technology, juxtaposing life-enhancing and life-destroy-ing technologies to demonstrate that although modern science can save lives, it also destroys them. While her brother's operation ends successfully, news re-ports alert her to the fact that the entire food chain may have been contaminated by the nuclear fallout. Children, she learns, should not be given fresh milk, spi-nach or lettuce and should not be allowed to play outside. This is due to the in-teraction of radioactive material from the accident with natural phenomena, such as the wind, which causes radioactivity to be spread indiscriminately via rain clouds without regard for human-made political borders. This interaction between wind and radioactivity illustrates the material ecocritical awareness – explained by Iovino and Oppermann – that all material forms, whether 'visible or invisible, socialized or wild,' emerge in combination with forces, agencies and other matter, and in so doing, 'their more-than-human materiality [...] tells us something about the world we inhabit'.[38] According to material ecocritics, all forms of matter have agency, and in their interactions with other forms and forces, they cause change, spreading harm or goodness, as the case may be, and demonstrating that human beings are no less or more a part of this materi-al/spiritual universe than all other life forms. Wolf's awareness of the environ-mental damage that can be caused by the interaction of material forms and nat-ural forces – the poisoning of vegetation and water, for example – demonstrates that she shares this understanding with material ecocritics. This in turn points her in the direction of a post-humanist view of the world, with its concern for more than just human matters.

The narrator of *Störfall* is particularly preoccupied with the change that the nuclear accident has wrought on objects of nature, especially clouds. Once sym-bols of purity and beauty, the radioactive particles they now contain have turned clouds into an ominous threat not only to the health of the planet, but also to human culture: 'Eine unsichtbare Wolke von ganz anderer Substanz hatte es übernommen, unsere Gefühle – ganz andere Gefühle – auf sich zu ziehen. Und sie hat [...] die weiße Wolke der Poesie ins Archiv gestoßen' [An invisible cloud of a completely different substance had seized the attention of our feelings – completely different feelings. And [...] it has knocked the white cloud of poetry into the archives].[39] Besides poems that feature clouds, many other descriptions of natural phenomena in literature have now also been consigned to the past, the narrator laments. For example, phrases such as 'die Kirschbäume sind explo-diert' [the cherry trees have exploded] and references to 'der strahlende Himmel'

---

38 Iovino and Oppermann, 'Introduction', p. 1.
39 Wolf, *Störfall*, p. 62.

[the radiant sky] can no longer be uttered – at least not with the meaning they once had.[40] Her awareness of how the meltdown has altered what language signifies, and that even the arts have been affected, illustrates Iovino and Oppermann's idea that meaning and matter are inextricably linked, and that matter tells a story.

Störfall also revisits many of the ecocritical themes explored in Wolf's earlier works. As in 'Selbstversuch', the narrator of *Störfall* rejects hierarchical dualisms and the notion that the domestic realm of caring for family should remain the exclusive domain of women, since such situations damage women's career possibilities as well as the emotional lives of both women and men. She reflects further on the alienation that occurs when human beings are unable to meet their deepest longings: 'dann schaffen wir uns Ersatzbefriedigung und hängen uns an ein Ersatzleben, Lebensersatz, die ganze atemlos expandierende ungeheure technische Schöpfung Ersatz für Liebe' [we create substitute gratification and cling to a substitute life, a substitute for life, the entire breathlessly expanding monstrous technological creation, a substitute for love].[41] Like Kassandra, *Störfall's* narrator also expresses her appreciation for the everyday aspects of life – 'Die haltbaren Genüsse' [imperishable pleasures][42] – for favourite meals enjoyed with family and friends and for beloved sights, smells and sounds of the natural world in which she lives. Furthermore, the narrative reveals once again how the public realm – inhabited by nuclear scientists and governmental officials – affects private individuals. In this way, as Katharina Gerstenberger points out, Wolf reveals that 'the personal is the position from which nuclear disaster can and must be confronted' and demonstrates her 'commitment to individual intervention in political processes'.[43] Wolf closes her novel with a very personal statement that accentuates her appreciation for life and reminds us of the importance of learning to love. She says to her brother – telepathically, as always in the novel – 'Wie schwer, Bruder, würde es sein, von dieser Erde Abschied zu nehmen' [How difficult it would be, brother, to take leave of this earth].[44] This personal realization not only reflects the grief associated with (almost) losing her brother or anticipating her own death, but also the immense sadness she would feel – we should all feel – if we had to accept irreversible damage to our planet, damage that had been caused by a lack of love and foresight.

---

40 Ibid., pp. 9 and 28.
41 Wolf, *Störfall*, pp. 38–39.
42 Wolf, *Störfall*, p. 14.
43 Katharina Gerstenberger, 'Störfälle. Literary Accounts from Chernobyl to Fukushima', *German Studies Review*, 37.1 (2014), pp. 131–148.
44 Wolf, *Störfall*, p. 118.

Conclusion: Searching for Liveable Alternatives in a Post-Humanist World

'Wieder einmal, so ist es mir vorgekommen, hatte das Zeitalter sich ein Vorher und Nachher geschaffen' [Once again, so it seemed, our age had created a Before and After for itself].[45] With this reflection, the narrator of *Störfall* describes the nuclear accident in Chernobyl as one in a series of sobering events that gave her – or rather, her creator, Christa Wolf – deeper insight into the disappointing options that she, as a socialist humanist, had been confronted with throughout her life. Disillusioned with Nazi ideology as a young adult and critical of the exploitation and alienation characteristic of capitalism, Wolf had accepted socialism as the system that could endow human beings with the means to achieve self-realization. Over time, however, governmental policies that compromised artists and intellectuals' attempts to participate in her society's development showed Wolf – with ever increasing clarity – that real-existing socialism in the GDR could not provide her with the desired alternative to capitalism. Like other utopian socialists, she sought a 'third way' that would present a liveable alternative to the many false ones she had repeatedly faced. Wolf's concept of an ideal society became more and more ecological as her concern about the development of nuclear warfare and the threat of nuclear contamination grew. Having already addressed the necessity of finding an alternative to 'killing or dying' in *Kassandra*, Wolf indicates in *Störfall* that human beings around the globe are encountering difficult environmental choices – for example, between living 'mit der Radioaktivität oder mit dem Waldsterben' [with radioactivity or with the dying woods];[46] between giving up our 'creature comforts' or destroying the planet;[47] and between drinking contaminated water or dying of thirst.[48] Insights of this nature reveal that Wolf was a trendsetter in terms of ecofeminist awareness. She was at the forefront of the ecocritical literary movement, even in advance of many of her North American counterparts and well before most German literary scholars. When GDR citizens seized the opportunity to reform their country in the autumn of 1989, Wolf continued to advocate for nature, calling for a socialist alternative to the Federal Republic that was both humanist *and* ecological – that would defend not only peace, freedom and social justice for all of its

---

45 Wolf, *Störfall*, p. 43.
46 Wolf, *Störfall*, p. 79.
47 Ibid.
48 In *Störfall*, the narrator recalls the fairy tale 'Little Brother, Little Sister', with its choice between turning into a wild beast after drinking the cursed water or dying of thirst (p. 80).

citizens, but also the preservation of the environment. This idea, expressed in the appeal 'Für unser Land',[49] corresponds to the themes contained in the texts examined in this chapter. From 'Selbstversuch' through *Störfall*, Wolf's socialist humanist vision has expanded over time to include opposition to hierarchical dualisms and delusional thinking that harm not only human beings, but the entire planet. Her works thus contribute to the post-humanist awareness that we are not the only material-spiritual agents inhabiting this living earth.

---

49 Christa Wolf, 'Für unser Land', in *Im Dialog. Aktuelle Texte* (Frankfurt a. M.: Luchterhand, 1990), pp. 170–171.

Sabine von Mering

Nature, Power and Literature: Rereading Christa Wolf's *Störfall. Nachrichten eines Tages* as 'Ecological Force' in Times of Climate Crisis

Störfall. Nachrichten eines Tages[1] – Christa Wolf's response to the 26 April 1986 nuclear disaster in Chernobyl, Ukraine – is by some accounts her most outspoken political book.[2] It is also one of the earliest works by a German author of fiction that raises questions about the danger of atomic energy and the problems of high energy consumption and environmental degradation.[3] Thirty years later, Wolf's questions have become even more pertinent. On 26 January 2017, the world's most distinguished atomic scientists of 'The Bulletin' moved the symbolic 'Doomsday Clock' to two-and-a-half minutes to midnight, the closest it has been to existential catastrophe since 1953.[4] The scientists added warnings of a new threat multiplier: climate change. How today's human-made crises exacerbate each other is depicted powerfully in the 2016 documentary film *The Age of Consequences*.[5] Human responsibility for climate change was not yet widely understood in the 1980s, but Wolf's exploration of the underlying tendencies in human nature that seem to propel humanity towards catastrophe, though in-

---

1 Christa Wolf, *Störfall. Nachrichten eines Tages* (Berlin: Luchterhand, 1987). English translation: *Accident. A Day's News* (Chicago: University of Chicago Press, 1989).

2 See, for example, Brigitte Rossbacher, *Illusions of Progress. Christa Wolf and the Critique of Science in GDR Women's Literature* (New York: Peter Lang, 2000), p. 8.

3 Earlier examples include Monika Maron's *Flugasche* (1981). More recent examples are Ilia Trojanow's *Eis Tau* (2011), Dirk C. Fleck's *Maeva!* (2011), and the 2015 *Weather Stations – Writing Climate Change Project* (https://cdn.freewordcentre.com/legacy/files/Weather_Stations_Writing_Climate_Change_ALL.pdf).

4 Peter Holley, Abby Ohlheiser and Amy B. Wang, 'The Doomsday Clock just moved two-and-a-half minutes to midnight thanks to Trump', *Washington Post*, 'Speaking of Science', 26 January 2017 (https://www.washingtonpost.com/news/speaking-of-science/wp/2017/01/26/the-doomsday-clock-just-moved-again-its-now-two-and-a-half-minutes-to-midnight/?utm_term=.2bd26157bd5b).

5 See TheAgeofConsequences.com. For an introduction to the climate crisis, see Joseph Romm, *Climate Change. What Everyone Needs to Know* (Cambridge, MA: Harvard University Press, 2015).

https://doi.org/10.1515/9783110496000-007

spired by the Chernobyl accident, also applies to human-made ecological crises in general.[6]

For Axel Goodbody, one of the pioneers of German ecocriticism, the ecological crises of our time also represent a new responsibility for literary scholars. He suggests we must define 'the roles which literary imagination, art, and writing might play in contributing to the development of a new subjectivity and culture [...] and of identifying creative possibilities and aesthetic forms fit for the task'.[7] Although ecocriticism only started to emerge a few decades ago, recent years have seen a tremendous growth in ecocritical scholarship, also in German studies.[8] Hubert Zapf's *Literature as Cultural Ecology. Sustainable Texts* provides a particularly useful theoretical framework for a rereading of *Störfall* in the context of the climate crisis.[9] Zapf positions his approach in close proximity to Serenella Iovino and Serpil Oppermann's version of 'material ecocriticism'.[10] Still, he cautions that 'a radicalized material ecocriticism risks to disempower human culture and creativity to a point where anonymous material processes of nature/culture entanglements are replacing personally and socially responsible forms of human agency as shaping forces of political, economic, social, scientific, and artistic developments'.[11] According to Zapf, literary texts have the potential to function as 'ecological force', a concept similar to Greg Garrard's idea of 'transformative discourse'.[12] Both terms – 'ecological force' and 'transformative discourse' – assert literature's key role in the radical eco-social transformation that modern societies have to embrace in order to prevent ecological collapse. Zapf's threefold model of literature as cultural ecology aims to describe 'the ecological function of literature within the larger system of cultural discourses: as a cultural-critical metadiscourse, an imaginative counterdiscourse, and a reintegrative interdis-

---

6 More recently, Harald Welzer has written about the climate crisis as a crisis that has its origins in basic human aggression. See Harald Welzer, *Klimakriege. Wofür im einundzwanzigsten Jahrhundert getötet wird* (Frankfurt a. M.: Fischer, 2008).
7 Axel Goodbody, 'Telling the Story of Climate Change. The German Novel in the Anthropocene', in *German Ecocriticism in the Anthropocene*, ed. by Caroline Schaumann and Heather Sullivan (New York: Palgrave Macmillan 2017), pp. 293–314 (p. 296).
8 See Schaumann and Sullivan.
9 Hubert Zapf, *Literature as Cultural Ecology. Sustainable Texts* (London: Bloomsbury, 2016).
10 See Serenella Iovino and Serpil Oppermann, *Material Ecocriticism* (Bloomington, Indiana: Indiana University Press, 2014).
11 Zapf, *Literature as Cultural Ecology*, p. 87.
12 Greg Garrard, *Ecocriticism*. (London: Routledge, 2004), p. 7.

course'.[13] In the following ecocritical rereading of *Störfall*, I use Zapf's model to explore how Wolf exposes the underlying tendencies in human nature to reveal the connection between humanity's insatiable hunger for knowledge and power on the one hand, and our propensity for (self)-destruction on the other. My reading illustrates how Wolf's *Störfall* functions as an 'ecological force' and thus serves as one model for how literature can tackle problems even as complex as climate change.

Wolf describes her understanding of writing fiction in close proximity to and interaction with her own life as 'subjective authenticity'.[14] This also effects the very genre of the text. It oscillates between ego-document and philosophical essay, which creates a unique version of 'imaginative counterdiscourse' that is particularly appropriate for the text's function as 'ecological force' in the face of an invisible threat like climate change, which most people cannot fully comprehend. Wolf never mentions Chernobyl, the Soviet Union or the GDR. Her text simply represents a powerful indictment of a failed system. Whereas the Soviet Union and the GDR no longer exist, Wolf's text sustains its 'ecological force' to this day. According to Zapf, art and literature do not just *help* us create a better world, they actually *create* it: 'art itself, and especially literary art, constitutes a form of sustainable aesthetic and textual culture'.[15]

Wolf presents her 'imaginative counterdiscourse' through a female narrator's stream-of-consciousness account of detailed descriptions of quotidian life; alone in a pastoral setting, she tries to make sense of the nuclear accident and its repercussions. Her emotional engagement and careful descriptions of ordinary tasks contrast sharply with the enormity of the accident.[16] There are two main 'cultural-critical metadiscourses' that expose 'petrifications of the dominant cultural system'[17] in *Störfall:* a metadiscourse about power and knowledge, to which we can subsequently add climate change; and a metadiscourse about the dichotomy of human nature, determined by the struggle for knowledge and power. Finally, a 'reintegrative interdiscourse' becomes visible in Wolf's understanding of the role of literature through her discussion of nature poetry. Together, these discourses confirm the text's power as a sustained 'ecological force'.

---

13 Hubert Zapf, 'Ecological Thought and Literature in Europe and Germany', in *A Global History of Literature and the Environment*, ed. by John Parham and Louise Westling (Cambridge: Cambridge University Press, 2016), p. 269–285 (p. 280).
14 Christa Wolf, *Die Dimension des Autors* (Berlin: Aufbau, 1986), p. 325.
15 Zapf, *Literature as Cultural Ecology*, p. 21.
16 The contrast also extends to the experience of the garden. See Heather Sullivan, 'The Dark Pastoral. A Trope for the Anthropocene', in Schaumann and Sullivan, pp. 29–44 (p. 35).
17 Zapf, 'Ecological Thought', p. 281.

Knowledge, Energy, Power and Climate Change

The first 'cultural-critical metadiscourse' in *Störfall* connects the text to discourses on knowledge, energy and power and allows us to draw a link to climate change. During the Cold War, these discourses were closely linked to the power dynamics determining the politics between the USA and the USSR. Christa Wolf herself had already been worried about nuclear power before Chernobyl.[18] For many, the obvious link between the so-called peaceful use of nuclear energy and nuclear weapons raised concerns about the dangers of nuclear power in general, and the proliferation of nuclear weapons in the wake of the *NATO-Doppelbeschluss* [NATO 'Double-Track Decision'] motivated hundreds of thousands to join anti-nuclear protests in West Germany.[19] There are many parallels to the present moment, as discussions about nuclear arms and nuclear energy are assuming new relevance, which should draw renewed attention to Wolf's text: despite reductions of the nuclear stockpile agreed upon in the New Start Treaty of 2010,[20] both Vladimir Putin and Donald Trump have expressed interest in expanding nuclear arsenals again in their respective countries, renewing the spectre of a potential nuclear war that had initially subsided after the end of the Cold War, and there are of course additional fears around potential nuclear threats from North Korea and Iran.[21] The broader discourse around energy and climate also connects the present moment with the period at the end of the Cold War. The 1970s and 1980s had been the world's fastest-growing production period for nuclear power plants. Chernobyl marked the abrupt end of the purported golden age of safe, cheap, unlimited nuclear energy and initiated a steady decline in the construction of nuclear plants worldwide until 2011.[22] The 25 years

---

18 Anna Kuhn writes that Chernobyl 'confirmed Wolf's worst fears about nuclear catastrophe.' See Anna K. Kuhn, *Christa Wolf's Utopian Vision. From Marxism to Feminism* (Cambridge: Cambridge University Press, 1988), p. 167.

19 For example, 500,000 people protested in Bonn on 22 October 1983. Protests continued for decades and were re-energized after Fukushima in March 2011.

20 See US Department of State, *Diplomacy in Action. New START* (https://www.state.gov/new start).

21 See 'Trump Says U.S. Should "Expand" Nuclear Ability', *New York Times*, 'Politics', 23 December 2016, p. A1; Stephen Collinson and Jeremy Diamond, 'Trump, Putin both seek to boost their nuclear capability', *CNN.com* 'Politics', 23 December 2016 (http://edition.cnn.com/2016/12/22/politics/donald-trump-strengthen-expand-nuclear-capability/).

22 For details, see Mycle Schneider's award-winning World Nuclear Report (http://www.world nuclearreport.org/World-Nuclear-Industry-Status-on-1-235.html). The *Umweltbibliothek* [environmental library] in Berlin's Zionskirche (Church of Zion) that was begun as a result of Chernobyl ended up playing a major part in the 1989 revolution (http://zionskirche-berlin.de/english).

between the Chernobyl accident and the March 2011 Fukushima disaster saw the consolidation of a broad public consensus against nuclear power in Germany. The country is set to phase out all of its nuclear plants by 2022.[23] In the United States, however, the merits of nuclear energy continue to be hotly debated, even among environmentalists.[24] A similar divide exists between proponents of geo-engineering and those who warn that it would only exacerbate humanity's unethical intrusion into natural processes.[25]

From Ukraine to Sweden, in the wake of the Chernobyl accident, people struggled to come to terms with the invisible transformation of nature around them: familiar vegetables and greens in their backyard – from lettuce to rhubarb to spinach to mushrooms – were suddenly deemed too dangerous to consume. Nature literally explodes in *Störfall:* 'Das Grün explodiert: Nie wäre ein Satz dem Naturvorgang angemessener gewesen' [The green is exploding. Never would such a sentence have been more appropriate in describing the progress of nature].[26] With this brutal metaphor, the narrator visualizes the realization that nature's powerful beauty had suddenly been rendered suspect. The accident at the distant power plant has disrupted the familiar environment. Confusion about the facts of the nuclear accident also upset the existing power structure: even former Soviet leader Mikhail Gorbachev himself, whose administration was heavily criticized at the time for withholding information about the accident, came to view Chernobyl as the beginning of the unravelling of the Soviet Union.[27] Wolf's text questions the authorities' handling of the crisis in subtle

---

23 The controversial consensus reached by the bipartisan parliamentary commission in April 2016 committed billions of euros to nuclear power plant operators for safe dismantling and storage. The process is expected to take decades to complete. See, for example, 'Fragen und Antworten zum Atom-Deal', *Welt.de*, 'Newsticker', 27 April 2016 (https://www.welt.de/newsticker/dpa_nt/infoline_nt/thema_nt/article154810086/Fragen-und-Antworten-zum-Atom-Deal.html); 'Atommüll-Entsorgung. Kompromiss für 23 Milliarden Euro', *tagesschau.de*, 15 December 2016 (http://www.tagesschau.de/wirtschaft/atomausstieg-129.html).

24 See, for example, Environmental Progress, 'An Open Letter on Nuclear Energy to President-elect Trump and Governor Rick Perry' (http://www.environmentalprogress.org/trump-letter/); see also Yale University's assessment: 'Is a nuclear fix for warming worth it?' (http://www.yaleclimateconnections.org/2016/08/is-a-nuclear-fix-for-warming-worth-it).

25 See, for example, Naomi Klein, *This Changes Everything. Capitalism vs the Climate* (New York: Simon and Schuster, 2014).

26 Wolf, *Störfall*, p. 9; *Accident*, p. 3.

27 'The nuclear meltdown at Chernobyl twenty years ago this month, even more than my launch of perestroika, was perhaps the real cause of the collapse of the Soviet Union five years later. Indeed, the Chernobyl catastrophe was an historic turning point: there was the era before the disaster, and there is the very different era that has followed'; Mikhail Gorbachev,

ways – for example, when she ridicules the 'mushrooming' of the number of 'experts' who are paraded in front of the TV in order to allay people's fears, or when she demonstrates the futility of following the so-called experts' advice.[28]

As Kate Rigby has shown, ecocriticism is also interested in literary analysis that pays attention to the political ramifications of our growing energy needs.[29] Christa Wolf's *Störfall* spurred heated discussions about nuclear power and its alternatives when it first appeared in 1987.[30] The author herself rejected the notion that the text deals primarily with the question of energy, however, and scholars have so far agreed with her. Other issues were considered more relevant.[31] Yet Hubert Zapf reminds us that rereading a text in new historical circumstances allows literature to unfold its power as an ecological force: it is 'a potentiality of texts that only comes alive through its ever new actualizations within always changing historical, social, and individual conditions'.[32] Read through this lens thirty years later, in the context of potential nuclear rearmament and the mounting climate crisis, *Störfall* clearly 'comes alive' with new significance.

Wolf's narrator accuses the scientists who pursued the development of nuclear power of negligence: 'Hätten sie es rechtzeitig anders wissen können?' [Could they have known otherwise in time?].[33] She answers her rhetorical question in the affirmative by allying herself with the young people who successfully protested against nuclear power plants already at the beginning of the 1970s. Those protestors, she remembers, had been 'verlacht, reglementiert, gemaßregelt' [ridiculed, rebuked, reprimanded][34] for highlighting the dangers of the allegedly peaceful use of atomic energy long before Chernobyl. Such negligence compares to US President Donald Trump's rejection of the scientific consensus and his support for the fossil fuel industry at a time of sea level rise, severe

---

'Turning Point at Chernobyl', *Project Syndicate*, 14 April 2006, p. 1 (https://www.project-syndi cate.org/commentary/turning-point-at-chernobyl?barrier=true).

28 See, for example *Störfall*, p. 11; *Accident*, p. 5.

29 See Kate Rigby, 'Confronting Catastrophe. Ecocriticism in a Warming World', in *The Cambridge Companion to Literature and the Environment*, ed. by Louise Westling (Cambridge: Cambridge University Press, 2013), pp. 212–225.

30 Wolf herself organized readings and discussions, including several at nuclear power plants, some of which are anthologized in Christa Wolf, *Verblendung. Disput über einen Störfall* (Berlin/ Weimar: Aufbau, 1991).

31 See, for example, Damian Rzezniczak, *DDR-Staatsdichterin oder Autorin von Gesamtdeutschem Rang. Christa Wolf im Rampenlicht des kulturpolitischen Lebens der DDR* (Hamburg: Diplomica, 2005), pp. 44–45.

32 See Zapf, *Literature as Cultural Ecology*, p. 26.

33 Wolf, *Störfall*, p. 37; *Accident*, p. 30.

34 Ibid.

droughts, fires, storms and floods. Trump's decision to make the former CEO of Exxon his Secretary of State while Exxon is being investigated by several state attorneys general for deceiving investors and consumers over decades about the dangers of climate change also indicates highly problematic conflicts of interest. *Störfall* is written against those who knowingly allowed a preventable accident to occur – exactly what attorneys in now eighteen US states are accusing ExxonMobil of having done.[35] Wolf's depiction of those in power who deny facts, neglect their duty to protect people and the planet and obstruct transparency for their own gain makes *Störfall* a highly relevant 'ecological force' for young readers engaged in environmental and climate activism today.

Given how proud the GDR was of its nuclear industry, expressing fears about the technology's safety was an act of courage in itself. As reviewer Jutta Krug writes: '[Christa Wolf] hat [...] den Mut, in einem Land, in dem Kernkraft-Optimismus gepredigt wird, Chronistin und schreibende Kassandra zu sein' [Christa Wolf has the courage to be a chronicler and a writing Cassandra in a country which preaches optimism about nuclear power.][36] Still, some reviewers were less impressed and wanted much more vocal criticism.[37] The Belarusian investigative journalist and Nobel laureate Svetlana Alexievich would no doubt agree. Her collection of interviews *Voices From Chernobyl. Oral History of a Disaster* (1997) paints a far darker picture than Wolf's text.[38] In February 1990, the news magazine *Der Spiegel* exposed the catastrophic conditions of all the nuclear power plants in the GDR,[39] which makes Wolf's critique seem tame in retrospect. She could have been more forceful, but she deserves credit for triggering a public de-

---

35 The investigations began in New York in 2015. See Justin Gillis and Gifford Kraus, 'Exxon Mobil Investigated for Possible Climate Change Lies by New York Attorney General,' *New York Times*, 6 November 2015, p. A1 (http://www.nytimes.com/2015/11/06/science/exxon-mobil-under-investigation-in-new-york-over-climate-statements.html).

36 Jutta Krug in *Hamburger Abendblatt*, 24 April 1987. All translations, except where otherwise indicated, are my own.

37 See, for example, Ingrid Strobl's critical review 'Zucchini mit Wolke', *Konkret*, 5 (1987), pp. 6–7.

38 See also Rachel Donadio, 'Svetlana Alexievich, Nobel Laureate of Russian Misery, has an English-language Milestone' *New York Times*, 'Books', 20 May 2016 (https://www.nytimes.com/2016/05/21/books/svetlana-alexievich-a-nobel-laureate-of-russian-misery-has-her-english-debut.html?_r=0).

39 See 'Zeitbombe Greifswald' *Spiegel Special*, 1 February 1990 (http://www.spiegel.de/spiegel/spiegelspecial/d-52397652.html). The dossier calls the history of atomic power in the GDR a 'Horrorchronik' and the power plant Lubmin near Greifswald 'ein atomares Pulverfass' [an atomic powder keg].

bate about nuclear power and energy consumption with *Störfall*. This debate is anthologized in *Verblendung. Disput über einen Störfall*.

Thirty years after Chernobyl and five years after Christa Wolf's death, the questions she raises in *Störfall* produce a 'cultural-critical metadiscourse' which, in turn, can inform contemporary discussions. The doomsday scenarios of the 1970s are no longer being ridiculed today.[40] Germany, though celebrated worldwide as a climate champion and united in its commitment to end the use of nuclear power, still has to respond to justified criticism related to its continued mining of the most dangerous fossil fuel, lignite coal.[41] Developing its function as an effective 'ecological force' under new socio-political circumstances, Wolf's text thus illuminates the fact that pertinent discourses can evolve long after the time of publication.

Between Good and Evil: The Dichotomy of Human Nature

In describing the unique contribution of German literature and philosophy to ecological thought, Hubert Zapf mentions Wolf's *Störfall* as part of a long history of literary engagement with the dichotomy of human nature – which, as in Goethe's *Faust*, is marked by 'the conflict between an egocentric will to knowledge and power and a deeper culture-nature connectivity'.[42] This metadiscourse has programmatic relevance for Wolf's text, and she places it in an epigraph at the beginning of the text in two quotations: the first by Carl Sagan – 'Die Verbindung zwischen Töten und Erfinden hat uns nie verlassen. Beide entstammen dem Ackerbau und der Zivilisation' [The connection between murder and invention has been with us ever since. Both derive from agriculture and civilization]; and the second by Konrad Lorenz – 'Das langgesuchte Zwischenglied zwischen dem Tier und dem wahrhaft humanen Menschen sind wir' [The long-sought missing link between animals and the really humane being is ourselves].[43]

---

40 See Kai F. Hünemörder, 'Kassandra im Modernen Gewand. Die Umweltapokalyptischen Warnrufe der frühen 1970er Jahre', in *Wird Kassandra heiser? Die Geschichte Falscher Ökoalarme*, ed. by Frank Uekötter and Jens Hohensee (Stuttgart: Franz Steiner, 2004), pp. 78–97 (p. 97).
41 See, for example, German climate activist Tadzio Müller's portrayal in Jared P.Scott's short documentary *Disobedience*. (https://www.youtube.com/watch?v=Tdtc7ltYB8E).
42 Zapf, 'Ecological Thought', p. 275.
43 Sonja Hilzinger identifies the origins of the quotations as follows: Carl Sagan, *The Dragons of Eden. Speculations on the Evolution of Human Intelligence* (New York: Random House, 1977). Lorenz's quotation appears in Konrad Lorenz, *Das sogenannte Böse. Zur Naturgeschichte der Aggres-*

Sagan sees both human aggression and ingenuity as inevitable products of civilization. Lorenz suggests that modern humankind bridges a continuum between nature/animal and ideal humanity.[44] Wolf's narrator discusses the human proclivity for brutality and wilful ignorance without sparing herself.[45] Indeed, she connects the nuclear accident with her growing sense of her own 'Lebenslüge' [living a lie].[46] The political dimension emerges when she recalls an argument with her scientist brother, who reminds her that, as a writer, she too would use her powers in potentially destructive ways, if only to avoid being irrelevant:

> Ob ich denn innehalten könnte. Ob ich nicht mal zu ihm gesagt habe, Worte könnten treffen, sogar zerstören wie Projektile; ob ich denn immer abzuwägen wisse – immer bereit sei, abzuwägen – wann meine Worte verletzend, vielleicht zerstörend würden? Vor welchem Grad von Zerstörung ich zurückschrecken würde? Nicht mehr sagen, was ich sagen könnte? Lieber in Schweigen verfallen?

> [Whether I would be able to stop. Whether I hadn't once told him that words could wound, even destroy, like projectiles; whether I was always able to judge – always willing to judge – when my words would wound, perhaps destroy? At what level of destruction I would back down? No longer say what I could? Opt for silence?][47]

These rhetorical questions force the reader to confront their own complicity with the status quo, but also implicate the author herself. It has been noted that the autobiographical is only thinly veiled in *Störfall*, which makes it difficult to distinguish between narrator and author.[48] On 17 August 1986, Wolf writes in a letter to the Polish writer Halina Ludorowska that she very much saw her own writing as a product of her diaries, and that the text she was working on at the time was

---

sion (Vienna: Dr. G. Borotha-Schoeler, 1963). See *Werkausgabe in 12 Bänden*, ed. by Sonja Hilzinger (Munich: Luchterhand, 1999–2001), vol. 9: *Störfall. Nachrichten eines Tages/Verblendung. Disput über einen Störfall* (2001), p. 388.

44 Brigitte Rossbacher analyses the two quotations in detail. See Rossbacher, *Illusions of Progress*, pp. 145–146.

45 In a letter to the author, Elisabeth Lenk, on 1 February 1987, Wolf writes: 'Ich habe in [*Störfall*] das Thema auch umkreist, [...] unter dem Gesichtspunkt, der mir zu einer wirklichen Bedrängnis geworden ist: Wo liegt mein Anteil am "Bösen" unserer Tage?' [I circled that topic in *Störfall* as well, in the aspect that became a true dilemma for me: What is my contribution to the "evil" of our time?]. See Christa Wolf, *Man steht sehr bequem zwischen allen Fronten. Briefe 1952–2011*, ed. by Sabine Wolf (Berlin: Suhrkamp, 2016), p. 530.

46 Wolf, *Störfall*, p. 103; *Accident*, p. 93.

47 Ibid., p. 55; p. 48.

48 For a more detailed discussion of the distinction between narrator and author in Wolf's work, see Karin Eysel, 'History, Fiction, Gender. The Politics of Narrative Intervention in Christa Wolf's Störfall,' *Monatshefte*, 84.3 (Fall 1992), 248–289.

based on a day in her life, which she had spent by herself juggling the news of Chernobyl with that of her brother's brain surgery.[49] Subtle hints throughout *Störfall* suggest Wolf's own growing disillusionment with those in power in the GDR, referred to only as 'they' in the narrator's phone conversations with her daughters.[50]

The realization that she herself is not free from destructive tendencies marks the 'Drehpunkt des Tages' [turning point of the day][51] for the narrator at the very centre of the novella. She goes on to describe how she catches herself absent-mindedly putting dirty dishes back into the cabinet before erupting into a violent outburst, repeatedly throwing wooden salad servers on the floor:

> So. Und so. Und so. Euch werde ich es zeigen. Euch habe ich so satt. Satt. Satt. Mit Genug-tuung habe ich mir zugesehen. Die Wut, der Hass in meinem verzerrten Gesicht.

> [And again. And again. Take that. And that. And that. I'll show you. I'm so fed up with you. Fed up. Fed up. I observed myself with satisfaction. The rage, the hate in my distorted fea-tures.][52]

The narrator's satisfaction with seeing her own rage is meant to be disconcerting, not reassuring: on the one hand she seems relieved, almost proud of her own explosion in reaction to the overwhelming feeling of helplessness that she can-not squarely blame on anyone. On the other hand, the absence and anonymity of the 'enemy' in this scene renders her rage and hate potentially self-destructive.

Wolf's engagement with the discourse about the German past represents one of a number of other 'cultural-critical metadiscourses' in *Störfall*. Wolf frequently posed questions about guilt and responsibility as a German of her generation in her work – most prominently in *Kindheitsmuster*.[53] As Harald Welzer's work has shown, there are obvious intersections between these three metadiscourses – that is, between the dichotomy of human nature; knowledge, energy and power; and the German past: all three deal in some way with denial, responsi-bility and resistance.[54]

---

49 See Christa Wolf, *Briefe 1952–2011*, p. 519.
50 See, for example *Störfall*, p. 22; *Accident*, p. 16.
51 Wolf, *Störfall*, p. 55; *Accident*, p. 48.
52 Ibid., p. 56; p. 48.
53 Many scholars have pointed out Wolf's discussion of the German past in this text. Most re-cently, see for example, Katharina Gerstenberger, 'Störfälle. Literary Accounts from Chernobyl to Fukushima', *German Studies Review*, 37.1 (2014), 131–148.
54 See Welzer, *Klimakriege*, and his earlier work: Harald Welzer, Sabine Moller and Karoline Tschuggnall, *Opa war kein Nazi. Nationalsozialismus und Holocaust im Familiengedächtnis* (Frankfurt a. M.: Fischer, 2002).

There are also attempts at conjuring a more optimistic 'imaginative counter-discourse' in *Störfall*. Wolf highlights the dichotomy of human nature in her text by juxtaposing the narrator's coming to terms with the meaning of the nuclear accident with her beloved brother's brain surgery – a surgery that employs radio-activity for positive ends and thus celebrates the human drive for knowledge and control of nature. Humanity, Wolf seems to say with Lorenz in the epigraph preceding the fictional text, is right to strive for an ideal of progress. The narrator also repeatedly evokes an alternative, feminine-inflected realm made up of peaceful and constructive activities such as gardening, doing laundry, cutting bread and making compote.[55] In addition, there are surreal moments in the text that can be attributed to Wolf's attempt to disrupt the dominant, rational patriarchal epistemology with an ecofeminist wisdom that foregrounds nature, myth and superstition rather than science and progress. For example, the narrator repeatedly claims to be linked to her brother by a supernatural bond that magically allows her to influence his wellbeing from afar,[56] which eventually makes her sing Beethoven's 'Ode to Joy', supposedly at exactly the same moment as he reclaims his eyesight.[57]

Yet these positive counterdiscourses are overshadowed by a depiction of nature and the animal kingdom that constitute forces we humans ignore at our peril. This is shown in the narrator's description of a scene in the kitchen. The brutality with which the narrator describes her handling of an eel brought over by a neighbour contrasts sharply – indeed almost ironically – with her professed peacefulness:

> Ich habe dann, nachdem Frau Umbreit gegangen war, angefangen, den Aal in Stücke zu schneiden, der wenn ich ihn mit dem Messer berührte, heftig zu zucken begann. Eines der kopflosen, enthäuteten Aalstücke sprang mir vom Tisch und führte auf den Fliesen einen grotesken Tanz auf. Mir ist eine Gänsehaut den Rücken hoch bis in die Haarwurzeln gelaufen, ich habe laut gesagt: Das sind ja nur die Nerven!, habe einen Lappen genommen, jeden Aal fest gepackt und zerschnitten. Danach habe ich meine verbissenen Kiefer kaum auseinanderbekommen.

> [Then, after Frau Umbreit left, I began to chop up the eel, which twitched violently whenever I touched it with the knife. One of the headless, skinned pieces jumped off the table

---

55 For a discussion of gender issues in the text, see for example, Thomas C. Fox, 'Feminist Revisions. Christa Wolf's *Störfall*', *German Quarterly*, 63.3–4 (1990), 471–477.

56 See, for example, 'Da ist etwas passiert, was mich veranlaßt hat, stehenzubleiben. He, Bruder. Was ist los? Läßt du dich jetzt gehen? Jetzt hör mir mal gut zu' [Something happened that caused me to stop. Hey, brother. What's going on? Are you letting yourself go? Now you listen to me]; Wolf, *Störfall*, p. 19; *Accident*, p. 13.

57 See p. 64; *Accident*, p. 56.

and performed a grotesque dance on the tiles. I had goose pimples all the way up my spine to the very roots of my hair. I said out loud: It's only their nerves!, took a rag, firmly grabbed hold of every eel and cut it up. Afterwards I could hardly pry open my set jaws.][58]

This elaborate and slightly ironic depiction of a lonely woman's slaughter of an eel produces a certain discomfort in the reader and elevates the scene to what Timothy Morton has called an 'enactive dance' – a concept which Serpil Oppermann describes as 'a dynamic coming together in which the nonhuman is intimately instated into the human fields'.[59] In reality, the eel poses no threat to the narrator, but the 'intimacy' and the killing generate feelings of guilt and uneasiness that the narrator describes in physical terms. Her attempt to reassure herself that the animal's movements are not signs of pain but 'just nerves' contrasts with the 'goose pimples' and her clenched jaw, proof that the ostensibly harmless, (womanly) routine activity of preparing a meal masks the routine slaughter of a fellow creature. Embedding this elaborate 'murder scene' in a philosophical meditation about human aggression, Wolf confronts her readers with their complicity in the anthropocentric privileging of humans over all other creatures.

The few scenes in which the narrator interacts with non-human nature are characterized by violent outbursts. Right at the beginning of the text, she expresses anger over her neighbour's hens, which annoy her 'wie jeden Morgen' [as (...) every morning]: 'Das beste, was man von ihnen sagen kann, ist, daß sie auf mein Klatschen und Zischen hin angstvoll, wenn auch verwirrt reagieren' [The best you can say about them is that they react to my clapping and hissing with fear, though confused].[60] Later on, she struggles with a certain weed she cannot name, 'ein klebriges, zielbewußtes Kraut' [a sticky, single-minded weed],[61] but whose ubiquity she is determined to destroy:

> dieses vermaledeite Kraut. Dir werd ich! habe ich laut gesagt. Dir werd ich! – So hat mein Großvater mütterlicherseits gesprochen. Daß dich der Deikert! Wie mag mein Großvater sich den Teufel vorgestellt haben. Dich, sage ich zu dem Kraut, dich rotte ich aus. Das versprech ich dir. Ohne Rückhalt auf die Erhaltung der Arten.
>
> [that damned weed. Just you wait! – That was the way my maternal grandfather used to talk. To the devil with you! I wonder how my grandfather pictured the devil. You, I say

---

58 Wolf, *Störfall*, p. 101; *Accident*, pp. 91–92.

59 Serpil Oppermann, 'From Ecological Postmodernism to Material Ecocriticism. Creative Materiality and Narrative Agency', in Iovino and Oppermann, pp. 21–36 (p. 28).

60 Wolf, *Störfall*, p. 9; *Accident*, p. 3.

61 Ibid., p. 32; p. 26.

to the weeds, I'm going to wipe you out! That's a promise. Regardless of the survival of the species.][62]

The narrator's sudden, irrational aggression – which turns an otherwise perfectly harmless weed into a devilish adversary – makes sense only if read in conjunction with the equally random reference to the grandfather, who represents the German past and thus German aggression towards others and the *Ausrottung* [extermination] of the Jews. Both represent parts of Wolf's metadiscourse. Our aggression as a human species, Wolf seems to suggest (linking back to Sagan), though random and irrational, is deeply ingrained in our humanity. A humanity which, in turn, is linked to our 'wild' animal origins:

> An irgendeiner Stelle, oder an vielen Stellen haben wir jene Wildheit, Unvernunft, Tierischkeit in die Kultur hineinnehmen müssen, die doch gerade geschaffen wurde, das Ungezähmte zu bändigen. Die Echse in uns schlägt mit dem Schwanz. Das wilde Tier in uns brüllt. Verzerrten Gesichts stürzen wir uns auf den Bruder und bringen ihn um. Dann möchten wir uns das Gehirn aus dem Kopf reißen und den wilden Punkt suchen, um ihn auszubrennen. Amok laufen, weil unser Gehirn durchbrennt.

> [At some point, or at many points, we had to accept the wildness, irresponsibility, animality into our culture, although it had been created to tame the untamed. The lizard in us wags its tail. The wild animal in us roars. With distorted faces we attack our brother and kill him. Then we want to pull out our brain and look for the wild dot to burn it away. To run amok, because our brain has run away with us.][63]

Here Wolf's text again suggests that culture had failed to civilize the wildness in human nature from the start – as symbolized in the biblical story of Cain and Abel.

Humanity's failure to civilize in harmony with nature is a function of our ostensible superiority and part of Wolf's 'cultural-critical metadiscourse'. But, as Hubert Zapf reminds us, literature – which he calls 'a medium of radical civilizational critique'[64] – also has the 'ecocultural potential' to counter that failure and contribute to 'the survival of the cultural ecosystem in its long-term co-evolution with natural ecosystems'.[65] Finally, Wolf's use of nature poetry contributes the 'reintegrative interdiscourse' in *Störfall*.

---

62 Ibid., p. 33; p. 26.
63 Ibid., p. 100; pp. 90–91.
64 Zapf, *Literature as Cultural Ecology*, p. 28.
65 Ibid., p. 25–26.

The Power of Literature as Cultural Ecology

According to Zapf, 'German nature poetry is another important source of ecological awareness, prefigured in Goethe's early poems'.[66] Christa Wolf saw an important role for literature in discussions about environmental challenges as well. In *Störfall*, Wolf presents nature poetry as the proverbial canary in the coal mine. She intersperses the text with one-line quotes from German poetry of different epochs and discovers, as Kate Rigby points out, 'their words, and the cultural memories that they encode, have grown radically incongruous',[67] thus alerting Wolf's readers to the fact that something must be seriously wrong with the human relationship to nature. Goethe's 'Mailied' [May Song] – the beautiful love poem and song about nature's eternal cycle of life, which celebrates and elegizes the power of nature – hence becomes a representative of all endangered species. This 'reintegrative interdiscourse' serves multiple purposes: to express solidarity with nature by creating an alliance with art and poetry, to trigger an emotional response in readers and to entreat them to protect nature.

> *Wie herrlich leuchtet mir die Natur.* Vielleicht ist es nicht die dringlichste Frage, was wir mit den Bibliotheken voller Naturgedichte machen. Aber eine Frage ist es schon, habe ich gedacht.

> [*Marvellous nature shining on me!* Perhaps the problem of what to do with the libraries full of nature poems is not the most urgent. But it is a problem all the same, I thought.][68]

Zapf's notion of literature as 'ecological force' connects back to earlier critics' readings of Wolf's work. Literature, writes Carsten Gansel, serves Wolf as 'aufstörende Instanz' [disruptive authority].[69] Anna Kuhn attributes to Wolf 'a passionate belief in the ability of human beings to change'[70] and suggests that reading literature motivated Wolf herself, and writing was her way of motivating

---

66 Zapf, 'Ecological Thought', p. 275.
67 Kate Rigby, 'Tragedy, Modernity, and Terra Mater. Christa Wolf Recounts the Fall' *New German Critique*, 101 (2007), 115–141 (p. 125).
68 Wolf, *Störfall*, p. 44; *Accident*, p. 37. A powerful visualization of this function of art and literature can be seen in Franny Armstrong's 2009 film *Age of Stupid*, in which a spaceship containing a digital archive of all of human culture is the only memory left of humans on planet earth.
69 Carsten Gansel, 'Erinnerung, Aufstörung und "blinde Flecken" im Werk von Christa Wolf', in *Christa Wolf. Im Strom der Erinnerung*, ed. by Carsten Gansel with Sonja Klocke (Göttingen: Vandenhoeck and Ruprecht, 2014), pp. 15–41 (p. 26).
70 Anna K. Kuhn, *Christa Wolf's Utopian Vision*, p. 169.

others to become agents of change in a world full of challenges.[71] Carol Anne Costabile-Heming, who discusses *Störfall* in the aftermath of the Fukushima disaster, acknowledges that Wolf's was not a text to openly incite civil disobedience against the GDR regime, but Costabile-Heming might agree that it promotes the idea of 'long-term co-evolution', as Zapf describes it above.[72]

Wolf knew that in order for literature to be an effective force for good, it would have to inspire positive action. In her contribution to a literary conference in December 1981, she encouraged young authors above all to write critically: to point out to society what it would need to live and to survive.[73] On 4 May 4 1986, a week after the Chernobyl accident and after having begun work on *Störfall*, she writes in a letter to the author Brigitte Soubeyran:

> Ich denke all die Tage über, daß wir etwas tun müssen. Ich weiß nicht genau, was. Nicht *gegen* etwas oder jemanden – *für* etwas, für das Fortbestehen von diesem Himmel und diesem Löwenzahn und diesen verdammten Holunderbüschen und Brennesseln, die ich auszurotten versuche.[74]

> [I am thinking all the time these days that we must do something. I don't know exactly what. Not *against* anything or anyone – *for* something, for the continued existence of this sky and this daffodil and this damn holly and nettles, which I am trying to eradicate.]

Yet a few months later, her essay 'The White Circle', written for the exhibition and subsequent publication *Save Life on Earth* (with images and texts by artists from twenty-one different countries, including the USSR and the US), ends with a deep sense of resignation: 'It seems to me that in recent years everything that could be said about this statement has been said', and yet 'Save Life on Earth. Yes, we reply fervently. Of course. Unconditionally. And then we hear within ourselves the question: But how? How?'[75] In the end, successful human agency is

---

71 Ibid.
72 Carol Anne Costabile-Heming, 'Rereading Christa Wolf's *Störfall* following the 2011 Fukushima Catastrophe', in *Catastrophe and Catharsis. Perspectives on Disaster and Redemption in German Culture and Beyond*, ed. by Katharina Gerstenberger and Tanja Nusser (London: Camden House, 2015), pp. 90–105 (p. 101).
73 Christa Wolf, 'Berliner Begegnung', in Hilzinger, vol. 8: *Essays, Gespräche, Reden, Briefe 1975–1986* (2000), pp. 220–225 (p. 225).
74 Christa Wolf, *Man steht sehr bequem zwischen allen Fronten. Briefe 1952–2011*, ed. by Sabine Wolf (Berlin: Suhrkamp, 2016), p. 514.
75 Christa Wolf, 'The White Circle', in *Save Life on Earth*, ed. by Nyna Brael Polumbaum (Berlin: Elefanten Press, 1986), pp. 104–105 (p. 105). Her feelings of resignation may have been connected to the exhaustion she expressed in a letter to Alfred Lechner in January 1986, in which she observed feeling increasingly tired with age. See Christa Wolf, *Briefe 1952–2011*, p. 500. Anna Sawko-von Massow believes that Wolf's text can serve as a starting point for a debate about

measured by positive outcomes. The power of literature, Zapf reminds us, is to reveal what otherwise remains hidden or denied: it 'constantly transgresses and shifts the boundaries of what can be known, said, and thought within a culture by opening them toward their excluded other, toward what remains unsayable and unknowable within its rules of discourse.'[76] In doing so, literature and art force us to confront our blind spots. With *Störfall*, Wolf presents us with a powerful 'ecological force' that urges us to reflect unflinchingly upon the big questions of our time – about the fragility of peace, our individual responsibility for all creatures on planet earth, the importance of honest self-criticism, the need to speak truth to power and the need to seek safe and sustainable solutions to the growing demand for energy on a planet with finite resources.[77]

---

the meaning of progress. See Anna Sawko-von Massow, 'Katastrophenbilder. Ein Störfall und seine Folgen in der deutschen Literatur', in *Sprache und Literatur im Spannungsfeld von Politik und Ästhetik. Christa Wolf zum 80. Geburtstag*, ed. by Sabine Fischer-Kania and Daniel Schäf (Munich: Iudicium, 2011), pp. 98–111 (p. 111).

76 Zapf, *Literature as Cultural Ecology*, p. 93.

77 See 'Earth Overshoot Day' (http://www.overshootday.org). A work that uses a similar approach to a similar effect is Doris Dörrie's 2016 film *Grüße aus Fukushima* [Fukushima, Mon Amour].

Roswitha Skare
Literature and Visual Art in Christa Wolf's *Sommerstück* (1989) and *Was bleibt* (1990)

The East German edition of Christa Wolf's 1963 novel *Der geteilte Himmel*[1] already included images by Willi Sitte that were meant to be more than simple illustrations of the text:

> Uns war er [Willi Sitte] eine so interessante Figur, daß wir absichtlich in die ersten Auflagen des *Geteilten Himmel* Zeichnungen von ihm aufnahmen. Sie waren nicht als Illustrationen gedacht, sondern wir haben Zeichnungen gewählt, die uns dem Geist nach paßten zur Tendenz und zur Stimmung des Buches.[2]

> [We thought him such an interesting character that we purposely included drawings by him in the first editions of *Der geteilte Himmel*. They were not meant to be illustrations; rather, we chose drawings whose spirit we thought matched the book's drift and atmosphere.]

In later years, this interest in the juxtaposition and interplay of literature and visual art led the Wolfs to cooperate closely with artists, both when designing Christa Wolf's books[3] and at her readings.[4] The Wolfs also introduced numerous artists to a wider audience through exhibitions and publications.[5]

---

1 An English translation by Joan Becker was first published under the title *Divided Heaven. A Novel of Germany Today*, by Seven Seas Verlag in 1965. A new translation by Luise von Flotow has been available since 2013. On this, cf. Luise von Flotow, 'Another Time, Another Text. From Divided Heaven to They Divided the Sky', in *They Divided the Sky. A Novel by Christa Wolf* (Ottawa: University of Ottawa Press, 2013), pp. v–xxiv.
2 'Was uns mit den Malern freundschaftlich verbindet... Gerhard und Christa Wolf im Gespräch mit Peter Böthig', in Christa Wolf and Gerhard Wolf, *Unsere Freunde, die Maler. Bilder Essays, Dokumente*, ed. by Peter Böthig (Berlin: Janus, 1996), p. 9.
3 See, for example, artists's books, such as *Was nicht in den Tagebüchern steht* (1994), *Im Stein* (1998), and *Wüstenfahrt* (1999), as well as Nuria Quevedo's etchings in the Reclam edition of *Kassandra* (1984) or Hartwig Hamer's images in the Aufbau edition of *Sommerstück* (1989).
4 An example would be Christa Wolf's reading of *Medea* in November 2002 in the Berliner Ensemble. Besides Christa Wolf, other artists involved in this staged reading of excerpts of *Medea* included Helge Leiberg (live painting/overhead projections), Lothar Fiedler (guitar, electronics) and Heiner Reinhardt (clarinet, saxophone). A similar performance had already taken place in January 2000, when Christa Wolf read her text *Im Stein* in the Schloßtheater Rheinsberg and Helge Leiberg painted on an overhead projector. On this, cf. Christa Wolf, *Eine Biographie in Bildern und Texten*, ed. by Peter Böthig (Munich: Luchterhand, 2004), p. 213.

https://doi.org/10.1515/9783110496000-008

Despite Christa Wolf's obvious affinity for art, most literary research on her writings focuses only on her texts. Her book covers, which vary from edition to edition, and the relationship between text and image are seldom studied. This is somewhat surprising, as we can assume that, at least during the 1980s, Christa Wolf exerted a comparatively strong influence upon the design of her first editions with the East German publishing house Aufbau-Verlag and was concerned with both the aesthetic and the material aspects of these editions.[6]

The present study thus investigates the interaction between word and image in the original editions of *Sommerstück* and *Was bleibt*, taking Roland Barthes's two 'functions of the linguistic message with regard to the (twofold) iconic message'[7] – anchorage and relay – as its point of departure. As Barthes argues, in modern society almost all images (iconic messages) are accompanied by text (linguistic messages). Images are polysemous and thus open to multiple meanings and interpretations. Therefore the linguistic message can be considered an anchoring technique 'intended to fix the floating chain of signifieds in such a way as to counter the terror of uncertain signs'.[8] Anchorage occurs when text is used to focus on one of an image's multiple meanings, or at least to direct the viewer towards this meaning. Barthes uses the example of a Panzani advertisement to explain anchorage: the image shows a half-open string bag containing packets of pasta, a tin of sauce, a sachet of Parmesan cheese and some tomatoes, onions and mushrooms. Our reading of the image is supported by the caption ('Pates – Sauce – Parmesan. A L'Italienne De Lux') and the labels of the products;[9] the text helps the beholder to understand the image in the manner intended by the producer of the advertisement. Relay, on the other hand, is less common, according to Barthes. In this case, the text does not simply repeat what is presented in the image but adds extra meaning, rendering the image even more ambiguous. Relay, according to Barthes, 'can be seen particularly in car-

---

5 On this, cf. Christa Wolf and Gerhard Wolf, *Unsere Freunde, die Maler*; and Christa Wolf and Gerhard Wolf, *Malerfreunde. Leben mit Bildern. Essays. Reden* (Halle: Projekte-Verlag Cornelius, 2010).

6 In letters to her editor Angela Drescher at Aufbau, Christa Wolf discusses print space, paper quality and the cover of *Sommerstück*, for example. On this, cf. Roswitha Skare, *Christa Wolfs 'Was bleibt'. Kontext – Paratext – Text* (Münster: LIT, 2008), p. 140. I was unable to find any materials in the archive confirming a similarly close cooperation between author and publisher when designing the licensed editions.

7 Roland Barthes, 'Rhetoric of the Image', in *Classic Essays on Photography*, ed. by Alan Trachtenberg (New Haven: Leete's Island Books, 1980), pp. 269–285 (p. 274).

8 Ibid., p. 274.

9 Ibid., pp. 270–273.

toons and comic strips', where 'text (most often a snatch of dialogue) and image stand in a complementary relationship'.[10]

Furthermore, in this article, images will be considered as paratextual elements, to employ the term coined by Gérard Genette in *Paratexts. Thresholds of Interpretation*. Genette states that a book's paratext is 'what enables a text to become a book and to be offered to its readers and, more generally, to the public.'[11] Genette uses numerous examples to demonstrate the role played by paratexts – such as the title, subtitle, foreword and cover blurb – in interpreting a text and also addresses other types of paratexts, such as an author's position, celebrity, age and gender. Genette points out that most often

> the paratext is itself a text: if it is still not *the* text, it is already *some* text. But we must at least bear in mind the paratextual value that may be vested in other types of manifestation: these may be iconic (illustrations), material (for example, everything that originates in the sometimes very significant typographical choices that go into the making of a book), or purely factual.[12]

Paratextual elements such as format, cover design and illustrations not only present a text to a potential readership; they also attempt to steer the way the text is read in a particular direction.[13] Accordingly, this article discusses the importance of images for our reading and understanding of Wolf's messages, showing that both cover images and images within the text itself are more than mere embellishments.

Sommerstück and *Was bleibt:* 'Branches of the Same Tree'[14]

Christa Wolf's *Sommerstück* was published in March 1989; *Was bleibt* followed in the summer of 1990, instigating the so-called *deutsch-deutscher Literaturstreit*

---

10 Ibid., p. 275.

11 Gérard Genette, *Paratexts. Thresholds of Interpretation* (Cambridge: Cambridge University Press, 1997), p. 1.

12 Ibid., p. 7.

13 On this, cf. also Jonathan Gray, *Show Sold Separately. Promos, Spoilers, and Other Media Paratexts* (New York/London: New York University Press, 2010), p. 79.

14 On this, cf. Anna K. Kuhn, '"Zweige vom selben Stamm"? Christa Wolf's *Was bleibt, Kein Ort. Nirgends,* and *Sommerstück*', in *Christa Wolf in Perspective*, ed. by Ian Wallace (Amsterdam/Atlanta: Rodopi, 1994), pp. 187–205.

[German-German literary dispute].[15] However, Wolf produced the first drafts of these two works as early as the late 1970s and early 1980s.[16] Both texts address the topics of East German society's stagnation as well as a farewell to utopian ideas of a better form of socialism, delineating the characters' withdrawal back into themselves, to their families and friends. The question of what remains plays a pivotal role in both texts.[17]

In this 'prose of memory',[18] we encounter protagonists who are writers and bear a resemblance to the author herself. In *Sommerstück*, Ellen spends the summer in the countryside with her family and a few friends. Like the first-person narrator in *Was bleibt*, Ellen finds it hard to concentrate on her writing. Ellen's escape to the country after a 'wüsten Winter' [desolate winter][19] in the city seems to be marked by resignation: she is running away from the East German state in which she finds herself constantly oscillating between hope and hopelessness. Like most of her friends, she belongs to the older generation who had lived in the young GDR, aware that they were building a new and better society, but whose enthusiasm has long since given way to disappointment. The first-person narrator in *Was bleibt* is similarly disappointed and resigned. The twenty-four hours recounted in this novella, in which scarcely anything unusual happens, are marked by a sense of being controlled, by a feeling of distrust and especially by the protagonist's internal dialogue with her inner censor and her growing inability to focus upon her writing. In both texts, the protagonist eventually finds her way back to her creative work and is able to overcome the crisis in her life and her writing. Despite the signs of everyday terror, dissolution and decay,[20] both texts thus end optimistically.

---

15 On this, cf. *Der deutsch-deutsche Literaturstreit oder 'Freunde, es spricht sich schlecht mit gebundener Zunge'. Analysen und Materialien*, ed. by Karl Deiritz and Hannes Krauss (Hamburg: Luchterhand, 1991); and *'Es geht nicht um Christa Wolf'. Der Literaturstreit im vereinten Deutschland*, ed. by Thomas Anz (Munich: edition spangenberg, 1991). These two volumes summarize this ongoing literary dispute and assess the results it has produced up to the time of publication, but also intervene in it by presenting their own evaluations and comments. For Christa Wolf's own thoughts on the *Literaturstreit*, cf. Christa Wolf, *Ein Tag im Jahr. 1960–2000* (Munich: Luchterhand, 2003), p. 467.

16 On this, cf. Sonja Hilzinger, 'Entstehung, Veröffentlichung und Rezeption', in Christa Wolf, *Sommerstück. Was bleibt*, pp. 313–333 (p. 313).

17 On this, cf. Skare, *Christa Wolfs 'Was bleibt'*, pp. 221–243.

18 Sonja Hilzinger, 'Nachwort', in Christa Wolf, *Sommerstück. Was bleibt* (Munich: Luchterhand 2001), pp. 303–312 (p. 311).

19 Christa Wolf, *Sommerstück* (Berlin: Aufbau, 1989), p. 178.

20 Cf. for example, Wolf, *Sommerstück*, p. 93: 'Dieses Haus verfiel nicht, es wurde zerstört. Wie wir um das Haus herumgingen, konnten wir sie ausmachen, die Stadien der Zerstörung. [...]

In the present article, my focus lies on the images in *Was bleibt* and *Sommerstück*.[21] Elsewhere, I have covered the significance of the whole range of other paratextual elements[22] contained in the original edition of *Sommerstück* published by Aufbau: its dedication ('Allen Freunden jenes Sommers' [To all the friends of that summer]) and its motto (Sarah Kirsch's poem 'Raubvogel süß ist die Luft' [Bird of prey sweet is the air]) as well as a postscript, which states explicitly that none of the characters are identical to living or deceased persons and that the episodes described do not correspond to actual events.[23] By contrast, the paratextual elements in *Was bleibt* remain restricted to the book's format and its cover, which bears only that information which is strictly necessary: the title, the author's name and the publisher. Because of this comparative paucity of paratextual elements in *Was bleibt*, the drawing on the front cover of the Aufbau edition by Christa Wolf's son-in-law, Martin Hoffmann, is particularly striking.

Martin Hoffmann's Cover Drawing for *Was bleibt*[24]

Was bleibt – which was edited and published at a time when social conditions, and thus conditions in both the public sphere and the book market, were changing significantly – was the last of Christa Wolf's works to be published more or

---

Woher der Haß auf unbeschädigte Dinge.' [This house had not decayed, it had been destroyed. As we walked around the house, we could spot them, the stages of destruction. (...) Where did this hatred of undamaged things come from.]

21 Cf. on this also Roswitha Skare, 'Was bleibt, sind Bilder. Bilder als paratextuelle Elemente in Christa Wolfs 'Sommerstück' und 'Was bleibt', in *Text + Kritik*, 46, 'Christa Wolf', ed. by Nadine J. Schmidt (Munich: edition text + kritik, 2012), pp. 97–106.

22 The present article will not analyse all of these elements in detail, but focuses primarily on the images. For further details on the motto, dedication and postscript, cf. Roswitha Skare, 'Unsere Freunde, die Maler. Zum Verhältnis von Text und Bild in Christa Wolfs *Sommerstück*', in *Neulektüren – New Readings. Festschrift für Gerd Labroisse zum 80. Geburtstag*, ed. by Norbert Otto Eke and Gerhard P. Knapp (Amsterdam/New York: Rodopi, 2009), pp. 273–291.

23 On this, cf. Christa Wolf, *Sommerstück* (Berlin: Aufbau, 1989), p. 191: 'Alle Figuren in diesem Buch sind Erfindungen der Erzählerin, keine ist identisch mit einer lebenden oder toten Person. Ebensowenig decken sich beschriebene Episoden mit tatsächlichen Vorgängen' [All characters in this book are invented by the author, none of them are identical with any living or deceased persons. Similarly, none of the episodes described correspond to actual events]. These sentences are signed with the author's initials, 'C. W.' On this, cf. also the opening of Christa Wolf, *Kindheitsmuster* [*Patterns of Childhood*] (Berlin/Weimar: Aufbau, 1976).

24 The cover is reproduced in line with the German Act of Copyright and Related Rights, Art. 51 (1) and the kind permission of the artist.

Figure 1: Aufbau edition of *Was bleibt* with drawing by Martin Hoffmann

less at the same time by Aufbau and in a licensed edition by Luchterhand.[25] As this was already a time of economic instability for many East German citizens, Aufbau decided to publish the book as a paperback, but Wolf's wishes were still taken into account when designing the cover. Thus the contract specifies that Wolf wanted an illustration by Martin Hoffmann on the cover of the book.

---

25 As licensed editions were no longer necessary after German unification, both publishing houses agreed that Aufbau should be given all rights (including West German rights) to the texts of Anna Seghers, while Luchterhand would be given all rights (including East German rights) to Christa Wolf's texts.

Hoffmann had already produced the cover designs for the Aufbau editions of some of Wolf's earlier books, such as *Kassandra* and *Störfall*.[26]

Martin Hoffmann created this drawing especially for *Was bleibt*.[27] The size of the Aufbau edition was adapted to the measurements of the drawing, which, according to the artist, is only slightly bigger than the book's cover.[28]

Hoffmann's coloured pencil drawing shows a street lined with houses. The doors and windows are scarcely visible; only the contours of the rows of houses can be seen. Both sides of the street are lined with streetlamps; the pavement and the street itself are completely empty. The absence of lit windows increases the impression that this area is uninhabited, and only the light of the streetlamps suggests that there might be people living in the houses or the town. The view of the street ends to the left, a quarter of the way up the image and a quarter of the way across from left to right. Thus our attention is drawn to the vanishing road, to what cannot be seen; only the light – especially the light of the streetlamp in front – and the contrasting black text are able to pull the focus towards the image's upper right-hand corner.

Along with the paratext's material aspects – format and typography – and combined with the author's name and the title, Hoffmann's drawing introduces potential readers to the text, setting first associations in motion. Both the deserted, lit street and the range of colours used in the image suggest the early morning or the late night. The brightness of the streetlamps, especially of the largest one in the foreground of the picture, draws our attention. Christa Wolf's name and the title, *Was bleibt*, are aligned with the right-hand border of the page. The black lettering forms a contrast to the white of the streetlamps and the brown and greenish-grey colours of the houses, the street and the sky. Printed in capital letters, the author's name catches the eye first. Genette asserts that the size of the author's name on the cover depends 'on the author's reputation; [...] the better known the author, the more space his name takes up'.[29] However, Aufbau chose not to make Christa Wolf's name markedly larger than the title,

---

26 On this, cf. Martin Hoffmann, 'Grafiker' (www.grafiker-hoffmann.de). On the cooperation between Hoffmann and Wolf, cf. also Christa Wolf, 'Gang durch Martin Hoffmanns Räume', in Martin Hoffmann, *Reflexe aus Papier und Schatten* (Berlin: Janus, 1996), pp. 103–105 (p. 105): 'Es macht Spaß, mit ihm am Computer zu sitzen und seine Vorschläge zu diskutieren, zuzusehen, wie er auf Wünsche eingeht, wie er Entwürfe nebeneinander stellt, Farbwerte verändert' [It is fun to sit at the computer with him discussing his suggestions, to see how he takes account of requests, sets drafts side by side, changes colour values].

27 On this, cf. Wolf, 'Gang durch Martin Hoffmanns Räume', p. 103. Here, the cover drawing for *Was bleibt* is reproduced without the text. 1989 is given as the year the drawing was created.

28 Personal e-mail communication with the author (2 December 2016).

29 Genette, *Paratexts*, p. 39.

perhaps in order not to detract from the drawing. There is no biography of the author, neither on the cover nor inside the book. As Wolf was one of East Germany's most popular writers, the publishing house may well have assumed that readers were familiar with her. A consideration of the extent to which the GDR's command economy and the planned distribution of Wolf's books may have influenced such design decisions goes beyond the scope of this article. However, it is interesting to note that, in this case, the finished product does not correspond to Genette's generalization about font size and author status.

Initially, the cover drawing strikes one as detailed and realistic, much like a photograph. According to Hoffmann, 'it is (at first) easy to recognize, an ostensibly 'correct' reproduction'. Only at a second glance does one realize that the objects depicted in the image are 'actually 'tidier' and more rectangular'[30] than the ones we behold in reality. This prevents or at least hinders a simple equation of reality and image; an interpretation with only one meaning becomes one of several possible readings. Hoffmann does not draw an actual, recognizable street in Berlin, but 'something imagined, designed, constructed',[31] and thus the area depicted cannot be linked to any concrete historical period or to a particular place.

Although Hoffmann's drawing was produced as an illustration of the text,[32] the relationship between image and linguistic message on the front cover is by no means one of simplistic duplication, but rather of multiple possible readings. Neither the drawing nor the title steer our interpretation in a clearly marked direction; rather, both are ambiguous. Image and title are only anchored by the text on the back cover, which draws them towards one possible theme. Instead of a summary of the content or information about the author, a quotation from *Was bleibt* is presented, albeit without citing the source. This quotation speaks of the 'wirklichen Fragen [...], die, von denen wir leben und durch deren Entzug wir sterben können' [the real questions (...) the ones which give us life and can mean

---

30 Hoffmann, *Reflexe aus Papier und Schatten*, p. 34, 58.

31 Ibid., p. 18. Also cf. Martin Hoffmann, *Köpfe. Räume. Collagen. Zeichnungen* (Berlin: Janus, 2011), p. 15 on the drawings: 'Als Kontrapunkt zu den Collagen bemühe ich mich hier um sogenannt Alltägliches, um Wiedererkennbarkeit, um die Wertschätzung von leicht Übersehenem. Es geht mir nicht um "Fotorealismus" [...], sondern um die Konzentration auf die dargestellten Situationen, die ich nicht durch eine wie auch immer gewollte "künstlerische Handschrift" stören möchte' [As a counterpoint to the collages, here I am searching for the so-called everyday, for recognizability, for appreciation of what is often overlooked. I am not concerned with 'photographic realism', but with concentrating on the situations depicted, which I do not want to mar with any kind of intentional 'artistic hand'].

32 On this, cf. Hoffmann, *Reflexe aus Papier und Schatten*, p. 103: '1989. Umschlagzeichnung für *Was bleibt*' [1989. Cover drawing for *Was bleibt*].

death if taken away from us]. The title and the quote allude to the novella's ex-istential topic and influence both our view of the cover image and our expecta-tions of the text we are about to read. Furthermore, if we regard not only the title and the text on the back cover, but also Christa Wolf's entire literary text as lin-guistic messages, their anchoring function in relation to Hoffmann's drawing be-comes evident. On the very first page, we read about a 'Berliner Zimmer'[33] [Berlin apartment], which anchors Hoffmann's rather abstract drawing in a clear geo-graphical location. Even though the drawing provides no concrete indicators of Berlin, the mention of the city in the story links text and image for the reader, and we associate the first-person narrator's everyday activities in Berlin with this street. By reading and interpreting Hoffmann's drawing in conjunction with the literary text, we are able to people the drawing with the persons and actions we encounter in the novel. As I have suggested above, because the drawing is open and abstract, it enables a considerable number of quite different interpretations. Thus Heinz-Peter Preußer – who, to my knowledge, is the only scholar to take account of the cover design in his work on the text – describes the illustration as follows:

> On the cover of the Aufbau edition of *Was bleibt*, we see a melancholy, foggy row of houses, grey on grey, through which – as if through a veil – we perceive a faint hint of colourful pastel. The line of the road itself provides scarcely any light, and the sky is also depicted in the same tone. But it is a free space upon which to project, if you will, a funnel out into the open, into freedom. It is no coincidence that this is where the title is printed: *What Re-mains*.[34]

We can certainly agree with this description, even though the 'faint hint of col-ourful pastel' is hard to make out. However, the interpretation that follows is based – or so I claim – upon Preußer's knowledge of Christa Wolf's political views:

> The image could be interpreted as an allegory. Only that which, vision-like, elevates the negativity of the present is able to grow upon the soil of East German reality. Hope lives. It breaks through the grey, as life and growth fight against and break open that which seals them off.[35]

---

33 Christa Wolf, *Was bleibt* (Berlin/Weimar: Aufbau, 1990), p. 5. English translation: Christa Wolf, *What Remains*, trans. by Heike Schwarzbauer and Rick Takvorian (Chicago: University of Chicago Press, 1993), p. 231.
34 Heinz-Peter Preußer, *Mythos als Sinnkonstruktion. Die Antikenprojekte von Christa Wolf, Hein-er Müller, Stefan Schütz und Volker Braun* (Cologne: Böhlau, 2000), p. 404.
35 Ibid., p. 404.

Here, Preußer's factual knowledge of Wolf's political attitudes and convictions shapes his interpretation of Hoffmann's image, which he understands above all as an illustration underlining Christa Wolf's political and thus authorial message.

The standardization of book printing often leads us to overlook the significance of format, typography, paper quality and – not least – cover design.[36] Nevertheless, we should bear in mind that various interpretations – in this case, of *Was bleibt* – may depend upon which paratextual elements readers take into account and which they neglect or even overlook. Here, a focus upon the open and abstract qualities of Hoffmann's drawing expands the scope for interpreting the text. In contrast, undue attention to other paratextual elements – such as knowledge about Christa Wolf's political convictions or the social conditions at the time of publication – may restrict our reading, as I argue is the case with Preußer's analysis. The fact that the covers of later editions of *Was bleibt* also used works of art or excerpts of works of art suggests that taking cover illustrations into consideration yields more complete understandings of the narratives. Looking at the different editions side by side reveals the significance of the various images for the book's reception, as I have examined in greater detail elsewhere.[37]

The influence of paratexts becomes visible not least in translations, of which I will provide one example here. Naturally, not only the text itself, but also paratextual elements are translated. These aim to address the audience in the respective target culture, encouraging them to buy the book. Thus the cover of the US edition[38] takes up the topic of a woman under surveillance: like Martin Hoffmann's drawing, illustrator Adam McCauley's image shows a street lined with houses. However, McCauley's image is less realistic, not least because of the proportions of the woman in the picture – she takes up nearly the entire street. Furthermore, the houses on both sides of the street take on the shapes of heads or

---

36 Cf. Genette, *Paratexts*, p. 34: 'no reader should be indifferent to the appropriateness of particular typographical choices, even if modern publishing tends to neutralize these choices by a perhaps irreversible tendency toward standardization'.

37 For a detailed account of this, cf. Skare, *Christa Wolfs 'Was bleibt'*, pp. 100–133.

38 Christa Wolf, *What Remains and Other Stories*, trans. by Heike Schwarzbauer and Rick Takvorian (Chicago: University of Chicago Press, 1995). The cover image can be viewed on the following website: https://www.abebooks.com/What-Remains-Stories-Wolf-Christa-University/14095486897/bd. The English translation of *Was bleibt* was already published in its entirety by the US publishing house Farrar, Straus and Giroux in 1993, also under the title *What Remains and Other Stories*, but as a hardback and with a comparatively nondescript cover. Cf. http://www.bokrecension.se/0374288887.

faces; the illuminated windows become eyes, following the woman's movements.

Both Christa Wolf's name and the title are printed in white, standing out from the darker background and forming a circle around the woman in the centre of the picture, to whom our attention is first drawn. While the brown, red-brown and orange colours radiate warmth, the schematized way the houses are represented, turning them into watchful heads the woman is unable to escape, creates a menacing atmosphere. The street separates the houses and the woman; the destination towards which she is moving appears to be far off, away from the faces. But as far as the eye can see, she is being watched and kept under surveillance.

The format of the US edition is larger (227 × 151 cm) and longer (304 pages), because it includes not only *What Remains*, but also other texts by Christa Wolf ('Exchanging Glances', 'Tuesday, September 27', 'June Afternoon', 'Unter den Linden', 'The New Life and Opinions of a Tomcat', 'A Little Outing to H.' and 'Self-experiment'). Although *Was bleibt* is emphasized in the title, the texts are ordered chronologically; accordingly, the context created by reading the other texts may influence the reception of *Was bleibt*. Thus the text's significance is relativized and put in relation to earlier texts, several of which also recount the events of a day in the narrator's life.

The US press's decision to refer to *Was bleibt* as a 'story', like the other texts in the book, and to categorize the entire volume as 'fiction'[39] clearly steers readers' expectations towards fictionality. Neither the texts' possible autobiographical elements nor their documentary character are emphasized explicitly. However, while McCauley's image is much more abstract and less realistic than Hoffmann's cover drawing, it draws our expectations of the text in a particular direction – namely, towards control and surveillance.[40] This reading is further encouraged by the text on the back cover, with its focus on East Germany and the *Staatsicherheit* (Stasi), the East German secret police:

> 'What Remains', the title story, powerfully describes what it is like to live under surveillance by the Stasi police and how such a life gradually destroys normalcy for a writer. An interior

---

39 In the German editions, the genre descriptor 'Erzählung' [short story, novella] is only used in the Luchterhand licensed edition and later new editions based upon the Luchterhand edition.
40 The surveillance by the *Staatssicherheit* is obviously the text's most striking aspect. However, Wolf's drafts and their various titles show that her main concern was not the phenomenon of observation, as the title 'Observation' was considered but then rejected in favour of *Was bleibt*. On this, cf. Skare, *Christa Wolfs 'Was bleibt'*, pp. 81–95.

monologue reveals the fear and self-consciousness of the author as the secret police eventually disrupt the balance of her life.[41]

Readers may know that Christa Wolf was actually under surveillance, which would strengthen this interpretation further, establishing an even closer connection between the first person narrator in *Was bleibt* and Christa Wolf in their minds. While this US paratextual combination arguably runs this risk, as did Preußer's interpretation of the image in relation to Wolf's politics, such biographical interpretations need not constitute an overly simplistic equation of author and narrator of the kind seen in the *Literaturstreit*.

Genette points out that in many cases, the question of the extent to which a text is fictional can only be answered by drawing upon the 'resources of the paratext'.[42] Doing so does not imply that the author's intentions can necessarily be perceived and understood as such by readers. Particularly considering the divisiveness of the political situation in the summer of 1990, the distinct signals engendered by the different paratextual ensembles may have contributed to the different positions taken in the *Literaturstreit*, for 'the stance we adopt towards a text while and after reading it depends on the view we hold of the motives leading to its production'.[43] At the same time, precisely because of this highly polarized debate, the influence of the cover images is almost certainly limited. As elaborated above, Hoffmann's drawing should highlight the openness of the text and thus lead to varied and ambiguous interpretations. However, the *Literaturstreit* showed that the main focus was not on the literary text and the interplay of text and cover. While the material and iconic paratextual elements were largely ignored, extra-literary, factual paratextual aspects – such as the author's gender and the social conditions in the summer of 1990 – were the main focus for many critics.[44] In hindsight, it could perhaps be argued that other paratextual elements, such as a preface or an afterword commenting on the work's title and genesis, could have prevented at least some parts of the literary dispute.[45]

---

41 Christa Wolf, *What Remains and Other Stories*.
42 Gérard Genette, *Fiction and Diction*, trans. by Catherine Porter (Ithaca, NY: Cornell University Press, 2000), p. 50.
43 Axel Bühler, 'Autorabsicht und fiktionale Rede', in *Rückkehr des Autors. Zur Erneuerung eines umstrittenen Begriffs*, ed. by Fotis Jannidis and others (Tübingen: Niemeyer, 1999), pp. 61–75 (p. 72).
44 On this, cf. Anna K. Kuhn, 'Rewriting GDR History. The Christa Wolf Controversy', *GDR Bulletin*, 17 (1991), 7–11 (p. 10).
45 The pre-texts of *Was bleibt* in the Christa-Wolf-archive shed light on two important issues in the literary debate: the date of publication and the choice of title. On this, cf. Skare, *Christa Wolfs 'Was bleibt'*, pp. 134–153. See also Hilzinger, 'Entstehung, Veröffentlichung und Rezeption',

Perhaps both Christa Wolf and her publisher paid too little attention to the changing social conditions between first drafts in 1979, Wolf's decision to publish the text in the autumn of 1989 and its publication in the summer of 1990.[46]

Hartwig Hamer's Images in *Sommerstück*

As mentioned above, *Sommerstück* contains of a whole range of textual paratextual elements, such as the dedication, the motto and the postscript. However, the textual elements on the cover are restricted to the title and the author's name – in other words, only the most necessary information, as was the case for *Was bleibt*. The drawing on the cover of *Was bleibt* was detailed and realistic at first sight, while the cover of the original edition of *Sommerstück*, published by Aufbau, uses an abstract watercolour. Hartwig Hamer's watercolour gives no indication of the literary text's content. Reproduced without an anchoring title – the only reference to the artist and the work of art is the short note on the inside of the cover: 'Book jacket design by Michael Roggemann, using a watercolour by Hartwig Hamer' – the cover illustration is open to all kinds of interpretations, but its dark colours suggest the opposite of an idyllic scene in the countryside.

What is striking in the case of *Sommerstück* is that only the original Aufbau edition also contains illustrations by Hartwig Hamer. These images within the text then reappear only in the Cornelius edition, published in 2011.[47] The Cornelius edition not only has a larger format, but also includes new images and an afterword by Hartwig's brother, Detlef Hamer, that draws attention to the changes made:

---

pp. 320–333. The Italian edition contains an introduction written in November 1990. Cf. Christa Wolf, *Che cosa resta*, trans. and with an introduction by Anita Raja (Roma: edizioni e/o, 1991), pp. 7–25.

46 Christa Wolf's editor Angela Drescher at Aufbau wrote in an e-mail (29 October 2001): 'Der Kritikerstreit hat uns sehr überrascht. Wir hatten nicht ahnen können, wie platt das Buch interpretiert werden würde und wie ungenau und vorurteilsbeladen die Kritiker lesen würden' [The critical dispute came as a great surprise. We could not have guessed how banal the interpretation of the book and how imprecise and prejudiced the critics' readings would be]. Christa Wolf herself called the dispute a witch hunt. Cf. Claudia Mayer-Iswandy, 'Between Resistance and Affirmation. Christa Wolf and German Unification', *Canadian Review of Comparative Literature*, 22 (1995), 813–835 (p. 824).

47 Christa Wolf and Hartwig Hamer, *Sommerstück/Landschaften* (Halle: Projekte-Verlag Cornelius, 2011).

Five further recently produced works have been added, including the panorama of a small town and the steep Baltic coastline. [...] Based on the premise that the prints, which were created specially for this purpose, are by no means illustrations in the traditional sense, the series was given the overarching title 'Landscapes' to underline both the internal and external parallels between text and images.[48]

This afterword draws our attention to the history of *Sommerstück's* publication and the relationship between text and images. Even though there is no explanation of what characterizes 'illustrations in the traditional sense', it seems likely that such illustrations are seen as mere embellishments of the text, without any significance for its interpretation. Gerhard Wolf's remarks on the use of works of art in literary texts go in the same direction: the images give *Sommerstück* 'a further charming dimension [...] that has nothing in common with the usual kind of illustration'.[49] As Roland Barthes emphasizes, however, illustrations can both 'duplicate certain of the informations [sic] given in the text by a phenomenon of redundancy' as well as 'add [...] fresh information.'[50] Hamer's afterword and the remarks quoted here on the role of the images point readers explicitly towards the latter category, in which text and images complement and add new dimensions to one another. This may also result in at least some readers devoting greater attention to the images.

The interpretation of the images as more than mere ornamentation is also emphasized several times in the new edition published by Cornelius. While the Aufbau edition only mentions the artist in the colophon, the cover of the Cornelius edition contains both Hamer's name and the name of the series – 'Landschaften' – in the same size as and thus on an equal footing with the author's name and the title 'Sommerstück'. This doubles the number of the textual paratextual elements on the cover and draws our attention to the coexistence of literature and visual art embodied in author and painter. There are no images on the cover; the signatures of the author and the artist are the only decorative elements. Furthermore, all illustrations within the text contain Hamer's signature and the note 'E. A.' (limited artist's copies), giving additional weight to their status as independent works of art. The publisher obviously wanted to stress that the images are independent of Christa Wolf's text. Format, cover design and the reproduction of the images with the artist's signature encourage this reading.

---

48 Detlef Hamer, 'Nachbemerkung', in Christa Wolf and Hartwig Hamer, *Sommerstück/Landschaften*, pp. 161–166 (p. 165).
49 Ibid., p. 164.
50 Barthes, 'Rhetoric of the Image', p. 273.

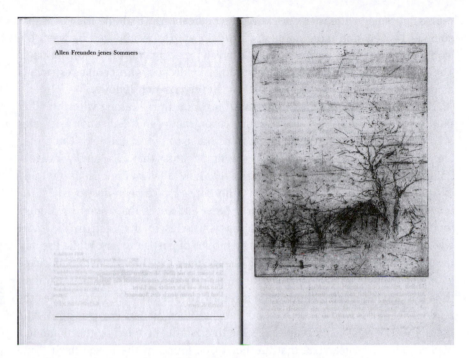

Figure 2: Aufbau edition of *Sommerstück* with etching by Hartwig Hamer

The following example of a particular image – the first one inside the book – illustrates the relationship between text and image in the original Aufbau edition in greater detail.[51] On the one hand, it demonstrates that Christa Wolf's *Sommerstück* can act as an anchor for the reception of Hamer's images, while on the other hand, it illustrates that the literary text can also function as a relay text and lead to multi-layered, ambiguous readings of both image and text.

Hamer's etching – listed in his catalogue of works as 'Haus hinter Bäumen'[52] [house behind trees] – reveals a low-roofed cottage and trees of varying sizes. In the original Aufbau edition of *Sommerstück*, Hamer's image is reproduced without its original title. Even though this descriptive and clearly anchoring title is unavailable to readers, most beholders will be able to make out both the house and the trees. The extent to which they associate them with a northern German landscape depends on their individual experience and knowledge. By

---

51 The image is reproduced with the kind permission of the artist.
52 Hartwig Hamer, *Meine Landschaft*. Grafische Bläterr. Mit einem Werkverzeichnis der Radierungen, ed. by Detlef Hamer (Berlin: Janus, 2003), p. 38.

replacing Hamer's title with Christa Wolf's dedication, 'To all the friends of that summer', a new and more ambiguous relationship is established between the iconic message of the image and the linguistic message on the following page. The dedication leads us to expect a summer landscape with people, especially as the friends of that summer are present in the text that follows.[53]

This first image precedes the 'actual' text and thus – along with the other paratextual elements, such as the title, cover, motto and dedication – creates a threshold that readers need to cross in order to get to the text. Once they cross this threshold, they discover in the first chapter that this 'merkwürdige[r] Sommer' [strange summer] is in the past, that now 'alles zu Ende ist' [everything is over] and 'die Häuser zerstört sind' [the houses have been destroyed].[54] The image of the house precedes the literary text and yet is discovered by readers to be an image of something that already belongs to the past, in the same way that Wolf's narrative is about her memories of past summers. While the narrator remembers her friends spending the summer together, Hamer's landscape is untouched by humans to a large extent; no persons are visible. The illustration thus not only duplicates information given by the literary text, but provides the readers-beholders with a kind of blank canvas. When readers engage with Wolf's literary text, Hamer's landscapes become temporarily peopled by the characters of *Sommerstück*; 'meanings that are not to be found in the image itself'[55] are added by the text, functioning as a relay.

This example demonstrates how the text and images are interdependent 'in the mind of the reader-beholder', while at the same time, the juxtaposition of text and image creates a kind of dialectic synthesis and 'verbal-visual relation'.[56] Hamer's landscapes become anchored by the literary text; viewers might recognize the 'heilen Flecken' [places where all is well][57] of which Irene speaks in *Sommerstück* and which already belong to the past. At the same time, however, Wolf's text also functions as a relay text, constituting a more 'costly message'[58] that requires effort on the part of the readers. Hamer's etchings and Wolf's text enter into a synthetic relationship, in which each complements the other and makes possible the emergence of something new and different, something

---

53 Cf. Christine Cosentino, 'Sarah Kirschs Dichtung in der DDR. Ein Rückblick', *German Studies Review*, 4 (1981) 1, 105–116.
54 Wolf, *Sommerstück*, p. 9.
55 Barthes, 'Rhetoric of the Image', p. 276.
56 Kibedi A. Varga, 'Criteria for Describing Word-and-Image Relations', in *Poetics Today*, 10 (1989) 1, pp. 31–53 (p. 42).
57 Wolf, *Sommerstück*, p. 120.
58 Barthes, 'Rhetoric of the Image', p. 276.

'das man mit Sprache allein nicht mehr sagen kann' [that can no longer be said through language alone].[59]

In this instance, then, the different media complement one another without their creation necessarily being interdependent. Gerhard Wolf wrote of their genesis: 'Die Grafiken von Hamer zum *Sommerstück* hatten wir übrigens eigens von ihm erbeten, da wir Übereinstimmungen sahen, ohne daß er sich konkret auf den Text bezog' [We asked Hamer specially for his images for *Sommerstück*, as we saw correspondences without Hamer having referred specifically to the text][60] This quote does not reveal the extent to which Hamer's images emerged from his knowledge of the text or whether they were based only on conversations with Christa and Gerhard Wolf. Detlef Hamer's afterword in the Cornelius edition describes the cooperation between author and graphic artist in greater detail:

> It was agreed with Christa and Gerhard Wolf that they would follow the stages and sketches from the selection of motifs to the first artist's proofs. [...] Upon his next visit, the artist was told what images the narrator thought particularly fitting for her text, so that gradually a series of nine sheets emerged. Ultimately, eight etchings were included in the first edition. [...] The incomparable aura of the Mecklenburg landscape is always dominant, not the representation of the subject-matter.[61]

It would seem that the northern German element was important to the work of both Wolf and Hamer; it synthesized the literature and the visual art. Nevertheless, this quotation also reveals Christa Wolf's dominant role in prioritizing certain images above others. By choosing figurative but still ambiguous illustrations, Wolf contributed to a combination of text and image that can open up fresh perspectives on both forms of art.

Conclusion

Choosing a particular edition, with or without illustrations, is often a matter of price as well as taste; however, in the case of Christa Wolf, illustrated editions are more than bibliophile collectors' items. Even though *Was bleibt* and *Sommerstück* were produced before and independently of the images, the interplay of literature and visual art forms an ideal starting point for new interpretations in both cases.

---

59 *Unsere Freunde, die Maler*, p. 46.
60 Ibid., p. 54.
61 Hamer, 'Nachbemerkung', pp. 164–165.

As demonstrated in the present article, the literary texts and the images stand in reciprocal relationships of anchorage and relay that lead to new ways of seeing and to multi-layered readings. While Barthes's essay assumes that the interpretation of ambiguous images is anchored using text (linguistic message) and the images thus gain particular meanings, the examples here demonstrate that images can also impact the readings of literary texts.

Together with the other paratextual elements, the combination of text and image creates links between readers, author and context. The examples discussed here show that images as paratextual elements do not necessarily steer a text's reception in one particular direction. Indeed, literary texts – which, like the visual arts, are usually ambiguous and open to a range of interpretations – can gain further layers of meaning through visual art, as is the case with Christa Wolf's *Was bleibt* and *Sommerstück*. By favouring artworks that are not superficially realistic reflections of diegetic reality, but that instead reveal polysemous visions of this reality,[62] Christa Wolf decisively contributed to this multiplicity of interpretation. Moreover, the book format (as paratext to the image) not only renders works of art accessible to a larger audience; they also gain new layers of meaning themselves. The interplay between image and text potentiates new and multiple meanings for both forms of art.

---

62 On this, cf. 'Was uns mit den Malern freundschaftlich verbindet', p. 9. Here, Gerhard Wolf speaks of a 'platten, illustrativen Realismus' [dull, illustrative realism] that they wanted to challenge and open up.

Anna Horakova

Learning from the Underground: Christa Wolf and the Fourth Generation of GDR Writers

Critical Amelioration of Socialism in *Was bleibt*

The belated publication of *Was bleibt* (June 1990) – Christa Wolf's autobiographical novella, first penned in 1979 – triggered a public attack on her long-standing reputation as a constructive dissident writer in the GDR. Wolf's enduring efforts to reform the socialist state from within entailed, for instance, opposing repressive cultural measures that the SED [Sozialistische Einheitspartei Deutschlands; Socialist Unity Party of Germany] adopted at the Eleventh Plenum of their Central Committee in 1965[1] and petitioning against the expatriation of the poet and songwriter Wolf Biermann in 1976. Moreover, five days before the collapse of the Berlin Wall, she called for the creation of a socialism that would differ radically from the one the SED pursued – a more desirable form of socialism that people would have no wish to abandon.[2] *Was bleibt*, on the other hand, portrays a socialist reality devoid of original socialist ideals – a socialism that hardly motivated one to stay in the GDR. Its readers become privy to the effect of Wolf's surveillance at the hands of the Stasi in the late 1970s and to oppressive and harsh retribution against dissenters. As a result, Wolf faced reprimands immediately after the publication of the novella for staging herself as the victim of a system she allegedly supported.[3] The criticism culminated in 1993, after Wolf made public her involvement as an unofficial informer (IM) of the Stasi. However, in her capacity as an IM between 1959 and 1962, Wolf never disclosed information that differed from what she published in GDR mainstream media at the time.

---

1 Christa Wolf, 'Diskussionsbeitrag', in *Kahlschlag. Das 11. Plenum des ZK der SED 1965 – Studien und Dokumente*, ed. by Günter Agde (Berlin: Aufbau, 1991), pp. 334–344.

2 Christa Wolf, 'Sprache der Wende. Rede auf dem Alexanderplatz', in Christa Wolf, *Werkausgabe in 12 Bänden*, ed. by Sonja Hilzinger (Munich: Luchterhand, 1999–2001), vol. 12: *Essays/ Gespräche/Reden/Briefe 1987–2000* (2001), pp. 182–184. Wolf remained firm in her political commitments, spearheading a movement for a socialist alternative to the Federal Republic – which was, however, met with ridicule.

3 See, for instance, Frank Schirrmacher, '"Dem Druck des härteren strengeren Lebens standhalten": Auch eine Studie über den autoritären Charakter: Christa Wolfs Aufsätze, Reden und ihre jüngste Erzählung *Was bleibt*', *Frankfurter Allgemeine Zeitung*, 2 June 1990.

https://doi.org/10.1515/9783110496000-009

Scholars such as Anna Kuhn have demonstrated that the heated public debates surrounding those revelations primarily sought to delegitimize Wolf's oeuvre and the GDR more generally.[4]

In agreement with Kuhn, I argue that Wolf's choice of a narrator who belongs to the same generation as the author has a twofold effect: firstly, *Was bleibt* reflects on what appears to be Wolf's inability to articulate effective societal critique; and secondly, the novella indicates the possibility of just such a critique. The latter happens both in the innovative writings of the 'Girl' – a figure based on Wolf's real-life mentee, the artist, poet, political activist and former associate of the East German underground scene, Gabriele Stötzer-Kachold (b. 1953) – and in the manner in which Wolf writes the fictionalized figure of the Girl into her own text.[5] In *Was bleibt*, Stötzer is represented as belonging to what Wolfgang Emmerich characterizes as a fourth and final generation of GDR writers, while the narrator has her place in the second generation.[6] Typically, this generational structure represents members of the second generation as committed socialists and the fourth generation as anti-socialist dropouts. Eroding such political boundaries between the generations, however, Wolf prompts us to reconsider the status of fourth-generation writers, notably Stötzer, in relation to East German socialism. Wolf thereby both upholds and undermines the chronological categorization and generational paradigm of GDR literature that Emmerich iden-

---

4 Anna K. Kuhn, 'Christa Wolf. Literature as an Aesthetics of Resistance', in *Literature and the Development of Feminist Theory*, ed. by Robin Truth Goodman (Cambridge: Cambridge University Press, 2015), pp. 155–171 (p. 156).
5 Since divorcing her husband, Dietmar Kachold, Gabriele Stötzer-Kachold goes by Stötzer.
6 With 'fourth generation GDR writers' I draw on Wolfgang Emmerich's classification of GDR writers, developed in his seminal *Kleine Literaturgeschichte der DDR* from 1996. His study differentiates between a first generation of GDR writers (e. g., Bertolt Brecht and Anna Seghers), who are defined as both those who most adhere to the prevailing socialist-realist doctrine of historical optimism as well as those most dedicated to the struggle against Germany's fascist past. The second generation, which was born between 1915 and 1930, consists of authors such as Franz Fühmann, Heiner Müller and Christa Wolf. Emmerich describes them as having experienced fascism at a young age. Generally, as children these authors had been either 'naïve enthusiasts or fellow travellers' with regard to the National Socialist regime. The second generation later unreservedly adopted the GDR's foundational anti-fascist myth and understood themselves primarily as 'writers on duty' for the socialist cause. The third generation of authors, who were born between 1930 and 1950 and included, for instance, Wolf Biermann and Volker Braun, were critical of socialism's shortcomings but fundamentally willing to participate in its construction. The fourth and final generation consists of authors who were born 'into' the already existing East German state after 1950, towards which they ostensibly adopted an attitude of utter disavowal ('Aussteigertum'). See Wolfgang Emmerich, *Kleine Literaturgeschichte der DDR* (Leipzig: Kiepenheuer, 1996), pp. 403–404.

tifies. Wolf's thematization of a writing style such as Stötzer's and its effects in the public sphere suggest that *Was bleibt* offers more than a mere attempt at self-exculpation on Wolf's part. My archival research reveals the significance of Wolf's dialogue with Stötzer, a connection that scholarship on Wolf has hitherto overlooked. Advancing an intertextual reading of Stötzer's text *Dabei sein und nicht schweigen* [Being present and not silent] (1978–1979) and its appearance in *Was bleibt*, I argue that Wolf's novella aims to legitimate and augment the voices of young East German female authors as well as the socialist ideals the second and fourth generations of GDR writers share for the unified Germany about to emerge. In what follows, I examine Stötzer's and Wolf's respective literary engagement with the oppressive surveillance and harsh retributions to which dissenters were typically subjected. These were two especially salient problems that both authors ultimately lay out with an eye to socialism's reform, rather than its defeat. I demonstrate that Wolf's novella does not simply establish a binary conflict between the GDR's 'real-existing socialism' and socialist ideals by limiting a commitment to the latter only to the second generation of GDR writers. Rather, *Was bleibt* articulates a more heavily imbricated, intergenerational relationship between these two registers of GDR socialism than most scholars have suggested – in both its 'real-existing' and its ideal forms.[7]

Was bleibt portrays a day in the life of the autobiographical narrator-protagonist, through a series of quotidian events, interspersed with themes of surveillance, censorship and general cultural malaise. We first encounter the protagonist, an established author strikingly similar to Christa Wolf, distractedly pacing through her apartment in East Berlin as she checks for signs of ongoing surveillance by Stasi agents, who have been monitoring her from cars parked outside of her window. We learn that the protagonist suspects that her walls and telephone line have been bugged, and that the Stasi has broken into her apartment. Returning from running errands, she encounters a 'Girl' on her doorstep. Following a brief conversation, the Girl hands the protagonist her prison writings, a portion of which the fictionalized author reads on the spot and de-

---

7 Alluding to the term "real-existing socialism" coined by Erich Honecker in 1973 to point to the discrepancy between the utopian socialist promise and the problematic conditions prevailing in the GDR, Rudolf Bahro, one of the GDR's most prominent dissidents, picked up the term in 1977 to hold East German socialism accountable for falling short of the ideals it ostensibly pursued. See Rudolf Bahro, *Die Alternative. Zur Kritik des real existierenden Sozialismus* (Cologne: Europäische Verlagsanstalt, 1977).

clares to be 'wahr' [true].[8] The Girl then leaves, and that evening the protagonist gives a public reading of an unspecified text, likely not the Girl's manuscript.[9] Both the protagonist and the event's organizers anticipate the reading with trepidation: while the author scans the audience for Stasi agents, the organizers fear that the event might become an open political forum. After a young woman asks about the possibility of a viable future arising from the status quo, a free discussion erupts among members of the audience, and the organizers promptly end the event. On her way out, the protagonist learns that police dispersed the peaceful gathering of young people outside the venue and arrested some of them.

Throughout the novella, the protagonist is preoccupied with the task of finding a language that would enable her to reconcile the experience of her surveillance with her commitment to the fundamental preservation of the socialist state. Building on the scholarly work of Gunhild Samson, I argue that this pursuit of a new language in *Was bleibt* draws on knowledge Wolf derived from her connections to the cultural underground that formed in the late 1970s in the GDR's urban centres – such as Dresden, Erfurt, Leipzig and East Berlin – and with which the novella explicitly engages.[10] Between 1979 and 1989, this underground scene consisted primarily of disaffected young writers. Emmerich describes this generation as having been 'born into' an already established socialist state between the mid-1950s and the early 1960s and thus as the fourth and final generation of East German authors. For them, socialism presented not hope for an alternative to fascism, but rather a 'deformed reality'.[11] While members of the second generation – such as Christa Wolf – placed critical demands on state socialism from a position of principled support, fourth-generation writers sought to distance themselves from the shared cultural and linguistic space of the GDR. They foregrounded their own, radical critique of language, which they considered an ostensible precondition for criticizing the state's social and ideological

---

8 Christa Wolf, *Was bleibt. Erzählung* (Frankfurt a. M.: Luchterhand, 1990), p. 76. All translations are taken from Wolf, *What Remains and Other Stories*, trans. by Heike Schwarzbauer and Rick Takvorian (London: Virago, 1993).
9 Interview with Stötzer on 13 June 2015. Stötzer claimed that Wolf would have been far too 'überlegt und vorsichtig' [judicious and careful] and would have therefore protested in a language that was more palatable to the authorities. Stötzer also added that Wolf would have not staged her protest in such an unoriginal way. All translations from this interview are my own.
10 Gunhild Samson, 'Die "neue Sprache" bei Christa Wolf. Utopie und Wirklichkeit', in *Germanica*, 25 (1999) (http://germanica.revues.org/2342).
11 Emmerich, *Kleine Literaturgeschichte der DDR*, p. 404. Here, as in the case of other texts that have not yet appeared in English translation, I use my own translation.

structures.[12] Since a Party decree banned this literature from official publication soon after it had emerged, the authors circulated their work mostly via unauthorized yet tolerated *samizdat* journals produced in Dresden, Erfurt, Leipzig and the East Berlin neighbourhood of Prenzlauer Berg.[13] From the late 1970s until the so-called *Wende* of 1989–1990, Christa Wolf and her spouse, the writer and publisher Gerhard Wolf, mentored several of these critical young authors, often attempting to reintegrate them into the official literary landscape. Throughout the 1980s, Christa Wolf provided several of these young authors, including Stötzer, with mentorship, financial support and protection, while Gerhard Wolf wrote reviews about their work and later published underground poets – such as Stefan Döring, Jan Faktor and Bert Papenfuß-Gorek – in the official Aufbau Press series Außer der Reihe [Out of Line].[14]

At times, these ties evolved into multidirectional rather than hierarchical relationships between mentors and mentees. One such exchange, which forms the historical crux of *Was bleibt*, took place between Christa Wolf and Stötzer.[15] In Wolf's novella, Stötzer assumes the fictionalized form of the Girl, a former convict and an aspiring writer, who hands the protagonist a manuscript containing highly divisive subject matter: it centres on the prison sentence the Girl served as a result of her protest against Wolf Biermann's expatriation. While Wolf, too, had protested against the Biermann affair, and both authors had objected with inde-

---

12 See David Bathrick, *The Powers of Speech. The Politics of Culture in the GDR* (Lincoln: University of Nebraska Press, 1996), p. 237.

13 Prenzlauer Berg literature was banned at a meeting of the Secretariat of the Central Committee of the Communist Party in November 1981, which ruled the emergent literary scene in Prenzlauer Berg to be 'außerhalb der durch die Kulturpolitik unserer Partei formulierten Erwartungen und Anforderungen an Literatur' [outside of the expectations and demands our Party's cultural politics places on literature]. See Peter Böthig, *Grammatik einer Landschaft. Literatur aus der DDR in den 80er Jahren* (Berlin: Lukas, 1997), p. 63. 'Samizdat' is a neologism coined by the Russian poet Nikolai Glazkov from a combination of the words *сам* and *издать*; it literally means 'self-published' or 'self-publishing'. The term designates a grassroots method of reproducing and disseminating otherwise unavailable texts. See Sergei Alex Oushakine, 'The Terrifying Mimicry of Samizdat', *Public Culture*, 13.2 (2001), 191–214 (p. 194).

14 Christa Wolf provided financial support for the young underground authors Gabriele Stötzer and Harriet Wollert. Stötzer imparted this information in an interview with me on 13 June 2015 in Erfurt, Germany. In addition to promoting underground authors in the Aufbau Press series, Gerhard Wolf composed literary essays on the Prenzlauer Berg underground scene. These include a four-part essay titled 'Zu einem Aspekt junger Lyrik', first published in the *samizdat* journal *ariadnefabrik*, 2 (1986), and reprinted in Gerhard Wolf's collected works.

15 Birgit Dahlke pointed out the encounter between Stötzer and Wolf as well as Stötzer's fictionalized form as the Girl in: *What Remains*, Papierboot. *Autorinnen aus der DDR – inoffiziell publiziert* (Würzburg: Königshausen and Neumann, 1997).

pendent petitions, only Stötzer was imprisoned. Wolf, on the other hand, enjoyed a degree of protection that derived from what many read as her fundamental loyalty towards the state, her attendant privilege and international reputation – even though Wolf's victim files, which document the increased surveillance of Wolf and her family in the aftermath of the Biermann affair, also attest to the limitations of that protection.[16]

Emergent Language in *Was bleibt*

Two years before Gabriele Stötzer's visit to Wolf in 1979, the very visit we become privy to in Wolf's novella, the then-twenty-three-year-old was given the choice between retracting her protest against Biermann's expatriation or bearing the consequences of her actions.[17] After refusing to recant, she was sentenced to a year in prison. Soon after her release, Stötzer composed an autobiographical account of her incarceration and showed Wolf the thirty-page typescript. As Stötzer informed me in an interview, the established author reportedly warned her mentee not to publish the piece officially or unofficially – that is, through the underground's *samizdat* journals. Wolf encouraged her 'nach [Stötzers Heimatstadt] Erfurt zurückzukehren und das Buch in ein Schubfach zu legen' [to return to (Stötzer's home town of) Erfurt and put the manuscript in a drawer].[18] Wolf allegedly presented East Berlin to her as a 'gefährliches Pflaster' [dangerous terrain], largely because of the heightened presence of the Stasi and state representatives. Here Wolf appears to have been concerned for Stötzer's safety in general,

---

16 *Akteneinsicht. Christa Wolf – Zerrspiegel und Dialog*, ed. by Hermann Vinke (Hamburg: Luchterhand), 1993, p. 266. Wolf later recalled having feared potential imprisonment in connection with the Biermann affair in her 2010 autobiographical novel *Stadt der Engel oder The Overcoat of Dr. Freud*. During the *Literaturstreit*, a particularly vocal proponent of the view that Wolf was fundamentally loyal to the GDR was the prominent literary critic Marcel Reich-Ranicki.
17 The circumstances surrounding Stötzer's visit to Wolf are reconstructed from my interview with Stötzer conducted on 13 June 2015 in Erfurt, Germany as well as correspondence with Stötzer, her autobiographical writings and a 2014 publication of her Stasi files. See also Ulrike Bestgen, 'ein anderes stück leibverantwortung: Lebensthema Haft in Sprache und Bild bei Gabriele Stötzer', in *Gabriele Stötzer. Schwingungskurve Leben* (Weimar: Klassik Stiftung Weimar, 2013), pp. 21–30.
18 Though Stötzer never published the volume officially, she showed her text to several members of the East German underground, including the Stasi IM Sascha Anderson, who then passed Stötzer's manuscript on to the Stasi. This information, including Stötzer's paraphrases of what Wolf had reportedly told her, are transcribed from my interview and correspondence with Stötzer.

rather than suspecting that the Stasi had gained access to the Prenzlauer Berg scene. The public learnt about this infiltration only in 1991, when the poet and media artist Sascha Anderson, together with the poet and underground publisher Rainer Schedlinski, were exposed as long-time Stasi informants. Accordingly, Stötzer contends that in 1979, Wolf mainly associated the underground scene at Prenzlauer Berg with hopefulness.

Throughout the 1980s, Wolf continued to provide Stötzer with material support, but as the latter recently remarked, this generosity did not always entail backing the younger author and her oeuvre: 'Wolf war mit mir als Frau solidarisch. Meine Literatur hat sie erst mal nicht akzeptiert' [Wolf's solidarity was with me as a woman. She did not accept my writing at first].[19] Here, Stötzer refers to Wolf's initial refusal to recommend zügel los [un bridled] (1989), a collection of Stötzer's texts, for official publication. That collection approaches writing as a way of working through both the author's incarceration and the limits of traditional gender norms and patriarchal language. Wolf allegedly considered the prose 'wolkig und gegenstandslos, Schriften von Frauen aus dem Westen gleich' [excessively idealistic and unfounded, akin to Western women's writing].[20] This supposed rejection tallies with Wolf's larger view of feminism as a movement specific to Western capitalist contexts. As Anna Kuhn explains, however, from the 1970s onwards, Wolf helped advance a 'historically grounded feminist critique of social relations in the GDR [...] that called for the emancipation of both men and women from patriarchal power structures'.[21] Therefore, Wolf likely found Stötzer's feminist writing to be lacking in proper historical and economic context and to conceive of men as necessary purveyors of patriarchy.[22] Though Wolf may have rejected Stötzer's texts on these grounds at first, the collection eventually had a very successful debut in June 1989, after the young author reportedly talked to the Wolfs in person. Stötzer's text sold out immediately and garnered praise from critics in both the GDR and the FRG. Yet the second edition of the volume, together with Stötzer's second book from 1992, failed to sell – a fact that Stötzer attributes to the post-Wall atmosphere, in which 'keiner [...] mehr etwas von der DDR lesen oder erfahren [wollte]' [nobody wanted to learn or read about the GDR anymore].[23] The short shrift Stötzer's texts received

---

19 Ibid.
20 Gabriele Stötzer, 'Gier nach Leben', in Stimmen der Freunde. Gerhard Wolf zum 85. Geburtstag, ed. by Friedrich Dieckmann (Berlin: Verlag für Berlin-Brandenburg, 2013), pp. 169–172.
21 Kuhn, 'Christa Wolf. Literature as an Aesthetics of Resistance', p. 156.
22 Ibid., p. 156.
23 Gabriele Stötzer, 'Gier nach Leben', p. 171.

in unified Germany corresponds to the larger tendency to marginalize voices from the former GDR after reunification.[24]

When examining the fate of GDR authors in reunified Germany, Wolf's substantial engagement with Stötzer and her prison writings in *Was bleibt* must not be overlooked. The established author's strategy of placing the younger writer and her manuscript intertextually in *Was bleibt* counteracts her marginalization not only before, but also after 1989. Set in 1979, the novella has the protagonist – trying to dissuade the Girl from putting herself in harm's way by publishing the manuscript – stating, 'es sei nicht wahr, daß [...] noch in zehn Jahren Menschen Sätze würden lesen wollen, wie sie sie [das Mädchen] schrieb' [it wasn't true that (...) people would still want to read sentences like the ones she (the Girl) was writing in ten years' time].[25] Thus carving out space in her own writing for Stötzer's marginalized voice, Wolf utilizes her position as an established author in both Germanies and abroad to counteract this prognosis. To clarify the complex intertextual relationship between Wolf's *Was bleibt* and Stötzer's little-known work, it is necessary to examine parallels in the handling of plot as well as the type of writing the younger woman produced during her time in prison.

Stötzer composed her prison writings, *Dabei sein und nicht schweigen*, between 1978 and 1979 as a predominantly factual report on the procedures and conditions of her incarceration, prefaced with a condemnation of the public sphere and penal law in the GDR. In the opening section of this unpublished text, Stötzer sets out to counter two oppressive forces that have compounded the secrecy surrounding the GDR's penitentiaries. These are, on the one hand, the complacency of the public – which, as the author writes, either refuses to discuss with former convicts their incarceration or broaches the topic only out of curiosity, as opposed to wishing to effect social change. The second mechanism, censorship, is imposed on the inmates when they are obliged to sign a document stating that they will not publicly disclose their prison experiences. Disregarding both mechanisms, Stötzer's text testifies to the dehumanizing conditions of imprisonment – detailing, for instance, the practice of solitary confinement before a trial. Stötzer's text relates the material conditions of imprisonment, such as the precise size of the prison cell: 'Ein Rechteck mit den Maßen von 2 ½ und 3 ½ Metern' [a quadrangle measuring 2 ½ by 3 ½ metres], and further details the inventory of an inmate's possessions: 'ein Zahnputzbecher, ein Plastebrettchen, eine Plastetasse, ein Plastemesser, ein billiges Stück Seife,

---

24 For in-depth discussion of this post-Wall phenomenon, see Paul Cooke, *Representing East Germany since Unification. From Colonization to Nostalgia* (Oxford/New York: Berg, 2005).
25 Wolf, *Was bleibt*, p. 77.

Zahnpasta' [a toothbrush cup, a plastic tray, a plastic cup, a plastic knife, a cheap piece of soap, toothpaste].[26] It likewise describes the prison routine, including labour norms, food rations and medical malpractice, which Stötzer experienced firsthand. Yet despite the harrowing circumstances of Stötzer's imprisonment, her text is an exercise in objectivity and an attempt to convey a sphere that the majority of East Germans did not experience. Stötzer employs a third-person, heterodiegetic narrator and a dispassionate tone, striving to relate information as accurately as possible, and diverging only rarely from her objective style – through, for instance, slight perspectival shifts and the use of figurative language.

Replete with facts, Stötzer's text buttresses the personal experiences with reports, statistics and official documents. She strings them together in the preface, in which she impugns the criminal justice system and the socialist status quo for having violated the 'Grundfreiheiten des Individuums wie Rede-Presse-Versammlungsfreiheit' [individual's basic freedoms, such as freedom of speech, of the press and of assembly].[27] These basic liberties – 'überhaupt jede Form individueller Aktivitäten' [actually all forms of individual activity] – Stötzer continues, are 'nur erlaubt "im Sinne der Verfassung", das bedeutet, solange sie die gegenwärtigen Machtverhältnisse nicht antasten oder gefährden' [authorized only 'in terms of the constitution', in other words, as long as they do not interfere with or jeopardize the existing power relations].[28] Stötzer's emphatic defence of individual freedom in the face of state infringement is couched in terms of a rights-based discourse. In accord with a common vernacular of Central and Eastern European dissidents since the Helsinki Accords of 1975, socialist systems shunned the language of human rights – not simply because their regimes frequently violated civil liberties. Rather, as Jonathan Bolton points out, traditional Marxism considers human rights relative to economic structures and the freedoms they safeguard (such as freedom of expression) to be distractions from more insidious forms of oppression and exploitation by, for instance, the capitalist market.[29] As

---

26 Gabriele Stötzer, *Dabei sein und nicht schweigen*, unpublished typescript, pp. 2–4. Stötzer granted me permission to access the typescript located in Erfurt, Germany.

27 Ibid., p. 1.

28 Ibid.

29 In his study of Czech dissident cultures, Jonathan Bolton points out that, from the ratification of the Helsinki Accords (1976), which obliged Western and Eastern European states alike to respect fundamental human rights, a rights-based political discourse became an alternative for many left-wing intellectuals with which to critique Central and Eastern European communist regimes. See Jonathan Bolton, *Worlds of Dissent. Charter 77, the Plastic People of the Universe, and Czech Culture under Communism* (Cambridge, MA: Harvard University Press, 1992), p. 25.

Bolton further explicates, however, Eastern European dissidents of all political stripes often deployed a rights-based discourse as an 'Esperanto of resistance'.[30] At times, this form of resistance served as a basic tool for addressing the failings of socialist regimes in the interest of promoting public debate and potentially reform as opposed to undercutting socialism. Stötzer's use of a human rights discourse in the GDR thus transgresses the linguistic conventions of permissible speech, taking it into an ostensibly anti-socialist realm. In so doing, however, she also mobilizes this discourse to effect what she calls 'public discussion and contestation' of the state's incarceration of political dissidents and the place of incarceration within socialism in general.[31]

In *Was bleibt*, the female author under surveillance and the Girl each represent the divergent attitudes of two distinct generations of East German writers towards dissent. The autodiegetic narrator emerges as a second-generation author, who carefully negotiates the terms of her writing under the threat of surveillance and potential repercussions, yet is also loyal to an ideal of the socialist state she has sought to perfect by operating within the shifting boundaries of an acceptable public voice.[32] As the protagonist states, she has thus far been able to transgress the 'Grenzen des Sagbaren' [borders of the sayable] in her writing, and thereby justifies her life as an officially sanctioned author.[33] However, the protagonist admits that she fails to reconcile her two interests – critiquing and simultaneously constructing socialism. After all, she struggles to divulge the implications her surveillance has for her socialist ideals. For example, the narrator surveys the concomitant and coincidental aspects of her observation with detailed descriptions of the colours and parking patterns of the Stasi cars, making a futile effort to penetrate beyond observable surfaces. Yet she is also aware that it is probably foolish to attempt to derive 'irgendeine Bedeutung' [any meaning at all] from such descriptions.[34] Baffled, she then seeks to normalize the experience of being observed. For instance, she supplements these descriptions with imagined aspects of the Stasi men's routine, speculating about the contents of their lunch boxes and whether 'sie, wie andere Werktätige, jeder eine Thermosflasche voll Kaffee mit[führten]' [they each bring along a ther-

---

30 Ibid., p. 26.
31 Gabriele Stötzer, *Dabei sein und nicht schweigen*, p. 1.
32 Here, I am paraphrasing David Bathrick, according to whom 'drawing upon a discourse that [...] would at once be acceptable to and yet subversive of the language of power itself' was a hallmark of Wolf's generation. Bathrick, *The Powers of Speech*, p. 226.
33 Wolf, *Was bleibt*, p. 22.
34 Wolf, *Was bleibt*, p. 12.

mos of coffee, like other working men].[35] At times, the narrator's observations mimic the gaze of her observers in an act of temporary subversion by using her position behind the window to conduct her own act of 'surveillance' – observing the Stasi officers in return. We read how, for example, from her elevated standpoint by the window, the protagonist sees 'die beginnende Glatze des jungen Herrn […], eher als seine eigene Frau, die womöglich nie derart aufmerksam auf ihn herabsah' [the encroaching baldness (of one of the young men), even before his own wife, who presumably never studied him so attentively from above].[36] Simultaneously, the text thus neutralizes, normalizes and subverts surveillance in a series of contradictory gestures. These gestures are akin to the structure of self-censorship discussed by Wolf in an interview from 1974, in which she describes the mechanism underlying self-censorship as a conflict that 'entangles an author in mutually exclusive demands'; Wolf further identifies this conflict as an impediment to artistic production.[37] Representing the social and political crisis of East German socialism, of which her oppressive surveillance is symptomatic, as a conflicted internal dialogue, the narrator-protagonist in *Was bleibt* partially mitigates – that is, self-censors – the extent of this crisis.

In contrast to the paralyzed protagonist, the Girl emerges as someone who cannot be held back from acting. The narrator describes her as 'unberührt von den gläsernen Blicken der jungen Herren' [unmoved by the glassy stares of the gentlemen] as she walks by them. She likewise disregards the protagonist's recommendation not to publish her manuscript because, as the protagonist surmises, she wants to 'etwas aufzuschreiben, was einfach wahr sei. Und dies dann mit anderen zu bereden. Jetzt. Hier' [write down the truth as she knew it. And then to talk about it with other people. Now. Here].[38] Gunhild Samson has remarked that, with the Girl's arrival, the protagonist glimpses in her prison writings a coveted, new language that would help overcome the paralysis imposed by the conflict she experiences between the Stasi surveillance and her self-censorship.[39] As the novella opens, the fictionalized author claims to have this new language 'im Ohr' [in my ear] but not yet 'auf der Zunge' [on my tongue], and we see her still searching for it by the time the novella comes to an end.[40] Elsewhere, we learn that her future expression will be more 'zupackend' [gripping]

---

35 Wolf, *Was bleibt*, p. 17.
36 Ibid.
37 Christa Wolf, as cited in Bathrick, p. 236.
38 Wolf, *Was bleibt*, p. 78.
39 Samson, 'Die "neue Sprache" bei Christa Wolf', p. 2.
40 Wolf, *Was bleibt*, p. 7.

and 'härter' [tougher] than the narrator's current writing and thinking.[41] Pitting this new expression against her insufficient, existing one, the protagonist – to add to Samson's analysis – describes her nascent speech as one that would be able to 'gelassen das Sichtbare dem Unsichtbaren opfern; würde aufhören, die Gegenstände durch ihr Aussehen zu beschreiben – tomatenrote; weiße Autos, lieber Himmel! – und würde, mehr und mehr, das unsichtbare Wesentliche aufscheinen lassen' [sacrifice the visible to the invisible; would stop describing objects by their appearance – tomato-red, white cars, good heavens! – and would increasingly allow their invisible essence to emerge].[42] In other words, the new language would enable the protagonist to articulate the causal complexes underneath the surface of East German life, instead of superficially reproducing the façade by means of atomized description. It would make social and political diagnoses, which, for the time being, she cannot attain with her existing linguistic means alone. In an indirect comparison, the protagonist positions her own inadequate critique of the Girl's text after she skims through its first few pages:

> Es war mir nicht gegeben, einen guten Text für schlecht zu erklären oder die Autorin eines guten Textes nicht zu ermutigen. Ich sagte, was sie da geschrieben habe, sei gut. Es stimme. Jeder Satz sei wahr. Sie solle es niemandem zeigen. Diese paar Seiten könnten sie wieder ins Gefängnis bringen. Das Mädchen wurde vor Freude weich, es löste sich, begann zu reden. Ich dachte: Es ist soweit. Die Jungen schreiben es auf.[43]

> [It wasn't for me to call a good text bad or not to encourage the author of a good text. I said that what she had written was good. It was no lie. Every sentence rang true. She shouldn't show it to anybody. These few pages could land her in prison again. The girl's pleasure at learning this softened her; she loosened up and started to talk. I thought, The time has come. The young people are writing it all down.]

Here, the established author at once praises the Girl's writing for being of both high aesthetic and moral quality and discourages her from 'show[ing] it to anybody' out of her concern for the Girl's safety. The Girl's happiness at the protagonist's praise betrays the mentee's admiration for her mentor. However, her writing also departs from her mentor's, as the last sentence of this passage makes evident. The protagonist comes to a key realization: 'The young people are writing it all down'. Tellingly, the sentence uses the elliptical 'it' in lieu of articulating the object of this writing. It thus points out the inadequacy of the established

---

41 Wolf, *Was bleibt*, pp. 15, 11.
42 Wolf, *Was bleibt*, p. 15.
43 Wolf, *Was bleibt*, p. 76.

author to articulate a direct and perspicacious critique that would adequately address the ongoing erosion of the East German socialist project. The narrator attributes the Girl's ability to verbalize such criticism to her experience as a victim of political repression, but also to her distinct position as a member of the fourth generation of East German authors. Though the troubled protagonist continues to search for a new language until the end of the novella, this linguistic renewal is textually indexed as having already taken place in the writing of authors such as Stötzer. Despite the protagonist's fictionalized intertextual entanglement with Stötzer's writing, however, the linguistic renewal stops short in the protagonist's texts because of her deeply engrained fear that the new language would identify the state of East German socialism as being beyond repair. Stötzer and the fourth generation of GDR authors, however, possess a more effective language for critiquing socialism and are not afraid to use it, as Wolf admits. Incidentally, Wolf confessed her awareness of both her shortcomings and the younger generation's courage at a time when the collapse of the GDR's institutions enabled discussions about crimes committed in the name of socialism on the grounds of a rights-based discourse. And Stötzer herself played an active role. On 4 December 1989, Stötzer – together with Sabine Fabian, Kerstin Schön, Tely Büchner and Claudia Bogenhardt – occupied the Stasi headquarters in Erfurt and prevented the total destruction of the Stasi's victim files, which had been underway. The events in Erfurt set a precedent and prompted the occupation of the Stasi headquarters in Leipzig, East Berlin and other East German towns and cities, laying the foundation for a collective coming to terms with recent German history.[44]

Conclusion: Wolf's Socialist Ideals

In his essays about fourth-generation underground poetry in the GDR, Gerhard Wolf praises the ability of these voices to renew language by means of their innovative ways of writing, thinking and perceiving reality.[45] Similarly, in her novella, Christa Wolf entrusts the writing of the fourth generation with the task of recuperating social and political critique of the GDR – a critique in which her own language cannot really participate. Even though *Was bleibt* is the work of an author who belongs to the second generation, the *novella* restores this critique

---

44 Stötzer was a founding member of an Erfurt-based women's civic rights group that, on 4 December 1989, stormed the Stasi headquarters in Erfurt to prevent the destruction of the Stasi files. See Ulrike Bestgen, 'ein anderes stück leibverantwortung,' p. 30.

45 Gerhard Wolf, 'Zu einem Aspekt junger Lyrik,' p. 2.

in an indexical register and by actively instantiating this language in its fiction-alized portrayal of the Girl. Given that Wolf published her novella at the time of the imminent collapse of the East German state and its impending integration into the Federal Republic, *Was bleibt* suggests that examining socialism's failures is key – not only for the process of post-Wall reconciliation, but also for identi-fying aspects of the East German past that can and ought to 'remain'. Wolf places Stötzer and her ostensibly anti-socialist discourse on the generational axis of East German writers who, in accord with the foundational conception of the GDR as a *Literaturgesellschaft* [society of literature], both created and contested the GDR's ever-evolving social and political form. That is to say, *Was bleibt* ren-ders the fictionalized persona of Stötzer as simultaneously belonging to the fourth generation of GDR authors, on account of the Girl's critique of existing re-lations via unorthodox discursive means, and to the second generation, on ac-count of her concerns for improving rather than defeating socialism through open and courageous debate – as in Stötzer's real-life writing, which the novella indexes.

In an interview with Therese Hörnigk from 1987/1988, Wolf explains her dis-illusionment with the GDR – a state in which society's socialist ideals, as she had to learn, cannot be realized.[46] She elaborates that the sense of hope her gener-ation of authors – for whom socialism had long represented the only alternative to fascism – had originally possessed had evaporated. This, however, is not the case with authors of the younger generation. Even though at the time she en-countered Stötzer, Wolf fundamentally agreed with the younger woman's assess-ment of the poor state of East Germany's socialist project, Wolf's generationally conditioned adherence to the socialist alternative kept her from sharing Stötzer's more radical critique. Thus, even though Stötzer's critique of East German social-ism identifies contradictions within this system, her emphasis on an open debate about its faults constructively interrogates the system in the hope of a socialism yet to come. *Was bleibt* presents the two characters, the narrator-protagonist and the Girl, as both fundamentally desiring to preserve socialist ideals in the new social and political circumstances in Germany after 1989.

In the final scene of Wolf's novella, what otherwise appears as a rigid gen-erational divide constitutes and expresses the desire for the implementation of socialist ideals as reaching across generations. At the end of the fictional au-thor's reading, members of the audience who have never met before freely en-gage in a conversation about future possibilities – 'auf welche Weise aus dieser

---

46 Christa Wolf, 'Unerledigte Widersprüche. Gespräch mit Therese Hörnigk', in Wolf, *Werke*, vol. 12: *Essays*, pp. 53–103.

Gegenwart für uns und unsere Kinder eine lebbare Zukunft herauswachsen solle'
[how a livable future for ourselves and our children was going to grow out of this
present situation].[47] While this question remains unanswered, this closing scene
functions as a nascent expression of a utopian socialism that may come to be.[48]
Was bleibt both refers to this appeal to openly discuss and question the system
and presents it as a call to action. With remarkable courage, the Girl in the earlier
scene indefatigably pursues such a challenging of the system. In this way, she
functions as a fictionalized version of Stötzer and her generation and as a
model for the kind of critique promulgated by the novella. This intertextual
and intergenerational appeal is perhaps what is to remain for the post-Wall reader. Wolf's fictionalized account of historical surveillance addresses its appeal to
readers who can acknowledge the faults of East German socialism and nevertheless articulate utopian hopes for a collective socialist imaginary.

---

47 Wolf, *Was bleibt*, p. 95.
48 According to Sonja E. Klocke, the young woman's question is 'central' to the novella and of
relevance to the time when the novella was published – in the transition period between the fall
of the Berlin Wall and the demise of the GDR. In Klocke's view, by taking over the discussion at
the reading despite the Stasi's infiltration of the audience, the young woman temporarily liber-
ates the protagonist-intellectual from 'her role as defender of moral values'. See Sonja E. Klocke,
Inscription and Rebellion. Illness and the Symptomatic Body in East German Literature (Rochester,
NY: Camden House, 2015), p. 64.

John Pizer

From Pan-German Cosmopolitanism to Nostalgic National Insularity: A Comparative Study of Christa Wolf's *Kassandra* and *Medea*

Much critical literature has been devoted to comparing Christa Wolf's two novels based on Greek myth: *Kassandra* (1983) and *Medea. Stimmen* (1996).[1] The appeal of such comparisons is obvious; both novels focus on female figures from Greek mythology ignored or distorted by male authors. Both eponymous heroines are shunned by their respective communities. As Sonja Klocke has noted: 'The two books are linked by the protagonists' feelings of alienation: they feel connected to their communities despite the lack of empathy they receive'.[2] *Kassandra* is appropriately treated within the Cold War context during which it was composed, whereas scholars often read *Medea* as a critique of what Wolf considered the West's virtual colonization of the former German Democratic Republic. Indeed, in a 1992 essay composed in Santa Monica when she was researching *Medea*, Wolf draws a subtle but clear parallel between the Western colonization of the GDR and that of ancient Colchis, the portrayal of which latter process she was pondering for her 1996 novel.[3]

Despite much comparative analysis of the two novels, a significant contrast has been ignored. *Kassandra* was written when both East and West Germany were subject to the stationing of missiles on their respective soils and were thereby threatened with annihilation. The rivals in the Trojan War are treated as uni-

---

1 What follows is a list of some of the most notable of these comparisons: Heinz-Peter Preusser, 'Medea-Kassandra/Kassandra-Medea. Apokalyptik und Identitätssuche bei Christa Wolf', *Literatur für Leser*, 28 (2005), 241–262; Corinna Viergutz and Heiko Holweg: '*Kassandra*' und '*Medea*' von Christa Wolf. *Utopische Mythen im Vergleich* (Würzburg: Königshausen and Neumann, 2007); Markus Winkler, '"Kassandra", "Medea", "Leibhaftig". Tendenzen von Christa Wolfs mythologischem Erzählen vor und nach der 'Wende', in *Wende des Erinnerns? Geschichtskonstruktionen in der deutschen Literatur nach 1989*, ed. by Barbara Beßlich and others (Berlin: Schmidt, 2006), pp. 259–274; Helen Bridge, 'Christa Wolf's *Kassandra* and *Medea*. Continuity and Change', *German Life and Letters*, 57 (2004), 33–43.
2 Sonja E. Klocke, *Inscription and Rebellion. Illness and the Symptomatic Body in East German Literature* (Rochester, NY: Camden House, 2015), p. 72.
3 Christa Wolf, 'Santa Monica, Sonntag, den 27. September 1992', in *Auf dem Weg nach Tabou. Texte 1990–1994* (Cologne: Kiepenheuer and Witsch, 1994), pp. 232–247 (p. 244).

https://doi.org/10.1515/9783110496000-010

fied through such martial bellicosity. Wolf wrote *Medea* in the wake of unification, which she regarded as a troubled process that fused two highly disparate
nation-states. An unbridgeable divide seems to separate the two geographic en-
tities in the novel, Colchis and Corinth. Building on these observations, this
essay focuses on a striking antithesis, ignored by previous scholarship, between
the two novels. The Cold War novel *Kassandra* entails an advocacy of pan-German solidarity. In *Medea*, on the other hand, Wolf no longer evokes this inner-
German cosmopolitanism – the representation of the people of both East and
West Germany as constituting a single community. Instead, Wolf's second
myth novel evinces the embrace of a now-lost, discrete Colchis culture. This culture allegorizes that of the GDR and underscores the unbridgeable social divide
between the GDR and the Federal Republic of Germany, the historical antecedent
of which in the novel is Corinth. In addition to focusing on the historical conditions prevalent when *Kassandra* and *Medea* were composed, I draw on race and
gender theory to elucidate Wolf's disparate approaches to East-West German relations in the respective novels.

Kassandra relates the fall of Troy from the perspective of the eponymous narrator, imprisoned in Mycenae and awaiting execution while she retrospectively
tells her tale. The novel portrays the intrigues leading to the war between Troy
and Mycenae, the concomitant elision of female voice in the Trojan Kingdom
and the annihilation of Troy after war breaks out. *Medea*, on the other hand,
uses multiple narrative voices to develop the tale of the pursuit of the Golden
Fleece in Colchis by the Corinthian Jason, aided by Medea, who rebels against
her father's increasingly authoritarian rule. She and other Corinthians accompa-
ny Jason and his Argonauts to Corinth, but not long after her arrival, Medea and
her fellow Colchians become estranged, culminating in Medea's banishment to
the Corinthian mountains on trumped-up evidence that she has murdered the
sons resulting from her union with Jason.

In *Kassandra*, the Greeks regard the Trojans as their kin, and the reverse is
also evident, at least with respect to ethnic and racial ties. On the other hand, as
the narrative develops, the two camps become ever more hostile towards one another, latent racism is made manifest and this ill will ripens into murderous mutual hatred. Christa Wolf asserted that the stationing of medium-range ballistic
missiles at the beginning of the 1980s inspired her to write *Kassandra*.[4] The nov-

---

4 See, for example, the third of Wolf's Frankfurt lectures on poetry, entitled 'Ein Arbeitstage-
buch über den Stoff, aus dem das Leben und die Träume sind', *Voraussetzungen einer Erzählung.
Kassandra*, 2nd edn (Darmstadt: Luchterhand, 1983), pp. 84–125; and the opening of Wolf's interview 'Zum Erscheinen des Buchs *Kassandra*. Gespräch mit Brigitte Zimmermann und Ursula

el's national figuration is made plausible by the Trojan inhabitation of Asia Minor, in close geographic and ethnic proximity to the Greeks. In *Medea*, by contrast, the Colchians – whose ancestral homeland was in the Caucuses – were geographically and ethnically alien to the Corinthians. This latter text underscores the racial, religious and cultural alterity of the Colchians who live in Corinth. For the native Corinthians, Colchis is at the edge of the world – a land of dark-skinned barbarians. In *Medea*'s somewhat overdetermined figuration, the Colchians also signify the dark-skinned residents of the new Berlin Republic. In other words, in *Medea*, Wolf portrays a conflict between two groups completely alien to each other racially, religiously and geographically. In *Kassandra*, on the other hand, she constellates the rivalry of the Trojans and the Greeks as a fraternal dispute despite the tragic mutual hatred between these two peoples.

A Fraternity Based on Fear and Hatred: The Men of *Kassandra*

In her comparison of *Kassandra* and *Medea*, Helen Bridge asserts that the first novel is focused on the diametrically opposed worldviews of the two cultures, the irreconcilability of which makes war unavoidable, whereas the later work portrays the subtler conflicts between an apparently autochthonous culture and an immigrant culture. This clash allows a single figure, Medea, to emerge as a scapegoat.[5] While I agree with Bridge, the annihilation of Troy in *Kassandra* and the contrasting lack of war in *Medea* might lead one to conclude that the rift between the Greeks and the Trojans in *Kassandra* is more profound than that between the Corinthians and Colchians in *Medea*. However, this is not the case. The animosity between Colchians and Corinthians in *Medea* is due to the unbridgeable social, ethnic and religious divisions between them – in most respects bitterer than that between the Trojans and the Greeks in *Kassandra*, who are not separated by such distinctions.

Because Cassandra narrates the downfall and destruction of her homeland retrospectively, as a prisoner of the Greeks facing imminent execution, the impression might arise that this development is predestined, reflecting the predilection of Greek tragedies such as Aeschylus's *Agamemnon*, the most well-known ancient rendering of the tale. This sense of fatedness is enhanced (as it

---

Fröhlich', in *Die Dimension des Autors. Essays und Aufsätze, Reden und Gespräche 1959–1985* (Darmstadt: Luchterhand, 1987), pp. 929–940 (p. 929).
5 Bridge, 'Christa Wolf's *Kassandra* and *Medea*', p. 34.

is, of course, in Aeschylus's tragedy) by the circumstance that Cassandra is a seer condemned to be ignored and even despised, a curse placed upon her by Apollo because she refused him. Nevertheless, Bridge is correct to note that Wolf's *Kassandra* goes against the mythic grain in conveying the insight that humans have full authority over the myths they circulate and that history results from human mediation, especially by those in power.[6] Because Wolf's Cassandra communicates this truth to her people, and they fail to heed her, Wolf's Trojans are not subject to a hopeless fate imposed by the gods. Since the Greeks and the Trojans resemble each other quite closely in worshiping the same gods, occupy contiguous territories, are ethnically indistinguishable in appearance and are governed by similar political and social structures, their enmity is all the stronger. In the traditional version, the primary trigger for this hostility – which takes on the contours of a civil war because it is a fraternal conflict – is the abduction of Helen, the wife of the Spartan king Menelaus, by Cassandra's brother, Paris. In Wolf's novel, however, it is the royal advisor Eumelos who brings the crisis to a boiling point. Reflecting the behind-the-scenes manoeuvring by the rival Cold War alliances at the height of the German missile crisis, in which the GDR and the FRG were effectively pawns, war between the Trojans and the Achaeans results from political intrigues. In her essay 'Von Kassandra zu Medea' ['From Cassandra to Medea'], Wolf provides this background historical circumstance of her first myth novel. She claims that in *Kassandra*, she was pondering the issue of how the self-destructive tendency of the West could have emerged – a tendency manifest, in her view, early in the 1980s. This is because missiles were deployed on both sides of the inner-German border, and military as well as political leaders calculated that atomic warfare in Central Europe might create a positive solution to the tensions between the NATO and the Warsaw Pact blocks.[7] The Western deployment began after a Warsaw Pact military build-up in the late 1970s. In response, NATO issued a 'Double Track Decision' in December 1979, proposing a limitation to the stationing of medium-range ballistic missiles by both sides. Consistent with this decision, NATO deployed more missiles in West Germany after the Eastern Block did not agree to the terms.

Cassandra comes to view the Greeks as 'the enemy' who has plundered her homeland.[8] Her contempt for the Greek army is directed most intensely towards

6 Ibid., p. 33.
7 Christa Wolf, 'Von Kassandra zu Medea', *Hierzulande. Andernorts. Erzählungen und andere Texte 1994–1998* (Munich: Luchterhand, 1999), pp. 158–168 (p. 160).
8 Christa Wolf, *Kassandra. Erzählung* (Darmstadt: Luchterhand, 1983), p. 113. All translations are taken from: Wolf, *Cassandra. A Novel and Four Essays*, trans. by Jan von Heurck (New York: Farrar, Straus and Giroux, 1984), p. 99.

Achilles, the 'brute', whom she wishes 'a thousand deaths' because she regards him as primarily culpable for the murderous profanations resulting in the deaths or psychic destruction of many of her family members.[9] Nevertheless, she recognizes that Eumelos is primarily responsible for the catastrophe befalling her country. Through his edicts, the Trojans are compelled to cease regarding the Spartan king Menelaus as a friendly guest at court. Instead, Eumelos's edicts transform Menelaus into an enemy and a spy. The war created by turning the Greeks into foes, which destroys Troy, reflects Wolf's fears that the machinations of both NATO and the Warsaw Pact might lead to a destructive martial conflict.

Menelaus comes to Troy to end the plague in his kingdom of Sparta by making sacrifices at the graves of two Trojan heroes. He had enjoyed the right to hospitality at Priam's court and table until Eumelos and his 'Royal Party' use intrigues to transform him into an enemy. Cassandra regards the soldiers of both armies as united by a common fear. The war itself and the mutual fear these soldiers seek to hide, symptoms of the patriarchalism characterizing the social and political power structures of both sides, create a common denominator uniting both foes through what one might term a 'negative cosmopolitanism'. Wolf uses the identical aspects of their conflict to represent them as a single community united by mutual hatred. In 'Von Kassandra zu Medea', Wolf argues that the Western tendency towards self-destructiveness is already evident in antiquity and, in her time, led to the stationing of medium-range missiles along the inner German borders.[10] In antiquity as well as in her time, the uninterrupted domination of a patriarchal world order creates the tendency towards war and mutual annihilation. Sabine Wilke finds that women in *Kassandra* are victims of the patriarchal war machinery embraced by most of the men in the novel because of their own psychological uncertainty.[11] Wolf once more reaffirms that the opposing sides, soldiers and victims alike, are united by this male militarism – as are, by projection, the populaces in the two German states in the early 1980s.

---

9 Wolf, *Kassandra*, p. 95. Wolf's narrator, Cassandra, reflects the author's perspective, so it is a sign of pessimism when the first-person narrator of Wolf's last novel – inspired by the writer's residence in Santa Monica, which is this work's primary setting – remarks that, due to narrative traditions maintained over centuries, Achilles is only allowed to appear in literature as a hero. See Christa Wolf, *Stadt der Engel oder The Overcoat of Dr. Freud* (Berlin: Suhrkamp, 2010), p. 61.
10 Wolf, 'Von Kassandra zu Medea', p. 160.
11 Sabine Wilke, *Ausgraben und Erinnern. Zur Funktion von Geschichte, Subjekt und geschlechtlicher Identität in den Texten Christa Wolfs* (Würzburg: Königshausen and Neumann, 1993), p. 92.

A Female Utopia: The Women of *Kassandra*

Wolf portrays the men on both sides of the conflict in *Kassandra* as often iden-
tical through their fear, martial aggression and subjection of women, reflecting
Wolf's view of the militaristic, patriarchal governments on both sides of the
Iron Curtain. While the men thereby create a dystopian cohesion, the productive,
peaceful coexistence of the novel's women constitutes the text's utopian strain.
They enjoy a brief communal existence towards the end of the war and the narrative. When Wolf declares in the second of her Frankfurt poetry lectures that the
Troy she envisions is a model for utopian society, she has the female utopia outside the Trojan city walls in mind. The novel and the lectures are intertwined, a
technique related to Wolf's engagement in an Eastern feminist praxis, involving
the dissolution of generic boundaries. Thomas Beebee and Beverly Weber elucidate the link between *Kasssandra* and the *Frankfurter Poetik-Vorlesungen* [*Frankfurt Poetic Lectures*] of which it was originally a part, arguing that for Wolf, there
is no valid separation between the modes of discourse she employs in the *Poetik-
Vorlesungen*; diary entries, letters, travelogue and the novel itself constitute a cohesive unit.[12] Beebee and Weber close by noting that the original work as a total-
ity, entitled *Voraussetzungen einer Erzählung* [*Conditions of a Narrative*], 'represents a thinking "outside the system" or "through the body"', so that
'women's literature may be the beginning of an aesthetic of resistance for
Wolf'.[13] This development in Wolf's writing indicates a proximity to Western feminists, such as Hélène Cixous.[14]

Jane Gallop's notion that the body is more than a 'physical envelope', but
also 'exceeds and antedates consciousness or reason or interpretation'[15] bears
a similarity to the holistic, somatic approach Wolf takes in *Kassandra* and
other works, though her holism is unique with respect to literary forms. In her
essay 'Berührung' ['Touching'] – published in 1977 as the preface to another
genre-bending work, Maxie Wander's *Guten Morgen, du Schöne* [*Good Morning,
You Beauty*] – Wolf notes the importance of preserving the insight that women

---

12 Thomas O. Beebee and Beverly M. Weber, 'A Literature of Theory. Christa Wolf's *Kassandra*
Lectures as Feminist Anti-Poetics', *German Quarterly*, 74 (2001), 259–279.
13 Ibid., 276. On Wolf's conscious self-distancing from Western feminism during the existence
of the GDR, see also Anna K. Kuhn, 'Christa Wolf. Literature as an Aesthetics of Resistance', in
Literature and the Development of Feminist Theory, ed. by Robin Truth Goodman (Cambridge:
Cambridge University Press, 2015), pp. 155–170, esp. pp. 155–156.
14 Beebee and Weber, 'A Literature of Theory', 272–273.
15 Jane Gallop, *Thinking Through the Body* (New York: Columbia University Press, 1988), p. 13.

must conceptually grasp ['begreifen'] with their entire body,[16] suggesting her affinity with feminists such as Cixous and Gallop. However, when Wolf concludes her essay by noting that female relationships made it possible for women to develop a consciousness endowed with the capacity for cooperation rather than a need to dominate, control and subjugate,[17] she evinces her own original feminist priorities as they emerge in *Kassandra*. According to Wolf, men lack this ability to develop solidary relationships because they are more damaged by capitalism than women – a view rather alien to Western feminism.[18]

Georgina Paul has justly described this novel's non-hierarchical female society beyond Troy's boundaries as a 'counter-model' to male authoritarian social structures and the quest for heroism – a quest even ultimately embraced by Cassandra's lover, Aeneas.[19] The women are driven towards each other because, as the narrator proclaims, 'schienen die Männer beider Seiten verbündet gegen unsre Frauen' [the men of both sides seemed to have joined forces against our women].[20] This unofficial male alliance against women underscores the fact that only superficial matters divide the Trojans and the Greek soldiers into enemy camps. Among the female commune residents are Greek slaves and Amazons. A fundamental component of the cosmopolitan utopian constellation of this group is the diverse geographic, ethnic and social origins of these women. The demise of this commune is triggered by the women's brutal murder of a Greek priest in revenge for the desecration of the Amazonian queen Penthesilea's corpse by Achilles.

Wolf draws together the characters in the novel to reflect the innate interconnectedness of the Greeks and Trojans, to demonstrate that both sides are inherently – beyond the realm of existing politics – members of a single community. She seeks to reveal the solidarity of the Greeks and the Trojans, both negatively (male dystopia) and positively (female utopia). Wolf evokes the parallels between the Trojans and the Greeks on other occasions as well. The carceral atmosphere, extending to the sky above her prison in harmony with the heavens above her homeland, is similar in Mycenae and Troy.[21] Cassandra perceives the smile of the Mycenaean queen Clytemnestra as identical to hers, leading the Trojan woman to believe that, under other circumstances, the two royal figures could

---

16 Christa Wolf, 'Berührung. Maxie Wander', in *Die Dimension des Autors*, pp. 196–209 (p. 204).
17 Ibid., p. 207.
18 Ibid.
19 Georgina Paul, *Perspectives on Gender in Post-1945 German Literature* (Rochester, NY: Camden House, 2009), p. 202.
20 Wolf, *Kassandra*, p. 119.
21 Ibid., p. 79.

have called each other 'sister'.[22] Translated into the political situation of the early 1980s, the dialectic of utopianism and dystopianism as well as the similarities between characters suggest the underlying unity of the citizens of the two Germanys at a time when missiles stationed on both sides of the German-German border threatened the existence of all Germans – indeed all Europeans. Under other circumstances, the populaces on both sides of the Iron Curtain could constitute a unity, as they had before 1949, when the FRG (in May) and, in response, the GDR (in October) were founded. Portraying the rivals in the Trojan War, Wolf adds a feminist twist to the political situation: *Kassandra* highlights the significance of masculine striving for prestige, heroism and absolute power as the decisive factor in the division of Germany. The novel thus reveals patriarchal structures as systemic and generated at the state level on both sides of the Wall.

Polyperspectivism, Hybridity and Colonialism in *Medea*

The milieu of inner-German cosmopolitan fraternity in *Kassandra* constitutes the binding of two intertwined peoples under an *undivided* heaven[23] – populaces who had been divided according to the title and purport of Wolf's first widely acclaimed novel, *Der geteilte Himmel* (1963). However, this poetically evoked underlying harmony is rendered impossible by the polyperspective narrative strategy Wolf employs in her second myth novel, *Medea. Stimmen.* The diverse voices referred to in the subtitle, which highlights the use of multiple narrating figures in this text, works against the sort of overarching harmonious ambience enabled by *Kassandra*'s homophonous narrative structure. The lack of such a unifying, omniscient narrative voice intensifies the profound geographic and ethnic chasm dividing the Corinthians and the Colchians in *Medea*. In *Kassandra*, it is the protagonist's uncontested presence as narrator that brings to expression the unity behind the superficial division between the two rival parties. The German unification Wolf evokes as an underlying telos in her first myth novel was indeed realized at a political level in October 1990, but the inner strife still dividing the country is refracted in the fragmentation of narrative voice in the second myth novel. It is only the title figure, Medea, who perceives the commonality of the two nationalities, but other 'voices' in the novel often blind her insight.

---

22 Ibid., p. 49.
23 Ibid., p. 79.

Whether the novel takes place in Corinth or Colchis, it consistently evokes the sense that the characters, outside their native land, are in utterly foreign territory.

The first 'voice' of the novel belongs to the title character, and near the beginning of her narration, Medea describes Corinth as a country 'das mir immer fremd geblieben ist und immer fremd bleiben wird' [that has always seemed alien to me and will stay that way forever].[24] It must be noted that she also feels alienated from her own homeland because of the machinations of her father, Aietes, the king of Colchis. Therefore, she aids the Corinthian Jason and his Argonauts in their furtive quest for the Golden Fleece and accompanies them back to Corinth. However, a relationship based on mutual love and understanding never develops between Medea and Jason, and Medea's premonition that she will always remain an outsider in Corinth proves to be accurate. In Santa Monica, where Wolf resided when she conducted much of her research for the novel at the Los Angeles Getty Center, she became uneasy as she read about violence against foreigners and minorities in unified Germany. Given the sense of alienation Wolf also felt in Santa Monica,[25] the figure of Medea – who, like the asylum seekers in Germany, was forced into a permanent exile but experienced deep alienation there – was particularly sympathetic for her. Like Medea, Wolf suffered profound disillusion in the Berlin Republic, and the Colchians' sense of estrangement reflects the emotions she and many fellow GDR intellectuals shared after 1990. Wolf's casting of the Colchians as dark-skinned victims of Corinthian mistreatment also reflects her sympathy with asylum seekers. Thus the Colchians stand in, at the same time, for former GDR citizens and current asylum seekers in recently unified Germany. In an interview, Wolf expressed her identification with the victimized asylum seekers. She notes that when she was composing *Medea*, she realized her countrymen always fell into the same pattern of behaviour at times of crisis: marginalizing certain people and making them scapegoats. These people, perceived as outsiders, are conjured as enemies to the point that reality becomes insanely distorted.[26] In *Medea*, the title figure is the victim of such distorted perception when the Corinthians make her responsible for the castration of Turon, a Corinthian aid to her enemy, Akamas, the chief astronomer to King Creon. However, Medea had sought to protect

---

24 Christa Wolf, *Medea. Stimmen* (Munich: Luchterhand, 1996), p. 19. All translations are taken from: *Medea. A Modern Retelling*, trans. by John Cullen (New York: Doubleday, 1998).

25 Wolf, 'Begegnungen Third Street', in *Hierzulande. Andernorts*, pp. 7–41.

26 Christa Wolf and Petra Kammann, 'Warum Medea? Christa Wolf im Gespräch mit Petra Kammann am 25.1. 1996', in *Christa Wolfs Medea. Voraussetzungen zu einem Text. Mythos und Bild*, ed. by Marianne Hochgeschurz (Berlin: Janus, 1998), pp. 49–57 (pp. 49–50).

Turon from the vengeance of Colchian women, whose sacred grove he had violated by chopping down a tree there. Their mood during the celebration of a spring festival had been ecstatic prior to Turon's profanation because, as Medea puts it, 'Endlich waren wir ganz bei uns, endlich war ich ganz bei mir' [At last we were one with ourselves, at last I was one with myself].[27] In contrast to the female utopia in *Kassandra*, the women's joy at the festival for Demeter is enabled by the national/ethnic exclusivity of the celebrants; they are all Colchians.

Indeed, the circumstance that the Colchians and Corinthians have diverse religious orientations – while the Trojans and the Greeks in *Kassandra* are portrayed as sacrificing to the same gods – is a further sign of the chasm separating the two populaces in *Medea*. The Artemis festival of the Corinthians alienates Colchian women such as Lyssa, Medea's foster-sister and companion. Lyssa is disturbed when Medea tells her she will attend the festival as an act of reconciliation.[28] Likewise, the Corinthians see in a lunar eclipse a sign that their gods are punishing them for allowing the alien gods of Colchis to be brought into their city.[29] When he is in Colchis in pursuit of the Golden Fleece, Jason finds the land and its people alien and barbaric.[30] Thus, from a religious, ethnic and geographic perspective, the division between the Colchians and Corinthians in *Medea* is deeper than the politically manufactured dispute between the otherwise similar Greeks and Trojans in *Kassandra*.

On the ship to Corinth, Medea hears the word 'Flüchtlinge' [refugees], a word the Argonauts use to disparage their Colchian passengers.[31] The Corinthians always maintain a distance between themselves and the Colchians. Gail Finney notes that the equality of the sexes and a relative economic sameness within the population are elements marking their distinction from the Corinthians – attributes intended to evoke parallel differences between the GDR and the FRG, respectively.[32] The term 'Flüchtlinge' may also reflect the resentment some East Germans felt when they left the GDR for the FRG in droves after the fall of the Berlin Wall in search of better opportunities and were frequently treated by Westerners as abject, second-class citizens.[33] At the same time, the distinctions be-

---

27 Wolf, *Medea*, p. 207.
28 Ibid., pp. 191–192.
29 Ibid., p. 205.
30 Ibid., pp. 45–46.
31 Ibid., p. 36.
32 Gail Finney, *Christa Wolf* (New York: Twayne, 1999), pp. 123–125.
33 See, for example, Ben Gook, *Divided Subjects, Invisible Borders. Re-Unified Germany after 1989* (London: Rowman and Littlefield, 2015).

tween the groups are constituted so that the Colchians can be read as ciphers for the ethnic minorities attacked by right-wing Germans soon after unification.

Most violence against refugees took place in the East. Problematically, Wolf seems to elide this circumstance in conflating the identities of former East Germans and contemporary refugees in the unified republic in *Medea*. Both novels explore the psychopathology of bellicosity, yet they treat its origins in distinct ways. *Kassandra* underscores similarities between the Trojan and Greek rivals in politics, religion, ethnicity and militarism – an identity rooted in a patriarchal worldview held by the men of both nations. In reinterpreting the Medea myth, by contrast, Wolf appears primarily interested in exploring the timeless search for scapegoats.[34] In analogy to the political events in unified Germany in the early 1990s, Wolf stages Medea and the other Colchians' racial alterity as prerequisites to instrumentalizing them as scapegoats. Once racially marked, nothing stands in the way of driving Medea into exile and convincing the Corinthians she is guilty of her sons' murder. However, the sons were sacrificed to rid Corinth of a plague that had befallen the kingdom, and powerful Corinthians also wanted to rid the kingdom of Jason and Medea's sons because they – one blond like Jason, one dark and curly-haired like Medea[35] – were the embodiment of coexistence between both nationalities.

Euripides's version of the Medea tale gave rise to the myth that Medea herself murdered her sons, and Wolf was pleased to discover that the Greek playwright, rather than historical evidence, was the source of Medea's murderous reputation.[36] In an article on *Medea*, Wilke brings together the critical discourses of postcolonialism, orientalism and Homi Bhabha's concept of hybridity to demonstrate how Wolf transforms the traditional image of the Colchian leader as an insanely jealous murderess into a warrior for gender equality and minority rights.[37] According to Wilke, hybridity in the novel results not from the intersection of disparate cultures or miscegenation, although these tendencies lead to the initial conceptualization of hybridity. The fate of the Colchians and the twin sons of Jason and Medea make such traditional hybridity impossible. Rather, the voices of Medea and her former pupil, the Colchian Agameda, are hybrid secondary manifestations resulting from their extended residency in Greek Western Corinth. Agameda sees through the colonialism of her new homeland but uses her insights to her own advantage by rejecting her Colchian heritage and

---

34 Wolf, 'Von Kassandra zu Medea', p. 116.

35 Wolf, *Medea*, p. 120.

36 See Jörg Magenau, *Christa Wolf. Eine Biographie* (Berlin: Kindler, 2002), p. 422.

37 Wilke, 'Die Konstruktion der wilden Frau. Christa Wolfs Roman *Medea. Stimmen* als postkolonialer Text', *German Quarterly*, 76 (2003), 11–24.

embracing her new Corinthian identity. Her hybridity manifests itself in this manner. Pushing Wilke's argument further, one can add that Agameda's shrewdly calculated adoption of the colonial guise reflects not only a form of secondary hybridity, but also mimicry. In *The Location of Culture*, Bhabha establishes that the colonized double unsettles colonial authority through an adaptation of colonial discourse, operating at the interstice 'between mimicry and mockery'.[38] Agameda's conscious embrace of Corinthian identity for her own selfish purposes demonstrates Wolf's own 'mockery' of the West's vision of itself as embodying transcendent norms. Agameda's mimicry, to paraphrase Bhabha, transforms 'resemblance' into a 'menace' to the West's belief in its superiority.[39] This consciously acquired resemblance is not motivated by genuine admiration for the colonizer's self-assumed inherent merit, but by the colonized's recognition that this adaptation will bring personal gain.

Agameda's loss as an ally to Medea makes the latter's role as a mediator between the rival parties even more difficult. Medea cannot create peaceful coexistence between the Corinthians and the Colchians. This inability is not only due to the machinations of her Corinthian enemies, but also to the Corinthians' perception that she constitutes a disturbing foreign threat from the East. While the tragedy of Cassandra in Wolf's first myth novel results from her status as a clairvoyant priestess living among two conflicting powers bound together by blind paternalism and enmity towards her, Medea is condemned to an equally grim fate through her foreignness; she is banished to the Corinthian mountains. Her tragic destiny most likely results from her discovery of the Corinthian king Creon's secret execution of his young daughter. With this deed, he wanted to prevent her accession to the throne and thus matriarchal rule. King Creon's attitude results from the now-dominant patriarchalism in Corinth. Gail Finney is correct in noting that Wolf's portrayal of the respective social structures in Colchis and Corinth reveals a stark contrast. Significantly, Colchian women have substantially more autonomous power than Corinthian women. For example, it is striking to Akamas that, in Colchis, women are the astronomers[40] – a group that occupies a politically and socially powerful position in both Colchis and Corinth. This discrepancy in the roles of the sexes contributes to difficulties in integrating Colchians into Corinthian society. Nevertheless, as Wolf explained in an interview, she did not intend to portray Colchis as an ideal antithesis to Corinth.[41] After all, Medea leaves her homeland because Colchis itself is transitioning from matriar-

---

38 Homi Bhabha, *The Location of Culture* (London: Routledge, 2004), p. 123.
39 Ibid., p. 123.
40 Finney, *Christa Wolf*, p. 123.
41 Wolf and Kammann, 'Warum Medea', p. 50.

chal to patriarchal rule. Still, Wolf also emphasized that she perceived Colchis as a city-state with traces of matriarchal relations while regarding Corinth as thoroughly imbued with paternalism.

In notes to her manuscript, Wolf claims that her research for *Medea* provided her with insights into the overlap of elements from diverse times and value systems. In the earliest stage of the Medea myth, however, one finds traces of a dominant matriarchy and evidence that Medea herself was a strong, independent woman.[42] This remark helps decipher a passage that appears to contrast with the novel's tendency to portray Colchis as a society the Corinthians refuse to integrate into their own national structure. Here, Agameda announces her intention to blend into Corinthian society, and reference is made to a diminutive, brown-skinned race living in the surrounding villages, towards whom the city-dwelling Corinthians display an attitude of superiority. These rural Corinthians regard the racially similar Colchians as their kin and want to integrate them into their villages through intermarriage, an attempt which Agameda repulses, but which not all Colchian women resist. The rural Corinthians maintain a legend that they are the original settlers of the region.[43] Given Wolf's emphasis on early matriarchy, which left more significant traces in Colchis than in Corinth, the brief presence in *Medea* of a populace similar in appearance to the Colchians highlights the autochthony of the original matriarchal values in both nations. If we were to search for a more profound reason for the presence of this autochthonous populace in the novel, we might conclude that, through their physical similarity to the Colchians as well as their rural lifestyle, they are designed to evoke Corinth's primeval matriarchy. The autochthonous Corinthians' racial proximity to the Colchians, as well as their agricultural way of life, evokes – through analogy – the matriarchal origins of both kingdoms.

Katrin Sieg notes that, in the transitional period in which the GDR was dissolved and incorporated into the FRG, East German youth wore Palestinian scarves. This sign of solidarity represented 'the GDR youths' symbolic identification with an ethnic minority struggling for recognition, autonomy, and statehood', which 'reflected their own situation as citizens of a vanishing state'.[44] Such identification may be at work in Wolf's establishment of the Colchians as a dark-skinned people, whom one can interpret as the 'vanishing' populace of the GDR's citizenry. On the other hand, it is possible to associate the Colchians

---

42 Wolf, 'Notate aus einem Manuskript ab 1. Februar 1993', in *Christa Wolfs Medea*, pp. 40–48 (p. 47).

43 Wolf, *Medea*, pp. 78–79.

44 Katrin Sieg, *Ethnic Drag. Performing Race, Nation, Sexuality in West Germany* (Ann Arbor: University of Michigan Press, 2002), p. 145.

with dark-skinned immigrants who arrived in Germany before and after 1990. Wolf contrasts the autochthonous residents of Corinth, described as 'kleinwüchsige braunhäutige Menschen' [people who are short of stature and brown of skin], with the taller, fairer-skinned urban Corinthians and their sense of superiority over the village residents.[45] Such racialized language, in conjunction with the obvious analogy with contemporary politics in the 1990s, supports readers' awareness of the increasing racism taking hold in Germany soon after unification. It also links the social position of former GDR residents and the colonized indigenous people of her novel.

Wolf's strategy of introducing the racial element seems tied to her anti-colonial stance. Among his articulations of hybridity, Bhabha argues that this postcolonial technique 'reverses the effects of the colonialist disavowal, so that other "denied" knowledges enter upon the dominant discourse and estrange the basis of its authority'. In citing this passage, Robert J. C. Young notes that hybridization undermines the dominance of the colonial power, revealing 'the trace of the other' and showing this colonial power to be 'double-voiced'.[46] Wolf's polyperspectivism gives voice to both the colonialist Corinthians and the internally colonized Colchians, but the autochthonous dark-skinned Corinthians are only presented through the sympathetic narrator Medea, who racially identifies with them. The space Wolf gives them in the narrative undermines the authority of the dominant, lighter-skinned Corinthians. By evoking their presence, Wolf – through Medea – reveals the originary 'trace' of their alterity among the Corinthians and suggests a kind of hybridization in foregrounding the union of some Colchian women with these Ur-Corinthians, a hybridization that challenges the light-skinned Corinthians as the colonial authority. She thereby allegorically questions this authority, both with respect to the FRG finalizing its 'colonization' of the GDR when she wrote the novel, and with respect to the Caucasians of the united Germany, who sought to deny even a presence to racial minorities in that country.

Conclusion

Utopian elements influence both of Wolf's myth novels. In *Kassandra*, the female utopia is destroyed because, like the residents of both German lands at the time

---

45 Wolf, *Medea*, p. 78.
46 Quoted in Robert J. C. Young, *Colonial Desire. Hybridity in Theory, Culture and Race* (London: Routledge, 1995), p. 23.

the novel was composed, two groups of male combatants are too like each other and thereby make the destruction of Troy inevitable. Yet the ideal glimpse of social harmony evoked in the atelier of Medea's lover, the sculptor Oistros, who ignores the social and ethnic origins of the individuals who mingle there, proves unattainable. This attempt at a model life in harmony comes to an end because the Corinthian and Colchian masses become more intolerant of each other. While both novels end tragically, the evocation of the sameness of GDR and FRG citizens in *Kassandra* gives way in *Medea* to renewed esteem for the GDR's now-lost, discrete identity. This nation, as in Oistros's studio, still tolerated alterity – a toleration that seemed to disappear after unification.

Beverly M. Weber
Christa Wolf's Trouble with Race

Fragen Sie ihn, ob er die alten Landkarten kennt, mit ihren vielen weißen Flecken, auf die man kurzerhand schrieb: Hic sunt leones. Fragen Sie ihn, ob er, als er mir ins Fleisch schnitt, als er meine Wunden öffnete, meine faulen Stellen bloßlegte: ob er da auf jene weißen Flecken gestoßen ist, die mir selber unbekannt, die unerforscht und unbenannt sind [...] an diesen resistenten Flecken [muss] jede Immunabwehr der Welt zuschanden werden.

[Ask him if he knows those old maps with all the white areas where people simply wrote 'hic sunt leones.' Ask him if, when he was cutting into my flesh, when he was opening my incisions and exposing my rotten places, he came upon any of those white spots, unknown even to me, that are unexplored and unnamed (...) every immune mechanism in the world will come to grief against those resistant spots.][1]

The narrator of *Leibhaftig* utters these words in response to doctors' bewilderment at her failing immune system. The *terra incognita*, the 'white spots' that she imagines, might be read in many directions: as acknowledgment of the narrator's complicity in violence, as markers of unacknowledged histories, as 'blind' spots that evidence a lack of knowledge. Those white spots, by being unmappable, are deemed unknowable, unthinkable and unspeakable. In many Wolf texts, the danger produced by the limits of the speakable is at its most severe when her various protagonists are tempted to give themselves up to these limits – in *Leibhaftig*, a danger expressed particularly through the inability to desire life itself.

Wolf's last novel, *Stadt der Engel oder The Overcoat of Dr. Freud* (hereafter *Stadt der Engel*), reveals one of those white spots to be whiteness itself, which – as bell hooks argues – often expresses among white anti-racists as 'a deep emotional investment in the myth of "sameness", even as their actions reflect the primacy of whiteness as a sign informing who they are and how they think'.[2] Sara Ahmed suggests that whiteness, as a consequence of racialization, is an 'ongoing and unfinished history, which orientates bodies in specific directions, affecting how they "take up" space'.[3] Whiteness exists as a structural advantage in racially structured societies[4] and as a set of norms – both institutional

---

1 Christa Wolf, *Leibhaftig* (Munich: Luchterhand, 2002), p. 98. All translations are taken from Christa Wolf, *In the Flesh*, trans. by John Barrett (Boston: David R. Godine, 2005).
2 bell hooks, *Black Looks. Race and Representation* (Boston: South End Press, 1992), p. 167.
3 Sara Ahmed, 'A Phenomenology of Whiteness', *Feminist Theory*, 8.2 (2007), 149–168 (p. 150).
4 Frankenberg, Ruth. 'Mirage of an Unmarked Whiteness', in *The Making and Unmaking of Whiteness*, ed. by Birgit Brander Rasmussen and others (Durham, NC: Duke University Press, 2001), pp. 72–96.

https://doi.org/10.1515/9783110496000-011

and somatic – that reproduce social relations;[5] it allows some bodies to be more at home and to move more easily in the world than others.[6] Approaching Wolf's oeuvre from a perspective informed by critical ethnic studies and its multivalent critiques of whiteness enables an approach to Wolf that can resituate her many contributions to post-1945 German literature within the post-War trouble with race. Wolf's earlier work engages with anti-Semitism and Eurocentrism in ways that continually lead Wolf's narrators back to a discussion of shared humanity while prohibiting explicit engagement with racism. Wolf's trouble with race in *Stadt der Engel*, alternatively, becomes a more extensive troubling of race: a complex, incomplete revelation of the entanglements of race at the heart of what is considered to be 'Western civilization'.

In her third *Kassandra* lecture, Wolf opens by posing the question: 'Die Literatur des Abendlandes, lese ich, sei eine Reflexion des weißen Mannes auf sich selbst. Soll nun die Reflexion der weißen Frau auf sich selbst dazukommen? Und weiter nichts?' [The literature of the West (I read) is the white man's reflection on himself. So should it be supplemented by the white woman's reflection on herself? And nothing more?].[7] With this question, Wolf briefly acknowledges the violence of whiteness. The imbrication of literature of the 'West' in structures of white patriarchy plays a role in two key Wolf projects in particular: the excavation of memory in a Benjaminian redemptive sense – that is, as a way of imagining alternative futures; and critiques of the violence of rationalized/instrumentalized Western masculinity in the name of progress, often expressed in the exclusion of women's voices from the public sphere, as well as in the environmental impact of advanced technology. Wolf's strategy of response was not to develop a unified aesthetics or poetics, but to represent a fragmented struggle towards an adequate politics of emotion as a counter to this violence. Yet although Wolf's interrogation of 'Western civilization' is extensively elaborated in her work, the role of racialized bodies in the construction of the fully human in Western thought is left largely unarticulated. Thinking through race and its emergence in tandem with modern colonialism have been key to several scholarly bodies of work that would seem to align with Wolf's critiques of the West, yet race haunts Wolf's texts rather ambiguously. It erupts, at times more

5 Sara Ahmed, *On Being Included. Racism and Diversity in Institutional Life* (Durham, NC: Duke University Press, 2012), p. 38.
6 Ahmed, 'A Phenomenology', p. 160, 162.
7 Christa Wolf, *Werkausgabe in 12 Bänden*, ed. by Sonja Hilzinger (Munich: Luchterhand, 1999–2001), vol. 7: *Kassandra. Voraussetzungen einer Erzählung* (2001), p. 108. All translations are taken from Christa Wolf, *Cassandra. A Novel and Four Essays*, trans. by Jan Van Heurck (New York: Farrar, Straus and Giroux, 1984).

visibly than others, to disappear again amidst a humanism that emphasizes sameness in the face of violence.

We might see *Kindheitsmuster*, Wolf's *Kassandra* lectures, *Leibhaftig* and *Stadt der Engel* as touchstones that mark Wolf's trouble with whiteness. In particular, whiteness produces problems for a particular ethics of empathetic feeling that emerges as part of Wolf's attempt to construct a politics of emotion. In seeking such an ethics, Wolf sets up identifications with the victims of anti-Semitism, racism and imperialism, resulting in equivalencies of victimhood that obscure the workings of whiteness. Wolf's narrative worlds have much in common with feminist projects that seek to highlight the role of emotions in knowledge, recognizing the epistemic authority accorded to white men as a consequence of the exclusion of emotion from epistemology.[8] Yet, given the lack of a language with which to articulate white women's participation in whiteness, Wolf's emphasis on emotion results in an ethics of empathy that easily slides into a conceptual exclusion of white women from whiteness and an identification with the target of racism that can, in turn, reify racism. As Sara Ahmed suggests, empathy can 'sustain the very difference that it may seek to overcome'.[9]

Stadt der Engel marks a critical turn by which Wolf's trouble with race is rendered visible. The protagonist's repeated attempts to establish a politics of empathetic feeling through her engagement with various 'others' in the text fail repeatedly. The novel is troubled by and troubles race,[10] in part because of Wolf's insistence on describing most characters in the text according to racialized categories – as white, Jewish, Black, Puerto Rican, Native American, for example – even as she fails to explicitly engage race; and in part due to the mockingly critical voice of her Black angel, Angelina, who challenges the narrator's appropriations of victimhood.

---

8 See, for example, Alison M. Jaggar, 'Love and Knowledge. Emotion in Feminist Epistemology', *Inquiry*, 32.2 (1989), 151–176.

9 Sara Ahmed, *The Cultural Politics of Emotion* (New York: Routledge, 2004), p. 30.

10 I am using trouble here partly inspired by Carrie Smith-Prei and Maria Stehle's work on trouble and the importance of staying *with* trouble. To trouble, they suggest (after Judith Butler), is to destabilize and de-essentialize, but to stay with trouble is to enact a feminist politics that does not seek to 'work through' trouble, but to use it as an ever-shifting starting point from which feminist action can issue. See Carrie Smith Prei and Maria Stehle, 'WiG-Trouble', *Women in German Yearbook. Feminist Studies in German Literature & Culture*, 30 (2014), 209–224.

Anti-fascism and Anti-Semitism in Christa Wolf's Work

The trouble with race begins with Wolf's engagement with the history of anti-Semitism under fascism, particularly starting with *Kindheitsmuster*. The protagonist of *Kindheitsmuster*, named Nelly as a child but an unnamed first person narrator as an adult, examines Nelly's ideological and emotional commitment to fascism, but also suggests that patterns of fascism continue in the present. The narrative can be clearly located in the tradition of East German anti-fascist narrative, even as Wolf explicitly challenges official state narratives of anti-fascism. Nelly's coming of age accompanies a maturity into anti-fascism and into a new political position as a Communist. Yet her work highlights how a certain view of history by GDR rulers refused to engage the past *as collaborators*, rather than as Communist victims of fascism.[11] Critical as Wolf was of the GDR in so many of her works, her embedding in a GDR context also contributes to some of the 'blind spots', the 'white spots' of Wolf's work.

The anti-fascist narrative of East Germany not only refused to engage East Germans as collaborators, but also to recognize that Jewish victims of fascism were targeted *as racialized others*, not only as Communists. Much has been written about the emphasis in cultural narratives on the Communist victim over the Jewish victim[12] – or at the very least, the repression of the Holocaust in literature, sometimes even in works by Jewish Communists, such as Anna Seghers.[13] In the context of early post-War purges of Jewish figures from public life, Jewish Germans who were also committed Communists thus found themselves called on by the cultural politics of the GDR to ignore the recent trauma of the Holocaust.[14] This is, perhaps, a specifically East German variant of the silence around race that occurs throughout Western Europe as well in the decades after the Second World War. Many Western European countries viewed racism as a force coming

---

11 Konrad H. Jarausch, 'The Failure of East German Antifascism. Some Ironies of History as Politics', *German Studies Review*, 14.1 (1991), 85–102 (pp. 85–88).
12 The most comprehensive account of the marginalization of anti-Semitism and the Holocaust in East Germany remains Jeffrey Herf's *Divided Memory*. Unfortunately, there is little space here to probe other historical silences about other groups targeted by fascism; these silences are nearly total in Wolf's work as well.
13 Julia Hell, *Post-Fascist Fantasies. Psychoanalysis, History, and the Literature of East Germany* (Durham, NC: Duke University Press, 1997), p. 89; Anke Pinkert, 'Pleasures of Fear. Antifascist Myth, Holocaust, and Soft Dissidence in Christa Wolf's Kindheitsmuster', *German Quarterly*, 76.1 (2003), 13–32.
14 Hell, *Post-Fascist Fantasies*, pp. 89–91.

from the outside, one that derailed the 'naturally' anti-racist bent of modern democracy. A restoration of right democratic principles, in other words, would lead to the end of racism.[15] In West Germany, the language of race virtually disappeared, even as Jews came to be conceptualized as members of an ethnicity rather than a race.[16] Anti-Semitism became understood as something other to and separate from racism. Racism, in turn, became refigured as xenophobia (in references to West Germany, racism has been often seen as a US phenomenon). These processes have epistemological and scholarly consequences, producing work that replicates the very difference it seeks to explain.[17]

The East German silencing of race incorporated elements of both processes. Race and racism were generally seen to exist in another time and place.[18] Racism was often constructed as the product of fascism that had thus ended with victory over fascism; and/or as restricted to fascism's perceived inheritor, West Germany; or as a phenomenon that existed in the United States. The early purges of Jewish 'cosmopolitans' from East German public life were viewed by the state as political developments that had nothing to do with anti-Semitism. Even the prominent trial of Paul Merker – a returned emigré who was not Jewish, but was committed to establishing an East Germany founded on remembering the Holocaust and fighting anti-Semitism – was a clear sign that Jewish identity and public life in East Germany would be incompatible.[19] Later, foreign labourers from African and Asian communist countries as well as Cuba were referred to with a public

---

15 Alana Lentin, 'Racism, Anti-Racism and the Western State', in *Identity, Belonging and Migration*, ed. by Gerard Delanty and others (Liverpool: Liverpool University Press, 2008), pp. 101–119.
16 Rita Chin and Heide Fehrenbach, 'Introduction. What's Race Got to Do with It? Postwar German History in Context', in *After the Nazi Racial State. Difference and Democracy in Germany and Europe*, ed. by Rita Chin and others (Ann Arbor: University of Michigan Press, 2009), pp. 1–29 (p. 3).
17 Rita Chin and Heide Fehrenbach, 'German Democracy and the Question of Difference, 1945–1995', in Chin and others, pp. 102–136 (pp. 129–131).
18 The phenomenon of the East German *Indianerfilme* in the mid-1960s to the 1980s serves as a further example of temporal and geographic displacement of racism in the GDR. The East German iterations of these films imagined racism as a US phenomenon explainable by the logics of imperialism and colonialism. The films promoted an identification of East German audience members with Native Americans as anti-fascist resistance fighters. See Gerd Gemuenden, 'Between Karl May and Karl Marx. The DEFA Indianerfilme (1965–1983)', *New German Critique*, 82 (2001), 399–407. Such displacement renders a discussion of East German racism unimaginable.
19 Sander L. Gilman, *Jurek Becker. A Life in Five Worlds* (Chicago: University of Chicago Press, 2003), pp. 36–37.

rhetoric of 'socialist friends' that enabled an official disavowal of East German racism.[20]

Kindheitsmuster both replicates and challenges East German anti-fascist narratives. Wolf rejects a rhetoric that assigns responsibility for recognizing complicity with fascism solely to citizens of the FRG. Yet her characters' encounters with Jewish survivors and non-Jewish camp survivors are depicted with a narrative structure that allows a certain shared post-War refugee experience to obscure the narrator's ongoing imbrication in whiteness.

For example, when the adult narrator of *Kindheitsmuster* reads from a draft of a book chapter to an audience in Switzerland, she imagines a powerful difference between Holocaust memory in East and West. An audience member suggests that it is time to 'finally' get past this obsession with the fascist past; a Jewish German survivor contradicts him. In a later conversation alone with the émigré, the narrator emphasizes how important 'people like him' were in the years after the War for her, then insists that a demand to end the engagement with the fascist past could not be verbalized in 'her' country.[21] In this way, the narrative of an anti-fascist East Germany is validated even as the narrator constructs a narrative probing everyday complicity with fascism and seeking an empathetic connection to the survivor.

The narrator's/Nelly's encounters with concentration camp inmates are elaborated in undifferentiated ways; indeed, encounters with concentration camp inmates are narrated as a learning about the suffering of Communists under fascism. As Nelly and her family flee west before the advancing Soviet army, they encounter concentration camp inmates from Sachsenhausen who were freed when their captors fled. Nelly's first encounter with a concentration camp survivor is when one approaches a bonfire the refugees have built. In a conversation with this survivor, Nelly's mother expresses disbelief that people were interned in camps as Communists; 'Wo habt ihr bloß alle gelebt?' [Where on earth have you been living?] he responds.[22] The structure of this incident, explicitly repeated later in the book, reveals the blind spots constructed by the East German anti-fascist narrative. Each recounting is surrounded by reflections on the appearance of concentration camps in local newspapers at the time of their founding and other ways in which everyday Germans were exposed to knowledge of the

---

20 *Germany in Transit. Nation and Migration, 1955–2005*, ed. by Deniz Göktürk, David Gramling and Anton Kaes (Berkeley: University of California Press, 2007), pp. 67–69.
21 Wolf, *Christa Wolf Werke*, vol. 5: *Kindheitsmuster* (2000), p. 450.
22 Wolf, *Kindheitsmuster*, p. 65. All translations are taken from Christa Wolf, *Patterns of Childhood*, trans. by Ursusle Molinary and Hedwig Rappolt (New York: Farrar, Straus and Giroux, 1984).

camps early on, as well as the supposed 'forgetting' of that knowledge. The second recounting of this incident within *Kindheitsmuster* follows directly on the heels of an encounter with an American soldier, a German Jew who had emigrated, who remains 'unheimlich' [uncanny] to Nelly.[23] This encounter is glossed over, as Nelly's learning becomes instead a learning about the persecution of Communists, while her mother's knowledge of Jewish persecution is effectively silenced.

Nelly's own coming of age as a Communist structurally aligns her with survivors, particularly as their journey collapses into that of a shared refugee experience. Throughout the text, Nelly, her family and others fleeing with them as the Soviet army advances in the east are the primary refugees in the text, while refugees from the concentration camps remain marginal. In only one case does the text represent a concentration camp survivor for a few paragraphs. In this case, Nelly and her family share the Frahm farmhouse with other refugees, including 'Concentration Camp Ernst', a camp survivor who refuses to explain how, where or why he was interned. In this way, he simply becomes one of the refugees, and a potential discussion of anti-Semitism or the differences in refugee experience is avoided.[24] As Anke Pinkert has suggested, through *Kindheitsmuster*, Wolf constructed an account of anti-Semitism that challenges official GDR anti-fascist narratives even as she suspends alterity in a vision of humanity – a kind of surrogate victimhood that Julia Hell, similarly, has viewed as an impossible desire for identification with Jewish victims.[25] Pinkert provides a valuable reading of this kind of empathy as rooted in a rejection of anti-Semitism as abjection of the Jewish body. A reading attentive to questions of race and its silencings in Europe suggests that empathetic identification also occurs because of a lack of language that can fully engage with anti-Semitism *as racism*, and therefore that could highlight the narrator's position of structural privilege.

In *Stadt der Engel*, the encounter with the Communist concentration camp inmate is repeated but relocated into a different context – no longer as a shared experience of being a refugee that subsumes the experiences of all concentration camp survivors.[26] The encounter is remembered through the narrator's relationship with Ruth, a 'hidden child' who meets the narrator at a gathering of survivors and survivors' children to which the narrator has been invited. Midway

---

23 Wolf, *Kindheitsmuster*, p. 480.
24 Ibid. p. 544.
25 Pinkert, 'Pleasures of Fear', pp. 28–30; Hell, *Post-Fascist Fantasies*, p. 216.
26 Christa Wolf, *Stadt der Engel oder The Overcoat of Dr. Freud*, 3rd edn (Berlin: Suhrkamp, 2010), p. 314. Unless otherwise noted, all translations are taken from Christa Wolf, *City of Angels. Or, The Overcoat of Dr. Freud* (New York: Macmillan, 2013).

through the text, the narrator discovers – quite accidentally – that Ruth herself is the person whom the narrator has been seeking throughout her stay. As Ruth relates a story of a German émigré, the narrator recalls the story of the Communist concentration camp inmate – internally, not out loud. But the retelling contains a major difference. The only point of contact here is that it is the story of the narrator's 'first encounter with a Communist in the flesh'.[27] The narrator's 'empathy' is not in any way expanded here to imagine a shared humanity based on experience as victims of fascism. Instead, the vast difference between the narrator and Ruth is allowed to stand. This recontextualisation, together with the unspoken form of this memory, prohibits the appropriation of the encounter with the concentration camp inmate in order to establish a shared experience with victims of anti-Semitism. Instead, the narrator's experience with survivor communities confronts her with her participation in racialized difference.

Such confrontation extends to forcing the narrator to engage with the new expressions of racism targeted at refugees and perceived refugees in Germany. When the Jewish director of the Holocaust Museum in Los Angeles asks her about the racist attacks occurring in the early 1990s in Germany, she must acknowledge a relationship to racialized violence, even as she feels her resistance to the invitation to speak for unified Germany. Invited to articulate a relationship between two forms of racism triangulated by the narrator's own participation in whiteness, the narrator retreats instead to a reflection on the loss of the GDR.

From Ingeborg to Kora Bachmann: Gender, Pain and the Problem with Empathy

Between *Kindheitsmuster* and *Stadt der Engel*, however, Wolf's engagement with Ingeborg Bachmann will demonstrate where gender is imagined in the politics of empathy. Bachmann served as a distant mentor and inspiration for Wolf's initial engagement with questions of gender; via those reflections, Bachmann also inspired Wolf's first references to whiteness. Wolf's *Kassandra* lecture on Bachmann, delivered as part of her *Frankfurter Poetik-Vorlesungen* (*Frankfurt Lectures on Poetics*), remains the most explicit mention of race and whiteness in her work. This *Kassandra* lecture, written in the form of a letter addressed to A., relies heavily on Wolf's reading of Bachmann's novel fragment *Der Fall Franza [The Book of Franza]*. Wolf cites from Bachmann's fragment extensively – omitting

---

27 Ibid., p. 313.

an important sentence in which Franza makes her identification with colonized peoples explicit, 'Ich bin Papua' [I am Papuan]:

> Man kann nur die wirklich bestehlen, die magisch leben [...] es ist eine tödliche Verzweiflung bei den Papuas, eine Art des Selbstmords, weil sie glauben, die Weißen hätten sich aller ihre Güter auf magische Weise bemächtigt ... Er hat mir [Franza] meine Güter genommen. Mein Lachen, meine Zärtlichkeit, mein Freuenkönnen, mein Mitleiden, Helfenkönnen, meine Animalität, mein Strahlen.
>
> [You can really steal only from people who live magically (...) There is a deadly despair among the Papuans, a kind of suicide, because they believe that the whites seized all their possessions by magical means ... He has taken my possessions from me. My laughter, my tenderness, my ability to feel joy, my compassion, my ability to help, my animality, my radiance.][28]

Wolf's citation of Bachmann illustrates the reliance on structures of empathy. Besides the fact that this expression of empathetic understanding has little to do with realities experienced by the indigenous people of Papua New Guinea,[29] the racialized experience of colonialism is constructed as parallel to the experience of white women vis-à-vis white men – only non-Europeans and women live 'magically', that is, beyond white, masculine (read: non-instrumentalized) rationality. 'The colonized' slip into 'I' seamlessly. Bachmann highlights colonialism even as she recolonizes through the easy identification of Franza with the Maori.[30] Wolf, in turn, doubles this epistemological recolonization through Kassandra's recognition of self in Franza and, therefore, in colonized peoples. This critique of violence proves quite different from that expressed in *Kindheitsmuster*, as Lennox points out: in *Kindheitsmuster*, race is never named, but the author/narrator probes her own complicity in structures of violence; in the fourth *Kassandra* lecture, whiteness is explicitly named, even as Wolf seems to excuse women from whiteness, uncritically stating that Franza must learn that women are colonized and of a 'lower race'.[31] This collapse of gendered and racialized

---

28 Wolf, *Kassandra*, p. 195.

29 Monika Albrecht, '"Es muß erst geschrieben werden". Kolonisation und magische Weltsicht in Ingeborg Bachmanns Romanfragment *Das Buch Franza*', in *'Über die Zeit schreiben'. Literatur- und kulturwissenschaftliche Essays zu Ingeborg Bachmanns Todesarten-Projekt*, ed. by Dirk Göttsche and Monika Albrecht (Würzburg: Königshausen and Neumann, 1998), pp. 59–91 (pp. 74–77).

30 Gisela Brinker-Gabler, 'Andere Begegnung. Begegnung mit dem Anderen zwischen Aneignung und Enteignung', *Seminar. A Journal of Germanic Studies*, 29.2 (1993), 95–105 (pp. 97–99).

31 Sara Lennox, *Cemetery of the Murdered Daughters. Feminism, History, and Ingeborg Bachmann* (Amherst, MA: University of Massachusetts Press, 2006), p. 61; Wolf, *Kassandra*, pp. 194–195.

others into one in order to achieve a certain sense of shared victimhood exists partly as a consequence of the lack of language with which to speak and recognize racism and racialization as part of the legitimation of imperialism.

And so, Wolf suggests, Kassandra's prophesy *today* would be the same as that expressed by Franza:

> Die Weißen kommen. [...U]nd wenn sie wieder zurückgeworfen werden, dann werden sie noch einmal wiederkommen [...S]ie werden mit ihrem Geist wiederkommen, wenn sie anders nicht mehr kommen können. Und auferstehen in einem braunen oder schwarzen Gehirn, es werden noch immer die Weißen sein, auch dann noch. Sie werden die Welt weiter besitzen, auf diesem Umweg.

> [The whites are coming. (...I)f they are repulsed again, they will return again once more. (... T)hey will come in spirit if they can no longer come in any other way. And they will be resurrected in a brown and a black brain, it will still always be the whites, even then. They will continue to own the world in this roundabout way.][32]

For Kassandra (and in this case, for the author herself), the ability to speak this terrifying occupation of land, spirit, brain and body opens up the possibility of understanding and *knowing* the Other as self. Wolf artificially delinks the effects of colonialism from racism, as 'the state-sanctioned or extralegal production and exploitation of group-differentiated vulnerability to premature death',[33] rendering colonialism an effect of Western masculine rationality. Wolf understands women to also 'live magically' – that is, to rely on a range of affects that extends their knowing beyond that of masculinized rationality. A discussion of colonialism and gender without a vocabulary of race has a range of effects: difference is reduced to a simple effect of either skin colour or gender; whiteness is rendered masculine, while white women are excluded from whiteness; the complexities of racist structures disappear; and women of colour are unthinkable and unrepresentable. The question 'Soll nun die Reflexion der weißen Frau auf sich selbst dazukommen? Und weiter nichts?' remains unanswered and unreflected. Instead, the fourth lecture, written in the form of a letter, issues an odd call to its addressee, A., to save whites from the curse on whites that Franza has declared with her final words. This odd imperative appropriates the experience of the colonized to establish a new imagined collective of action in order to rescue white men – a collective comprised of what appear to be white women rec-

---

32 Wolf, *Kassandra*, p. 196.
33 Ruth Wilson Gilmore, 'Race and Globalization', in *Geographies of Global Change. Remapping the World*, ed. R. J. Johnston, Peter J. Taylor and Michael Watts, 2nd edn (Malden, MA: Wiley-Blackwell, 2002), p. 261.

ognizing themselves as victims of white men: A., Bachmann, Franza, Kassandra and Wolf.

In *Leibhaftig*, Ingeborg Bachmann is explicitly replaced by another Bachmann – the 'dark woman', Kora Bachmann, introduced to the reader as a name with many associations.[34] The repeated use of the term 'dark woman' functions as a counterpoint to Ingeborg Bachmann's white ladies,[35] gesturing to the unfulfilled promise of *Kassandra* to move beyond a mere complementing of white male dominance with the voice of white women. Yet the portrayal of Kora Bachmann here largely leaves the workings of whiteness unchallenged. In *Leibhaftig*, based on Wolf's experience of repeated surgeries and a life-threatening infection after untreated appendicitis, Kora Bachmann is the narrator's anaesthetist. With the name Bachmann, she becomes the narrator's mentor as well as caretaker, staying with the narrator for hours, changing cold compresses as she battles fever. And with the name Kora, she references the Greek Persephone/Cora, the goddess of the underworld who here accompanies the narrator into darkness before every operation – and rescues her from the underworld to return her to the realm of the living.[36] Kora Bachmann also, however, prefigures Angelina in *Stadt der Engel* – while not an angel, Kora Bachmann nevertheless flies with the narrator over Berlin to question the narrator's self-destructive impulses and to further excavate the story of Lisbeth.

Lisbeth, as a character in both *Leibhaftig* and *Kindheitsmuster*, is based on Wolf's aunt Elfriede.[37] In *Kindheitsmuster*, in coded language, it is implied that her son may be the biological son of a Jewish doctor with whom she had an affair; in *Leibhaftig*, it is explicit. Between the writing of the two texts, the father of the child, Dr. Leitner/Lechner, writes and then visits Wolf to confirm the story.[38] In a remarkable conversation with Kora, the narrator links her inability to fight for her life to a Hitler quotation that hung on her wall at school: 'Wer leben will, der kämpfe also' [Those who want to live, let them fight].[39] The narrator then tells Kora the story of her aunt, Dr. Leitner and their child, then bursts into tears, while Kora comforts her.

The disturbing reference to a Hitler quotation also references a comment early in the book, when the narrator draws a connection between her body

---

34 Wolf, *Leibhaftig*, 37.
35 Lennox, *Cemetery*, pp. 269–296.
36 Wolf, *Leibhaftig*, p. 124.
37 Jana Simon, *Sei dennoch unverzagt. Gespräche mit meinen Großeltern Christa und Gerhard Wolf* (Berlin: Ullstein, 2013), pp. 30–32.
38 Ibid., pp. 31–32.
39 Wolf *Leibhaftig*, p. 81.

and those of the concentration camp survivors she witnessed as her family fled west: 'Und sie geben auf, wenn es ihnen an allen Mineralstoffen fehlt. Musel-männer. Ohne Kalium [...] fühlt man sich wie eine Padde, die von einer Astgabel im Genick in den Staub gedrückt wird' [And they give up when their minerals are depleted. Mussulmen. Without potassium (...) you feel like a frog pressed into the dust by a forked stick against the back of the neck].[40] The narrator equates her experience to that of concentration camp survivors using the trope of the *Musel-mann* – an antiquated word for Muslim, derived from the Arabic term for Muslim, which eventually became derogatory and which, together with its cognates in several languages, emerged in the language of the concentration camps to name the most abject figures who had lost the ability or will to live, figured as between life and death, unable to control many bodily functions. As Alexander Weheliye explores, the uncritical use of *Muselmann* was popularized further via the work of Georgio Agamben, who employed the term to figure a biopolitics *be-yond* racism.[41] Wolf's use of the figure here conjures this history. The incorpora-tion of Jewish suffering into her family history and into her very body triggers the appropriation of the 'dark lady' Bachmann to construct both good-feeling and health for the narrator by enabling mourning and providing comfort.

Leibhaftig thus participates in a post-unification trend that is often discussed in film as 'heritage cinema' – which, in the German context, often seeks to depict a German-Jewish reconciliation in order to 'clear historical debts so as to open a path for a normal German future'.[42] In *Leibhaftig*, a recovered German-Jewish symbiosis depends on contact with the Bachmanns, from Ingeborg to Kora, ob-scuring the contingency of pain by covering up the ways in which whiteness in-forms the narrator's position. In the narrator's imagination, her body quite liter-ally becomes that of the survivor because of her ability to 'know' their pain. This act becomes manageable, liveable, by the incomplete incorporation of Dr. Leit-ner into the family, made possible by Kora Bachmann.[43] In this odd triangula-tion, Kora – whose sole role in the text is to heal the narrator – is evacuated

---

40 Ibid, p. 16. My translation.

41 Alexander G. Weheliye, *Habeas Viscus. Racializing Assemblages, Biopolitics, and Black Fem-inist Theories of the Human* (Durham, NC: Duke University Press, 2014), pp. 63–65.

42 Lutz Koepnick, '"Amerika gibt's überhaupt nicht". Notes on the German Heritage Film', in *German Pop Culture. How American' Is It?* (Ann Arbor: University of Michigan Press, 2004), pp. 191–208 (p. 193).

43 For reasons of brevity, I omitted a discussion of the complicated ways in which Jews of Euro-pean heritage in Germany and the United States have come to occupy whiteness, uneasily, un-comfortably. Such whiteness, however, does not explain the workings of racialized empathy in Wolf's texts.

of a personal biography or a location in any social relationship. Her darkness is reiterated throughout *Leibhaftig*; she is only marginally represented as more human than the undifferentiated colonized peoples with whom Wolf/Kassandra/Ingeborg Bachmann/Franza have allied themselves in the *Kassandra* project.

Ahmed's thoughts on the contingency of pain and the ethics of a response are helpful here:

> I want to suggest here, cautiously, and tentatively, that an ethics of responding to pain involves being open to being affected by that which one cannot know or feel. [...] The ethical demand is that I must act about that which I cannot know, rather than act insofar as I know. I am moved by what does not belong to me. If I acted on her behalf only insofar as I knew how she felt, then I would act only insofar as I would appropriate her pain as my pain.[44]

In *Leibhaftig,* the points of contact between the narrator and her various Others remain appropriative empathy.

From Kora to Angelina – The Transformation of Wolf's Flying Guides

The work of the figure of Angelina in *Stadt der Engel*, however, does something very different, pointing to the possibility of rejecting the appropriation of the experience of racialized others. Angelina serves as a figure around which all the unspoken issues of race at work in Wolf's oeuvre crystallize. *Stadt der Engel*, like *Kindheitsmuster,* relies on a semi-autobiographical narrator who relentlessly examines her complicity in a structure of violence: in *Kindheitsmuster,* as a youth firmly committed to the ideology of National Socialism; in *Stadt der Engel*, as a collaborator with the Stasi from 1959 to 1963 (indeed, it is difficult not to read *Leibhaftig* as performing a similar examination, this time probing the urge to punish herself for both such complicity and its forgetting). And yet there is something different in *Stadt der Engel* that more explicitly reveals Wolf's trouble with race, embodied in the figure of Angelina.

Any angel other than Benjamin's angel of modernity (who also makes an appearance in *Stadt der Engel*) strikes one as a strange apparition in Wolf's decidedly nonreligious contemporary worlds; even the gods mentioned in Wolf's Greek worlds are never created as actual characters in the text. Angelina reveals the limits of the speakable to be particularly about race, as partially delineated

---

44 Ahmed, *The Cultural Politics of Emotion*, pp. 30–31.

by the lack of language and vocabulary with which to name and think race. One might argue that the figure of the black woman serves as the kind of racialized 'Other' Anke Pinkert identifies in post-unification discourses, who enables a negotiation with the new relationship between East and West and reveals the un-worked-through histories of race and racism.[45] Yet racialized characters also mark a shift in how the limits of the speakable are expressed in or haunt Wolf's texts, revealing the limits of her ongoing project to both construct a specifically East German memory of Germans as perpetrators during the Second World War as well as to construct a female voice in response to what she sees as the inherent violence of Western masculine rationality. Whereas in her earlier texts, narrator figures often sought points of identification with racialized forms of victimhood through empathetic relationships with racialized others, in *Stadt der Engel*, alterity is both allowed to stand and to become visible as a consequence of a set of social relationships. In this transformed politics of emotion, Wolf's texts begin to reveal the deeply problematic politics of empathy with victims of imperialisms and German racism. Instead of an identification with such figures, a relationship is forged through which Angelina challenges, criticizes and denies healing to the narrator through the *failure* of identification.

Angelina first enters the narrative about one-third of the way into the text, in a realistic episode – as a Ugandan immigrant working for the cleaning service at the hotel where the narrator has been placed for the duration of her fellowship at the Getty Museum in Los Angeles. On a hot day, the narrator offers the cleaning staff something to drink; Angelina, however, feels uncomfortable and refuses to join the narrator at her table.[46] Unusually for this text, Angelina's body is described in great detail. One recalls Wolf's third *Kassandra* lecture: 'Das Objektmachen: Ist es nicht die Hauptquelle von Gewalt?' [As for turning things into objects, isn't that the principal source of violence?].[47]

Angelina disappears from the text until the narrator attends a service at the First African Methodist Episcopal Church, the oldest African American congregation in Los Angeles, where her group of friends are the only white people in a group of 400. The narrator insists that this does not make her uncomfortable – she merely does not know how to act as the object of scrutiny as a white woman.[48] At this moment, the same observing eye that the narrator trained on

45 Pinkert, Anke. '"Postcolonial Legacies". The Rhetoric of Race in the East/West German National Identity Debate of the Late 1990s', *The Journal of the Midwest Modern Language Association*, 352 (2002), 13–32.
46 Wolf, *Stadt der Engel*, p. 164.
47 Wolf, *Kassandra*, p. 146.
48 Wolf, *Stadt der Engel*, p. 322.

Angelina much earlier on in the text is now imagined to be trained on her. The narrator quickly brushes away her sense of inhabiting whiteness, however, focusing instead on difference in faith as the more powerful caesura between the religious group and the deeply atheist narrator. Even this feeling of difference slips away quickly after the service, when they are greeted by the congregation: 'Zuerst umarmten uns unsere unmittelbaren Nachbarn, dann kamen entfernter Sitzende, sie standen in einer kleinen Schlange, ich spürte viele schwarze Wangen an meiner Wange, hörte viele Stimmen welcome sagen, ich begann zu lächeln, zu lachen, mich wohl zu fühlen' [First the people right next to us hugged us, then people sitting farther away came up and stood in a short line, I felt lots of black cheeks on my cheek, heard a lot of voices say Welcome, and I started to smile, to laugh, to feel good.]⁴⁹

This experience is notable within the text. There are many meaningful interactions with friends, with Holocaust survivor groups and refugee communities, and various encounters with scholars. Nevertheless, this moment at the church is unique, both due to the actual physical touch and because the narrator begins to feel 'wohl' [good]. For much of the text she is suffering from tremendous physical pain as well as psychological distress, both linked throughout the text to her sense of loss as a result of unification, betrayal upon finding out the extent to which she had been spied upon by friends, self-betrayal upon discovering the documentation of her own meetings with the Stasi as an IM in the 1950s and of course the relentless wave of criticism that began even before the discovery of the Stasi files. 'Wohl' as well-being – being-well. Not happy, or healthy, but able – for at least a moment – to be well.

This encounter could potentially stand as a deeply problematic construction of positive affect that locates the source of healing and trauma in the encounter with a group targeted by a racism that is, for the narrator, distanced. Stuart Taberner comes to a similar conclusion when he argues that Wolf has constructed an ethics of affective cosmopolitism that relies on assumptions of the knowability of the other.⁵⁰ A closer look at Angelina complicates such a reading, however. Angelina re-enters the text as a gently mocking figure who will incompletely serve as a corrective, highlighting the problem of this healing identification even as she shies free of identifying the narrator's embeddedness in a larger structure of whiteness. In short, Angelina will trouble Wolf's trouble and, in doing so, will make whiteness more visible even though it is not explicitly named.

---

49 Ibid.
50 Stuart Taberner, 'Memory, Cosmopolitanism and Nation. Christa Wolf's *Stadt der Engel* (2010) and JM Coetzee's *Disgrace* (1999)', *Comparative Critical Studies*, 11.1 (2014), 49–67 (p. 50).

Lost in memories of her last communion fifty years ago, at her own confirmation, the narrator finds herself being chided by Angelina, as an angel, immediately after the church service. Upon the narrator's demand for security in order to remember the feeling of joy, Angelina merely disappears rather than responds.[51] Later, she accompanies the narrator regularly during her last weeks in Los Angeles, and the narrator offers sympathy to Angelina as one of the cast-off 'dark angels'. Angelina responds with an obscene gesture. The narrator's condescending sympathy for Angelina, which began already with that proffered drink in the kitchen when they first met, is constantly rejected, undermined and thwarted, as are her demands that Angelina provide her with some sort of ongoing good-feeling. Even when she becomes sick, Angelina the angel denies her sympathy and watches her mockingly, although Angelina the housekeeper brings her tea and asks if she should call a doctor.[52]

Angelina continues to deny the narrator good-being/good-feeling during the narrator's experience in the American Southwest, where the narrator invites Angelina's validation of various theories and thoughts that would allow her to appropriate Native cultures for her own feeling-good. The narrator's first hope for transformation lies in her tour through the Canyon de Chelly, immediately after having been disappointed on her quest for the remains of matriarchy. Among the gorgeous views experienced at sunset and moonrise, she feels that something fundamental has transformed in her – that she is finally free. Angelina's response is: 'Ja was denn sonst' [Of course! What else would you be?][53] Angelina's laconic response undercuts the narrator's simplistic appropriation of Navajo culture as well as of the very landscape in which it is embedded. When the narrator tries again to establish some sort of connection inspired by her new 'knowledge', this time by wondering whether the Anasazi were 'more human' than today's rich whites, Angelina 'hielt auch nichts von Schuldgefühlen, sie war der Meinung, die würden einen nur daran hindern, drauflos zu leben und dabei Freude zu haben und, egal, was wir uns aus der Vergangenheit vorzuwerfen hätten, frischweg das zu tun, was heute nötig sei' [she considered guilt feelings worthless – in her view, they only kept you from being happy and living your life and going ahead and doing whatever was necessary today irrespective of what we have to reproach ourselves for in the past].[54] The angel, the narrator concludes, is far too simple to adequately apprehend the

---

51 Wolf, *Stadt der Engel*, p. 326.
52 Ibid., p. 334.
53 Ibid., pp. 383–384. I am using my own translation, since the official English translation of the text underplays this phrase.
54 Ibid., p. 388.

complicated psyche of modern humankind. The narrator sets up a grand theory for herself in her dreams about how 'wenn man tief genug hinabsinken lasse, verschwänden die Unterschiede zwischen den Menschen und Völkern' [when you go deep enough down the differences between people and between peoples disappear], then looks to Angelina for confirmation. Angelina remains silent.[55]

As the Southwest tour continues, the narrator seeks comfort in learning about and from the Hopi and the Navajo, expressed internally as hope and *Schadenfreude* that the 'West' has been unable to access 'das innere Geheimnis dieser in ihren Augen primitive Kultur' [the inner secret of, in their view, a primitive civilization].[56] The narrator's language here echoes the gendered appropriation of colonized peoples and their perceived connection to 'mystery' that was set up in the *Kassandra* lecture on Ingeborg Bachmann. This comparison of the experience of imperialism is no longer allowed to stand as essentially equivalent to women's experience – that lost matriarchy which the tour refuses to provide for the narrator – nor as equivalent. This also contradicts the equation of the experience of Native peoples with that of East Germans that was set up early in the book, when the narrator refers briefly to the 'colonization' of East Germans.[57]

Throughout this sequence of events, the narrator herself never acknowledges the workings of whiteness; it is primarily the narrative and the figure of Angelina that allow whiteness to become visible through Angelina's rejection of empathy. The distinction is particularly relevant when the narrator describes her prohibition from attending Hopi ceremonies as the first time she's experienced exclusion because of her skin colour. It is not her skin colour that has excluded her, of course, but her non-membership in a community which has been constantly subjected to an ethnographic gaze that appropriates other cultures in the interest of Western subject constitution – a gaze literalized in *Stadt der Engel* by the use of cameras against the wishes of the Hopi.

The Possibility of Fellow-Feelings

It is the impossibility, then, of 'empathy' between the narrator and Angelina, Ruth, the Hopi or the Navajo that points to a different possible cultural politics of emotion that remains unfulfilled within the novel. A political coalition would be rooted in the impossibility of sharing pain across racialized barriers – a pol-

---

55 Ibid., p. 398.
56 Ibid., p. 396. My translation.
57 Ibid., p. 16.

itics of coalition rooted not in a sense of 'I feel as if I am you', but 'I shall try to hear you, and I know that your pain is not mine'. Ahmed suggests that:

> The call of such pain, as a pain that cannot be shared through empathy, is a call not just for an attentive hearing, but for a different kind of inhabitance. It is a call for action, and a demand for collective politics, as a politics based not on the possibility that we might be reconciled, but on learning to live with the impossibility of reconciliation, or learning that we live with and beside each other, and yet we are not as one.[58]

Stadt der Engel never achieves an imagination of such a collective politics, but it does point to their necessity by marking the necessity of troubling race and a politics of empathy in the face of racialization. Unlike in *Leibhaftig*, the narrator's body in pain will not become a source of knowing the racialized other. Nor will a politics of feeling-good through contact with the other succeed.

It requires a particular practice of reading with the insights offered by critical ethnic studies to take the troubling a step further. If we return to the encounter in the church, for example, the moment of contact is a moment laden with possibility. That possibility lies not merely in the contact itself, which always contains the possibility of reinscribing violence. Rather, a practice of reading this encounter to attend to the workings of whiteness would require, in Ahmed's words, that the reader 'respond to injustice in a way that shows rather than erases the complexity of the relation between violence, power and emotion'.[59]

---

58 Ahmed, *The Cultural Politics*, p. 39; p. 41fn 9.
59 Ibid., 196.

Catherine Smale

Towards a Late Style? Christa Wolf on Old Age, Death and Creativity in *Stadt der Engel oder The Overcoat of Dr. Freud*

'Ich denke viel an den Tod, und es ist mir fast jeden Tag bewusst, dass die Frist, die mir noch bleibt, kurz ist. Während des Schreibens habe ich manchmal gedacht: Na, das werden sie mich vielleicht noch zu Ende schreiben lassen.' [I think a lot about death, and almost every day I am conscious that the amount of time I have left is short. As I've been writing, I've sometimes thought: Well then, perhaps they'll just about let me finish writing this.][1] These words are taken from an interview with the 81-year-old Christa Wolf, published in the German news magazine *Der Spiegel* in 2010. Wolf discusses the process of writing her final novel, *Stadt der Engel oder The Overcoat of Dr. Freud*, which was published that same year and hailed by some reviewers as an 'Alterswerk' – a work of old-age or late style.[2] In this passage, Wolf alludes to her experiences of aging and life-threatening illness as she was writing the novel, which led her to become acutely aware of her own mortality: she realizes that each day could be her last, yet she is determined to finish writing before her time runs out. Similar references to her sense of imminent death occur in Wolf's posthumously published life-writing project *Ein Tag im Jahr im neuen Jahrhundert*, particularly in the diary-like entries dating from around 2004 onwards: she describes how the thought of death 'unterfüttert fast jede Stunde' [underpins almost every hour][3] and often wonders how much time she has left in this life: 'Wie lange noch?' [How much longer?].[4] These frequent references to death raise questions about how one might read *Stadt der Engel* as a 'late work'. Does Wolf develop a self-consciously 'late' style in anticipation of her death? And if so, how does this manifest itself in her novel? How does her conceptualization of herself as 'writ-

---

1 Volker Hage and Susanne Beyer, 'Wir haben dieses Land geliebt. Interview mit Christa Wolf', *Der Spiegel*, 14 June 2010, pp. 134–138 (http://www.spiegel.de/spiegel/print/d-70940417.html). My translation.
2 See, for example, Joachim Güntner, 'Weich abgefederte Selbstbefragung. *Stadt der Engel oder The Overcoat of Dr. Freud* – Christa Wolfs kalifornisches Räsonnement', *Neue Zürcher Zeitung*, 22 June 2010 (http://www.nzz.ch/weich-abgefederte-selbstbefragung-1.6201888).
3 Christa Wolf, *Ein Tag im Jahr im neuen Jahrhundert*, ed. by Gerhard Wolf (Berlin: Suhrkamp, 2013), p. 143. My translation.
4 Ibid., p. 106.

https://doi.org/10.1515/9783110496000-012

ing in the proximity of death'[5] relate to broader concerns about societal and epochal belatedness in the twenty-first century? And in what ways might an analysis of Wolf's specific approach to lateness enable new light to be shed on the
concept of late style per se?

In this chapter, I address these questions by focusing on the depiction of
lateness and death in *Stadt der Engel*. Drawing both on Edward Said's influential
writings on late style and on Walter Benjamin's 1936 essay 'Der Erzähler. Betrachtungen zum Werk Nikolai Leskows' ['The Storyteller. Reflections on the
Works of Nikolai Leskov'], I demonstrate how the prospect of the narrator's
death operates as both a thematic and a structuring principle in Wolf's novel.
I suggest that her engagement with the imminence of the narrator's death evokes
a future anterior tense – a sense of 'this will have been' – which highlights the
transitoriness of the present and raises questions about the post-mortem legacy
of the writer and her work.[6] In doing so, I move away from Said's understanding
of an artist's late style as a gesture of leave-taking, an indication of the subject's
impotence in the face of death. Instead, I develop an alternative understanding
of the concept, inflected by Benjamin's conception of *Erzählen* [narrating or
storytelling] as an art form which situates the subjective experiences of an individual amongst those of past and future generations, transmitting these experiences beyond that individual's immediate death.[7] I argue that, for Wolf, the imminence of death paradoxically lends greater legitimacy to her work, lifting it out
of the sphere of the purely personal and into the realm of shared historical experience.

Stadt der Engel oder the Overcoat of Dr. Freud is a loosely autobiographical
novel which recounts a research visit to Los Angeles undertaken by the author in

---

5 Here, and elsewhere in the chapter, I use the term coined by Gordon McMullan in *Shakespeare
and the Idea of Late Writing. Authorship in the Proximity of Death* (Cambridge: CUP, 2007). Wolf
also frequently refers to her experience of writing 'in Todesnähe' [in the proximity of death].
6 Here and throughout this chapter, I regard the Wolf-like narrator in *Stadt der Engel* as an autobiographical persona, through which Wolf explores the different faces of her public role as a
writer, the elusiveness of the self and the relationship between writing and historical experience.
In this respect, I follow Dennis Tate's observation that, time and again, we see the same autobiographical narrator in Wolf's oeuvre. See Dennis Tate, *Shifting Perspectives. East German Autobiographical Narratives Before and After the End of the GDR* (Rochester, NY: Camden House,
2007), pp. 226–227.
7 Walter Benjamin, 'Der Erzähler. Betrachtungen zum Werk Nicolai Lesskows', in *Gesammelte
Schriften*, ed. by Rolf Tiedemann and Hermann Schweppenhäuser (Frankfurt a. M.: Suhrkamp,
1977), vol. 2, pp. 438–465. All translations are taken from Walter Benjamin, 'The Storyteller',
in *Selected Writings*, ed. by Howard Eiland and Michael W. Jennings (Cambridge, MA: Belknap,
1999–2004), vol. 3, pp. 143–166.

1992–1993.[8] During that time, the news of Wolf's Stasi involvement broke in the German press, and she consequently experienced a reactive period of severe depression.[9] The narrative operates on several different temporal levels, interweaving memories of the narrator's time in the USA with references to her present, roughly fifteen years later, and details from her childhood and her adult life, commenting as it does so on the complex workings of memory.[10] The novel has therefore been regarded as an intertext to Wolf's earlier autobiographical work *Kindheitsmuster* (1976), because it continues that text's process of personal scrutiny and incisive self-reckoning.[11] Like *Kindheitsmuster*, *Stadt der Engel* is clearly influenced by Walter Benjamin's writings on the philosophy of history. The angel in the title alludes in part to Benjamin's 'Angelus Novus' figure, while the novel is prefaced by a citation from his essay fragment 'Ausgraben und Erinnern' ['Excavating and Remembering'] (1932) and contains references to his essay 'Über den Begriff der Geschichte' ['Theses on the Philosophy of History'] (1940). Benjamin also features in the text in the guise of the unnamed phi-

---

8 Wolf later claimed that the designation 'Roman' [novel] was 'smuggled in' by the publisher without her permission. She noted that she nevertheless found this genre designation appropriate, despite the clear biographical resonances which the novel contains. See Carsten Gansel and Christa Wolf, 'Zum Schreiben haben mich Konflikte getrieben. Ein Gespräch', in *Christa Wolf. Im Strom der Erinnerung*, ed. by Carsten Gansel with Sonja Klocke (Göttingen: Vandenhoeck and Ruprecht, 2014), pp. 353–366 (p. 353). This strategy of fictionalization based on her own life experiences is not unusual in Wolf's writing and is linked to her concept of 'subjective authenticity'. See Tate, *Shifting Perspectives*, pp. 194–236.
9 Kaleen Gallagher describes this as a 'crisis of shame'. See Kaleen Gallagher, 'The Problem of Shame in Christa Wolf's *Stadt der Engel oder The Overcoat of Dr. Freud*', *German Life and Letters*, 65 (2012), 378–397. Anna Kuhn reads the narrator's crisis as form of psychic trauma from which she gradually recovers. See Anna Kuhn, 'Of Trauma, Angels and Healing. Christa Wolf's *Stadt der Engel oder The Overcoat of Dr. Freud*', *Gegenwartsliteratur*, 10 (2011), 164–185.
10 On the depiction of memory in the novel, see Franziska Bomski, '"Moskauer Adreßbuch". Erinnerung und Engagement in Christa Wolfs *Stadt der Engel oder The Overcoat of Dr. Freud*', in Gansel with Klocke, pp. 257–282; Daniela Colombo, '"Die Zeitgeschichten, durch die ich gegangen bin". Christa Wolf in ihren autobiografischen Texten *Kindheitsmuster* und *Stadt der Engel oder The Overcoat of Dr. Freud*', in *"Die Mauer wurde nebenbei eingerissen". Zur Literatur in Deutschland und Mittelosteuropa nach 1989/90*, ed. by Stephan Krause and Friederike Partzsch (Berlin: Frank and Timme, 2012), pp. 195–202; Peter Paul Schwarz and Sebastian Wilde, '"Und doch und doch...". Transformationen des Utopischen in Christa Wolfs *Stadt der Engel oder The Overcoat of Dr. Freud*', in Gansel with Klocke, pp. 231–244.
11 Gallagher, 'The Problem of Shame', p. 379. See also Michael Haase, 'Christa Wolfs letzter Selbstversuch. Zum Konzept der subjektiven Authentizität in *Stadt der Engel oder The Overcoat of Dr. Freud*', in Gansel with Klocke, pp. 215–231 (p. 217); and Michael Minden, 'Social Hope and the Nightmare of History. Christa Wolf 's *Kindheitsmuster* and *Stadt der Engel*', *Publications of the English Goethe Society*, 80 (2011), 196–203 (p. 196).

losopher whom the protagonist's friend, Peter Gutman, is researching, and many of the metaphors Wolf uses to depict the workings of memory can also be found in Benjamin's work (including archaeological layers, vortices, and blind spots).[12] Wolf's engagement with Benjamin in her fictional autobiographies not only reveals what Aija Sakova-Merivee terms her concern with a '[personally] experienced past versus official historiography',[13] it also highlights her preoccupation with questions of historical relations, utopian thinking and – in *Stadt der Engel* – with the possibility of messianic redemption.[14]

On Late Style

The concept of late style is perhaps most famously set out in Edward Said's posthumously published study, *On Late Style. Music and Literature Against the Grain* (2006). Influenced by the philosophers of the Frankfurt School, and in particular by Theodor Adorno's unfinished essays on late Beethoven, Said identifies an apparent 'relationship between bodily condition and aesthetic style'.[15] There is, he suggests, a widespread assumption that the passage of human life – and aesthetic reflections of this – are characterized by 'a general abiding *timeliness*',[16] a perception that there are certain behaviours, beliefs and aesthetic styles that are appropriate to particular times of life and to particular historical times. Thus, it is commonly assumed that late works, 'produced in the last or late period of life', come to 'reflect a special maturity, a new spirit of reconciliation and serenity',

---

12 Sabine Wilke has analysed the Benjaminian conception of history in *Kindheitsmuster*. See Wilke, *Ausgraben und Erinnern. Zur Funktion der Geschichte, Subjekt und geschlechtlicher Identität in den Texten Christa Wolfs* (Würzburg: Königshausen and Neumann, 1993). On the significance of the epigraph to *Stadt der Engel*, see Aija Sakova-Merivee, 'Die Ausgrabung der Vergangenheit in *Stadt der Engel oder The Overcoat of Dr. Freud*', in Gansel with Klocke, pp. 245–256.
13 Sakova-Merivee, 'Die Ausgrabung der Vergangenheit', p. 248.
14 To date, relatively little attention has been paid to Wolf's engagement with the religious strand in Benjamin's thought. In fact, Sabine Wilke suggests that, in *Kindheitsmuster*, Wolf's materialist thinking leads her to reject Benjamin's messianism in favour of a reworking of his dialectical historiography. See Sabine Wilke, '"Dieser fatale Hang der Geschichte zu Wiederholungen". Geschichtskonstruktionen in Christa Wolfs *Kindheitsmuster*', *German Studies Review*, 13.3 (1990), 499–512 (p. 510). However, *Stadt der Engel* is replete with religious imagery and references to salvation, paradise and the second coming, which, I suggest, prompt a reconsideration of Wolf's engagement with Benjamin's messianic conception of history and its political significance.
15 Edward W. Said, *On Late Style. Music and Literature Against the Grain* (London: Bloomsbury, 2006), p. 3.
16 Ibid., p. 5.

which corresponds to society's 'accepted notion of age and wisdom'.[17] What interests Said most, though, are late works which do not conform to this perceived norm – works characterized above all by 'intransigence, difficulty, and unresolved contradiction'.[18] These late works are often fundamentally *un*timely: they stand in a contradictory relationship to the condition of the artist and the period in which they were produced, establishing what Said terms a 'sort of deliberately unproductive productiveness going *against...*'.[19] For Said, then, late style can be regarded as 'a form of exile', which occurs when the artist 'abandons communication with the social order of which he is a part and achieves a contradictory, alienated relationship with it'.[20]

Stuart Taberner draws on Said's notion of 'deliberately unproductive productiveness' in his book *Aging and Old Age Style in Günter Grass, Ruth Klüger, Christa Wolf and Martin Walser*. Identifying what he describes as an 'old-age style' – an 'aesthetic mode that is willed, perhaps even wilful'[21] – he suggests that Wolf engages in a 'literary performance' of old age, which enables her to undertake 'a reediting of her lifelong commitment to the ideal of socialism that is both self-critical *and* reparative'.[22] Taberner's study usefully situates Wolf's late work in the context of a generation of writers, born in the mid-to-late 1920s, whose careers have, to some degree, become synonymous with the cultural politics of East and West German history in the twentieth century. However, Taberner bases his analysis on what I see as uncritical gender categories – concluding, for example, that the old-age style in the texts he addresses is characterized by 'self-monumentalization' in the case of male writers and 'self-healing' in the case of female authors; in this regard, he reasserts precisely the stereotypes of the late writer as an aging male genius that his study sets out to question.[23] Moreover, Taberner does not systematically differentiate between 'late style' and 'old-age

---

17 Ibid., p. 6.

18 Ibid., p. 7.

19 Ibid., p. 17.

20 Ibid., p. 8.

21 Stuart Taberner, *Aging and Old Age Style in Günter Grass, Ruth Klüger, Christa Wolf and Martin Walser* (Rochester, NY: Camden House, 2013), p. 25.

22 Ibid., p. 97.

23 Ibid., p. 99. By contrast, Karen Leeder argues that old-age and late style are best regarded as contingent and context-bound. See Karen Leeder, 'Figuring Lateness in Modern German Culture', *New German Critique*, 125 (2015), 1–29 (p. 8). A similar observation is made in Karen Painter, 'On Creativity and Lateness', in *Late Thoughts. Reflections on Artists and Composers at Work*, ed. by Karen Painter and Thomas Crow (Los Angeles: Getty Research Institute, 2006), pp. 1–11. On national specificities in critical conceptions of late style, see Ben Hutchinson, *Lateness and Modern European Literature* (Oxford: Oxford University Press, 2016), pp. 1–30.

style', consequently overlooking the political implications of late style which underpin Said's analysis.[24] Late style is not limited to old age and can, in fact, be produced by a writer *at any age*; it is a critical category most commonly imposed on a body of work in retrospect, after a writer's death, rather than something necessarily inherent in the work itself.[25] Indeed, death does not always appear explicitly as a theme in late works – as Said suggests, it frequently appears 'in refracted mode', as allegory, irony, anachronism or anomaly.[26] Following Adorno, Said argues that late works of art are characterised by a gesture of 'subjectivity [taking] leave of the work'; they are 'touched by death' and thus 'set free' from the 'masterly hand' that created them.[27] In this sense, artistic conventions undergo a kind of 'hollowing out', which leaves in its wake a trace of the subjective presence that fashioned them; the late work can thus be regarded as 'a mould created by the removal of subjectivity',[28] its form a 'memorializing' of the absent subject who created it.[29]

Inherent in this view of late style is a tension between what Said terms 'the idea of surviving beyond', the notion that there remain in the artistic work vestiges of subjectivity which can be recuperated for the future, and 'the idea that one cannot really go beyond lateness at all' – that there is, in fact, no possibility of transcendence, and that the project of recuperation is always doomed to fail.[30] Adorno's writings on late style, on which Said draws heavily, sought to move away from biographical criticism, focusing instead on the relationship between artistic form and historical processes; as such, his work resonates with Walter Benjamin's vestigial utopianism, the notion that artistic form itself contains

---

24 Taberner suggests that 'the author's performance of life review as old-age style may *become* late style once it generalizes individual biography to intervene itself in a collective sense of epochal lateness'; see Taberner, *Aging and Old Age Style*, p. 199. However, his focus on 'old-age' style as opposed to 'late' style situates his work in the field of literary gerontology, along with other studies, such as *Aging and Gender in Literature. Studies in Creativity*, ed. by Anne M. Wyatt-Brown and Janice Rossen (Charlottesville: University Press of Virginia, 1993); Kathleen Woodward, *Aging and Its Discontents. Freud and Other Fictions* (Bloomington: Indiana University Press, 1991); and Miriam Seidler, *Figurenmodelle des Alters in der deutschsprachigen Gegenwartsliteratur* (Tübingen: Narr, 2010).

25 On occasion, the term is used while an author is still alive, but in such cases, the work is read through the lens of the author's anticipated death, thus creating a future anterior perspective and imposing a sense of teleological order on his or her oeuvre.

26 Said, *On Late Style*, p. 24.

27 Theodor W. Adorno, *Essays on Music*, ed. by Richard Leppert (Berkeley: University of California Press, 2002), p. 566. Cited in Said, *On Late Style*, p. 9.

28 Hutchinson, *Lateness and Modern European Literature*, p. 258.

29 McMullan, *Shakespeare and the Idea of Late Style*, p. 41.

30 Said, *On Late Style*, p. 13.

traces or fragments of lost potential that can be retrieved and recuperated for the utopian project.[31] Viewed in this light, late works can be seen to gesture beyond the individual subject who created them towards the possibility of recuperating what has been lost or oppressed in the past. As Gordon McMullan observes in his recent study on lateness, this conception of late style can be regarded as an eschatology, a way of thinking about the place of the individual in relation to historical temporality and the concept of the end of days.[32] Since late style is characterized by the dissolution of the subject and is no longer underpinned by a biographical connection to the individual ego, it comes to symbolize the notion of historical lateness in a broader, epochal sense, signalling both a sense of belatedness, of coming after a key historical period or moment, and an anticipation of coming to the end of an era. The notion of historical lateness thus sustains two opposing temporalities: one consists of a retrospective connection to the past, to what has been, while the other is an anticipation of what will be – or rather, what will have been.

What makes Wolf's case so pertinent to this discussion of late style is her self-conscious thematization of her own exemplarity. This does not, in fact, mean that she regards herself as an idealized example to be followed, but rather that she understands her own life to have been influenced by patterns of historical configurations which she seeks to uncover and comprehend through her writing. As Anna Kuhn notes, Wolf's writing 'address[es] superindividual phenomena',[33] since it gives expression to the ways in which the experiences of those in her generation have been shaped by the social, political, and economic forces of the period.[34] This idea is expressed in the title of *Kindheitsmuster*, which was initially translated into English as *A Model Childhood* but subsequently altered to *Patterns of Childhood* when the translation was reprinted. The earlier title wrongly conveys exemplarity in the sense of the protagonist's childhood being worthy of imitation, as something which is laid down in advance for others to copy; the later one refers rather to the 'patterns of behaviour [which] become

---

31 Benjamin develops this train of thought in several of his works, but I have been particularly influenced here by his *Passagen-Werk* [*Arcades Project*] (1927–1940), his *Charles Baudelaire. Ein Lyriker im Zeitalter des Hochkapitalismus* (1939) and his essay 'Über den Begriff der Geschichte' ['Theses on the Philosophy of History'] (1940).

32 See McMullan, *Shakespeare and the Idea of Late Writing*, p. 42.

33 Anna Kuhn, *Christa Wolf's Utopian Vision. From Marxism to Feminism* (Cambridge: Cambridge University Press, 1988), p. 108.

34 Dennis Tate usefully situates Wolf's concern with the relationship between individual subjectivity and historical circumstances in the context of GDR debates about autobiographical practice and form. See Tate, *Shifting Perspectives*, pp. 194–236.

ingrained [...] in a child',[35] to the specific combination of circumstances which constitute a life and which can be perceived in retrospect through self-examination. This theme is taken up further in *Stadt der Engel* when the protagonist notes that she regards herself as an 'Exempel' [example][36] because she engages in the contradictory movement of focusing in on herself while also moving beyond herself to examine the general historical circumstances which have determined the pattern of her life. In this text, the narrator's exemplarity is evident above all in her awareness that her own personal old age coincides with the end of the GDR, the fall of Communism, and what Francis Fukuyama famously – if inaccurately – termed 'the end of history'.[37] Her physical deterioration, evidenced by her painful joints and difficulty in walking, appears as a symptom not only of her individual senescence, but also as a manifestation of a broader epochal decline. She comments repeatedly on her perception that she is living in an 'Endzeit' [end times],[38] a term which conveys both the approaching end of civilization and an anticipation of redemptive, messianic visitation. Above all, the prospect of the narrator's imminent death, which is referenced frequently in the novel, thus connects the personal with the historical, raising questions about what will happen to the traces of both her subjective experience and her utopian vision once she has 'taken leave' of her works.

Writing in the Proximity of Death

Towards the end of *Kindheitsmuster*, the narrator reflects on the fact that the death of Hitler, and the perceived 'end of the world' which it represented, marked a significant caesura for her and her generation:

> Das Ende der Welt mußte nicht den eigenen Tod bedeuten. Sie lebte. Das war sicherlich unwürdig, doch auch interessant. Entschieden aber war noch lange nicht, ob sie durch Melancholie [...] sich selbst zerstören oder ob es ihr gelingen würde, die verkümmerte Fähigkeit, Erfahrungen zutreffend zu deuten, zu entwickeln und zu überleben.

---

35 Kuhn, *Christa Wolf's Utopian Vision*, p. 108.
36 Christa Wolf, *Stadt der Engel oder The Overcoat of Dr. Freud* (Berlin: Suhrkamp, 2010), p. 356. Most of the translations are taken from Christa Wolf, *City of Angels. Or, The Overcoat of Dr. Freud*, trans. by Damion Searls (New York: Farrar, Straus and Giroux, 2013). However, where indicated, I have used my own translations because the published translation does not convey the full sense of the German original.
37 See Francis Fukuyama, *The End of History and the Last Man* (New York: Avon Books, 1992).
38 Wolf, *Stadt der Engel*, p. 125.

[The end of the world didn't mean one's own death. She was alive. It was surely shameful, but also interesting. But it wouldn't be decided for a long time whether she would destroy herself with depression (...) or if she would succeed in developing her atrophied faculties to interpret experience properly and survive.][39]

Here, the narrator makes an important distinction between 'leben' [living] and 'überleben' [surviving or, literally, living beyond]. She has remained alive despite having experienced what she perceives to be an apocalypse; now she must try to ensure that she lives beyond this by developing the ability to analyse and interpret her experiences in the light of new value systems and beliefs. In *Stadt der Engel*, the narrator explicitly links the capacity to survive and live beyond seemingly catastrophic events with the very act of narrating: 'Ohne die wohltätige Gabe des Erzählens [hätten wir] nicht überlebt und nicht überleben können' [Without the benevolent gift of storytelling, we would not have survived and would not be able to survive].[40] More specifically, it is its capacity to penetrate different temporal layers, looking both forwards and back,[41] that makes the act of narrating so crucial for the survival of the self; past events can be recalled and worked through in the present, in anticipation of the future. The writer engages in a 'Selbstversuch' [self-experiment], an intensive process of 'sich selbst kennenlernen, bis auf den Grund' [getting to know oneself down to the bottom],[42] while the prospect of ending this process is likened to the 'Abbruch einer lebenserhaltenden Therapie bei einer schweren Krankheit' [stopping a life-sustaining treatment in the course of a serious illness].[43]

Like the narrator of *Kindheitsmuster*, the protagonist of *Stadt der Engel* is conscious of the fact that she has outlived her country; she travels to the US with the passport of an obsolete state[44] and becomes the object of curiosity at the Getty Institute precisely because she comes from a country that has ceased to exist.[45] However, while the narrator of *Kindheitsmuster* is still an adolescent when she experiences epochal transition, the protagonist of *Stadt der Engel* is conscious that she is entering old age: 'Ich wußte nun, daß ich sterben mußte. Ich wußte, wie gebrechlich wir sind. Das Alter begann' [Now I knew

---

39 Christa Wolf, *Kindheitsmuster* (Berlin: Aufbau, 1976), p. 418. The translation is taken from Christa Wolf, *Patterns of Childhood*, trans. by Ursule Molinaro and Hedwig Rappolt (New York: Farrar, Straus and Giroux, 1980).
40 Wolf, *Stadt der Engel*, p. 13. My translation.
41 Ibid. My translation.
42 Ibid. My translation.
43 Ibid., p. 233. My translation.
44 Ibid., p. 10.
45 Ibid., p. 15.

that I had to die. I knew how fragile we are. Old age began].[46] Whereas the protagonist of *Kindheitsmuster* has the bulk of her life still ahead of her, that of *Stadt der Engel* perceives herself existing in a liminal position between a past which is 'versunken' [sunk] and a future which does not concern her.[47] This position of liminality seems to resonate with Said's description of the late artist as an anachronistic figure who is no longer fully part of the time in which he or she lives. However, for the protagonist, this liminality is experienced as something entirely unproductive: her perception of reality becomes increasingly fragmented as she no longer has the possibility of situating her past experiences in the context of a narrative which connects them to an envisaged future for herself.[48] And, although she tries to cling to the project of writing despite her awareness that she is moving into the final phase of her life, she experiences resistance and long periods of writer's block, which threaten to destabilize her existence.[49]

Right from the outset of the novel, Wolf highlights the protagonist's experience of aging through the retrospective temporal perspective of the narrative. In an entry in *Ein Tag im Jahr im neuen Jahrhundert* dating from 2008, when Wolf was working on the manuscript of *Stadt der Engel*, she describes her own eightieth birthday as the 'Grenze zwischen Alter und Todesnähe' [boundary between old age and proximity to death].[50] Thoughts of death, she writes, are now a constant presence in her life, as is the 'Bewußtsein, daß die Jahre jetzt auf ihn zulaufen' [awareness that the years are now running towards it].[51] This position of proximity to death also shapes the outlook of the narrating voice in *Stadt der Engel*. The narrator frequently looks back on her younger self in Los Angeles and comments on how she has changed in the intervening time period, and as she does so, her awareness of death's presence becomes increasingly apparent. Early in the novel, for example, she reports a conversation with a friend about the possibility of life after death:

> Ohne Übergang fragte sie mich: Was denkst du über den Tod. [...] Ob der Tod wirklich das Ende von allem sei, wollte sie wissen. Ob ich das glaube. Ja, sagte ich, erinnere ich mich, leichtfertiger, als ich es heute sagen würde. Das glaube ich, aber es bekümmere mich nicht. Noch nicht, dachte ich damals, aus dem 'Noch nicht' ist inzwischen ein 'Jetzt' geworden.

---

46 Ibid., p. 335.
47 Ibid., p. 367.
48 Ibid.
49 Ibid., p. 107.
50 Wolf, *Ein Tag im Jahr im neuen Jahrhundert*, p. 128.
51 Ibid., p. 131.

[Without explaining the connection, she asked me: What do you think about death? (...) She wanted to know if death was really the end of everything, if that's what I believed. I do, I said, I remember, more flippantly than I would say it today. I do believe that but it doesn't bother me. Not yet, I thought at the time, and that 'not yet' has since turned into a 'now'.][52]

For the narrator, what was once the future has now become the present; she has become conscious of the prospect of death in a way that her past self did not envisage. Gradually, this sense of impending death also comes to influence the protagonist in the narrated level of the text, as she becomes aware that her narrative project offers her the only possible means of recording and communicating her thoughts and feelings in the face of her death: 'Ist dir eigentlich klar, daß der ganze Inhalt deines Kopfes verlorengeht, wenn du stirbst? [...] Außer dem, was du aufgeschrieben hast' [Do you realize that everything in your head will disappear when you die? (...) Except for what you've written down].[53]

Two-thirds of the way through the text, the narrator explicitly links the prospect of her own death with the potential completion of her narrative project:

Ich spüre einen Sog vom Ende her, ich muß mich dagegen stemmen und noch bisher Verschwiegenes oder jedenfalls nicht Erwähntes in mir aufsteigen lassen und zu Papier bringen. ‚Sog vom Ende her'. Jetzt erst bemerke ich den Doppelsinn dieser Metapher, lasse sie aber stehen, obwohl – oder weil – sie auch in ihrem zweiten Sinn, dem Sog auf das Lebensende, nicht nur auf das Ende dieses Textes hin, zutrifft.

[I feel a pull from the end and have to brace myself against it, have to let things I have kept my silence about until now, or at least haven't mentioned yet, rise up in me and have to put them down on paper. 'A pull from the end': only now do I notice the double meaning of this metaphor, but I let it stand, even though – or because – it applies in both senses. The pull from the end of life, and not just from the end of this book.][54]

The double meaning of the term 'a pull from the end' only becomes apparent to the aging narrator, not to her younger self; it refers both to a pull towards the end of her text – conveying, as Michael Minden observes, 'a post-modern self-referentiality, as if the text is developed purely to complete itself'[55] – and to a pull towards her own death. By resisting the pull of textual completion, by conjuring up everything that she has not yet said in order to put it to paper, the protagonist is also, by implication, resisting the onset of her death. Her anticipation of death is thus ambivalent: while, on the one hand, it appears as a looming threat to the

---

52 Ibid., p. 109.
53 Ibid., p. 410.
54 Ibid., p. 309.
55 Minden, 'Social Hope', p. 202.

protagonist, it also lends impetus to her creative endeavour, enabling her to engage more productively with her literary project in anticipation of its final closure.

This connection between narrative and death resonates with some of the claims made by Walter Benjamin in his essay 'Der Erzähler'. For Benjamin, the 'Erzähler' [narrator or storyteller] is someone who 'nimmt, was er erzählt, aus der Erfahrung' [takes what he tells from experience] and 'macht es wiederum zur Erfahrung derer, die seiner Geschichte zuhören' [in turn makes it the experience of those who are listening to his tale].[56] Benjamin refers here to the communicability of experience from the individual to the collective via the medium of storytelling. He then goes on to highlight death as one of the main sources of legitimation for the storyteller's authority: 'Nun ist es aber an dem, daß nicht etwa nur das Wissen oder die Weisheit des Menschen [sic] sondern vor allem sein gelebtes Leben – und das ist der Stoff, aus dem die Geschichten werden – tradierbare Form am ersten am Sterbenden annimmt' [Characteristically, it is not only a man's knowledge or wisdom, but above all his real life – and this is the stuff that stories are made of – which first assumes transmissible form at the moment of his death].[57] According to Benjamin, the proximity of death instigates in the dying person a succession of images which reveal new perspectives on his life, and it is precisely this pre-mortem moment of insight that renders the experiences of his life transmissible to others.[58] As a result, death is 'die Sanktion von allem, was der Erzähler berichten kann. Vom Tode hat er seine Autorität geliehen' [the sanction for everything that the storyteller can tell. He has borrowed his authority from death].[59] However, as Peter Brooks notes, Benjamin's argument also highlights a fundamental paradox: namely, that while death creates the very possibility of narrative by rendering communicable on an imaginative level the experiences of an individual's life, it also signals the end of narration, since death is the ultimate 'nonnarratability'.[60] On the one hand, an individual's experiences are communicated to others by means of a narrative which survives beyond his or her own death. On the other hand, though, the moment of death marks the conclusion of the individual's life and the end of the very possibility of narrating. Narrative thus gains legitimacy

56 Benjamin, 'Der Erzähler', p. 439.
57 Ibid., p. 449.
58 I am keeping to the masculine grammatical form used by Benjamin, although it should be noted that, both here and in Benjamin's essay, the dying person can be male or female.
59 Ibid., p. 450.
60 Peter Brooks, *Reading for the Plot. Design and Intention in the Narrative* (New York: Vintage, 1985), pp. 107–108.

through its relation to death, but it also becomes an attempt to forestall the clo-sure brought about by death. Marked by an impulse like that of the Freudian Death Drive, it tries to resist its end point while also being pulled inexorably to-wards it.

In Wolf's case, the death in question is, in fact, that of the narrator herself, who appears to borrow her authority from her own impending death; at this point her life *will have achieved* a form that is transmissible to the reader. There is an implied future anterior tense here, like that evoked in much of Ben-jamin's work on historical materialism: the past is understood to contain latent meaning that can only be recognized at some point in the future. In Wolf's case, the narrator, quoting her younger self, comments on the apparently revelatory perspective ['Aufklärung'] offered by her old age: 'WIE VOM ENDE HER ALLES SICH AUFKLÄRT. WIE MAN, WENN MAN MITTEN DRIN STECKT, DURCH KEINE ANSTRENGUNG DAS MUSTER ERKENNEN KANN, DAS UNTER DEN ER-SCHEINUNGEN ARBEITET' [How everything is revealed as if in hindsight. How there is no way, no effort you can make, to see the pattern that underlies the ap-pearances when you are stuck in the middle of it].[61] However, the life which she looks back on does not appear to her as a coherent, readily transmissible whole, like that accessible to Benjamin's 'Erzähler'; rather, it seems to be a 'patchwork life', with individual pieces 'sloppily stitched together'.[62] The image of scraps of cloth being pieced together in a rather haphazard way might recall the figure of the ragpicker in Walter Benjamin's *Passagen-Werk* [*Arcades Project*] (1927–1940), whose impulse is to recover remnants from the past and find unexpected uses for what has been left behind. As someone who collects and pieces together what has been left behind, the ragpicker becomes a metaphor for the poet – an outcast figure who 'recuperate[s] the fleeting images of modernity' and 'recycle[s] the lin-guistic scraps, the forgotten, the unnoticed, the leavings of modern society'.[63] The image is also fitting as a metaphor for Wolf's narrative practice in *Stadt der Engel*: recalling fragmentary memories and piecing together scraps from her notebooks and journals, she attempts to construct a transmissible 'patch-work' narrative, one which reflects the contradictions, illusions and missed op-portunities in her past experiences.

---

61 Wolf, *Stadt der Engel*, p.121. My translation.
62 Ibid., p. 367.
63 Carlo Salzani, *Constellations of Reading. Walter Benjamin in Figures of Actuality* (Bern: Peter Lang, 2009), p. 192.

Utopian Visions

Wolf creates this 'patchwork' effect in part by disrupting linear temporality in her narrative, juxtaposing the narrator's memories with dream-like visions and reflections on what might have happened had historical circumstances been different. Towards the middle of the novel, the protagonist engages in one of many conversations with her friend, Peter Gutman. Recalling her family's flight from the Red Army in 1945, she sets out a series of seemingly insignificant events which, if altered, would have meant that she would have ended up living in the West:

> Es war um Stunden gegangen: Wären die Pferde nicht so ausgepumpt gewesen, daß sie selbst durch Peitschenhiebe nicht mehr anzutreiben waren – ich hätte ein vollkommen anderes Leben gelebt. Ich wäre ein anderer Mensch geworden. So war das damals in Deutschland, ein Zufall hatte dich in der Hand.
>
> [It came down to a couple of hours: if the horses hadn't been so worn out that even blows of the whip couldn't get them to move any faster – I would have lived a completely different life. I would have been a different person. That's how it was in Germany then. You were entirely in the hands of chance.][64]

The notion of *Zufall* [contingency] is a recurrent theme in Wolf's work, and it reveals her preoccupation with the tension between the teleology inherent in Marxist conceptions of history and the possibility of reducing human existence to a matter of chance.[65] Here, in the depths of her depression, the protagonist latches onto the idea that she might have had an alternative life. When asked by Peter Gutman whether she would like to go back and become the person that she might have been, she answers indirectly by envisaging this other life and highlighting the fact that, had she lived it, she would now be free of guilt;[66] she would not be having to face the consequences of her involvement with the Stasi, and she would not be grieving the loss of the country in which she had invested so much hope.

This conversation forms part of a thematic strand in the novel in which the protagonist reflects on and questions the validity of her utopian beliefs and the

---

64 Wolf, *Stadt der Engel,* pp. 242–243. My translation.
65 Michael Minden has explored this tension in relation to *Kindheitsmuster.* See Minden, 'Social Hope', p. 198.
66 Wolf, *Stadt der Engel,* p. 243.

confidence she had in the early GDR.[67] She recalls her love for this country[68] and describes how, in the early years of the GDR, she and her fellow activists were brimming over with utopian desire: 'Wir platzten vor Utopie. [...] Wir mochten unser Land nicht, wie es war, sondern wie es sein würde' [We were bursting with utopia (...). We didn't like our country the way it was but the way it would be'].[69] Then, referring to the period after the high-profile expatriation of the dissident poet and songwriter Wolf Biermann in 1976,[70] she describes how this desire changed: 'Die Hoffnung verkam, die Utopie zerbröckelte, ging in Verwesung über. Wir mußten lernen, ohne Alternative zu leben' [The hope crumbled, utopia fell apart and started to rot. We had to learn to live without alternatives].[71] In the post-GDR context of her stay in Los Angeles, the aging protagonist repeatedly asks whether her earlier hopes were simply illusions[72] and wonders whether every utopia has become risible.[73] In fact, these utopian beliefs are held so deeply that her questioning of them casts doubt on her whole existence: 'Ist unser Leben umsonst gewesen?' [Was our whole life for nothing?],[74] she asks, and a few pages later, she and Peter Gutman come to the tentative conclusion that 'alles war umsonst, und alles war unvermeidlich' [it was all for nothing, and it was all inevitable too].[75]

Central to the protagonist's recovery from her depression are her reflections on the origins of the GDR and the unrealized potential of its political system. In the course of her stay in Los Angeles, she becomes increasingly preoccupied with the material legacy of German émigrés who fled to the US in the 1930s and 1940s. This includes thinkers associated with the Frankfurt School, such as Theodor Adorno and Max Horkheimer, as well as other left-wing intellectuals, such as

---

67 Schwarz and Wilde argue that, in *Stadt der Engel*, 'fragments of utopian thinking' take the place of coherent utopian ideas. See Schwarz and Wilde, 'Transformationen des Utopischen', pp. 243–244.

68 Wolf, *Stadt der Engel*, p. 73.

69 Ibid., p. 258.

70 The publication of *Was bleibt* (1976/1990), Wolf's semi-autobiographical documentation of her surveillance by the Stasi following Biermann's expatriation, was the central trigger for the so-called *Literaturstreit* [literature quarrel] of the early 1990s. She has discussed the Biermann affair and her subsequent disillusionment with the GDR in several press interviews. See, for example, Jana Simon, '"Weder hier noch dort gut". Interview mit Christa Wolf', *Die Zeit*, 'Kultur', 23 April 2015 (http://www.zeit.de/2015/17/christa-wolff-flucht-ddr).

71 Wolf, *Stadt der Engel*, p. 258.

72 Ibid., p. 266.

73 Ibid., p. 89.

74 Ibid., p. 291.

75 Ibid., p. 310.

Thomas Mann, Bertolt Brecht, Marta Feuchtwanger, Hans Eisler, Karl Zuckmayer, Erich Maria Remarque and Ludwig Marcuse. As inhabitants of this 'New Weimar under the Palms',[76] these figures represent, for the protagonist, the true intellectual heritage of the GDR: 'ich hielt [die DDR] für die legitime Nachfolge jenes Anderen Deutschland, das in den Zuchthäusern und Konzentrationslagern, in Spanien, in den verschiedenen Emigrationsländern, verfolgt und gequält, schrecklich dezimiert, doch widerstand' [I saw (the GDR) as the legitimate successor to this Other Germany, the one that, in all the prisons and concentration camps, in Spain, in the various countries of emigration – persecuted, tortured, horribly decimated – nevertheless resisted].[77] Some of these intellectuals, however, are in danger of falling into obscurity in the new, reunified Germany,[78] just as the protagonist sees herself one day succumbing to the 'vortex of being forgotten'.[79] By visiting the houses of these exiled intellectuals and immersing herself in their works, she attempts to recuperate some of the lost potential of this tradition and ensure that its ideals are not erased from memory.[80]

Towards the end of the text, the older narrator, writing around fifteen years after her time in California, surrounds herself with books written by these émigrés and finds herself drawn to them once again:

EIN SOG GING VON DIESEN BÜCHERN AUS.
Noch einmal gerate ich in diesen Sog, indem ich mich in die Bücher vertiefe, welche die Emigranten später, sich erinnernd, nach ihrer Rückkehr ins Nachkriegsdeutschland oder eben nach ihrer Nicht-Rückkehr geschrieben haben. [...] Ich suche die Stellen, an denen ihre Autoren beschrieben, was das Exil ihnen angetan hat. Was es hieß, wurzellos zu sein.

[A GRAVITATIONAL PULL EMANATED FROM THESE BOOKS.
And once again I am drawn back into this pull when I immerse myself in the books that the émigrés, remembering, wrote after their return to post-War Germany or likewise after their non-return. (...) I seek out the passages in which the authors describe what exile has done to them. What it meant to be rootless.][81]

While the narrator makes it clear that, for her, emigration to the USA is not an option, she nevertheless sees certain similarities between her situation and that of the exiles in the 1930s and 1940s. As a figure whose voice is not heard in the political context in which she now lives, she seeks refuge in these earlier

---

76 Ibid., p. 338.
77 Ibid., p. 347.
78 Ibid.
79 Ibid., p. 317. My translation.
80 Ibid., p. 347.
81 Ibid., p. 345. My translation.

accounts of rootlessness and banishment. Her reading of their work suggests an attempt to validate her own writing by drawing implicit parallels between the anti-fascist resistance of these intellectuals and her critique of capitalist society following the collapse of Socialism in Europe. The gravitational pull emanating from these books draws the protagonist in a different direction from the 'pull from the end' described elsewhere: rather than propelling her forward in time, towards her death, it actually draws her back towards the past, to a time when the project of Socialism was still an aspiration. Chiming with Walter Benjamin's redemptive vision of the historian who 'kindles the sparks of hope in the past',[82] the image signals the protagonist's desire to embrace and reawaken what might have been, had this project been fully realized in the GDR.

Conclusion

In the final pages of the novel, the protagonist travels to the emblematically named Death Valley with some friends from the Research Centre. In the inhospitable surroundings of the desert, she experiences a final vision, in which she flies over the valley towards Los Angeles, the so-called 'city of angels', accompanied by Angelina, her rather whimsical guardian angel.[83] Floating over a barren landscape filled with ghostly figures from the protagonist's past, who emit an uncanny pull,[84] it becomes clear to the protagonist that this is a leave-taking, a gesture of farewell towards Angelina, Los Angeles and, perhaps, her past life: 'Eine Arbeit ist getan, Angelina, aber warum bleibt das Gefühl der Vollendung aus?' [A piece of work has been finished, Angelina, but why is there no sense of completion?].[85] There is no obvious sign of conclusion here, no glimpse of what Said describes as the 'harmony and resolution' often associated with old age; nor is there a sense of what he terms the 'deliberately unproductive

---

82 Walter Benjamin, 'Über den Begriff der Geschichte', in *Gesammelte Werke*, ed. by Tiedemann and Schweppenhäuser, vol. 1.2, pp. 691–704 (p. 695). Translations are taken from Benjamin, 'On the Concept of History', in *Selected Writings*, ed. by Eiland and Jennings, vol. 4, pp. 389–411.
83 Angelina is, in many respects, reminiscent of the figure of Kora Bachmann in Wolf's novella *Leibhaftig* (Munich: Luchterhand, 2002).
84 Wolf, *Stadt der Engel*, p. 413. This recalls both the 'pull from the end' described earlier in the text and the gravitational pull towards death which the protagonist of *Leibhaftig* experiences. See Wolf, *Leibhaftig*, p. 162.
85 Wolf, *Stadt der Engel*, p. 413. My translation.

productiveness' of the late writer.[86] Instead, the narrator introduces a tension between competing conceptions of time:

> Müßte ich jetzt nicht eine große Schleife fliegen? sagte ich. Zurück auf Anfang?
> Mach doch, sagte sie [Angelina] ungerührt.
> Und Jahre Arbeit? Einfach wegwerfen?
> Warum nicht?
> Das Alter, Angelina, das Alter verbietet es.
>
> [Shouldn't I now fly in a great loop? I said. Back to the beginning?
> Go on then, she (Angelina) said, unmoved.
> And years of work? Just throw them all away?
> Why not?
> Old age, Angelina. Old age won't let me.][87]

The protagonist is encouraged by Angelina to follow her wishes and return to the
beginning, to recover the utopian potential which was not realized in the GDR
and build on the intellectual heritage of the émigré writers to whom she is so
attached. However, this cyclical notion of time, expressed spatially in the
image of the loop, is juxtaposed with a linear model, according to which the protagonist's old age and proximity to death cannot simply be reversed. Unlike Angelina, who is unaffected by the passage of time, the protagonist is ultimately
bound to her aging body and unable to escape being pulled towards her final
demise.

Wolf's narrative thus depicts the narrator being drawn in two different directions, pulled unstoppably towards her death while nevertheless longing to pause
and recover the lost potential in the past, to undo what will have been and revive
what might have been. These competing temporalities coalesce in the image of
the Paul Klee's 'Angelus Novus', which Benjamin describes in his 'Über den Begriff der Geschichte' ['On the Concept of History'], the figure of the Angel of History who is blown backwards into the future while gazing at the wreckage of
modernity left behind him. Benjamin's angel longs to linger, awaken the dead
and piece together what has been smashed; however, he is driven irrevocably onwards by a storm blowing from paradise. Wolf refers explicitly to this image at
two points in *Stadt der Engel*, as the protagonist reflects on her past in conversation with Peter Gutman. In particular, Wolf appears to evoke the figure in
order to comment on the discrepancy between the broad-scale utopian narrative
to which she subscribes and the particularity of individual experience, which

---

86 Said, *On Late Style*, p. 7.
87 Wolf, *Stadt der Engel*, p. 414. My translation.

does not always fit into this narrative. Strikingly, her version of the Angel of History is 'blind to horror'; he perceives neither the chaos which he leaves behind, nor the 'hindered lives' created by human civilization.[88] By distinguishing the image in this way from Benjamin's Angel of History, Wolf seems to be raising the question of how – and indeed whether – it is possible to recover the remains of lived experience that cannot be incorporated into the utopian narrative: how might the specificity of individual subjective experience be recuperated so that 'something always remains'?[89]

To conclude, I return here to Said's writing on late style, to ask whether this notion can be reconfigured through an engagement with Wolf and Benjamin. The narrative of *Stadt der Engel* engages quite explicitly with what Said, following Adorno, terms 'subjectivity [taking] leave of the work'.[90] Wolf reflects on what will happen to the text once its direct connection to the subjectivity of a living narrator has passed. Moreover, she engages with this question on a formal level, creating a 'patchwork' narrative whose structure enables new patterns to be created from the disjointed remainders of the narrator's past experiences, from the specific individual experiences which the Angel of History is unable to perceive. These experiences are opened up to the possibility of reconfiguration according to new patterns; they attain a semblance of coherence, yet, crucially, this coherence is one in which gaps, seams and contradictions remain visible. Evoking Benjamin, Wolf is concerned with resisting totalizing historical narratives and creating the possibility of recuperating the revolutionary potential of past moments through her writing; by reflecting on what will have been and what might have been, she offers glimpses of a 'Jetzt-Zeit, in welcher Splitter der messianischen eingesprengt sind' [now-time in which splinters of the messianic are interspersed].[91] However, the narrative of *Stadt der Engel* remains highly ambivalent, calling into question this possible messianism even as it articulates it. Like so much of Wolf's work, this text ends on an equivocal note, with Angelina and the protagonist journeying together into the unknown. Its final pages gesture towards the possibility of rehabilitation, even redemption, yet this remains tentative and, ultimately, deeply uncertain.

---

88 Ibid., p. 141. My translation.
89 Ibid., p. 316.
90 Adorno, *Essays on Music*, p. 566. Cited in Said, *On Late Style*, p. 9.
91 Benjamin, 'Über den Begriff der Geschichte', p. 704.

Birgit Dahlke

The Protocol of Barriers to Thinking? Wolf's *Moskauer Tagebücher. Wer wir sind und wer wir waren* (2014)

The publication of the *Moskauer Tagebücher* from Wolf's posthumous estate generated expectations well beyond Germany. 'Moscow' was a hot-button term. Was
the author's confrontation of Stalinism finally to be found here – and in the medium of a diary, no less? The heterogeneous texts gathered under the above title
raise more questions than they answer. The sometimes hermetic nature of the
notes suggest *Denkblockaden* [barriers to thinking]. Between 1957 and 1989,
the author made ten trips – to Armenia in the Ukraine, to Abkhazia in Lithuania,
to the Volga, to Leningrad and Latvian Riga as well as to Moscow. In 1989, the

Author's Note: The following article relates to a publication whose title arouses expectations
that are not met: made available posthumously under the title *Moskauer Tagebücher* [Moscow
Diaries], it is a collection of heterogeneous sources that are more or less related to the Soviet
Union and to German-Soviet socialist history. Travel notes and exchanges of letters with Soviet
authors are set alongside excerpts from Christa Wolf's essays, speeches and prose texts, her
short diary excerpts placed with those of Brigitte Reimann and Max Frisch and each of the
ten trips is commentated by Gerhard Wolf. Added to this corpus are documents from the Lew
Kopelew Archive, a KGB report on Wolf's 1970 stay in Komarowo, and letters from Kopelew
and Etkind to Gerhard Wolf. Of the book's 270 pages, approximately 160 are by Christa Wolf,
of those, almost 100 are based on mainly handwritten original notes about her travels. Only
these 100 pages can be characterized as 'Travel Diaries'; at the same time, they do not refer
solely to travel to Moscow, as the book title suggests. Previously published forewords, essays,
memoires, discussions and speeches with and about Juri Kasakow, Vera Inber, Max Frisch, Efim
Etkind, Konstantin Simonow, Juri Trifonow and Lew Kopelew comprise the remainder. The 1987
journey is integrated with excerpts from a discussion between the translators Nina Fjodorowa
and Albert Karelski and the literary scholar and friend of the Wolf's Jewgenija Kazewa that
took place in June 1988 in Moscow. Despite its rather confusing textual basis, this publication
is to be welcomed, in part because it sets individual or previously inaccessible writings into a
broader context. I have used this philological basis to reflect on the status of 'Moscow' in Christa Wolf's authorial self-understanding. My caution results from the slender text base that this
Nachlass volume offers. These notes appear to me too contradictory and particularly too fragmentary to derive a thesis from them about Christa Wolf's more than three decades of changing
perspective on Soviet socialism, also and especially on the history of Stalinism. Regardless of
thematic affinity, diaries and fleeting travel notes must be read fundamentally differently than
passages disconnected from larger narrative structures, such as 'Farewell from Moscow' in *Stadt
der Engel*, particularly because Wolf 'never saw [her diaries] as part of her actual literary creation', as Gerhard Wolf recalls in his foreword.

https://doi.org/10.1515/9783110496000-013

year of the fall of the Berlin Wall and the collapse of real-existing socialism in Central and Eastern Europe, these trips broke off. If one reads Wolf's correspondence with Efim Etkind and Lew Kopelew from the 1980s as intertexts to the Stalinism passages in *Kindheitsmuster* (1976) and *Stadt der Engel oder the Overcoat of Dr. Freud* (2010), it cannot be overlooked: as much as the author admits to skirting the depths of Stalinism, she is unable to find an aesthetic form for dealing with this theme – which, for her, is second in importance only to National Socialism. Her easterly voyages can be regarded as a hermeneutic movement: shuttling to and fro between the Soviet and her own East, Wolf constantly undertakes an internal differentiation. This leads to her perception of the GDR as more 'Western' – from the perspective of her personal national identity – than has previously been recognized.

Wolf does not hide the blind spots in her own thinking; they are visible in her travel reports. The tone changes. While the perspective of the young, post-Second World War German Christa Wolf is primarily defined by the consciousness of historical guilt towards the Soviet people, the travel notes of her later decades allow one to see how, little by little, she begins to observe the everyday life of socialism in the Soviet Union critically. This farewell to her early idealization of the Soviet people and their way of living exclusively for the public good is painful. Wolf the observer repeatedly tries to explain what she saw as disturbing behaviours and circumstances, ascribing them to the material and moral cost of the gruelling war of defence against and liberation from the German attacker.

In contrast to what can be expected from the title, the *Moskauer Tagebücher. Wer wir sind und wer wir waren* [Moscow Diaries. Who we are and who we were] contains rather short travel reports as extracts from Wolf's extensive (and still not publicly accessible) diaries. The relationship to the Soviet Union is central to understanding Christa Wolf as an author. Although beginning in 1960, she already had the privilege of travelling to the Federal Republic of Germany, Finland, France and Sweden, and later to Austria, the United Kingdom and, from 1974, also to the USA, that centrality remains until the end of her life – when the Soviet Union as a political system no longer existed. Literary traces of the voyages reveal that she perceived the crossing of geographical boundaries – to the East as to the West – primarily geopolitically. Until 1989, the author acts as a representative of German perpetrators – East and West – towards the Eastern European victims of the Second World War. She takes on the responsibility for them which all Germans share. This pattern is by no means a unique case in the German remembrance discourse after 1945. A 1990 comparison of oral history interviews with East and West Germans led the historian Lutz Niethammer to the thesis that the different sides took on different groups of victims of the Second

World War: the West Germans took on the Jews, the East Germans the Russians.[1] Clearly this did not occur independently of the official views of histories and ideologies. Real historical facts also strengthen these ideologized memory grids: the Soviet Zone of Occupation (SBZ) had to pay reparations to the Soviet Union in the form of factories and raw materials immediately after 1945, while the Western occupation zones began reparation payments to Jewish survivors at the end of the 1950s.

Positive expectations on the part of the 28-year-old functionary of the Writers' Union mark Wolf's perception of Moscow on her first trip in 1957. Wolf writes in her travel notes: 'Das ist überhaupt etwas Auffallendes. Es gibt hier keinen Snobismus. [...] Ein großer Ernst [...] herrscht überall. [...] Das Volk ist hier wirklich ,Volk': Arbeiter und Bauern, arbeitende Menschen beherrschen das Straßenbild' [This is something notable. There is no snobbery. (...) a great seriousness (...) is everywhere. (...) Here, the people are really 'people': workers and peasants, working people dominate the streets].[2] The deictic gesture of the 'here'[3] casts the East-West paradigm in a social – in this case, decidedly antibourgeois – manner. The 'here' of the labouring Soviets references a 'there' in which these workers do not determine the picture: the (capitalist) West. Young people are foregrounded in the description and (as is typical of GDR 'Arrival Literature') are linked with the modernity of the new buildings and wide streets. The names Mayakovsky, Pushkin and Tolstoy give these quotidian impressions a cultural tradition and historical depth. For Christa Wolf's generation – which had been socialized into National Socialism and, after the capitulation of the German Wehrmacht, had to gradually recognize the crimes this ideologized education had enabled – ideas of a 'new start' and 'conversion' ('Wandlung') had become dominant concepts of intellectual self-actualization after 1945.[4] Both Christa Wolf and Uwe Johnson – and also, for example, Wolfgang Hil-

---

1 See Jörg Magenau, *Christa Wolf. Eine Biographie. Überarbeitete und erweiterte Neuausgabe* (Reinbek bei Hamburg: Rowohlt, 2013), p. 119; Lutz Niethammer, 'Juden und Russen im Gedächtnis der Deutschen', in *Der historische Ort des Nationalsozialismus. Annäherungen*, ed. by Walter H. Pehle (Frankfurt a. M.: Fischer, 1990), pp. 114–134; Jeffrey Herf, *Divided Memory. The Nazi Past in the Two Germanys* (Cambridge: Harvard University Press, 1997).
2 Christa Wolf, *Moskauer Tagebücher. Wer wir sind und wer wir waren. Reisetagebücher, Texte, Briefe, Dokumente 1957–1989*, ed. by Gerhard Wolf and Tanja Walenski (Suhrkamp: Berlin, 2014), p. 14 and 16.
3 See the keyword 'deixis' in: *Routledge Encyclopedia of Narrative Theory*, ed. by David Herman, Manfred Jahn and Marie-Laure Ryan (London/New York: Routledge, 2008), pp. 99–100.
4 Literary historiography labels GDR prose texts of the early 1960s as 'Literature of Arrival'. Their commonality is a concentration upon the everyday life of the new 'young' socialist society. Brigitte Reimann's novel *Ankunft im Alltag* (1961) is one example of this. The prose of Franz Füh-

big, who was a decade younger – would later develop a poetics of guilt and would search for an authorial positionality, which, from the position of a German after 1945, did not simply take for granted the authority of literary speech. Wolf's travel notes from 1957 are characterized by the need for a radical break and the search for an orienting non- or indeed anti-fascist historical grounding. She finds this orientation in the Soviet Union – the socialist state that freed Germany from National Socialist rule.[5]

The first travel report ends with a reference to 'Goethe: aufsteigende und verfallende Epochen' [Goethe: ascending and declining eras].[6] The ascendant ordering – young, large and new – transforms the topographic perspective into a topological one. To determine the Self through demarcation from the foreign / the Other is characteristic of identitarian thinking. Accordingly, it is not only socialist worldviews that are structured binarily. If younger generations (as mentioned, Wolf was 28 at the time) lean particularly towards binary models in their differentiation processes, it is because these models were dominant in the Cold War era. In the sixties, the East-West paradigm served all sides as a qualitative coordinate system. The geographical measures of east and west were deployed qualitatively in the public discourse of divided Germany, serving the purposes of reciprocal contrast and the attribution of meaning. During the first journey, Wolf's sensual experience of belonging to a supranational community of social transformation, together with the Soviet Union and the other socialist countries of Eastern Europe, becomes her final incentive to become a writer. This motivational push culminates in her intent to learn Russian,[7] a resolution that would be only partly successful.

Moskauer Novelle (1961) – Wolf's debut novella, which was never translated into Russian, and which she later rejected – actually goes back to her first encounters with a semantically overdetermined Moscow. That Christa and Gerhard Wolf worked on a film of this novel demonstrates the importance of the topic for the couple. Its realization by their friend, the director Konrad Wolf, was thwarted

---

mann, born in 1922, is placed in the rubric 'conversion' literature from the 1950s. See his early stories *Kameraden* (1955) and *Das Judenauto* (1962), as well as the long essay *Vor Feuerschlünden. Erfahrung mit Georg Trakls Gedicht* (1982).

5 See Birgit Dahlke, 'Vom Gewaltsymbol zum Verdrängungsnarrativ. Deutungskämpfe um die Chiffre '1945' im kollektiven Gedächtnis (nicht nur) der DDR', in *Gedächtnis und Literatur in den 'geschlossenen Gesellschaften' des Real-Sozialismus zwischen 1945 und 1989*, ed. by Carsten Gansel (Göttingen: V&R unipress, 2007), pp. 39–52.

6 Wolf, *Moskauer Tagebuch*, p. 19. In this manner, Goethe's comment is bound to a central paradigm of historical Marxist thought: the development of the history of humanity is conceptualized in its entirety as an ascending line of social progress.

7 Wolf, *Moskauer Tagebuch*, p. 18.

by opposition to the script on the part of Soviet censors.[8] From the beginning, brief references to Stalinist persecutions accompanied the perception of Moscow's present. When the note about a second trip to Moscow in 1959 describes a meandering walk with Willi Bredel – the communist exile[9] and author of *Verwandte und Bekannte* [Relations and Acquaintances] (1941), the GDR novel trilogy canonized as an anti-fascist foundational narrative[10] – one statement stands without comment: 'Er zeigte mir die Lubljanka' [He showed me Lubyanka]. For insiders, the signal word 'Lubyanka' – the name of the central Moscow prison in which important, innocent German Communists were imprisoned without cause – initiates a chain of associations that leads directly to the Stalinist persecutions and show trials.[11] At the same time, Christa Wolf solely articulates the keyword without going into more detail or making the connection between her anecdotal experience with the old Communist author and her visit to the notorious prison. This may be due to the character of the text as a travel note rather than to thinking barriers. In her last large novel, *Stadt der Engel oder The Overcoat of Dr. Freud* (2010), the author would come back to Bredel and give more space to the Hotel *Lux* and the Lubyanka prison:

> Bei der nächsten Gelegenheit [...] führte er dich durch das Moskau seiner Emigrantenzeit: das hier ist das Hotel Lux, da haben wir alle gewohnt, in der schlimmen Zeit der Säuberungen haben wir uns abends gegenseitig angerufen, um zu hören, ob der andere noch da ist, und wenn er sich meldete, schweigend aufgelegt. Und mancher der Genossen war eben nicht mehr ‚da'. – Und hier war die Lubljanka, die Zentrale des NKWD mit ihren vergitterten Fenstern, von hier aus wurden sie ins Lager verschickt, und von manchem hat man nie wieder etwas gehört.

---

8 See Gerhard Wolf in Wolf, *Moskauer Tagebuch*, p. 20.

9 Bredel, born in Hamburg in 1901 and an early member of the Spartacus Youth, had begun to write in prison in 1923. During the Second World War, he was a writer on the side of the Red Army and was one of the founders of the National Committee of Free Germany in 1941. In May 1945, he returned to Germany as an instructor for the KPD. From 1953 to 1957, he was editor-in-chief of the literary magazine *New German Literature* (NDL), and from 1962 until his death in 1964, he was president of the Academy of Arts. See, for example, *Lexikon sozialistischer Literatur. Ihre Geschichte in Deutschland bis 1945*, ed. by Simone Bark and others (Stuttgart/Weimar: Metzler, 1994).

10 On the role of authors such as Willi Bredel, Anna Seghers, Otto Gotsche and Hans Marchwitza in the establishment of a foundational narrative, see Julia Hell, *Post-fascist Fantasies. Psychoanalysis, History and the Literature of East Germany* (Durham/London: Duke University Press, 1997).

11 'Lubljanka' is the unofficial name for the central prison on the eponymous square in Moscow, built in 1897, in which – from 1920 onwards – the Soviet secret service had its headquarters. For decades, its extensive cellar rooms were used for interrogation and torture. See, for example, Karl Schlögel, *Terror und Traum. Moskau 1937* (Munich: Hanser, 2008).

[The next chance he had (...), he gave you a tour through the Moscow he remembered from his émigré years: That's the Hotel Lux, we all lived there. In the bad time, during the purges, we would call each other up at night to hear if the other person was still there, and when they answered we would hang up without a word. Some comrades weren't 'there' anymore ... And here's the Lubljanka, the NKVD headquarters with the bars on the windows; from here they were sent to the camps, and we never heard from some of them again].[12]

From the third trip in 1963, her first as a writer, Wolf's idealizing semanticization of Moscow gives way to critical, naturalizing metaphors. She notes the idea for a story: "'die grasüberwachsene Stadt". Ein Mensch, der in einer von innen her zu-wuchernden Stadt lebt, wehrt sich verzweifelt dagegen, auch selbst zu verstep-pen' ['the steppe-d city'. A man who lives in a city that is being overgrown from within desperately defends himself against becoming a steppe himself].[13] Wolf sketches a parable of a city that, little by little, gives up the cultural ach-ievements of civilization and reverts to nature from its core, rather than from out-side. The author connects this unconventional image with the threatening meta-phor that its inhabitants could also 'versteppen' [coarsen] and lose the capacity for sensitivity and initiative.

Increasingly, annotations follow the names of the people the traveller meets in Moscow and elsewhere in the Soviet Union: for example, 'fünf Jahre im Lager' [five years in the camps] or 'Vater 1937 verhaftet, nicht wiedergekommen' [father arrested in 1937, did not return].[14] In what form, Wolf asks sceptically, could the complexity of this experience between the construction of socialism, the daily life of war and camp detention be made literary? Instead of an answer, she refers to a comment by the Jewish historian Jerussalimski, a friend of the Wolfs, to the effect that Stalin needs a Shakespeare.[15] She also finds it '[i]nteressant, daß es keinen Emigrantenroman eines deutschen Autors aus der SU gibt' [(i)nteresting that there is no emigrant novel of a German author from the SU].[16] This restrain-ed note points to a significant imbalance in the history of literature and ideas within the exile literature tradition that is so central to GDR socialist literature. Although politically and racially persecuted German authors initially found little

---

12 Christa Wolf, *City of Angels. Or, The Overcoat of Dr. Freud*, trans. by Damion Searl (New York: Farrar, Straus and Giroux, 2013), p. 62. (*Stadt der Engel* [Berlin: Suhrkamp, 2010], p. 87).
13 Wolf, *Moskauer Tagebuch*, p. 46. The fragment of the unfinished text is part of the Wolf estate in the Christa Wolf Archive of the Academy of the Arts in Berlin, under the provisional signature CWA N 204/2.
14 Wolf, *Moskauer Tagebuch*, p. 66, 77.
15 Wolf, *Moskauer Tagebuch*, p. 44. Arkadi Jerussalimski (1901–1965) had participated as an ob-server at the Potsdam Conference in 1945.
16 Wolf, *Moskauer Tagebuch*, p. 91.

support in the Federal Republic, they became important guarantors and symbolic figures of the anti-fascist foundational narrative in the GDR's first decade.[17] In the SBZ, an exile such as Wolfgang Langhoff was appointed as director of the Deutsches Theater in 1946, and Bertolt Brecht even received his own theatre, the Berliner Ensemble. The work of Anna Seghers, who was doubly persecuted as a Jewish person and as a Communist, was published immediately after 1945.[18] She kept her Mexican citizenship until well into the 1950s.

Like many returning migrants, Seghers nevertheless remained an outsider; the feeling of foreignness – resulting from differences in experience as well as from the experience of persecution of a racist and political nature – was also not lessened by her various attempts to integrate into the newly established or re-established cultural institutions and networks. Most of these protagonists of German exile literature were involved in vehement debates over aesthetic and ideological questions in the raw climate of 1950s GDR cultural policy. In particular, modernist writing styles and theatre as well as concepts of art and music were confronted with the fierce resistance of political functionaries, whose societal origins and decades-long imprisonment had obstructed their attainment of higher education.[19] Nevertheless, those who had lived through persecution, expulsion and escape knew how to appreciate that, in spite of this attempted paternalism, the SBZ offered a *Heimat* [homeland]. Those persecuted by the Nazi regime received preferential treatment in the form of apartments, food and printing paper quotas.[20]

---

17 Many anti-fascist authors settled in the GDR upon their return from exile, such as: Willi Bredel, J.R. Becher, Erich Weinert, Friedrich Wolf, Adam Scharrer, Theodor Plivier, Anna Seghers, Ludwig Renn, Bodo Uhse, Alexander Abusch, Hans Marchwitza, Bertolt Brecht, Ernst Bloch, F.C. Weiskopf, Wieland Herzfelde, Stefan Heym, Arnold Zweig, Louis Fürnberg and many more.
18 Born in 1900, Anna Seghers came from the family of an Orthodox Jewish art dealer in Mainz. She emigrated with her young children in 1933, first to Zurich and then to Paris. After an exhausting journey, she finally landed in Mexico City. In 1947, she returned to Berlin, to the Soviet Occupied Zone. The novel *Transit* (written in 1941/1942, first published in 1944), as well as *Das Argonautenschiff* (1948) and *Post ins gelobte Land* (1947), which fictionalize the biographical experience of flight and persecution in highly artistic ways, are some of the most important books for Christa Wolf's personal canon, as evidenced in her essays and speeches.
19 See the short biographies of art functionaries collected and edited by Hauke Reich and Beatrice Vierneisel in *Kunstdokumentation SBZ/DDR 1945–1990. Aufsätze, Berichte, Materialien*, ed. by Günter Feist, Eckhart Gillen and Beatrice Vierneisel (Cologne: DuMont, 1996), pp. 855–888
20 Simone Barck, *Antifa-Geschichte(n). Eine literarische Spurensuche in der DDR der 1950er und 1960er Jahre* (Cologne/Weimar/Vienna: Böhlau, 2003); Elke Reuter and Detlef Hansel, *Das kurze Leben der VVN 1947–1953. Die Geschichte der Vereinigung der Verfolgten des Naziregimes in der SBZ und in der DDR* (Berlin: Edition Ost, 1997).

'A.S. [Anna Seghers] und die anderen haben keinen Mut zu ihren Erfahrungen… Was ich verstehe. Wir auch nicht, bis jetzt' [A.S. and the others do not have the courage to engage with their experience… which I understand. We have not either, until now].[21] What experience is Wolf referring to in 1966? The Soviet occupying force appears neither positively nor negatively in Seghers's tales. Significantly, a small text in which a German asks a Russian officer to return his watch, and in response, the officer shows the German his family, who were killed in the war, remained a fragment.[22] As it was for Brecht, for Seghers, the period she spent in the GDR was one of the most difficult and contradictory of her life. This is evident not only in Seghers's behaviour during the trial of Paul Merker in 1955,[23] or that of Walter Janka after 1956,[24] but also in her self-doubt as chair of the GDR Writers' Union from 1952 to 1978. Anna Seghers largely omitted from her writings precisely this dark side of her experiences in exile and her early days in the GDR, which included mistrust and anti-Jewish sentiment within the Communist movement. Wolf made standing up for one's own experience a life-long topic and a central poetic paradigm. This is the aim of her concept of subjective authenticity. In an interview in 1987, she would speak of the shock generated among the older comrades and colleagues who had been swept up

---

21 Wolf, *Moskauer Tagebuch*, p. 69.

22 Signature 546 in the Anna Seghers Archive of the Academy of the Arts in Berlin. Cf. Christiane Zehl-Romero, *Anna Seghers. Eine Biographie 1947–1983* (Berlin: Aufbau, 2003), p. 25fn59.

23 From 1931, Paul Merker (1894–1969) was in U.S. American and then Soviet exile. Interned in Le Vernet (France) 1941, he escaped to Mexico in 1942. Merker regularly wrote articles for the magazine *Freies Deutschland*. After 1946, he was a member of the politburo of the SED. In 1950, against the background of the Noel Field Affair and the Budapest Rajk Process, proceedings against Merker were opened. In 1955, he was sentenced by the supreme court of the GDR to eight years in prison for 'Zionist Positions'. After his early release in 1956, he was extorted into giving an incriminating statement in the show trial against Walter Janka. See, for example, Jeffrey Herf, 'East German Communists and the Jewish Question. The Case of Paul Merker', *Journal of Contemporary History*, 29.4 (October 1994), 627–661.

24 Walter Janka (1914–1994) was a dramaturge and publisher. Deported from the Gestapo prison to Czechoslovakia in 1935, he participated in the Thälmann Battalion in the Spanish Civil War from 1936 and was interned in Le Vernet from 1939 to 1941. He escaped to Mexico, where he founded the movement 'Free Germany' with Paul Merker and Alexander Abusch, and in 1942, he led the exile publishing house El Libro Libre. In 1947, he returned to Germany, and in 1948 he was the managing director of the DEFA, although he was quickly replaced in 1949. From 1950, he was the deputy managing director of the publishing house Aufbau, and he was its director from 1953. In 1956, he was arrested under accusations of counterrevolutionary conspiracy, and in 1957, he was imprisoned for five years in strict solitary confinement 'as a ringleader and a member of a counterrevolutionary group'. After his release in 1960, he was a dramaturge and a screenwriter at DEFA studios. In 1972, he renewed his membership in the SED. See Walter Janka, *Schwierigkeiten mit der Wahrheit* (Berlin: Aufbau, 1990).

in the Moscow emigration, by the Twentieth Party Congress of the CPSU in 1956, with Nikita Khrushchev's secret speech on the Stalinist *Säuberungen* [cleansings]:

> Ich fragte mich, wie es ihnen möglich gewesen war, alles, was sie dort erfahren oder selbst erlebt hatten, so weit zu verdrängen, dass sie ganz oder partiell gläubig bleiben konnten. Ich denke, ich habe dabei etwas gelernt: Meine eigene Gläubigkeit schwand dahin, künftig wollte ich zu meinen Erfahrungen stehen und sie mir durch nichts und niemanden ausreden, verleugnen oder verbieten lassen.
>
> [I asked myself how it would have been possible for them to suppress everything that they had discovered or experienced enough to remain faithful. I think I learned something through it: My own faith disappeared; in the future I wanted to stand behind my own experience and not allow anything or anyone to talk me out of, deny or prohibit it].[25]

The film project that Christa and Gerhard Wolf developed during their 1966 trip, which would take up material thematizing the inner connection between the National Socialist pre-history of the founding of the GDR and the role of the Soviet liberators, was never realized. Konrad Wolf, who had emigrated from Moscow, was to have been the main character.[26] *Ein Mann kehrt heim* [*A Man Returns Home*] could not be made in the wake of the Eleventh Plenary of the Socialist Unity Party in 1965.[27]

The sensory, concrete experience of alterity during these stays in the Soviet Union sharpened the early Christa Wolf's own perceptions. Seen from the East, the war crimes that were bound to German nationality after 1945 insert themselves nearly automatically into her texts: her detailed description of Lev Tol-

---

25 *Unerledigte Widersprüche. Gespräch mit Therese Hörnigk*, June 1987/October 1988, in *Christa Wolf. Werkausgabe in 12 Bänden*, ed. by Sonja Hilzinger, 13 vols. (Munich: Luchterhand, 1999–2001), vol. 12: *Essays, Gespräche, Reden, Briefe 1987–2000* (2001), pp. 53–102 (p. 73).
26 Wolf, *Moskauer Tagebuch*, p. 95. The fragment is located in the Gerhard Wolf Archive of the Academy of the Arts in Berlin (GWA AK 31, provisional signature), also with the treatment in several versions. Christa Wolf never finished the novel *Preisgericht*. The film director Konrad Wolf (1925–1982) was president of the Akademie der Künste Berlin from 1965 until his early death in 1982. Son of the playwright Friedrich Wolf, who was forced into exile as a Jew and a Communist, Konrad grew up in Moscow and, in 1945, was involved in the liberation of Berlin as a nineteen-year-old soldier of the Red Army. His 1968 film *Ich war neunzehn* addresses this experience.
27 The Eleventh Plenary of the Central Committee of the SED has gone down in history as the GDR's 'clear-cutting' plenary session. In the wake of the Eleventh Plenary, a whole cohort of feature films was banned. See *Spur der Filme. Zeitzeugen über die DEFA*, ed. by Ingrid Poss and Peter Warnecke (Berlin: Christoph Links, 2006). During this session, the young Christa Wolf courageously, publicly and largely extemporaneously spoke out against the threatening political climate that was developing. See *Kahlschlag. Das 11. Plenum des ZK der SED – Studien und Dokumente*, ed. by Günter Agde, 2nd edn (Berlin: Structure, 2000), p. 264.

stoy's apartment building in 1966 culminates in the phrase: 'Man kann sich nicht vorstellen, sage ich, daß aus solchen Häusern die SS-Leute von Auschwitz hätten hervorgehen können [One cannot imagine, I say, that the SS-men of Auschwitz could have emerged from these apartments].[28] That viewing an old Russian wooden house triggers such an associative arc to the SS murderers of Auschwitz indicates the extent to which the young author took on historical debt as individual and personal.

As sources, the diary excerpts must be interpreted with caution. The knowledge that surveillance by the Stasi led Christa Wolf to hide her diaries for the first time in 1968[29] means that we must read these partly fragmented passages not only as traces of barriers to thinking, but also as precautionary measures in light of the threat of surveillance. The excerpts from Wolf's correspondence with Efim Etkind[30] and Lew Kopelew[31] in the 1980s[32] recorded in *Moskauer Tagebücher*, however, illuminate the key position this confrontation with the Stalinist abyss holds in her own socialist thought. In letters, but also in *Ein Tag im Jahr* and in *Stadt der Engel*, Wolf repeatedly formulates what she saw as a pending task – to engage as intensively with Stalinist patterns as she had with National Socialist patterns in *Kindheitsmuster*. But the author lacks the power to develop an adequate form. The 2013 volume *Ein Tag im Jahr im neuen Jahrhundert 2001–2011*, published posthumously and edited by Gerhard Wolf, shows some of the reasons for this deficiency. The exhausting debates around *Was bleibt* (1990) may have prevented her from writing a large novel on Stalinism.

The constantly shifting understanding of 'the East' in Wolf's work demonstrates how the topographic becomes topological. Once the GDR is labelled 'the East'; another time it is an eastern Soviet republic, and later it is Siberia. The travel reports are each determined by a certain perspective: first from her own East towards the more eastern East, then from the GDR East – always polit-

28 Wolf, *Moskauer Tagebuch*, p. 61.
29 See Christa Wolf, *Ein Tag im Jahr 1960–2000* (Munich: Luchterhand, 2003), p. 477. The detailed diaries are referred to here. The author kept a diary for her entire life.
30 Efim Etkind (1918–1999) was a Russian Germanist and translator. In 1974, his professorship was withdrawn due to his contacts with Solženicyn and the poet Iossif Brodski. From then onwards, he lived in Paris.
31 Wolf met the Russian writer Lew Kopelew (1912–1997) through Anna Seghers in 1965. See her eulogy from 1997, reproduced in Wolf, *Moskauer Tagebuch*, pp. 255–258.
32 Over the course of these years, she also met Yuri Trifonow, Yevgeny Jewtuschenko, Grigori Baklanow and Constantin Simonov. Tamara Motylowa informed the Wolfs about the Party exclusion of Lew Kopelew, later they learned more details about criminal proceedings against Iosif Brodskij, Andrej Sinjawski, Juli Daniel and criminalization of Aleksandr Isaevič Solženicyn from her.

ically understood as more Western – into the extra-European East, and always back to her own. The ten voyages move her own East symbolically eastward, and in this way, they incrementally establish a different coordinate system.[33] In view of the vehement post-Wende normalization discourse that configured German history as the 'long road to the West',[34] East German writers pushed the memory of their past – the 'Inner East' – as far as Siberia. Christa Wolf's travel notes show signs of this process long before 1989; the East-West antagonism has already become the asymmetrical structure of periphery and centre. In one of her last interviews, in 2010, Wolf registers with a shake of her head 'wie viele Stunden wir damit verbracht haben, uns darüber klar zu werden, wo wir eigentlich leben [...]. Wir fuhren [1964 mit dem Schriftsteller Franz Fühmann durch Ungarn] auf der Donau und rundum um uns herum waren die schönsten Landschaften. Und wir haben über die DDR gesprochen. Die ganze Zeit [how many hours we have spent clarifying to ourselves where we actually live (...). We drove (through Hungary in 1964 with the writer Franz Fuhmann) along the Danube, and all around us were the most beautiful landscapes. And we talked about the GDR. The whole time].[35]

As in her literary prose, Wolf favours the process of thought over the result. In metaphors of motion (travel and flowing elements), hard-and-fast meanings are eluded. Topological patterns even structure the perception of personal encounters: as the Wolfs meet the Swiss Max Frisch during their Volga boat trip in 1968, the ship becomes a semiosphere of the East-West encounter.[36] In a 1981 essay, Wolf considers herself an Eastern European intellectual vis-à-vis the Swiss writer.[37] This contact with a soulmate colleague leads her back to herself. Why, she asks herself in the middle of the Volga, does he present himself so much more decisively, maturely and confidently? 'Man muß einmal untersuchen,

---

33 In post-GDR literature, the topos 'Sibiria' is doubly coded as Eastern: both as extra-European and as part of the former Eastern Bloc countries. See Asako Miyazaki, *Brüche in der Geschichtserzählung. Erinnerung an die DDR in der Post-DDR-Literatur* (Würzburg: Königshausen and Neumann, 2013), pp. 113, 134.

34 Heinrich August Winkler, *Der lange Weg nach Westen. Deutsche Geschichte*, vol. 2, 5th rev. edn (Munich: C. H. Beck, 2002).

35 Carsten Gansel und Christa Wolf '"Zum Schreiben haben mich Konflikte getrieben" – ein Gespräch (geführt am 8. Juli und 23. September 2010)', in *Christa Wolf. Im Strom der Erinnerung*, ed. by Carsten Gansel with Sonja Klocke (Göttingen: Verlag für Berlin-Brandenburg, 2014), pp. 353–366 (p. 363).

36 The Volga journey leads to Gorki, from Moscow to Leningrad and Vilnius. Wolf, *Moskauer Tagebuch*, p. 137.

37 Christa Wolf, 'Begegnungen. Max Frisch on this 70th Birthday (1981)', reprint in Wolf, *Moskauer Tagebuch*, pp. 143–148 (p. 143).

warum unsere Generation in Deutschland – speziell in der DDR – so lange braucht, um ‚fertig' zu werden. Der schreckliche Umweg über zwei ausschließliche – alles andere und leider auch die eigene Beobachtung ausschließende Ideen [We must examine why our generation in Germany – especially in the GDR – takes so long to be 'finished'. The terrible detour via two ideas that exclude everything else, and unfortunately also one's own observation].[38] Wolf always comes back to her generational affiliation. Christa Wolf was born in 1929. Her generation lived their childhood and youth in the National Socialist era and started their careers in the GDR's early days; these are two ideological influences whose contents are contradictory and which are formally more similar than those intellectuals who had been anti-fascistically re-educated and who sincerely held socialist convictions wished them to be. In *Kindheitsmuster* (1976), Wolf would highlight certain patterns of socialization that continued in the GDR as well. Within the GDR, this strand of her complex narrative structure was very delicately perceived.[39]

In 1990, as the collapse of socialism in Europe led to the rebuilding of the political coordinate system of many Eastern European intellectuals, memories were also retroactively topologically recoded: 'Die Orte, an denen wir uns begegnet sind, haben sich in meiner Erinnerung in Inseln verwandelt, gegen die die Flut ansteigt' [The places where we met have transformed in my memory into islands, against which the tide rises].[40] This apocalyptic, naturalizing imagery refers to Cold War times. The author dedicates a whole chapter to waters – as waters of a life – in her last novel, *Stadt der Engel* (2010). In addition to the Baltic Sea, the Black Sea emerges – but interestingly, it is no longer part of the East, as in the *Moskauer Tagebücher*, but is rather an 'erste Bekanntschaft mit dem Süden' [first acquaintance with the South].[41]

On her first trip to Moscow in 1957, Wolf was still inclined to concede to the Russian hosts who officially accompanied her that they had a 'Blick fürs Wesentliche' [an eye for the essential] with regard to the GDR.[42] As a German, she felt

---

38 Wolf, *Moskauer Tagebuch*, p. 137.

39 For more on this internal reception in the GDR, cf. Birgit Dahlke, 'Schreiben wider das Vergessen. Kindheitsmuster (1976)', in *Christa Wolf Handbuch. Leben, Werk, Wirkung*, ed. by Carola Hilmes and Ilse Nagelschmidt (Stuttgart/Weimar: Metzler, 2016).

40 Wolf, 'Begegnungen', p. 143.

41 It identifies the Baltic Sea, the Black Sea, the Atlantic from Brittany and Lisbon, the Mediterranean from Cannes and from the edge of Sicily, the Pacific Ocean, the lakes of Mecklenburg (with a 'Heimatsee'), the lake Zürichsee, the small Pleisse River, the Saale, the Spree, the Panke, the Moldova, the Rhine, the Thames, the Tiber and the Moskva River; see Christa Wolf, *Stadt der Engel*, p. 362.

42 Wolf, *Moskauer Tagebuch*, p. 16

particularly critically observed, and not only by Vladimir Steshenski, who had been a culture officer in post-War Berlin. By 1966, however, the comparison between daily life in the socialist Soviet Union and the socialist GDR more confidently favoured her own society. 'Eine geistige Erneuerung des Marxismus wird aus der SU wahrscheinlich kaum kommen – zuwenig Gärung, zuviel Resignation. Zuviel Leiden wahrscheinlich hinter ihnen, sie sind erschöpft. Zu groß die Trägheit des riesigen Landes [...] Der ‚neue Mensch' existiert gar nicht' [A spiritual renewal of Marxism is unlikely to come from the Soviet Union – too little foment, too much resignation. Probably too much suffering behind it; it is exhausted. The inertia of the vast country is too large (...) The 'new human being' doesn't even exist].[43] The expression 'the new human being' reflects a Marx-inflected image of humankind with which the first generation of the GDR had grown up. In a society based upon collective ownership of the means of production, the interests of the individual would largely dovetail with those of the collective, and vice versa. Important works of 1960s poetry, drama and film tell of the inner and outer conflicts of such disinterested 'heroes of labour' acting for the benefit of the community.

The question of the relationship between the needs and conditions of the socialist community and of individual self-realization became essential for Wolf. A seemingly minor sentence in the travel log of the fourth trip in 1966 shows an interesting perspectival shift that implies self-identification as a Western European woman: 'Ist nicht vielleicht dieser innere Kampf um die Erhaltung der Persönlichkeit eine typisch westliche Erscheinung, ein Ideal, auf wenige europäische Länder beschränkt? Und sonst überall geht es einfach um das nackte Leben?' [Is not perhaps this inner battle for the preservation of personality a typically Western phenomenon, an ideal, limited to a few European countries? And everywhere else the point is simply bare life?]. [44] At this time, Wolf was working on *Nachdenken über Christa T.,* a prose text that opposes the socialist pressure to adapt precisely by insisting on the maintenance of personality. If this position is 'Western', whence is it being spoken? Obviously, in asking these questions, the author must extend the East-West paradigm to the European versus the non-European in order to secure her own position as a socialist.

In the notes on the eighth and tenth trips in 1981 and 1989, the careful questions have become pronouncements: 'der Haupteindruck: der einzelne ist nicht viel wert' [the main impression: the individual does not count for much].[45]

---

43 Wolf, *Moskauer Tagebuch*, p. 84.
44 Wolf, *Moskauer Tagebuch*, p. 82.
45 Wolf, *Moskauer Tagebuch*, p. 198.

'Das Gefühl, die Person verschwinde je weiter gen Osten desto mehr hinter und in der Masse' [The feeling, that further eastward the person disappears more and more behind and in the mass].[46] What the author here pointedly observes about the 'more eastern East' had also been central to her own East in *Nachdenken über Christa T.* Early on, Christa Wolf registered scenes of general indifference, recklessness and hypocrisy in public interactions: 'Kein Lächeln übrig' [No smile available].[47] In 1987, in the midst of Perestroika and Glasnost, she particularly attends to the divergent positions of Russian conversation partners; anti-Semitism comes up for discussion multiple times. This sensitivity is remarkable – the longevity of anti-Jewish and anti-Semitic sentiment, even within the communist and workers' movements, remained taboo.

The key term is now 'polarization'. On the one hand, long-repressed themes can finally be publicly negotiated, and corresponding works of art become accessible. On the other hand, the economic situation across the huge country also becomes visible. Hopes and fears hold the balance. It is interesting to see what serves her as a standard of comparison to assess the mood: 'ohne Illusion und Überschwang: Das unterscheidet diese Perestroika von der Prager damals' [without illusion and exuberance: this is what distinguishes this Perestroika from that of Prague at the time].[48] The determination of an Eastern standpoint leads to the perception of her own intermediate positioning. At the height of Gorbachev's Glasnost policy, Wolf draws upon Eastern and Western thought patterns simultaneously: 'Die Russen auf der Suche nach ihrer Seele – Westler würden sagen: nach ihrer Identität' [The Russians seeking their souls – Westerners would say: seeking their identity]. She is the one who knows both discourses, who does not choose one of the two rhetorics but connects both in her literature. As a resident of a city that, in the form of the Wall, is daily and very directly confronted with the other part of Germany, she links the consciousness of the Western extension of the East with the eastward expansion of the Western horizon.

In a poem that Thomas Brasch – the son of Jewish Communists, born in exile in 1945 and living in West Berlin from 1976 – dedicated to Christa Wolf on the occasion of her 65th birthday in 1994, this intermediate position 'between here

---

46 Wolf, *Moskauer Tagebuch*, p. 213.
47 Wolf, *Moskauer Tagebuch*, p. 61.
48 Wolf, *Moskauer Tagebuch*, p. 202. See also: Jan Pauer, *Prag 1968. Der Einmarsch des Warschauer Pakts – Hintergründe, Planung, Durchführung* (Bremen: Edition Temmen, 1995); Vladimir V. Kusin, *The Intellectual Origins of the Prague Spring. The Development of Reformist Ideas in Czechoslovakia in 1956–1967* (Cambridge: Cambridge University Press, 2002); Dieter Segert, *Prager Frühling. Gespräche über eine europäische Erfahrung* (Vienna: Braumüller, 2008).

and again-there' becomes the axis of a paradoxical structure of identity assignment:

> Wünsche für C.
>
> 1
> Den Ort der zwischen Hier und Wiederdort
> dich immer gehen aber nie vergehen läßt.
> Bleib, ruft er dich, bleib endlich fort.
> Ich will dein Land sein. Sei mein Rest.
>
> 2
> Das Wort, das jeder buchstabieren kann,
> der es nicht schreibt, weil jeder es versteht.
> Nie heißt es Ich, oft Du und manchmal Wann
> hast du mich endlich mir ganz zugedreht.
>
> 3
> Die Zeit, die zwischen Jetzt und Dunkelheit
> sehr plötzlich unaufhörlich dauert, ja
> als öffne sie dir deine Türen einmal weit
> und steht. Jetzt bin ich wieder da.[49]

To write from an intermediate position becomes the object of desire. If one reads the poem precisely, one sees that Brasch respectfully and critically deploys the subjunctive voice, which is so typical of Wolf, against her. His word 'again-

---

[49] Thomas Brasch, „Die nennen das Schrei". Gesammelte Gedichte, ed. by Martina Hanf and Kristin Schulz. (Berlin: Suhrkamp, 2013), p. 387. A rough, literalist translation of this poem follows:
1
That which between here and again-there
Always lets you go but never lets you vanish.
Stay, he calls you, stay away at last.
I want to be your country. Be my place of rest.
2
The word that everyone can spell,
who does not write it, because everyone understands it.
It is never called I, often you and sometimes When
have you at last turned me completely to myself.
3
The time that between now and darkness
very suddenly continuously lasts, yes
as if it opens your doors to you wide once
and stands. Now I am back again'.
Wolf, Moskauer Tagebuch, p. 205.

there' references a trap. All the spatial vocabulary in this poem is bound to time; in the last of the three verses, time even 'stands'. The 'again-there' of the first line has become an 'again-here', and the desire has become a warning. The oxymoron in the title of Wolf's 1999 collection of stories – *Hierzulande. Andernorts* – enriches the deictic gesture through a dimension that can be most specifically determined through topologically understood alterity.

In the 1995 long-short story 'Begegnungen Third Street' [Encounters on Third Street] (entire passages of which would later be incorporated into *Stadt der Engel*), the first-person narrator speaks from and within the encounter. Her meetings with different people in Los Angeles allow her to perceive herself as an urbanite, a European, a German, an Eastern German, a woman and as white. At one point, because the author's own identity has been called into question by the historical break of 1989, the text works to assemble a new identity from various elements. The category of guilt becomes a connecting structure for these heterogeneous elements, in contrast to all the people – characterized as 'innocent' – whom the narrator meets on the Ocean Park promenade. Associative links with National Socialist crimes, GDR State Security and, finally, with the work on the *Medea* text drive her literary search. In the context of the narrative flow, the proper name 'Third Street' can be read as a chronotope[50] – one thinks, for example, of left-leaning reform debates about a 'third way' of democratic socialism,[51] or of Homi Bhabha's post-colonial critical concept of a 'third space'.[52]

Surprisingly, in Wolf's story about Los Angeles, 'Heimweh nach Moskau' [Homesickness for Moscow] suddenly appears, 'nach einem Moskau, das es nicht mehr gibt' [for a Moscow that is no longer there], with friends who now meet in Western cities.[53] The walk with Bredel to Lubyanka, mentioned in the 1959 travel notes, is mentioned again – and later she will also mention the drinking session with the old German Communist, in which tears erupted. Three times – from the different revisions of the 1959 travel notes, to the 1999 short story, to the 2010 novel *Stadt der Engel* – 'Moscow' is amalgamated into a very specific

---

50 'Die Merkmale der Zeit offenbaren sich im Raum, und der Raum wird von der Zeit mit Sinn erfüllt und dimensioniert.' Mikhail Bakhtin, 'Forms of Time in the Novel. Investigations on the Historical Poetry (1937/38 and 1973/75)', in *Chronotopos*, trans. by Michael Dewey, afterword by Michael C. Frank and Kirsten Mahle (Frankfurt a. M.: Suhrkamp, 2008), pp. 7–196 (p. 7).

51 See, for example, Dieter Klein, 'Demokratischer Sozialismus – ein transformatorisches Projekt', *Utopie Kreativ*, 147 (January 2003), 17–29.

52 For him, 'third space' is a largely unrecognized mental space, a transient 'Nicht-Ort' between personal and historical-specific origin. See Homi K. Bhabha: *The Location of Culture* (London/ New York: Routledge, 1994).

53 Christa Wolf, 'Begegnungen Third Street', in *Hierzulande. Andernorts. Erzählungen und andere Texte 1994–1998* (Munich: Luchterhand, 1999), pp. 7–41 (p. 15).

time, thus acting as a chronotope. No matter what the *story-here* forms or in which thematic context the respective narrative flow is situated, 'Moscow' is always part of the *discours-here*.[54] This chronotope is anything but accidental. Both in Christa Wolf's posthumous texts and in many other prose texts from 2000 onwards, central figures are portrayed via their relationship to Russians. The beginning of the new millennium forces a (re-)determination of their own identity, which is undertaken towards the East. The *Moskauer Tagebücher* record the traces of a long and contradictory path leading there.

Translated by Jennifer Ruth Hosek

---

54 In a path-breaking essay on chronotopes (literally, 'timespaces'), published in 1981, Mikhail Bakhtin (1938–1973) argued that time and space were best treated as an inseparable complex of parameters, with time supplying the 'fourth dimension of space', as in Einstein's theory of relativity'; see Sabine Buchholz and Manfred Jahn, 'Space in Narrative', in Herman, Jahn and Ryan, pp. 551–555 (p. 551). 'Story-HERE is the zero-point in the story space determining the use of deictic expressions such as "here", "there", "left", "right" etc. [...] Discourse-HERE, on the other hand, is the current point of orientation in discourse space, equivalent to the current physical location and the vantage point of the narrator' (p. 552).

Caroline Summers
Translating Subjective Authenticity from *Christa T.* to *Stadt der Engel* and *August:* Re-presenting Christa Wolf's Subaltern Voice

[O]b sie sich vielleicht ebenso wie ich als Darsteller vorkamen in einem ihnen fremden Stück, [...] dessen Sprache sie so korrekt wie möglich sprachen, eingelernte Dialoge, aber die eigene Sprache würde es niemals sein.

[If they felt as much like an actor in a foreign play as I did, [...] whose words they pronounced as correctly as possible, dialogue that would never be their own language.][1]

Since the publication of *Nachdenken über Christa T.* in 1968 and its English translation *The Quest for Christa T.* in 1970, Christa Wolf has been considered one of the most influential voices in German twentieth- and twenty-first-century literature and a representative of 'German' writing on the global stage. With almost all her narrative prose texts translated into English, Wolf's profile in the Anglophone literary context surpasses that of many of her contemporary German-language writers. Nonetheless, this internationally representative status is characterized by negotiation and compromise on a local level. Theories of translation as rewriting, for example, demonstrate how an author and her work are continually reframed by the new literary environments they enter in translation.[2] As André Lefevere's work reveals, the implications of such shifts are not inevitably negative; however, the 'hyper-central' status of the Anglophone literary field and its reputation for a hegemonic and aggressively monolingual approach to translation engender questions about the forms of negotiation or rereading Wolf's writing has undergone in its transition to the status of 'world literature'.[3]

---

1 Christa Wolf, *Stadt der Engel oder The Overcoat of Dr. Freud* (Berlin: Suhrkamp, 2010), p. 101; translation taken from Christa Wolf, *City of Angels. Or, The Overcoat of Dr. Freud*, trans. by Damion Searls (New York: Farrar, Straus and Giroux, 2013), p. 73.
2 See, for example, André Lefevere, *Translation, Rewriting, and the Manipulation of Literary Fame* (London: Routledge, 1992).
3 On the centrality of the English language to world literary systems, see Johan Heilbron, 'Towards a Sociology of Translation. Book Translations as a Cultural World-System', *European Journal of Social Theory*, 2 (1999), 429–444; and Gisèle Sapiro, 'Globalization and Cultural Diversity in the Book Market. The Case of Literary Translations in the US and in France', *Poetics*, 38 (2010), 419–439; on aggressive monolingualism, see Lawrence Venuti, *The Scandals of Translation. Towards an Ethics of Difference* (London/New York: Routledge, 1998), p. 310.

https://doi.org/10.1515/9783110496000-014

Wolf's texts explore a productive dialectic between self and other as fundamental to human experience, not only in their fluid narrative poetics, but also in their critical engagement with object/subject relations in the narrative act. Her characteristic 'subjective authenticity' constitutes a stylistic challenge to the norms of linguistic fluency and cultural domestication that have shaped translation practice in the Anglophone literary system. In addition, particularly in the USA and during the Cold War that contextualized the publication of *Nachdenken über Christa T.* and its translation, the affinity Wolf identifies between her poetics and her socialist worldview challenged an ideological norm of mainstream cultural production as divorced from politics. Studies of the early translations of her writing certainly reflect this challenge, demonstrating the considerable stylistic and interpretive shifts undergone by her texts in their translation into English.[4] Looking not only at the texts, but also at the discourse surrounding the translations, some of this research also demonstrates how other agents – such as publishers or reviewers – contribute to the rewriting and reinterpretation of her work through translation. Such shifts are significant specifically because of the close relationship between Wolf's politics and her writing: a move away from subjective-authentic style in a given translation implies the reformulation not just of her literary, but simultaneously also of her cultural-political voice.

Wolf's status in the GDR, where she occupied a relatively powerful (while also vulnerable) speaking position within institutional discourse, contrasts sharply with the extensive reconstruction of her literary voice in English translation. Such a reformulation of voice has significant implications for the author's ability to speak to readers through the English translations. In her work on the position of the subaltern outside hegemonic discourse, cultural theorist Gayatri Chakravorty Spivak describes the act of speaking as a transaction between speaker and listener: the subaltern, positioned outside normal channels of expression, is unable to speak because she cannot be successfully heard.[5] It

---

4 See Charlotte Koerner, 'Divided Heaven. By Christa Wolf? A Sacrifice of Message and Meaning in Translation', *The German Quarterly*, 57 (1984), 213–230; Caroline Summers, 'Patterns of Authorship. The Translation of Christa Wolf's *Kindheitsmuster*', *German Life and Letters*, 67 (2014), 378–398; Caroline Summers, *Examining Text and Authorship in Translation. What Remains of Christa Wolf?* (London: Palgrave Macmillan, 2017); Katharina von Ankum, 'The Difficulty of Saying "I". Translation and Censorship of Christa Wolf's *Der geteilte Himmel*', *Studies in Twentieth Century Literature*, 17 (1993), 223–241.
5 Donna Landry and Gerald MacLean, 'Subaltern Talk. Interview with the Editors', in *The Spivak Reader*, ed. by Donna Landry and Gerald MacLean (New York/London: Routledge, 1996), pp. 287–308; Leon de Kock, 'New Nation Writers Conference in South Africa', *Ariel. A Review of International English Literature*, 23 (1992), 29–47 (pp. 45–46).

would be inappropriate to assume a straightforward parallel between the relatively privileged position of Wolf in the GDR and the lives of the oppressed postcolonial subjects who are the focus of Spivak's work; however, Spivak's definitions of speech as a transaction and of the subaltern as a position of non-dominance, outside of the hegemonic discourse, resonate with the work of translation theorists – such as Lefevere – on translation as a rewriting or rearticulation of the source text. Spivak's highlighting of the subaltern can therefore help us towards a better understanding of Wolf's discursive position – in other words, that of a writer translated into the hegemonic literary language of English.[6]

The wealth of English translations of Wolf's writing, in contrast to other German-language writers who have explored subjectivity or written within a socialist cultural framework (Ingeborg Bachmann or Irmtraud Morgner, for example), makes her a significant case study for the application of Spivak's theory to the figure of the translated author. Wolf is a writer considered 'international' enough to appeal repeatedly to an audience beyond her immediate cultural context, but one whose voice has nonetheless undergone rearticulation for this new readership. Even in recent English translations of her later texts, which move closer than earlier translations to the distinctive and disruptive style of the German,[7] the reader's access to Wolf's voice continues to be curated by those beyond the translator who present the texts for the Anglophone reader. Applying this wider understanding of the translation process and acknowledging Spivak's reading of the subaltern as outside the hegemonic discourse, this chapter asks whether Wolf the world author might still be considered a subaltern voice in world literature.

The Translated Writer as Subaltern?

Spivak understands the subaltern as a speaking position without agency, from which the speaker unsuccessfully seeks to enter the hegemonic discourse. This leads to representation in the language of the discourse: Spivak discusses the German terms *vertreten* and *darstellen* as two dimensions of representation and observes that western cultural theorists often conceal the latter – the less explicit act of identity construction – behind the former, the more visible act

---

6 Gayatri Chakravorty Spivak, 'Can the Subaltern Speak?', in *Marxism and the Interpretation of Culture*, ed. by Cary Nelson and Lawrence Grossberg (London: Macmillan, 1988), pp. 271–313.
7 Caroline Summers, 'World Authorship as a Struggle for Consecration. Christa Wolf and *Der geteilte Himmel* in the English-speaking World', *Seminar*, 51 (2015), 148–172.

of speaking on someone's behalf.[8] The result of this, she notes, is that 'white men are saving brown women from brown men' – in other words, that the stories and experiences of subaltern populations are retold in the language and value systems of the dominant culture.[9] Spivak identifies the act of translation as the construction rather than the simple transfer of meaning, in which the sometimes disruptive relationship between the 'rhetoricity' and the 'logic' of the source text is crucial to the creation of agency.[10] In other words, the author may exploit expression in the source language to disrupt the accepted truths of the text or source-culture discourse. Spivak notes that, in translation, the temptation is to preserve logic at the expense of the expression or rhetoricity of the source text. This concern with the reshaping of expression by dominant norms of the target culture is echoed by voices in Translation Studies – such as Michaela Wolf, who identifies translation as a strategy for consolidating the cultural other, one that can imply 'the blocking of any autonomous dynamics of cultural representation'.[11]

Thus, while Wolf is considered representative of German literature, she is *represented* in translation by the reassignment of meaning in her writing. In the absence of rhetorical and logical frameworks that contextualize the German text, the author is left without agency to make her voice heard in an Anglophone literary field. Crucially, of course, this is not solely the responsibility of her translators: if being heard is a crucial element of the act of speaking, is not just the translator's choices, but also the readings offered by (for instance) reviewers that assign meaning to the text in the target system and prepare the reader to interpret the text.[12] Accordingly, Michaela Wolf argues that consolidation of the other 'can be observed, for instance, at different levels of the production of translations, from the selection of texts to be translated to the modes of distribution, all marked by power relations, including the translation strategies adopted'.[13] In-

---

8 Spivak, 'Can the Subaltern Speak?', p. 276.
9 Ibid., p. 296.
10 Gayatri Chakravorty Spivak, 'Translation as Culture', *Parallax*, 6 (2000), 13–24; Gayatri Chakravorty Spivak, 'The Politics of Translation', in *The Translation Studies Reader*, ed. by Lawrence Venuti, 3rd edn (London: Routledge), pp. 312–330 (p. 313).
11 Michaela Wolf, 'Culture as Translation – and Beyond. Ethnographic Models of Representation in Translation Studies', in *Crosscultural Transgressions. Research Models in Translation Studies II – Historical and Ideological Issues*, ed. by Theo Hermans (Manchester: St Jerome, 2002), pp. 180–192 (p. 188); see also for example Mohja Kahf, 'Packaging "Huda". Sha'rawi's Memoirs in the United States Reception Environment', in *Critical Readings in Translation Studies*, ed. by Mona Baker (London: Routledge, 2010), pp. 28–45.
12 Spivak, 'Translation as Culture', p. 22.
13 Wolf, 'Culture as Translation', p. 188.

stitutional agents in the target culture adopt the position of Spivak's western intellectual as they participate in the reframing (or *Darstellung*) of text and author. The subjective authenticity of the text, central to Wolf's literary voice, is thus exposed to potential rearticulation or rereading by numerous agents in the translation process. This has been apparent since the very earliest translations of Wolf's writing.

Translating Subjective Authenticity: *Nachdenken über Christa T.*

The authenticity of subjective experience as a medium for literary prose moved to the centre of Wolf's literary practice while she was writing *Nachdenken über Christa T.* in the late 1960s. It is discussed at length in her essays and interviews from that period, most significantly in 'Lesen und Schreiben' (1968) and in her 1973 conversation with the East German literary scholar Hans Kaufmann.[14] Wolf uses the term *subjektive Authentizität* to refer to a prose style in which the narrator is a visible practitioner of memory and narration, identifying a 'fourth dimension' in the text as that of the narrator.[15] This 'dimension' manifests itself, for example, in shifts of tense between the moments of experience and narration; in fragmented, incomplete syntax; or in the intrusion of character perspective into the narrative voice. The narrator, like her protagonist, is both a narrating and a narrated subject. Wolf's narrator in *Nachdenken über Christa T.*, attempting to reconstruct the life of a recently deceased friend, explores tensions between institutional ideology and individual experience by appealing to unofficial accounts, such as diaries and personal memory. Key to Wolf's subjective authenticity, then, is her questioning of the alignment of 'facts' with 'truth'.

---

14 Christa Wolf, 'Lesen und Schreiben', in *Werkausgabe in 12 Bänden*, ed. by Sonja Hilzinger (Munich: Luchterhand, 1999–2001), IV: *Essays/Gespräche/Reden/Briefe 1959–1974*, pp. 238–282; Christa Wolf, 'Subjektive Authentizität. Gespräch mit Hans Kaufmann', in *Werkausgabe in 12 Bänden*, ed. by Sonja Hilzinger (Munich: Luchterhand, 1999–2001), IV: *Essays/Gespräche/Reden/Briefe 1959–1974* (1999), pp. 401–437. Wolf had also experimented with unstable narrative form in her book *Der geteilte Himmel* (1963) and her short story 'Juninachmittag' (1967).
15 'Das ist die Koordinate der Tiefe, der Zeitgenossenschaft, des unvermeidlichen Engagements, die nicht nur die Wahl des Stoffes, sondern auch seine Färbung bestimmt' [this is the co-ordinate of depth, of contemporaneousness, of inevitable involvement that determines not only the choice of material, but also its colouring]; Wolf, 'Lesen und Schreiben', p. 265; translation taken from Christa Wolf, 'The Reader and the Writer', in *The Reader and the Writer*, trans. by Joan Becker (Berlin: Seven Seas Books, 1977), pp. 177–212 (p. 198).

The authentic in the text depends not on the unreliable 'facts' of the diegetic world, but rather on the sincerity of the experience narrated: '[Der Erzähler] entschließt sich, zu erzählen, das heißt: wahrheitsgetreu zu erfinden auf Grund eigener Erfahrung' [the narrator decides to tell, that is invent, truthfully on the foundation of her own experience].[16]

Focusing on the author as much as the narrator, Wolf advocates 'Schreiben als Vorgang' [writing as process][17] and borrows from Brecht to coin the term 'epic prose', indicating a diegetic rather than a mimetic gesture through which the reader is directly exposed to the author's efforts to know herself. The expression of individual experience within and beyond institutional structures supports what the East German poet and politician Johannes Becher terms the 'Zu-sich-selber-Kommen des Menschen' [human coming-to-self], implying the emotional and social completeness of the individual.[18] For Wolf, this process is enabled in part by dialectic exposure and discovery of the self through the other, as in subjective-authentic prose. She quotes Becher as an epigraph to *Nachdenken über Christa T.*, and a central theme of the book is the protagonist's (and also the narrator's) 'Schwierigkeit, "ich" zu sagen' [difficulty of saying 'I'] within the rigid institutions (of politics, of narration) that rule them.[19] Offering uncertainty, tension, complexity and moral ambiguity rather than unambiguously positive heroes, formulaic structure and an explicit political message, Wolf's approach to literary narrative positioned her at odds with the key principles of the socialist-realist literary model favoured by the cultural and political authorities of the GDR.[20]

Unsurprisingly, Wolf's critical engagement with 'real-existing socialism' antagonized those authorities. The introspection and ambiguity of the subjective-authentic text raised concerns about its political credentials, as reflected in the publication history of *Nachdenken über Christa T.* in the GDR.[21] Initially re-

---

16 Wolf, 'Lesen und Schreiben', p. 258; 'The Reader and the Writer', p. 193.

17 Wolf, 'Subjektive Authentizität', p. 408.

18 See Johannes R. Becher, *Auf andere Art so große Hoffnung. Tagebuch 1950. Eintragungen 1951*, in *Gesammelte Werke* 12 (Berlin/Weimar: Aufbau, 1969), p. 224.

19 For an exploration of this, see for example, Julia Hell's discussion of Wolf's location of the split voice 'between body and language' in Julia Hell, *Post-Fascist Fantasies. Psychoanalysis, History, and the Literature of East Germany* (Durham/London: Duke University Press, 1997), p. 140.

20 See George Buehler, *The Death of Socialist Realism in the Novels of Christa Wolf* (Frankfurt a. M.: Peter Lang, 1984); Colin E. Smith, *Tradition, Art, and Society. Christa Wolf's Prose* (Essen: Blaue Eule, 1987).

21 The publication history of *Nachdenken über Christa T.* is documented in *Dokumentation zu Christa Wolf 'Nachdenken über Christa T.'*, ed. by Angela Drescher (Hamburg: Luchterhand, 1991).

jected in 1968 on the basis of its apparently inadequate ideological commitment to socialism, it was finally approved for publication later that year, before production was stopped in December. Concerns about the text's pessimism continued to dominate public discourse surrounding Wolf and her writing for many years: ambivalent reviews called her politics into question whilst acknowledging her efforts to conform to some precepts of socialist realism, and her publisher, Heinz Sachs, was obliged to publicly distance himself from the text.[22] Meanwhile, the West German publisher Luchterhand had published it in spring 1969, with reviewers in the FRG welcoming it as a critique of GDR socialism.[23] This reading irritated Wolf and further antagonized her critics in the East, who interpreted it as confirmation that the text undermined socialist values. Wolf's impulse to 'overstep the boundaries here and there', using rhetoricity to challenge logic, was thus read as a rejection of socialism throughout the text.[24]

Nonetheless, Wolf conceives subjective authenticity as a direct literary response to the aims of an ideal socialist society: she explains that 'die tiefe Wurzel der Übereinstimmung zwischen echter Literatur und der sozialistischen Gesellschaft sehe ich eben darin: Beide haben das Ziel, dem Menschen zu seiner Selbstverwirklichung zu helfen' [I see in this the deep roots of conformity between genuine literature and socialist society: both have the purpose of helping man to realise himself].[25] The culture and politics of the GDR are essential contextual factors for Wolf, who conceived subjective authenticity as a means to embody socialist principles as much as it challenged the socialist-realist paradigm.[26] Like Brecht's epic theatre, Wolf's epic prose combats the alienation of the individual from society by encouraging a move away from fixed literary models. In her later interview with Kaufmann, she defends herself against the charge

---

22 Hermann Kähler, 'Christa Wolfs Elegie', *Sinn und Form*, 1 (1969), 2251–2261; Horst Haase, 'Nachdenken über ein Buch', *Neue deutsche Literatur*, 17 (1969), 174–185; Hans Sachs, 'Verleger sein heißt ideologisch kämpfen', *Neues Deutschland*, 14 May 1969.

23 Most famous among the West German responses is Marcel Reich-Ranicki's reading that Christa T. 'stirbt an der Leukämie, aber sie leidet an der DDR' [dies from leukaemia, but she suffers from the GDR]; Marcel Reich-Ranicki, 'Christa Wolfs unruhige Elegie', *Zeit*, 23 May 1969.

24 See Christa Wolf, *Moskauer Tagebücher* (Berlin: Suhrkamp, 2014), p. 153.

25 Christa Wolf, 'Selbstinterview', in Hilzinger (ed.) *Werkausgabe* IV, pp. 139–144 (p. 141); translation from Christa Wolf, 'Interview with Myself', in Becker, pp. 76–80 (p. 77).

26 Wolf's comments in an interview with Grace Paley from 1983 support this view: 'I'm a person who is very strongly rooted in the society in which I live, and what I usually write about are the conflicts between individuals and the societies in which they live – and the society is always shown as a very strong factor in the individual's life'; Christa Wolf, 'A Conversation with Grace Paley', in Christa Wolf, *The Author's Dimension. Selected Essays*, trans. by Jan van Heurck (Chicago: University of Chicago Press, 1993), pp. 271–282 (p. 272).

of subjectivism – or, in other words, the accusation that her writing destabilizes morality by implying that knowledge is determined by the individual. Wolf explains in her defence that exploration of the individual's material surroundings is coherent with Marxist principles, and she acknowledges her departure from the precepts of socialist *realism* specifically as an attempt to more fully engage with socialist *reality*. As Julia Hell has argued, Wolf's voice cannot be read as 'pure' in the sense of free from politics, but rather is inextricably embedded in its own historical and ideological context.[27]

While specifically informed by the historicity of her East German context, Wolf's intentions for her writing reached far beyond the GDR. In 1982, she explained to the scholar and journalist Frauke Meyer-Gosau how an institutional focus on forms of realism (not specifically socialist realism) obscures essential elements of human experience, which is where literature must step in: 'Institutionen [können sich] das Wesentliche nicht ausdenken, das rutscht zwischen den perfekten Strukturen durch [...]. Und da wird Literatur als ein Mittel der Selbstbehauptung benutzt' [institutions cannot imagine the essential things; they slip through the perfect structures (...). And so, literature is used as a means of self-assertion].[28] Here, Wolf is explicitly referring not just to the GDR, but also to the FRG, indicating that it is not just in the socialist context that literature can help individuals to process their experiences. For Wolf, the route to an understanding of broad, universal ideas is through particular experience. While (or perhaps specifically because) her intentions are inherently socialist, then, Wolf sees that her subjective-authentic writing has something to offer the reader outside of the GDR – exploring literature as a crucial link between the individual and society. Looking beyond the German context, however, Wolf's subjective authenticity has consistently presented a challenge to her translators working in different linguistic, literary and political systems.

Reading translation as the inevitable rewriting of a text for the poetics of another literary system, André Lefevere defines poetics as consisting of two elements: 'one is an inventory of literary devices, genres, motifs, prototypical characters and situations, and symbols; the other a concept of what the role of literature is, or should be, in the social system as a whole'.[29] This second element

---

27 Hell, *Post-Fascist Fantasies*, p. 145.
28 Christa Wolf, 'Projektionsraum Romantik. Gespräch mit Frauke Meyer-Gosau', in Hilzinger (ed.) *Werkausgabe* VIII: *Essays/Gespräche/Reden/Briefe 1975–1986* (2000), pp. 236–255 (p. 251); translation from Christa Wolf, 'Culture is What you Experience. An Interview with Christa Wolf', trans. by Jeanette Clausen, *New German Critique*, 27 (1982), pp. 89–100 (p. 98).
29 Lefevere, *Translation, Rewriting, and the Manipulation of Literary Fame*, p. 26.

is crucial to an understanding of how Wolf's early writing has been read in translation: while the German texts are written and read in contexts characterized by politicized literature as the norm, the English translations have been published in literary environments lacking mainstream norms of political art. The work of the social theorist Gisèle Sapiro, for example, identifies a literary tendency to eschew politics in the post-War USA (in comparison with France).[30] While groups of writers such as the Beat Generation had questioned the values espoused by capitalist and elitist literary culture and sought to use literature as a form of political protest, the comments of prominent contemporary literary figures – such as the writer Eudora Welty – suggest an enduring institutional tendency away from 'crusading' in literature.[31]

What is more, the norms of fluent and invisible translation that have traditionally dominated in publishers' and reviewers' attitudes to literary translation in English are anathema to the 'inventory of literary devices' that sustain instability and uncertainty in the subjective-authentic text. While non-standard expression in non-translated literature may be welcomed in the interests of style, voice and effect, translated literature has historically contended with the expectation that it must read 'well' in English (as Spivak identifies when she comments on the sacrifice of rhetoricity to logic). This emphasis on normative fluency is reflected, for example, in the historical rejection of idiomatic incorrectness and incoherence under the label of 'translationese'.[32] While translators are answerable for the words on the page, it is often other institutionally authorized arbitrators and commentators – such as reviewers and editors – who most emphasize this requirement of fluency.[33] Alongside the shift from the fundamentally politicized context of the GDR to the putatively apolitical norms of mainstream US literature in the 1970s, then, the literary devices (and other poetic elements) available to the Anglophone translator have conditioned the appearance of Wolf's texts in translation. This began with the English translation of *Nachdenken über Christa T.*, a key moment in the positioning of Wolf as a subaltern voice.

---

30 Gisèle Sapiro, 'The Debate on the Writer's Responsibility in France and the United States from the 1920s to the 1950s', *International Journal of Politics, Culture and Society*, 23 (2010), 69–83.

31 Eudora Welty, 'Must the Novelist Crusade?', in *The Eye of the Story. Selected Essays and Reviews* (New York: Vintage, 1979), pp. 146–158.

32 See, for example, Venuti's discussion of normative, domesticating translation practices and the traditional invisibility of the translator in Lawrence Venuti, *The Translator's Invisibility*, 2nd edn (New York: Routledge, 2008).

33 Lefevere, *Translation, Rewriting, and the Manipulation of Literary Fame*, pp. 14–17.

Christopher Middleton's *The Quest for Christa T.* (1970) is a landmark in Wolf's emergence as a world author, since it was the first Wolf text to be published in English translation outside of the GDR and introduced her literary voice to an extensive Anglophone audience of readers, reviewers and scholars.[34] The German text and its English translation are differentiated by many stylistic discrepancies, which are discussed in depth elsewhere.[35] Most significantly, the translation consolidates a boundary between the narrated past and the narrating present tenses, reduces interference in the narration from 'other' voices in the text by standardizing idiolect and clearly marking speech and shifts focalization away from character perspectives by reorganizing syntax. The resulting increase in narrative stability means that the translated narrator gains control of the story thanks to her critical distance from past events. The shifting of the unstable 'ich' identity is lessened, so that the narrator's subjective 'dimension' is no longer present, and the writing no longer functions as a process of the narrator's coming-to-self.

Meanwhile, it is exactly this kind of (apparent) distance that leads Wolf to doubt the adequacy of traditional literary structures for representing human experience: in her interview with Kaufmann, she questions the idea that 'was erzählbar geworden ist, ist überwunden' [what is tellable has been overcome] – that is, she contends that acts of writing and narrating belong to the process of overcoming experience rather than reflecting its completion.[36] She comments to Frauke Meyer-Gosau that contradictions and tensions in her writing play a crucial role in exploring productive relationships between individual experience and (socialist) society: in *Nachdenken über Christa T.*, this inherent conflict is apparent not solely in Christa's illness, but in the shifts of narrative identity between the narrator and Christa herself.[37] However, *The Quest for Christa T.*

---

34 See Marilyn Sibley Fries, 'Christa Wolf's "Ort" in Amerika', in *Zwischen gestern und morgen. Schriftstellerinnen der DDR aus amerikanischer Sicht*, ed. by Ute Brandes (Berlin: Peter Lang, 1992), pp. 169–182. A translation of Wolf's *Der geteilte Himmel* (1963) had been published in 1965 by the GDR publisher Seven Seas Books and was largely ignored by the Anglophone world until a new edition was published in 1971 by the American publisher Adler's Foreign Books.
35 For a full analysis of translation shifts in *The Quest for Christa T.*, see Summers, *Examining Text and Authorship in Translation*. Sonja Klocke also notes a number of examples of loss of nuance or resonance in the translation: see Sonja Klocke, *Inscription and Rebellion. Illness and the Symptomatic Body in East German Literature* (Rochester: Camden House, 2015), pp. 45, 55, 61, 66, 67, 68.
36 Christa Wolf, 'Subjektive Authentizität', p. 406.
37 'Um Missverständnisse auszuschließen: Es ist meine grundlegende Lebensform, in Widersprüchen zu leben – das wäre nichts, was ich negative finde oder je gefunden habe'; Wolf, 'Pro-

often does not offer the reader the opportunity to recognize these tensions. Most significantly, the translation is not able to reflect a socialist concern with individual coming-to-self, as demonstrated by the translation of a quote from Christa's thesis on Theodor Storm:

> Die Konflikte ergreifen den ganzen Menschen, zwingen ihn in die Knie und vernichten sein Selbstgefühl.[38]

> [The conflicts grip the whole human being, force him to his knees and destroy his sense of self.][39]

> The conflicts seize hold of the whole person, force him to his knees and destroy his sense of individuality.[40]

In the German, the concept of 'Selbstgefühl' as knowledge and understanding of the self recalls Becher's 'Zu-sich-selber-Kommen des Menschen'. Wolf's point is that the social and political conflicts determining the experience of the individual prevent her from reaching the desired state of completeness and maturity. The translation, however, focuses on individuality as that which is threatened. This shift towards the ideological frameworks of the target system (focus on individuality rather than the collective) results in a very different message that presents 'die Schwierigkeit, "ich" zu sagen' as a search for autonomy rather than selfhood. The translation of such individual statements characterizes the role of mainstream literature in the target culture as fundamentally different from Wolf's understanding of literature as a space for political resistance.[41] It is therefore not only the rhetoricity of the writing that goes astray, but also its logical resonance for Wolf's immediate readership.

As far as the general stylistic changes between the German text and the English translation are concerned, they generate a narrative voice in the translation that departs from Wolf's concept of subjective authenticity, as the narrator is re-

---

jektionsraum Romantik', p. 242 ('So as to preclude misunderstandings: living in contradictions is my fundamental form of life – it's not something I find or have ever found negative'; Wolf, 'Culture is what you Experience', p. 93).

38 Wolf, *Nachdenken über Christa T.*, in *Werkausgabe in 12 Bänden*, ed. by Sonja Hilzinger (Munich: Luchterhand, 1999–2001), II: *Nachdenken über Christa T.*, p. 110.

39 My translation.

40 Christa Wolf, *The Quest for Christa T.*, trans. by Christopher Middleton (New York: Farrar Straus Giroux, 1970), p. 97.

41 For a recent exploration of how Wolf's writing opens a space for cultural resistance, see Anna Kuhn, 'Christa Wolf. Literature as an Aesthetics of Resistance', in *Literature and the Development of Feminist Theory*, ed. by Robin Truth Goodman (Cambridge: Cambridge University Press, 2015), pp. 155–171.

positioned at a critical and authoritative distance from the narrated events. Other early Wolf translations – such as Ursule Molinaro and Hedwig Rappolt's translation of *Kindheitsmuster* (1976; *A Model Childhood*, 1980) – display similar tendencies, suggesting that stylistic moves away from Wolf's poetics are provoked not (or not only) by the taste or strategy of the particular translator, but rather (or also) by the poetics of the target system and the perceived need to avoid 'translationese'.[42] Thus the translator, who occupies a mostly invisible position behind a fluent narrative voice that does not appear as 'other' to the Anglophone reader, participates in the *Darstellung* of Wolf and her literary voice in the image of existing target-culture norms.

The reviews of Middleton's translation reflected a mixed response to the voice of the text: the *New York Review of Books* rated the translation highly, while the *Times Literary Supplement* was more cautious, admitting that, while the translation was ingenious in places, 'at times the magic of [Christa's] personality is baldly stated rather than felt. Or the extent to which she is bound to her particular region proves sheerly untranslatable'.[43] Reviews such as these demonstrate how the institutional norms and reader expectations of the target literary system shape the author's ability to speak to her target-culture readers through the translated text. As for the text's political significance, W. L. Webb's exhortation in *The Guardian*, 'do not under-value the individual human life, from which alone the collective draws its value', counters the simplistic elision of individuality with 'Selbstgefühl' as seen above. However, the reviews also reconfigure Wolf's text with claims that it reflects 'individual resilience in the face of evil and adversity', makes use of 'objective narration', or even that it is 'apolitical', demonstrating the author's 'disdain of politics'.[44] These interpretations are not sensitive to Wolf's voice, and the socialist dimension of the text – seen by Wolf as key to its ability to reach out to the reader – is consequently lost in the target system. Whilst seeming to speak for Wolf as *Vertreter*, these agents of translation nonetheless reshape her and contribute to her *Darstellung*.

Thus the translation of *Nachdenken über Christa T.* and its reception by reviewers contributed to the initial representation of Wolf's writing in the systemic poetics of the Anglophone literary system and demonstrated the difficulty of

---

42 See Summers, 'Patterns of Authorship', for a discussion of the Molinaro and Rappolt translation.

43 John Willett, 'The Quest for East Germany', *New York Review of Books*, 2 September 1971; Unknown author, 'The problems of purity', *Times Literary Supplement*, 13 August 1971.

44 W. L. Webb, 'Complex Fatality', *Guardian*, 27 May 1971; Margaret McHaffie, 'See no evil', *Times Literary Supplement*, 4 June 1982; Willett, 'The Quest for East Germany'; Ernst Pawel, 'The Quest for Christa T.', *New York Times*, 31 January 1971.

making her speech recognizable for Anglophone readers. The initial cost of participation in the hegemonic discourse (that is, of translation into English) seems to have been the appropriation of her voice by the target culture, placing Wolf in the subaltern position of not being able to truly 'speak' to the Anglophone cultural field. In subsequent years, Wolf occupied an increasingly prominent position in the international literary field, in particular thanks to the 1984 translation of *Kassandra*, which found popularity in English thanks to the text's pacifist and apparently feminist arguments.[45] Meanwhile, the end of the Cold War and the process of German unification marked seismic shifts in the geopolitical context surrounding international literary exchange. It might therefore be assumed that, over time, Wolf and her texts moved to a position within the hegemonic discourse, following the growth of her profile in English and the disappearance of the geopolitical binary that had categorized her as 'other'. However, we might now turn our attention to the most recent translations to consider whether Wolf, now an established world author, cannot continue to be seen as a subaltern voice in Anglophone literary culture.

Stadt der Engel and *August*

Both of the later translations examined here were published after the demise of the GDR in 1990 and after Wolf's death in 2011. These two significant events varied greatly in their impact on the representation of Wolf and her writing. Wolf's death saw her celebrated and mourned as an important figure in world literature, increasing her visibility just as she herself was no longer present to comment on her writing.[46] Meanwhile, whilst still palpably present in German-language discourse and in Wolf's writing after 1990, the GDR and its ideology have become increasingly invisible to Anglophone discourse since the fall of the Berlin Wall. The loss of the GDR as a reference point is a signal that Wolf's subaltern status may endure even as her credentials as a world author are affirmed by posthumous tributes: if her speech cannot be heard in the con-

---

45 For a discussion of feminist readings of *Kassandra* in English translation, see Summers, *Examining Text and Authorship in Translation*; see also Georgina Paul, 'Feminism in the German Democratic Republic. The Discreet Charm of the Bourgeois Literary Tradition', *Oxford German Studies*, 45 (2016), 62–82.

46 For Anglophone obituaries, see for example, David Binder and Bruce Weber, 'Christa Wolf Dies at 82; Wrote of the Germanys', *New York Times*, 1 December 2011; 'Christa Wolf', *Daily Telegraph*, 1 December 2011; Carolyn Kellogg, 'German Author Christa Wolf has Died', *Los Angeles Times*, 1 December 2011; Kate Webb, 'Christa Wolf Obituary', *Guardian*, 1 December 2011.

text of the discourse in which it is produced, her voice continues to be excluded from the hegemonic discourse.

Published in 2010, *Stadt der Engel oder The Overcoat of Dr. Freud* recalls Wolf's nine-month residency at the Getty Center in Los Angeles from 1992–1993, during which period the revelation of her early Stasi involvement made her the target of heavy criticism in the German press. Published at a remove of almost twenty years, *Stadt der Engel* intersects the narrator's remembered trauma with reflections on the strangeness of American culture, alighting on questions of language and identity provoked by her new surroundings. Among other challenges, she is prompted to consider her position as a representative of the GDR and of post-unification Germany. Her new acquaintances hold her accountable not only for the flaws of the GDR as they (mis)understand them, but also for the ongoing failure of unified Germany to move on from the Nazi past. She overhears the comments of one American Germanist to this effect and finds herself frustrated by the efforts of her new American acquaintances to read post-War cultural production exclusively as a response to the Third Reich.[47] While it was Wolf's last publication during her lifetime, the text exhibits clear links to Wolf's earlier texts: there are echoes of *Kindheitsmuster* in its visible enactment and problematization of the writing process alongside the use of fragments from various sources, such as dreams, newspaper clippings, letters, diaries and conversations. It also recalls *Nachdenken über Christa T.* in its attempt to piece together the life of the mysterious 'L.' from letters and to offer an accurate narrative of intimate experience.[48] Like Wolf's earlier writing, *Stadt der Engel* continues to exploit the boundary between fact and fiction, with reflections

---

47 'Was die westdeutsche Öffentlichkeit jetzt mit der DDR-Kultur und ihren Vertretern mache, könne man doch eigentlich nur aus dem Bedürfnis erklären, nachzuholen, was man bei der Abrechnung mit der Nazi-Kultur versäumt habe'; Wolf, *Stadt der Engel*, p. 105. ('The way the West German media were treating East German culture and its representatives these days really had only one possible explanation: it stemmed from a need to make up for what they had failed to do in settling their own accounts with Nazi cultural figures'; Wolf, *City of Angels*, p. 76.) See also *Stadt der Engel*, p. 209; *City of Angels*, p. 157.

48 For more detail on the links between *Stadt der Engel* and the two earlier texts, see for example, Michael Minden, 'Social Hope and the Nightmare of History. Christa Wolf's *Kindheitsmuster* and *Stadt der Engel*', *Publications of the English Goethe Society*, 80 (2011), 196–203; Kaleen Gallagher, 'The Problem of Shame in Christa Wolf's *Stadt der Engel oder The Overcoat of Dr. Freud*', *German Life and Letters*, 65 (2012), 378–397; Angelica Michelis, '"To Learn to Live without Alternatives". Forgetting as Remembering in Christa Wolf's *The City of Angels; or, The Overcoat of Dr. Freud*', *Journal of Literature and Trauma Studies*, 3 (2014), 63–80. Wolf herself also comments, for example, on the centrality of the diary form to both *Kindheitsmuster* and *Stadt der Engel* (amongst others) as a source of 'the authentic' in her writing; see Christa Wolf, *Ein Tag im Jahr* (Frankfurt a. M.: Suhrkamp, 2008), p. 650.

throughout the text on the difficulty of the writing process making it an enact-ment of subjective authenticity (the narrator's emotions and memories form the basis of a highly personal narrative) as well as a discussion of what it should be (she comments on the nature of the text as she writes it).

With similar links to earlier writing, *August* (2012) is a short prose text appa-rently written by Wolf in one sitting, as an anniversary present for her husband Gerhard, and published posthumously. The title character is Wolf's only male protagonist, whose childhood stay in a tuberculosis sanatorium brings him into contact with the (largely autobiographical) Nelly of *Kindheitsmuster*, appear-ing in this text as Lilo.[49] Like *Nachdenken über Christa T.*, the text shifts between two worlds of memory and present experience: the now aging and widowed Au-gust pieces together his own life while travelling through East Germany as a coach driver for a group of West German pensioners on holiday. His memories recall his brief acquaintance with Lilo and also reflect on his marriage to his late wife, Trude.

Crucially, while both these texts post-date the political and cultural water-shed of 1989/1990, they also demonstrate the continuing salience of Wolf's so-cialist values and her commitment to the now non-extant GDR as a contextual influence on her writing. In the opening passage of *Stadt der Engel*, the narrator uses her still-valid GDR passport to enter the USA, much to the confusion of the customs official; in *August*, it is specifics of GDR culture – such as the *Spätver-kaufstelle* [kiosk with later opening hours] where the protagonist first met Trude or the *volkseigener Betrieb* [state-owned company] at which he worked – that contextualize his memories. Alongside the thematic links to Wolf's earlier writ-ing, the two later texts also present a translator with some familiar stylistic chal-lenges. There is the same shifting temporality and multiplicity of voices, and Wolf's fragmented and often idiosyncratic use of syntax creates narrators who constantly question their own assumptions whilst trying to reconcile conflicts between their individual experience and the world around them.

Despite these continuities, the translators' approach to the texts is signifi-cantly different from that seen in *The Quest for Christa T.* Wolf's recent translators have been sensitive to the stylistic challenges posed by her writing and have also commented on this. *City of Angels. Or, The Overcoat of Dr. Freud*, translated by Damion Searls, appeared with Wolf's main US publisher, Farrar Straus Giroux, and attracted acclaim in the US through its nomination by the website Three Per-

---

49 This intertextual reference may well be lost on the Anglophone reader, since the translation of *Kindheitsmuster* renames the young boy 'Gus' when he appears in the narrative; see Christa Wolf, *A Model Childhood*, trans. by Hedwig Rappolt and Ursule Molinaro (New York: Farrar, Straus and Giroux, 1980), pp. 404–405.

cent to the longlist for the Best Translated Book Award in 2014. Meanwhile, Katy Derbyshire's 2014 translation *August* appeared with the independent publisher Seagull, based in Kolkata, which specializes in translated literature in English. In both cases, the translators' freely available comments on their work invite a reader to recognize the stylistic characteristics of the writing and the intervention by the translator in the text. Searls has explained, for example, that his priority was to preserve what he describes as Wolf's poised and subtle style, and Derbyshire, having read Molinaro and Rappolt's translation of *Kindheitsmuster*, describes how she was keen to avoid the 'clunkiness' she identified in their version of Wolf.[50] This visibility of the translation process as *Vertretung* and *Darstellung* draws attention to the otherness of the translated text rather than concealing it, and the translation strategies used also reflect a greater degree of visibility for the stylistic other of the translated text.

Looking back, one of the most far-reaching stylistic changes in the translation of *Nachdenken über Christa T.* is the standardization of the voices in the text through 'correction' of non-standard language and reorganization of syntax. Searls and Derbyshire stay much closer to Wolf's syntax and style, evoking the orality (and therefore the immediacy) of the narrative act and allowing ambiguity to interfere with the narrator's control:

Geruch von Benzin, von Abgasen. Eine lange Fahrt.[51]

[Smell of petrol, of exhaust fumes. A long journey.][52]

The smell of gas and exhaust. A long drive.[53]

Sie hatte Papiere bei sich gehabt, einen Brustbeutel mit Papieren, als man sie auffand.

[She had had papers with her, a neck pouch with papers, when she was found.]

---

50 Larissa Zimberoff, 'Damion Searls', in *Bomb Magazine*, 19 June 2013 (http://bombmagazine. org/article/7138/damion-searls); Katy Derbyshire, 'Lilo, Nelly and I. On Translating Christa Wolf's *August*', in *The Quarterly Conversation*, 10 March 2014 (http://quarterlyconversation. com/lilo-nelly-and-i-on-translating-christa-wolf%E2%80%99s-august). Luise von Flotow, whose new translation of *Der geteilte Himmel* was published in 2013, has also used spaces outside of the published translation to comment on her work as a translator of Wolf; see 'Creatively Retransposing Christa Wolf. They Divided the Sky', in *In Translation. Honouring Sheila Fischman*, ed. by Sherry Simon (Montreal: McGill-Queen's University Press, 2013), pp. 65–82.

51 Wolf, *Stadt der Engel*, p. 11.

52 My translation.

53 Wolf, *City of Angels*, p. 5.

She'd had papers on her, a pouch round her neck with papers, when they found her.[54]

Both the translations here support a subjective-authentic reading. Through temporal ambiguity and fragmented syntax, they echo Wolf's text to give the effect of emotive, remembered fragments rather than distant, organized narrative.

Derbyshire's translation is particularly sensitive to the multiple voices that feature in the text, such as those of the maternal but straight-talking head nurse and of August himself. This multiplicity comes out clearly in the third-person narrative through expressive choices:

> Die Oberschwester hörte nicht auf, den Behörden vorzuwerfen, dass sie Lungenkranke in eine Sumpfgegend verfrachtet hatten, in der im Herbst die giftigen Dämpfe aus dem Boden aufstiegen, und dass sie anscheinend vorhatten, sie alle jetzt im Winter erfrieren zu lassen.[55]

> *[The head nurse did not stop accusing the authorities of having bundled lung patients off to a marshland where poisonous fumes came up out of the ground in autumn, and of apparently planning to let them now all freeze to death in winter.]*[56]

> The head nurse didn't stop accusing the authorities of having dumped lung-disease patients in a marshland where poisonous vapours came out of the ground in autumn, and of apparently intending to let them all freeze to death now it was winter.[57]

> Weiterfahrt. Die Senioren sind munter geworden.[58]

> *[Onward journey. The senior citizens have become lively.]*[59]

> Back on the road. The pensioners have perked up.[60]

Here, the feelings of the nurse are brought to life in both the German and the English through the use of emotive language and the adverb 'jetzt', which positions the speaker and the reader in the same temporal moment. In the second example, the narrator momentarily sees the situation through August's eyes – in his cursory, elliptical syntax and the othering of his passengers as 'Senioren'

---

54 Christa Wolf, *August* (Berlin: Suhrkamp, 2012), p. 19; translation taken from Christa Wolf, *August*, trans. by Katy Derbyshire (Calcutta: Seagull Books, 2014), p. 30. Future references will be given as *August* (DE) and *August* (EN).

55 Wolf, *August* (DE), p. 13.

56 My translation.

57 Wolf, *August* (EN), pp. 14–15.

58 Wolf, *August* (DE), p. 27.

59 My translation.

60 Wolf, *August* (EN), p. 48.

that reflects his unwillingness to identify with them. In both of these examples, the translation captures the attitude of the character within the narrative voice and filters events through multiple perspectives.

However, this is a point on which the two translations differ in approach, as Searls makes some substantial changes to the voice of *Stadt der Engel* through his translation of Wolf's code-switching between English and German. This mixing of languages happens throughout the German text as an indicator of the new cultural and linguistic context in which the narrator finds herself. To mark these words and phrases as other for the Anglophone reader too, Searls italicizes everything that appears in English in Wolf's text. However, he also undermines the constant mixing of self and other when he standardizes language, opting to 'translate [Wolf's] English into English', so that it sounds authentic to the American reader:[61]

> Mike sagte düster: If Clinton doesn't win I have to leave my country. – Why that?[62]
>
> *[Mike said bleakly: If Clinton doesn't win I have to leave my country. – Why that?]*[63]
>
> If Clinton doesn't win I'll have to leave the country, Mike said gloomily. – Why?[64]

While Searls explains that he was keen to avoid distracting the reader and embarrassing the author with incorrect English, this decision reduces the multivoicedness of the narrative. In the above example, the use of 'incorrect' English highlights the narrator's feeling of otherness when communicating in English, and also her unreliability: Mike's words are quoted as direct speech, but the selection of tense suggests that the wording stems from the narrator (a non-native speaker of English). By correcting Wolf's English, the translation makes this dimension invisible to the reader. Searls thus both foregrounds and masks the instability of speaking positions in the narrative.

In both texts, as in *Nachdenken über Christa T.*, language marks the dialogue between identities. In *Stadt der Engel*, conscious of her awkwardness in English and her wariness of particular expressions in German, Wolf's narrator reflects on how the sense of otherness between a speaker and a language that is not her own can sometimes lead to greater self-expression.[65] Acting as a 'Schutzschild,

---

61 Zimberoff, 'Damion Searls'.
62 Wolf, *Stadt der Engel*, p. 26.
63 My translation.
64 Wolf, *City of Angels*, p. 16.
65 The narrator speaks of 'rückhaltloses Sprechen in der fremden Sprache'; Wolf, *Stadt der Engel*, p. 200 ('holding nothing back as I talked in a foreign language'; Wolf, *City of Angels*, p. 150).

auch als Versteck'[66] [shield, or hiding place],[67] the foreign language in some instances permits Wolf's narrator to express herself more effectively than her native tongue. In translation, the narrator's probing of the disparate meanings of apparently equivalent words in German and English loses much of its impact due to the gloss translations provided: 'on my way back to the MS. VICTORIA I thought about how this word "honest" could fit the German word *"ehrlich"* (candid, straightforward), but also *"redlich"* (fair) and *"aufrichtig"* (genuine)'.[68] The mixing of languages becomes an exercise in vocabulary rather than a demonstration of how identities are created through the power of language to express experience. Here again, Searls sacrifices the rhetoricity of the text to the logic of the target language.

In *August*, too, this important dialectic with otherness as the key to self is reflected in the language of the text. August's West German passengers are approximately his age, but the character-focalized moments of the narrative reveal his sense of difference from them, as shown above. In addition, the specifically East German reference points (*Spätverkaufstelle, volkseigener Betrieb*) that mark August's memories demonstrate the degree to which he sees himself as formed by his East German experience. He is aware of this, but also recognizes the importance of engaging with West German (and post-unification) otherness as a way of remembering what has disappeared with the GDR. To some extent, this linguistic foregrounding of tension between East and West German identities is lost in the translation: the German-ness of particular terms or references is often blended out in the interests of readability, so that the GDR-specificity of August's experience is less visible, and therefore the dialogue with other perspectives is less clear. In both texts, then, the identities created and maintained by specific linguistic frameworks seem 'untranslatable', as they are embedded in language that demonstrates its own historicity. This apparent untranslatability represents a degree of resonance lost to the Anglophone reader.

While there are areas in which both translations adapt to norms of the target language or literary style, in general the stylistic preservation of Wolf's voice in *City of Angels* and *August* maintains the interpretive potential of the texts as subjective-authentic prose. This is achieved in part by reflecting the experience of the characters in the words of the narrator to reveal the difficulty of articulating experience in 'correct' forms. In addition, the fragmentedness of the narrative

---

66 Wolf, *Stadt der Engel*, p. 218.
67 Wolf, *City of Angels*, p. 164.
68 Wolf, *City of Angels*, p. 164.

voice dismantles the temporal boundary between a tellable past and a stable narrating point in the present. One review of *August* notes this temporal division:

> Wolf directs the reader between the book's two time periods. There is no space, no signal nor set-up, August's mind simply glides from one to the other, sometimes even mid-thought. But this feels wonderfully true-to-life. The thresholds between the past and the present are never fixed, and the self is a constant time-traveller.[69]

As the above examples show, then, these later renderings of Wolf's texts into English embrace her poetic voice much more explicitly than *The Quest For Christa T.* This greater sensitivity extends not just to the practice of translation, but also to the texts' resonance in the target literary system. Particularly in the case of the well-publicized *City of Angels*, commentary on the translation indicates how the enactment of Wolf's subjective authenticity has been read in the more recent Anglophone context. The promotional material and reviews for *City of Angels* suggested that the fragmentedness and instability of Wolf's narrative voice, minimized by her earlier translators, are now actively appreciated as features of her writing. There was praise for Searls' translation, with reviewers commenting on the lightness of the prose and noting favourably that Wolf's text was 'fragmented but not sprawling'.[70] Frequently acknowledging the translator's input and his stylistic compatibility with Wolf, though also applauding him for some changes to the text, reviews reflected much less concern with 'translationese' and an increased openness to difference or otherness of style in a translated text.

However, despite this recognition of the 'other' poetic voice of Wolf's original, the reviews also reflected an ongoing desire to assign the text to target-culture literary categories. Picking up on the genre announced by the front cover of the translation, several referred to the book as a 'novel' and calibrated their expectations on this basis, sometimes concluding that the text fell short of the required model. Expressing doubts about the text's 'novel' status in view of the au-

---

69 Michelle Bailat-Jones, '*August* by Christa Wolf', in *Necessary Fiction* (http://www.necessar yfiction.com/reviews/AugustbyChristaWolftranslatedbyKatyDerbyshire).
70 Anna Altman, '*City of Angels*', *New Yorker*, 11 March 2013 (http://www.newyorker.com/mag azine/2013/03/11/city-of-angels); David L. Ulin, 'Christa Wolf relives a public scandal in the novel *City of Angels*', *Los Angeles Times*, 31 January 2013 (http://articles.latimes.com/2013/jan/31/en tertainment/la-ca-jc-christa-wolf-20130203); Malcolm Forbes, 'Speak, Memory. Christa Wolf in Los Angeles', in *LA Review of Books*, (https://lareviewofbooks.org/article/speak-memory-chris ta-wolf-in-los-angeles/#); Monica Carter, '*City of Angels. Or, The Overcoat of Dr. Freud* by Christa Wolf, Trans. by Damion Searls – Why This Book Should Win', in Three Percent (http://www.ro chester.edu/College/translation/threepercent/index.php?id=10572).

tobiographical content of the text, but at the same time assuming Wolf's involvement in selecting the genre label, the *Los Angeles Review of Books* concluded that

> [o]nly Wolf could have told us how much of her book is fiction and how much is fact, but as she is in no position to do so, we will have to go with what it says on the tin. However, this makes reading the book a somewhat bizarre experience.[71]

The term is, of course, a misleading one for any Wolf text: as early as 'Lesen und Schreiben', she dismantles the *Roman* as a genre too set in rigid tradition to be an effective prose model for modern society, and in her comments to Kaufmann, she resists the application of generic categories to her writing.[72] In this respect, then, publication norms have clearly contributed to the *Darstellung* of the author and her text. As far as the politics of Wolf's writing are concerned, some reviews commented either that the prose was occasionally 'preachy' or that Wolf's politics were untranslatable and could (or should) therefore be separated out from her literary style.[73] The *LARB*, again, was more explicitly condemnatory:

> You can take the girl out of the former German Democratic Republic, but, apparently, you can't take the former German Democratic Republic out of the girl. [...] Wolf wrote like Orwell, her politics ingrained in the prose. Those who find them unpalatable may view the novel as sullied.[74]

These brief examples suggest that, while the reviews of *City of Angels* encourage a reader to engage with the style of the text, they do not invite an understanding of (and under no circumstances sympathy for) the politics and the literary framework at the heart of Wolf's mode of narration.

So far, *August* has attracted less in the way of publicity: it has not been discussed in any of the major newspapers in the USA or the UK, although it was reviewed in *World Literature Today,* and a number of reader reviews are available online. These reviews all commented on the quality of the prose, with one iden-

---

71 Forbes, 'Speak, Memory'.
72 See Wolf, 'Lesen und Schreiben', pp. 261–262; and 'Subjektive Authentizität', p. 406. Use of the category 'novel' on the back cover of the Suhrkamp German edition was treated with scepticism by some German reviewers; see, for example, Richard Kämmerlings, 'Mein Schutzengel nimmt es mit jedem Raumschiff auf', *Frankfurter Allgemeine Zeitung*, Feuilleton, 18 June 2010.
73 Unknown author, '*City of Angels or, The Overcoat of Dr. Freud*', in Kirkus Reviews, 15 October 2012 (https://www.kirkusreviews.com/book-reviews/christa-wolf/city-of-angels-wolf/); Kevin Nolan, '*City of Angels* by Christa Wolf', in The Rumpus, 2 April 2013 (http://therumpus.net/2013/04/city-of-angels-by-christa-wolf/).
74 Forbes, 'Speak, Memory'.

tifying 'a 3rd person [...] so deeply connected to its subject it very often feels like it is masquerading as a 1st', reflecting the success of Derbyshire's translation in recreating the character focalization that is so important in Wolf's writing.[75] Like the *City of Angels* reviews, they also reflect a desire to allocate a target-culture genre label to Wolf's *Erzählung*. (Is it a novella or a 'long short story'?) In addition, while some comment on the emotive power added by the text's autobiographical context, there is little interest in its specific German-ness, perhaps reflecting the translation's tendency towards anglicizing references. Thus the complex sense of otherness – seen, for example, in the portrayal of the West German tourists as intruders in August's emotional and memorial landscape – seems lost on Anglophone readers. While they appreciate the personal story at the heart of the text, Anglophone commentators do not see it as bound to the particular context in which it is set and are more inclined to read it as an exploration of universal themes. This reading moves away from the subjective-authentic principle of Wolf's writing as an exploration of experience embedded in particular social and cultural conditions and leads instead towards an understanding of the text as simply a touching, nostalgic narrative. In both cases, then, Anglophone reviewers' fixation on genre labels and their reluctance (or failure) to recognize the values at the heart of Wolf's writing reflects the degree to which her texts continue to be *dargestellt* in the interpretive frameworks of the target system. While her voice may be more effectively heard on the page, the interpretive frameworks surrounding the translation exclude the author's agency in the text.

Concluding Remarks: Re-presenting the Representative

Henry fragte Ted, den Germanisten, [...] welches Thema er eigentlich gerade am Wickel habe. Wir würden wohl lachen, sagte er. Er arbeite mit einer Gruppe von Studenten über bestimmte Aspekte der Literatur in der DDR. Sehr praktisch, sagte Henry. Ein abgeschlossenes Forschungsgebiet.[76]

[Henry asked Ted, the German professor, (...) what topic he was working on at the moment. We would laugh if he told us, he said. He was working with a group of students on aspects of literature in East Germany. Very practical, Henry said. A research field with a clearly marked beginning and end.][77]

---

75 Bailat-Jones, '*August*'.
76 Wolf, *Stadt der Engel*, p. 104.
77 Wolf, *City of Angels*, pp. 75–76.

While Searls and Derbyshire give an Anglophone reader much closer access to Wolf's literary 'voice' than earlier translations, the representative acts of *vertreten* and *darstellen* are inherent in the practices of the literary system. It is clear from the evidence presented here that 'translating subjective authenticity' involves both the individual translator and the systemic frameworks and other agents that control and (re-)present the translated text. Reflecting on the disappearance of the GDR as a cultural context for the reading of GDR literature, Volker Braun famously comments that, without this frame of reference, 'unverständlich wird mein ganzer Text' [my whole text becomes incomprehensible].[78] This may also ring true in Wolf's case: while her recent translators in particular have been sensitive to the characteristics of her textual voice, the cultural-political resonance of her writing still shifts considerably when it encounters the representative models of the Anglophone literary system curated by publishers, reviewers and readers, amongst others. Acknowledging these differing readings is not a question of 'right' and 'wrong' interpretation, but rather of understanding how the process of translation alters the resonance of the text. While readings of Wolf's texts in German are more sensitive to the historicity and specificity of her voice, the English translations have encouraged a response to Wolf as a writer concerned with universal or target-culture themes independent of her local context.

Examining the translation of subjective authenticity in the most recent Wolf translations shows how the attitudes of translators, publishers and readers towards her style have changed since the earliest renderings of her writing in English. The translation of *subjektive Authentizität* draws attention to the way in which Wolf's representativeness as a German writer in the context of world literature has relied on her representation within the poetics of target literary systems – in particular those of the Anglophone literary world. In Spivak's definition, then, she arguably remains a subaltern voice. While the author herself moved from the position of relatively unknown foreign writer in 1970 to celebrated figure in international literature by 2013/2014, her texts continued (and continue) to speak from a position that is outside the hegemonic discourse of the powerful Anglophone system. The continuing dominance of the host poetics in the Anglophone literary system ensures that, paradoxically, the global circulation of Wolf's *texts* has not always enabled Anglophone readers to hear her *voice*.

---

78 Volker Braun, 'Das Eigentum', *Zeit*, 10 August 1990.

Yutian Chen and Fan Zhang

From Political-Realistic Reading to Multiperspectival Understanding: The Reception of Christa Wolf's *Der geteilte Himmel* in China

Christa Wolf was perhaps the best-known East German writer and also one of the leading figures of German letters after German unification. Characterized by profound themes and modernist ways of writing, her works have been a focus of study for Chinese scholars for more than 30 years. *Der geteilte Himmel* (1963), her first well-known book in both East and West Germany, has been continuously read and interpreted in China since the first Chinese translation was published in 1982. Since then, two new translations have been published, in 1987 and 2012 respectively. The interpretation and understanding of the novel has continuously shifted in relation to the transitions of Chinese society. Since the end of the Cultural Revolution, Chinese society has transformed from a politically centralized society into a society of diversity and individualism.

Since the establishment of reception aesthetics, research on the reception history of a literary work has become important for critics who are trying to explore literature's value and significance. This chapter employs the work of Hans Robert Jauss and Wolfgang Iser. According to Hans Robert Jauss, there is no such thing as an objective and eternal meaning inherent within the text itself – a meaning that is immediately accessible to any interpreter.[1] Instead, the potential significance of a text is gradually revealed and realized in historical changes to readers' 'horizons of expectation':

> The obvious historical implication of this is that the understanding of the first reader will be sustained and enriched in a chain of receptions from generation to generation; in this way the historical significance of a work will be decided and its aesthetic value made evident.[2]

This article was financed and supported by the 'Research Project under Academic Guidance of Advisors of Shanghai International Studies University'.

1 See Hans Robert Jauss, *Toward an Aesthetic of Reception*, trans. by Timothy Bahti (Minneapolis: University of Minnesota Press, 1982), p. 28.
2 Ibid., p. 20.

https://doi.org/10.1515/9783110496000-015

A core concept of Jauss's theory, the idea of a reader's horizon of expectation refers, in the first place, to the aesthetic horizon of a given reader; Jauss defines it
as the 'unity of a common horizon of literary expectations, memories, and antic-
ipations that establishes [the works'] significance'.[3] Because the author of a text
is also a reader of the literature of and prior to his or her time, the text itself car-
ries the general literary expectation of the time in which it is produced: the first
expectation of the text's author and its readers. The reconstruction of the horizon
of expectation of the time in which a literary work was produced 'allows one to
determine its artistic character by the kind and the degree of its influence on a
presupposed audience'.[4] Moreover, through the tension caused by the disparity
between an existing expectation and novel circumstances, a new literary work
can lead to changes in the horizon and – upon the condition of a creative reading – to the fusion of the past and the more contemporary horizons of expectation and a concomitant establishment of further aesthetic significance. As 'the
new literary work is received and judged against the background of other
works of art as well as against the background of the everyday experience of
life',[5] the horizon of expectation of a given reader consists not only of pre-exist-
ing expectations towards literature, but is also influenced by the reader's lived
experience. However, Jauss also points out that 'the question of the subjectivity
of the interpretation and of the taste of different readers or levels of readers can
be asked meaningfully only when one has first clarified which transsubjective
horizon of understanding conditions the influence of the text'.[6] This 'transsubjective horizon of understanding' can be understood as a sort of 'collective consciousness' that functions as the precondition of the act of reading.[7] Deploying
Jauss's reception theory, this article analyses the changes in expectations towards *Der geteilte Himmel*, reconstructs the literary horizon of expectation by
providing an historicized overview of Wolf reception in China and investigates
the interaction of the reception of the novel with the social and cultural context
in China, as well as the influence of the latter on its reception over time.

From after the period of the Cultural Revolution to contemporary times, the
reception of *Der geteilte Himmel* has shifted from a political-realistic reading to a
multiperspectival understanding. It is important and complex to describe the development of this process. The reception of the novel can be divided into three

---

3 Ibid., p. 38.
4 Ibid., p. 25.
5 Ibid., p. 41.
6 Ibid., p. 23.
7 Fang Weigui, 'Literary Interpretation is a Complicated Art. Introduction of the Reception
Theory', *Social Sciences Research*, 2 (2012), 109–137 (p. 117).

phases: the 1980s, the 1990s and the twenty-first century. The 1980s, just after the great social upheaval, saw a political-realistic reading of it; the 1990s saw no new interpretations; and since the twenty-first century, as Chinese society entered an era of opening and diversity, the novel has been read multiperspectivally.

According to Wolfgang Iser's reader-response theory, the meaning of a literary work does not exist within the text but is situated somewhere in-between it and its reader.[8] Iser attached great importance to the dialogue between the text and the reader in the act of reading. The text is a construction containing indeterminacy and blanks that impel the reader towards engagement; the reader is drawn towards using his or her imagination to realize the meaning of a work. Although readers can actively participate in the generation of meaning in the reading process, their imaginations are not arbitrary, but are rather affected by the textual structure.

Consider how these ideas relate to translation. In the translation process, the translator is not only a reader of the original text, but also the author of the translation. The scholar Ma Xiao believes that 'the original of a translation is not the original text, but a virtual text that has been generated in the dialogue between the text and the translator'.[9] This virtual text is the understanding or interpretation derived by the translator from the original in the attempt to reconstruct the horizon of expectation represented in the original, which is inevitably affected by the translator's present horizon of expectation of literature in general. In the process of creating the translation, the interpretation and the way the virtual text fulfils the textual structure of the original will affect the strategies the translator applies in creating the translation. Therefore, it is also important to analyse the translation strategies of the three translations of *Der geteilte Himmel* to determine the horizons of expectation in these different phases of reception.

---

8 See Zhu Liyuan, *Introduction to Reception Aesthetics* (Hefei: Anhui Education Press, 2008), pp. 69–70.

9 Ma Xiao, 'Literary Translation in the Light of Reception Aesthetics', *Chinese Translators Journal*, 2 (2000), 47–51 (p. 48).

The Reception of *Der geteilte Himmel* in the Context of General Wolf Reception in China

Christa Wolf's name was first mentioned in 1977 in a Chinese translation of an article by a US scholar,[10] but Wolf reception in China began in earnest in the 1980s. In the 1980s, foreign literature studies in China concentrated mainly on the translation and introduction of foreign works[11] in order to fill the research gaps caused by the Cultural Revolution. The Cultural Revolution, also known as the Great Proletarian Cultural Revolution, was a sociopolitical movement that took place from 1966 until 1976. The movement was started by Mao Zedong, the Chairman of the Communist Party of China, who overestimated administrative problems and social contradictions as existential threats to Chinese socialist society.[12] Mao saw class struggle as the best way to sustain the socialist system in China and called on the masses, especially young people, to participate in the campaign of the Great Proletarian Cultural Revolution[13] so as to purify the Party by purging Chinese society of remnants of the capitalist and feudal past, thereby preventing the restoration of capitalism. Mao appealed to the masses to take up the leadership of this process and coordinate an overwhelming social upheaval that, in his firm conviction, would lead to social prosperity.[14] However, when certain reactionaries – that is to say, the Gang of Four – assumed leadership, the nation fell into a time of political turmoil in which the extremely high political pressure turned everyone against each other. In the so-called 'decade of civil strife', most aspects of social life were damaged and some were even paralyzed. Public life was completely organized around 'class struggle', which was in fact an anarchic movement that persecuted both political dissidents and ordinary people.

Despite the end of the Cultural Revolution around the year 1976, its ultra-leftist ideas – particularly the idea that class struggle and social revolution were the

---

10 Wilma Iggers, 'From Socialist Realism to a New Individualism. Some Trends in Recent East German Literature', trans. by Ning Jing, *World Literature Recent Developments*, 9 (1977), 11–23 (p. 12).
11 See Ye Jun, *German Literature Studies and Modern China* (Beijing: Beijing University, 2008), p. 409.
12 See Jin Chongji, *Outline of Chinese History in the 20ᵗʰ Century*, 3 vols. (Beijing: Social Sciences Academic Press, 2009), pp. 995–996.
13 See ibid., p. 997.
14 See ibid., p. 996.

core tasks of political and social life[15] – still impacted foreign literature studies, at least until the 1980s. Particularly in the early 1980s,[16] ideas that were critical of this ultra-leftist ideology and measures aimed at restoring normal social production were hesitantly deployed, due to the continued fear of political sanction that was carried over from the late 1970s. However, as increasing numbers of relatively democratic policies aimed at correcting the mistakes made during the Cultural Revolution were implemented in the 1980s, Chinese society began to reflect on the disaster of the Cultural Revolution. Against this background, Chinese literature – which had been the vehicle of political ideology – began to attend to the trauma that individuals went through during that catastrophic period, to concern itself with how human nature was suppressed and distorted by the Cultural Revolution and to explore the essence of literature, which had been alienated by political ideology.[17] In fact, although this political ideology still impacted Chinese culture for quite some time, reflection upon past history, humanistic concern with individuals in history and engagement with modernist and postmodernist foreign literature and literary theories had been eagerly demanded in the study of both national and foreign literature in China since well before the end of the Cultural Revolution.[18]

It is particularly difficult to generalize about the 1980s, the time immediately after the end of the Cultural Revolution, as this was a new beginning for Chinese literature and the study of foreign literature. Two concepts can be used to describe the general literary conceptions of this time: realism and modernism. The first years of the 1980s witnessed a great eagerness to restore the old tradition of realism in Chinese literature – that is to say, the realism that was established and developed before the Cultural Revolution, during which time official literature, the so-called 'further development of realism',[19] was in reality either a hymn to the Cultural Revolution and the socialist system or a celebration of class struggle.[20] Due to the particular historical development of Chinese society and

---

15 See Wei Zhiliang, 'The Impact of Ultra-leftist Ideology on Developing Socialist Modernization', *Journal of Yan'an University (Social Sciences)*, 1 (2001), 8–11, 83 (p. 8).

16 See Zha Mingjian, Xie Tianzhen, *The History of Chinese Translation Works in the 21st Century*, 2 vols. (Hubei: Hubei Education Press, 2007), p. 76.

17 See ibid., p. 766.

18 See *Modern Chinese Literature from 1900 to 2010*, 3 vols., ed. by Zhu Defa and Wei Jian (Beijing: Renmin, 2012), pp. 1329–1337.

19 Zhang Xuezheng, *Realistic Literature in Contemporary China* (Tianjin: Nankai University Press, 1997), p. 30.

20 See Wolfgang Kubin, *Chinese Literature in the 21st Century*, trans. by Fan Jin and others (Shanghai: East China Normal University Press, 2008), p. 291.

the strong heritage of the realist spirit in traditional narrative literature,[21] realism and socialist realism – sometimes linked to revolutionary romanticism – constituted the mainstream literature of the twentieth century.[22] Throughout this period, Chinese literature aimed to reflect life, reality and a concern for humanity.[23] On one hand, due to the residual impact of the ultra-leftist ideas mentioned above, realist sensibilities generally converged with political-ideological understandings of literature. On the other, the alienation of literature during the ultra-leftist time gave rise to a new trend of learning from Western modernist literature – such as symbolist, futurist, stream-of-consciousness, surrealist and existentialist literature[24] – mainly through the translation and introduction of foreign works. Chinese literature concentrated more on the artistic skills and techniques of these streams than on their theoretical discussions,[25] as it was urgently in need of renewal; before the Cultural Revolution and in the early 1980s, the study of foreign literature was not robust, and outdated conceptions of literature still influenced it. Since the middle of the 1980s, there has been an ongoing interest in studying modernist and postmodernist theories and literature, which has profoundly changed Chinese literature.[26] Some Chinese avant-garde writers began to experiment with forms such as concrete poetry and the theatre of the absurd, and Foucault, Derrida and Lacan were passionately welcomed by Chinese writers and theorists.[27]

The first years following the end of the Cultural Revolution thus saw two parallel and distinct approaches to foreign literature: a political-ideological approach and a purely aesthetic, theoretical approach. The former never disappeared in the 1980s, but the latter set the tone for the study of foreign literature at that time and began thriving from the mid-1980s. The ambivalence of Chinese foreign literature studies in this decade is exemplified by the reception of Wolf and the interpretation of *Der geteilte Himmel*.

---

21 See Feng Xiaohua, *The Epochal Tension of Realist Literature. The Poetic Value of Chinese Realist Literature in the 20th Century* (Beijing: China Social Sciences Press, 2011), pp. 3–6.
22 See ibid., pp. 13–19.
23 See Yang Bin, O*n the Development of Novels in the New Era* (Beijing: People's Press, 2011), p. 3.
24 Jiang Lasheng, *Research on Contemporary Chinese Literature*, ed. by Yangyi (Beijing: China Social Sciences Press, 2011), p. 182.
25 See Yang Chunshi, *On Modernity and Chinese Literary Trends in the 20th Century* (Beijing: SDX Joint Publishing Company, 2009), p. 273.
26 See Lasheng, *Research on Contemporary Chinese Literature*, p. 187.
27 See Hong Zicheng, *An Outline of Chinese Contemporary Literature* (Beijing: Beijing University Press, 2010), p. 166.

Der geteilte Himmel was first referred to in an article by the Germanist Xie Ying- ying in 1980 that primarily treats the situation of West German literature after the Second World War. Xie acclaims Wolf as a distinguished writer who was also influential in West Germany and reviews the novel in a single sentence, as 'a description of personal life under the influence of national division'.[28] In the same year, the Germanist Ning Ying published an article addressing the new literary trends in East German literature of the 1960s and the 1970s. According to Ning, there were four main features of the new developments in East German literature during that time: simultaneous praise for socialist society and exposure and criticism of its social ills; attention to the relationship between individuals and society; more discussion of moral and ethical problems than was evident in the 1950s; and breakthroughs and development in forms of writing.

All of Ning's examples have political implications and, in general, convey the mainstream political ideology of the early 1980s. This makes it difficult to determine the extent to which they were affected by the political approach to literature resulting from the Cultural Revolution, during which time literature could be nothing but the vehicle of political ideology. In discussing the first three trends, however, Ning did emphasize that social problems and abuses were thematized in East German literature so as to reflect social reality authentically. He also paid special attention to the relationship of individuals to society as well as interpersonal relationships. Finally, in addressing the fourth trend, Ning argued that '[socialist realism] has produced some works of low literary quality and taken on some formulaic and rigid features. What's worse, some works are even only mouthpieces of political slogans and catchwords'.[29] In our estimation, Ning's observations regarding the new trends in East German literature were in fact an implicit criticism of the ideologization and functionalization of literature during the Cultural Revolution.

In his analysis of the first trend, Ning treats *Der geteilte Himmel*. While Western scholars generally classify *Der geteilte Himmel* as *Ankunftsliteratur*, such categorizations are not found in Chinese literary investigations of this period. Instead, Ning interprets the novel very concretely as a realistic work that describes some social problems but still recognizes the benefits of the socialist system:

---

28 Xie Yingying, 'A Brief Summary of German Literature after the Second World War', *Foreign Literature*, 3 (1980), 1–12 (p. 12).
29 Ning Ying, 'On Contemporary East German Literature in the 1960s and 1970s', *World Literature Recent Developments*, 3 (1980), 2–19 (p. 17).

The exposure of bureaucracy and dogmatism was a common theme in literature of this time. Wolf's *Der geteilte Himmel* described the indifference of the leaders towards the people and the impediments to technological innovation. [...] In *Der geteilte Himmel*, despite her loss of love, Rita finds her happiness in the collective by working together with other workers.[30]

In dealing with the fourth feature – the use of new literary forms – Ying mentions *Der geteilte Himmel* as a work with an original style that delicately depicts emotion, but he analyses modern artistic techniques solely in *Nachdenken über Christa T.*[31] His focus suggests that it is the theme and the content rather than the form and technique of *Der geteilte Himmel* that interested Chinese scholars in the early 1980s.

This supposition is even more evident in Bao Zhixing's interpretation of the novel. His article 'The Contemporary German Women Writer Christa Wolf and Her Works' (1981) was the first comprehensive introduction of Wolf's life and oeuvre, including a detailed review of *Kindheitsmuster* and *Der geteilte Himmel*. On *Der geteilte Himmel*, Bao writes:

> Since its publication, the book has consistently been welcomed by readers. Even today, it is still a thought-provoking and educational novel. The German nation was divided for historical reasons, which finally led to the parting of the two lovers. However, the theme of the novel is not the unfortunate love between the figures, but the question of which road young people should choose in life. Having finished reading the book, the reader will praise Rita for her firm goal, her clear political position, her ability to distinguish between right and wrong and her love for the socialist system. A few months after Manfred's escape from East Germany, Rita went to West Berlin to see him. It was the time for Rita to make her final decision and she took the right step. [...] She made the right decision between the two kinds of social systems. Since Rita had a highly developed political consciousness and could properly handle her romantic relationship, seeing her break-up with Manfred, readers would speak highly of her correct choice and could anticipate that, instead of being sad, she would be happy in the future.[32]

Bao's analysis clearly demonstrates a political-ideological approach to the novel.

---

30 Ibid., p. 6. All translations from Chinese are our own. We thank Jennifer Ruth Hosek for revision assistance with this article.
31 Ibid., p. 18.
32 Bao Zhixing, 'The Contemporary German Woman Writer Christa Wolf and Her Works', *World Literature Recent Developments*, 3 (1981), 47–60 (pp. 54–55).

As it was strictly forbidden during the Cultural Revolution to read and re-search most foreign literature,[33] contemporary foreign literature was new territo-ry for both Chinese scholars and Chinese readers. In order to rebuild foreign lit-erature studies in China and introduce foreign language literature to Chinese readers, the Chinese Academy of Social Sciences, in cooperation with publishing houses, organized the publication of many introductory overviews that intro-duced the history of literature of a certain country or a larger region, such as Eu-rope, as well as important contemporary writers.[34] Bao's political reading of Wolf's novel was preferred in such books. For instance, *Modern European and American Literature* (1981) similarly held that the old theme of love had been in-scribed with new political content in Wolf's novel.[35] This repeated, enthusiastic praise for the politically acceptable consciousness of the protagonist shows that the ideas typical of the Cultural Revolution – such as viewing literature as a ve-hicle for political ideology – left obvious traces in literary criticism during this time.

As Ning Ying had done, Bao Zhixing noted the disclosure of social contradic-tions and abuses in the tale – which, however, in this case, we do not read as criticism of the Cultural Revolution. The distinction lies in their assessments of Wolf's relationship to socialist society, as demonstrated in *Der geteilte Himmel*. Ning depicts Wolf's faith in the socialist system as a fact that Wolf's novel dem-onstrates, Wolf's simultaneous criticism of that system notwithstanding. In con-trast, Bao tends to defend Wolf's criticism by emphasizing that Wolf 'criticized severely but appropriately, seriously but with good intention; she not only ex-posed problems, but also let them be solved to a certain extent, which gave one the impression that things became better after characters struggled with their problems'.[36]

Bao Zhixing discusses certain aspects of Wolf's thoughts on literature, as well:

> Wolf emphasizes the social function and effects of literature. She believes that the ultimate goal of literature and socialist society is to help people realize themselves, which means literature and socialist society are always striving to make people complete by reforming and producing them. Another writing principle of hers is that, instead of being consistent with political trends in their writing, an author should create a work that is artistically and

---

33 See Zha Mingjian and Xie Tianzhen, *The History of Chinese Translation Works in the 21st Cen-tury* (Hubei: Hubei Education Press, 2007), p. 754.

34 See Ye, *German Literature and the Modern China*, p. 409.

35 See 'German Literature', in *Modern European and American Literature*, ed. by Sun Fengcheng and others (Beiing: Beijing Normal University, 1981), pp. 81–111 (p. 99).

36 Bao, 'The Contemporary German Woman Writer Christa Wolf', p. 54.

truly based on their own experience. In her opinion, a writer should write freely and independently, even if they are at risk. She regards the idea that socialist art should not express
feelings in life or characterize individual differences as ridiculous.[37]

As this passage demonstrates, Bao's analysis of Wolf's thoughts on literature
concentrated mainly on the function of literature and how a writer should
write under political restrictions, rather than on literature itself.

In contrast to his discussion of *Der geteilte Himmel* and Wolf's deliberations
on literature, in his analysis of *Kindheitsmuster*, Bao analyses the multi-layered
structure of the novel and its techniques, such as its multi-layered depiction of
memory interwoven with the diegetic present and stream of consciousness. Bao
regarded the novel as artistically far less valuable than *Der geteilte Himmel*, viewing it as too complicated for readers, owing to the many comments, inferences
and philosophical theories that speak with each other in forming the narrative.[38]
This assessment indicates that Bao still interpreted the novel according to realist
norms and that modernist literary forms and techniques had not yet entered his
aesthetic horizon of expectation. The special attention Ning and Bao paid to the
political aspects of the novel stood in the tradition of Chinese realist literature
going back to 1928.[39] Ning's article already deployed criticism and reflection,
while Bao's more cautious interpretation applied more political ideology.

In 1982, the novel *Der geteilte Himmel* was first translated and published in
the literary journal *Foreign Literature Quarterly*. Zhang Rongchang analysed the
form and techniques of the work in the foreword to his translation:

> The novel has a well-knit structure. The author fills the mainly chronologically arranged
> narrative with psychological reactions, impressions and feelings of the moment, inter-
> twines the past with present reality, memories with thoughts, thus creating a uniquely nat-
> ural, exquisite and sincere mood.[40]

Zhang's attention to the structure and the techniques of the novel indicates the
changing literary horizon of expectation, which was consistent with the enthusiasm for translating and interpreting modernist works from Western countries. At
the same time, to some extent, the impact of political ideology can still be seen
in his translation, as he applied some vocabulary and expressions that con-

---

37 Ibid., pp. 51–52.
38 Ibid., pp. 59–60.
39 See *Modern Chinese Literature from 1900 to 2010*, 2 vols., ed. by Zhu Defa and Wei Jian (Beijing: Renmin, 2012), p. 565.
40 Christa Wolf, 'The Divided Heaven', trans. by Zhang Rongchang, *Foreign Literature Quarterly*,
1 (1982), 3–106 (foreword p. 3).

tained political value judgments. For example, there is a scene in chapter 23 in which Manfred is irritated rather than encouraged after hearing the news that the Soviet Union has sent an astronaut into space. He complains about the over-blown propaganda and the celebration that is about to take place and argues that the great event will change nothing in people's daily lives. Rita recalls this scene long afterwards and believes that the motivation behind Manfred's argument was: 'Der Bodensatz der Geschichte is das Unglück des einzelnen', and she describes his thought as 'entnervend'.[41] Zhang translates this sentence as: 'Individual miseries are the foundation of historical development', and he translates 'entnervend' – which actually means unnerving or daunting – as 'deca-dent'.[42] At that time, 'decadent' was a derogatory word with strong ideological connotations, used to criticize capitalist individualism.

While examples such as this show that politics drove his translation at least in part, Zhang also made great efforts to make the translation flow in the Chinese language. The language it employed was quite sophisticated – that is to say, it used many Chinese idioms and expressions in classical Chinese. In his monograph *Modern Chinese and Modern Chinese Literature*, Gao Yu put forward the viewpoint that classical Chinese and modern Chinese mirrored two different systems of mental structure, and the latter, which featured modern ideas, was the deep foundation of Chinese modern literature.[43] Gao's view of the relation-ship between modern Chinese and modern Chinese literature suggests that the linguistic style of a translation also reflects literary ideas as well as the profound social and philosophical ideas behind them. Nevertheless, Zhang's attention to the narrative structure and techniques in *Der geteilte Himmel* solely highlighted the way they functioned to build 'a uniquely natural, exquisite and sincere mood', without pointing out how they influenced the expression of subjective perceptions of and feelings towards the outside world. This indicates that, de-spite his awareness of the new form and techniques of the novel that were differ-ent from those of socialist realism, Zhang still treated them as 'decoration' of the realistic story told in the novel. His writing about the novel generally focuses on the narrative itself, such as in this characteristic selection: 'Through the different figures in this story – cadres, workers and various groups of characters – the au-thor was able to reflect the social and political conditions, the mental states and lives of people truthfully and deeply'.[44]

---

41 Christa Wolf, *Der geteilte Himmel*, 3rd edn. (Berlin/Weimar: Aufbau, 1990), p. 169.
42 Wolf, 'The Divided Heaven', trans. by Zhang Rongchang, p. 77.
43 See Gao Yu, *Modern Chinese and Chinese Modern Literature* (Beijing: China Social Sciences Press, 2003), pp. 77–90.
44 Wolf, 'The Divided Heaven', trans. by Zhang Rongchang, preface, p. 3.

In the mid-to-late 1980s, Wolf's ideas about aesthetics and the artistic techniques of her works became the focus of reception in China. The articles 'Persistent Pursuit. On Christa Wolf's Literary Quest',[45] written by Ning Ying in 1987, and 'The Subject Awareness of Christa Wolf's Creation',[46] written by Wang Shidan in 1988, focus on Wolf's concepts of 'modern prose' and analyse some of her works based on these two ideas. Ning considered the concept of 'modern prose' as a modern way of renewing traditional narrative literature, and the essence of this concept lies in the idea of 'subjective authenticity'. To be subjectively authentic, a work of literature should reflect the subjectivity of the author – that is to say, a literary work should convey the reality that the subjectivity of the author has perceived in his or her life and experience.[47] With regard to *Der geteilte Himmel*, Ning analyses the structure of the novel in the following manner:

> *Der geteilte Himmel* [...] does not have linear structure, nor does it tell a story in a chronological way. It weaves together the past and contemporary reality, memories and thoughts in the story, which is divided into many parts. It is not only the story that the author wanted to tell, but she also wanted to express her feelings about all these occurrences, to analyse and to appraise them. The description is always interrupted by comments, and there are internal thoughts and reflections inserted into the development of the storyline. We can see the author behind a seemingly simple love story.[48]

With regard to the topic of realism, while Zhang regards the novel basically as a realistic work with some modern techniques, Ning's criticism here highlights new literary conceptions that are different from realism.

In 1987, at the end of the first decade after the great turmoil, the novel was translated again, this time by Diao Chengjun, and published in book form.[49] Diao characterized Wolf's writing in the foreword to his translation in the following manner:

> Christa Wolf is good at capturing great events in the real world and has the ability to reveal complex contradictions authentically. She applies techniques such as implication, symbolism and contrast to explore the mysterious inner world of the characters and reveal the

---

45 Ning Ying, 'Persistent Pursuit. On Christa Wolf's Literary Quest', *Foreign Literature Studies*, 1 (1987), 16–22.

46 Wang Shidan, 'The Subject Awareness of Christa Wolf's Creation', *Foreign Literature Review*, 4 (1988), 71–77.

47 See Ning, 'Persistent Pursuit', pp. 17–18.

48 Ning, 'Persistent Pursuit', p. 18.

49 Christa Wolf, *The Divided Heaven,* trans. by Diao Chengjun (Chongqing: Chongqing Press, 1987).

movement of their consciousness. The employment of modern techniques in her works – including stream-of-consciousness, montage and reversal and change of time and space dimensions – has earned her the reputation of 'the avant-garde modernist of the German Democratic Republic' in Western countries.[50]

While in the early 1980s, Zhang had noted forms and techniques that were new to socialist realism, several years later, Diao defined them as distinctly modernist and Wolf as a modernist writer. As Zhang had done, Diao privileged the normative expression of the Chinese language and seldom followed the unique grammatical structure of Wolf's original work. However, Diao's translation paid special attention to the psychology and inner thoughts of the protagonist. Unlike Zhang's translation, which does not differentiate between perspectives, Diao's work used oral language to describe thoughts and inner monologue and literary language to depict external circumstances and what the characters see. Diao's special attention to multiple perspectives and linguistic modes evinces an awareness of the form of the novel and reveals more facets of the novel than the first translation.

The two primary strands of literary interpretation that characterize the early and the late 1980s respectively indicate shifts in society and concomitant horizons of expectation among readers. The increasing reception of Wolf as a modernist writer led to the more modernist works *Nachdenken über Christa T.* and *Kassandra* becoming the focus of Wolf reception in China. But the retranslation of *Der geteilte Himmel* in 1987 demonstrates its popularity, as well. The novel certainly has a high aesthetic and philosophical value, but more than this, profound cultural and historical considerations may have led to its popularity at this time. We recall that the 1980s marked a complex transition in Chinese society. The end of the Cultural Revolution and the implementation of Chinese Economic Reform in 1978 had contributed to the collapse of both traditional Chinese values and ultra-leftist political dogma.[51] Fresh values and beliefs had yet to be constructed in this new historical context. In traditional Chinese culture, the collective was valued more highly than the individual, as a result of which there was little expression of subjectivity. In addition, 2000 years of feudal monarchy had led to great emphases on loyalty and servility.[52] The foundation of the People's Republic and the socialist system had led Chinese society to expect radical transformation. However, Marxism and class struggle had been increasingly mechanically

---

50 Ibid., preface, pp. 3–4.
51 See Zhou Xiaohong, 'The Changes in the Psychological State of Chinese Society. Another Reading of Chinese Experience', *Journal of Social Science in China*, 2 (2009), 1–11 (p. 2).
52 See ibid., p. 3.

interpreted and implemented, and Chinese society had gradually been integrated into politics, a synchronization that reached its peak during the Cultural Revolution. In fact, there had been genuine and sincere political belief at the foundation of both the Republic and the Cultural Revolution. The end of the Revolution marked the end of the time in which politics was the centre of social life. With the implementation of a series of relatively democratic policies to correct the mistakes made during the Cultural Revolution, and with the Chinese Economic Reform after 1978, the development of Chinese society began anew, and most Chinese people also regained hope for the country and the future.[53] Under these circumstances, humans were also recognized as subjects of history in the complex plenitude of their being, and their pain and misery under political coercion was seen as requiring expression and solicitude.[54] In the area of literature, for instance, while 'scar literature' and 'reflection literature' marked the first years of the 1980s and the restoration of the realistic tradition,[55] the second half of the decade witnessed another form of literary expression, with an upsurge in the study of modernist and postmodernist theories and literature as a rebellion against the restriction and suppression of humanity. In this context, the attention to the life of the individual, the social criticism and the sincere faith in socialism expressed in *Der geteilte Himmel* could well have met the expectations of the contemporary Chinese reader. That resonance may be why the novel was translated twice in the 1980s.

In the 1990s, Chinese Germanists mainly translated and researched those of Wolf's works written in that same decade. The paucity of research articles was caused by the attrition of researchers, due to people leaving their previous occupations to go into business; a generalized, utilitarian mindset in the new market economic system; and the retirement of the senior generation of Germanists.[56] In the 1990s, those older Germanists who were still active concentrated on canonical German writers – such as Goethe and Schiller, Franz Kafka, Thomas Mann and Hermann Hesse – and on compiling the history of German literature.[57]

---

53 See ibid., p. 5.
54 See Chen Xiaoming, 'Boiling Blood. Chinese Literature in the Past 60 Years', *Literature and Art Forum*, 7 (2009), 28–57 (p. 40).
55 See Hong Zichang, *History of Contemporary Chinese Literature* (Beijing: Beijing University Press, 2007), p. 200.
56 See Ye Jun, *German Literature and the Modern China* (Beijing: Beijing University, 2008), p. 409.
57 See Chen Zhongyi and others, 'Study of German Literature', in *Foreign Literature Studies in Contemporary China*, ed. by Cheng Zhongyi (Beijing: China Social Sciences Press, 2011), pp. 208–214.

The 1990s was a time of tumultuous social change in China. The socialist market economy that made China's economy part of economic globalization also massively promoted the modernization of society and turned it towards consumerism. While mainstream social culture in the 1980s was guided by rationality and humanity – that is to say, by the spirit of Enlightenment – after the 1980s, with the rise of popular and consumer culture, the central discourse of political ideology and the Enlightenment was gradually disassembled, and a culture of diversity, personalization and differentiation came into being.[58] In literary study, research on postmodernist literature and theories was the absolutely dominant trend, and many postmodernist theories were translated, introduced and researched. This is very likely the second reason that so little attention was paid to Wolf during this time; her works are not fundamentally postmodernist.

As for *Der geteilte Himmel*, the novel was mentioned in only one academic article – Xie Jianwen's discussion of East German literature. Xie advanced the concept of 'arrival literature' to describe the literature from the late 1950s to the mid-1960s – 'arrival' meaning the development of young people from their initial disorientation to a reconciliation with the problems of real-existing socialist society and faith in its future.[59] Xie did not count *Der geteilte Himmel* as 'arrival literature', but rather as literature that returned to the self and to everyday life, arguing that the novel 'reflected quite frankly the conflict between the individual and society and manifested a personalized writing style and a critical attitude towards reality'.[60] Xie also held the view that attention to daily life did not mean a reduction of literary quality, but rather the addition of thematic diversity and the demonstration of writing skills.[61] His differentiation of 'arrival literature' from other, subsequent literature demonstrates that he did not count *Der geteilte Himmel* as a realist work, and his emphasis on the return to self and everyday life suggests his awareness of the subjectivity expressed in the novel.

Der geteilte Himmel has gained more attention than ever in the twenty-first century. Scholarly enthusiasm for Wolf and her works in general has grown with the development of German literature studies in China and the increasing interest in female writers and feminist theories overall since the late 1990s in Chinese academic circles.[62] From the end of the Cultural Revolution until the

---

58 See Jiang, *Research on Contemporary Chinese Literature*, pp. 329–330.
59 See Xie Jianwen and Tian Yu, 'The Trails That Cannot be Wiped Out. The Transition of East German Literature', *Journal of Social Sciences of Xiangtan University*, 2 (1999), 53–56, p. 54.
60 Ibid., p. 54.
61 See ibid.
62 See Lin Xiaoyun, *The Power Discourse of the Second Sex. Characteristics of Contemporary Feminist Literary Criticism in China* (Beijing: Chinese Market Press, 2010), pp. 26–29.

1990s, Chinese scholars translated and introduced many German writers and works that had been forbidden during the Cultural Revolution as well as a vast number of modern and contemporary German writers and works. Even though some writers of modern German classics – such as Franz Kafka und Stefan Zweig[63] – were researched in depth, work on German literature was still mainly concentrated in the introduction and legitimation of foreign research. However, such translations, introductions and basic investigations laid a solid foundation for Chinese German literature studies. In the new century, this field developed very quickly, due to the expansion of colleges and universities and the growth of German as a major. Some scholars have summarized Chinese German literature studies between 2010 and 2012 as follows:

> The awareness of independence and question-oriented consciousness has clearly been enhanced. Some classical questions have been reinterpreted through new perspectives. The horizon of literary interpretation has been broadened, and investigations have more depth. In comparison with the past, researchers have shown more solid philosophical and theoretical knowledge.[64]

This statement not only describes new trends in Chinese German literature studies in the twenty-first century, but also their direction in general.[65] Chinese scholars have increasingly researched Wolf's narrative works from multiple perspectives. For example, Yin Zhihong has analyzed *Kassandra* from the perspective of the transcendent spirit of Zen and Taoism;[66] Qi Kuaige has applied Mikhail Bakhtin's idea of polyphony and dialogue to his examination of *Medea*;[67] Chen Xiaolan has considered *Kassandra* as a reconstructed myth that revealed

---

63 See *60 Years of Foreign Literature Studies in New China. Research on Foreign Novels*, vol. 1, ed. by Shen Dan and others (Beijing: Beijing University Press, 2015), pp. 164–198.
64 *The Frontier Academic Research Report on Literature and Linguistics*, ed. by Bureau of Scientific Research Management of the Chinese Academy of Social Sciences (Beijing: China Social Sciences Press, 2014), p. 225.
65 The scholar Feng Yalin defined the lack of theoretical knowledge, the narrowness of research perspectives and the lack of criticism and reflection in her article describing the general situation of Chinese German literature studies from 2001 to 2005 as three important problems of Chinese German literature studies during this time. See Feng Yalin and others, 'Chinese German Literature Studies from 2001 to 2005', *Journal of Sichuan International Studies University*, 2 (2007), 46–53 (p. 52.). From this observation and the summary of the academic situation from 2010 to 2012, it can be concluded that Chinese German literature studies have realized their problems and improved themselves in a positive way.
66 Yin Zhihong, 'The Pursuit of Subjectivity in *Kassandra* in the Light of Eastern Philosophy', *Contemporary Foreign Literature*, 3 (2002), 95–102.
67 Qi Kuaige, 'Polyphony and Dialogue. Research on Christa Wolf's *Medea*', *Contemporary Foreign Literature*, 3 (2002), 89–94.

the cultural roots and cultural-psychological motives behind wars and killings in Western culture and *Medea* as a work that weaves gender and racial conflict into myth;[68] Zhang Fan has noted that the imageries of illness among the women protagonists in Wolf's works were metaphors for social symptoms;[69] and Jin Xiuli has researched themes of memory and forgetting from philosophical and psychological perspectives in *Stadt der Engel oder The Overcoat of Dr. Freud*.[70]

As for *Der geteilte Himmel*, Chinese Germanists have approached it in many different ways. First of all, from 2000 to 2014, the anthologies *Appreciation of One Hundred Foreign Novels from the 20th Century*[71] and *Appreciation of Foreign Literature*[72] each incorporated an excerpt of *Der geteilte Himmel* and a detailed analysis and interpretation of both its content and its form. These two volumes were not edited by Germanists, but rather by scholars from other research fields, which suggests that Wolf had become established as a foreign writer in China. In 2012, the abridged version of *Der geteilte Himmel* was selected by the famous Germanist Ye Tingfang for the book *Understand German Literature in One Book*,[73] which contains a summary of the contents of twenty important works from German literary history. In addition, two versions of *History of German Literature* – written by Li Changke and Yu Kuangfu, respectively – also added new understandings of this novel in China. The former regards the text as an important example of the 'literature of arrival', defining the term in this way:

> Belief in socialism, love for socialism and sincere praise for life in socialist society is the basic position, conviction, choice and purpose of 'arrival literature'. Moreover, it borrows the narrative experience and plot patterns from the traditional novel of education to present the development of young people. It shows how their activities in work and life conflict with the demands that socialist society laid on individuals and how they finally develop

---

68 'Gender, Race and War. On Christa Wolf's *Kassandra* und *Medea*', in Chen Xiaolan, *Gender, City and Foreign Lands. Cross-Cultural Interpretation of Literary Themes* (Shanghai: Fudan University Press, 2014), pp. 37–54.

69 Zhang Fan, 'Women's Illness as Metaphors of Epochal and Social Symptoms. On the Illness Imageries in Christa Wolf's Works', *Yilin*, 4 (2009), 208–211.

70 Jin Xiuli, 'Oblivion and Memory. On *Stadt der Engel or the Overcoat of Dr. Freud*', in *German Literature and Literary Criticism*, 7 vols., ed. by Wei Yuqing (Beijing: People's Literature Publishing House, 2013), pp. 155–171.

71 Diao Chengjun, 'The Divided Heaven of Christa Wolf', in *Appreciation of One Hundred Foreign Novels From the 20th Century*, ed. by Tao Dezhen and Zhang Zhaoke (Shenyang: Liaoning University, 2000), pp. 333–341.

72 Sun Yue, 'The Divided Heaven', in *Dictionary of Foreign Literature Appreciation*, ed. by Zhang Hong (Shanghai: Lexicographical Publishing House, 2009), pp. 186–198.

73 *Understand German Literature in One Book,* ed. by Ye Tingfang (Beijing: Beijing Institute of Technology, 2012), pp. 269–279.

themselves – with the guidance of elder workers with high ideological awareness or the help of party cadres – to be relatively mature persons that have gained new ideological consciousness and are heading for a better future full of faith and hope. The spiritual background of the writers is optimistic, healthy and free, and their works glitter with the radiance of idealism. Their works [...] also attach great importance to uncovering the 'true reality' and do not avoid facing contradictions and problems.[74]

Li emphasizes that *Der geteilte Himmel* and other 'arrival literature' demonstrated the advantage of socialism over capitalism – hence, the first aspect he notes is ideological.[75] Li also emphasizes the ideological aspect of the construction of the Berlin Wall, noting that the novel showed 'how the building of the Berlin Wall tragically split the German nation and touched a sensitive emotional site for East and West Germany, and even the international community'.[76] Previous interpretations and introductions of the novel have only paid attention to the Berlin Wall as a backdrop to the love story. Li's equal focus on Rita's well-formed socialist stance and the historical significance of the construction of the Berlin Wall suggests Li's broad cultural and historical horizon in approaching the novel. Yu Kuangfu deemed the novel a love story and then noted that, 'at the same time, the novel also highlights the question of which road young people should take and what they think is the meaning and value of life – that is to say, the question of their outlook on life'.[77] Yu does not mention any specific political or historical connotations; the 'road' here is the general choice of an individual life.

In addition to this scholarly reception, in the article 'Collective Memories in *The Divided Heaven* and *The Wall* and *The Property* [by Volker Braun]', Yin Zhihong applies a theory of collective memory to analyse the novel, investigating 'such issues as literary condensation, the reader's refiguration of the text, the influence of politics and ideology and the relationship between split identity and collective memory',[78] with the novel as one of the examples. This contribution rearticulated the historical and cultural value of *Der geteilte Himmel*, deploying

---

74 See Li Changke, 'Arrival Literature', in *History of German Literature*, 5 vols., ed. by Fan Dacan and others (Nanjing: Yilin, 2008), pp. 365–370 (pp. 369–370).
75 See ibid., p. 369.
76 Ibid., p. 369.
77 'Wolf', in Yu Kuangfu, *German Literature*, 2 vols (Shanghai: Foreign Language Education, 2013), pp. 83–90 (p. 86).
78 Yin Zhihong, 'Collective Memories in *The Divided Heaven* and *The Wall* and *The Property*', *Contemporary Foreign Literature*, 4 (2011), 128–137 (p. 128).

a cultural approach to the text, which was defined by Feng Yalin as a new trend in Chinese German literature research.[79]

In 2012, *Der geteilte Himmel* was translated for the third time and published in book form. In comparison with the other two versions that seek to comply with standards of expression in the Chinese language, this twenty-first century version tends to follow the rules of German and leaves gaps in meaning due to the structural disparity between the German and the Chinese languages. Far fewer conjunctions are used, and there are more short sentences and phrases. The many full stops leave breaks within the narrative as well, which gives the reader more room for imaginative interpretation. According to Iser, 'the more modern a text is, the more indeterminacies and blanks it has'.[80] Zhao Dan's special attention to the gaps of meaning in the work shows that he sees *Der geteilte Himmel* as a modern text that contains more ambiguity than a realist text would.

In the twenty-first century, with China's accession to the World Trade Organization and the deepening of Chinese economic reform, China's economy and also its society and culture have been pulled into the processes of globalization.[81] Chinese society has gained more freedom and tolerance than it ever had before – that is to say, many different values, demands and lifestyles are now recognized and even encouraged.[82] The commercialization and popularization of Chinese society that began in the 1990s has developed to a new degree, and consumerism and entertainment have become the most important parts of the lives of the vast majority of Chinese people.[83] The production, publishing and reading of literary works is now closely connected to the market, and literature has also become a commodity that must meet customer demands. However, the dearth of spirituality does not mean that it is unnecessary for individuals in modern China.[84] The diversity of values in society may well lead to confusion in life, especially for young people, and the 'entertainmentization' of life can

---

79 Feng Yalin, 'German Language and Literature', in *Report on Foreign Literature and Related Disciplines 2006*, ed. by Wang Lunan (Chongqing: Chongping Press, 2007), pp. 76–81 (pp. 78–79).
80 See *Big Dictionary of Foreign Aesthetics*, ed. by Zhu Liyuan (Shanghai: Lexicographical Publishing House, 2014), p. 538. Terms such as 'modern' – used here in a direct quotation from Iser – 'postmodernism' and 'modernity' are as contested in China as they are elsewhere in the world. It exceeds the framework of this article to define them completely, and we rely instead on the incomplete definitions that their contextual use yields.
81 See Yi Junqin, 'The Cultural Logic of Globalization and the Situation of Chinese Culture', *Social Science Journal*, 1 (2001), 13–33 (pp. 13–14).
82 See ibid., p. 18.
83 See ibid.
84 Meng Xianli, 'The Reconstruction of Values in Contemporary China and the Rebuilding of Chinese People's Spiritual Life', *Probe*, 2 (2016), 171–177 (p. 171).

also result in a lack of meaning. In this context, the continued popularity of *Der geteilte Himmel* may be due to the way in which this simple and concise text – with its love story that touches the heart of the modern human being, its historical and cultural background that interests readers, its depiction of the attainment of an orientation towards life after a fierce struggle – attracts young people. It may also be its socialist idealism – and its correspondence with the idea that Chinese society may need to establish new central values – that has led to the popularity of this novel in the twenty-first century.

The reception of Wolf and her oeuvre in China extends over more than 30 years. As the only work that has been repeatedly translated, *Der geteilte Himmel* has never fallen from public or scholarly view. The changes in expectations towards the novel on the part of Chinese scholars – from reading it as a realistic narrative work to interpreting it as a modern novel – show how different political and aesthetic values have been recognized and highlighted in different Chinese cultural and historical contexts. In the meantime, the novel has established itself as a classic of modern German literature in China. Based on the reception of *Der geteilte Himmel* in the twenty-first century, we can anticipate that Chinese scholars will reveal more meanings of the text and that Chinese readers will continue to read the novel in more ways than ever.

Huynh Mai Trinh
Reading Christa Wolf in Socialist Vietnam

Vietnam has a special history; its people have gotten used to the state of war. They fought against the Chinese Empire for more than two thousand years, against France during their colonization for nearly 80 years and against America for 20 years. Therefore, patriotism has been a primary theme in Vietnamese literature.

From France's invasion of Vietnam in 1858 onwards, many rebellions on the part of the colonized fomented and failed. The French established full domination and a protectorate over Vietnam from the early twentieth century, modernizing the country in various political, social and cultural aspects.

Like many other parts of the world, Vietnam encountered great changes during the twentieth century. In 1945, Vietnam declared independence from France and soon afterwards tried to reclaim control over its country, causing the first Indochina War. Vietnam won the war in 1954, and the Geneva Convention divided Vietnam into two parts with two different political systems. North Vietnam followed socialism, and South Vietnam followed market republicanism. The war to unify the two parts of the country lasted until 1975, when the country was united under the Communist government. The hostilities caused horrible pain and loss for more than 20 years, which still haunts the country 40 years later. During Vietnam's separation, the Cold War had also divided the world into two camps. When socialism collapsed in the Soviet Union during the 1990s, Vietnam faced serious challenges to its political path, and the government finally decided in favour of Renovation (the Đổi Mới policy) in 1986 – an initiative that altered the country in many ways, notably through the institution of economic reforms and the integration of the country into post-Cold War world trade.

Sixteen years into the twenty-first century, Vietnam has made great strides in innovation, development and global integration. Generally speaking, despite inconsistent pacing over time, the modernization of Vietnam over the last century has brought the country much development.

Due to the many international and transnational relationships between state-socialist countries, many North Vietnamese students, researchers and workers spent a significant part of their lives in East Germany during the 40 years of its existence. Many university professors in Vietnam, some of whom are still working today, experienced the scientific environment of socialist countries such as the Soviet Union, East Germany, Czechoslovakia and Bulgaria in the 1980s and 1990s. Thanks to this assistance from other 'brother' socialist nations, Vietnam managed to build up its human resources to construct and develop the

https://doi.org/10.1515/9783110496000-016

country. A great number of intellectuals returned to Vietnam from the Soviet Union and Eastern Europe immediately after the reunion of North and South Vietnam. Despite its short 40-year existence, East Germany contributed greatly to the construction and development of Vietnam.

Exchange between the German Democratic Republic (GDR) and the People's Republic of Vietnam included robust cultural and literary connections. At first, texts were translated into Vietnamese according to the availability of skilled translators. Thus theoretical texts – such as those of Hans Robert Jauss, a representative of the famous Konstanz school – were first derived from other translations; in the case of Jauss, from Hungarian. After several decades, the essay 'Lịch sử văn học như là sự thách thức đối với khoa học văn học' ['Literary History as a Challenge to Literary Studies'] was translated directly from Jauss's German original and published in Vietnam in 2016. Similarly, the first German literature that came to Vietnamese readers was translated from French, although shortly thereafter, more and more works were translated directly from the German originals, thanks to increasing numbers of German-language translators.

Christa Wolf in Vietnam

Vietnamese readers were introduced to Christa Wolf through the novel *Bầu trời chia cắt*, translated by Vũ Hương Giang from Wolf's original *Der geteilte Himmel* and published in Vietnam in 1985, which was 10 years after the reunion of North and South Vietnam and 20 years after the original's first publication in German. This is the only novel by Wolf that has been translated and published in Vietnam. In 2010, her two books of essays and interviews, *Reden im Herbst* [Speeches in the Fall] and *Im Dialog* [In Dialogue], were translated into Vietnamese under the title *Sống hay là bị sống* [*To Live or to Be Lived*] by Thế Dũng and Trương Thiện, published only in Germany by VIPEN Verlag. VIPEN is a Berlin-based publisher whose customer base is Vietnamese, including Germans with Vietnamese roots living in Germany and Vietnamese living in Vietnam who spent time in Germany. In terms of criticism, Wolf was discussed in an article by Trần Đương, who reviewed her novel *Der geteilte Himmel* upon its first publication in Vietnam in 1985. This review was then reprinted in the book *Văn hoá Đức tiếp xúc và cảm nhận* [*Meet and Feel German Culture*] by Trần Đương, published by Thế Giới publishing house in 2010.

Christa Wolf experienced all the highs and lows of 40 years of East Germany, and these are reflected in the development of her public persona and literary identity. Introducing her to Vietnamese readers, Trần Đương wrote:

The female writer Christa Wolf, known to Vietnamese readers as the author of the novel *Bầu trời chia cắt*, is currently living in Berlin and still working non-stop. Her works contain profound and clever judgements of society and, therefore, are widely read and highly appreciated by readers from the two parts of Germany. She was even suspected of working for the Stasi (the Ministry of State Security of the GDR), but this suspicion was quickly discarded. After the reunion of Germany, she published numerous short stories, novels and essays, such as 'Auf dem Weg nach Tabou', *Medea. Stimmen*, 'Was bleibt', 'Hierbleiben', 'Hierzulande Andernorts' and 'Sommerstücke'. Her works focus on expressing her political hope and belief and her concern about the role of literature in society, containing both joy and sorrow, surprise and memories, and even severe pain.[1]

This quote shows that Trần Đương, a Vietnamese researcher who considers Germany his second homeland, has much interest in and holds much respect for Christa Wolf and her works. Considering the fact that Wolf was not widely known in Vietnam, Trần Đương's introduction significantly and positively influenced the choices and opinions of potential readers.

Our years spent studying the reception of German literature in Vietnam seem to have been a journey to discover the fate of German works and authors in this country – for example, why a particular writer was chosen for translation in North Vietnam but not in South Vietnam, and vice versa; why certain authors – such as Hermann Hesse, Heinrich Böll and Erich Maria Remarque – were so famous at one time but easily ignored at another time; and why writers such as Anna Seghers were translated in North Vietnam before 1975. The reception of Wolf is related to the overall uptake of German literature in Vietnam – a reception that may be described as 'unstable' in that it has fluctuated according to societal shifts. This adjective points to the differences in and inconstancies of the translation, review and evaluation of German works over time. From 1954 to 1975, cultural production and perceptions of it were extremely different in South and North Vietnam, due to their political differences. South Vietnam, following the republican model, created a liberal environment in which literary translation and study could develop in various manners and directions. Meanwhile, North Vietnam, following the socialist model, solely appraised literary works from other socialist countries that focused on patriotism and enthusiasm for revolution, fighting enemies and constructing socialist society. Since the union of South and North Vietnam, fewer German literary works of any political bent have been translated, and their quality is not as high as those translated

---

1 Trần Đương, 'Văn học Đức – Đôi nét phác thảo' ['A Brief Sketch of German Literature'], in *Văn hoá Đức tiếp xúc và cảm nhận* [*Meet and Feel German Culture*], (Hanoi: Thế Giới, 2010), pp. 20–21 (p. 21). All translations from Vietnamese are my own. I would like to thank Jennifer Ruth Hosek for her particular assistance in revising this article.

previously. From 1975 to nearly the end of the twentieth century, due to the special political situation, the market for literary translation was no longer as productive and diverse as it had been prior to 1975 in South Vietnam. Marxist theory was considered the only orthodoxy for decades, and this meant limited choices in translation, research and publishing. After Đổi Mới, people had more freedom to engage other literary trends and theories. Books translated before 1975 have been reprinted and retranslated. German writers or writers writing in German who had been familiar to South Vietnamese readers – such as Hermann Hesse, E. M. Remarque, Heinrich Böll, Thomas Mann, Günter Grass, Franz Kafka and Stefan Zweig – have been retranslated or have had their new works introduced to readers in both parts of the country.

GDR literature was nevertheless well represented in unified Vietnam after 1975. The works of Christa Wolf entered the country during this period, along with those of writers such as Erwin Strittmatter, Eduard Claudius, Bertolt Brecht and Helmut Sakowski. Vietnamese readers recognized Wolf for her concern about society, her great effort in building a literary career and her political role in the GDR. Anna Seghers was the most translated female writer of the GDR before 1975, and Christa Wolf became the most well-known female writer of the GDR in the subsequent period.

In recent years, a good number of works about German literature and culture have been translated into Vietnamese. Books of literary history, an example of which we will consider below, have contributed greatly to the reconsideration of earlier evaluations of writers such as Bertolt Brecht and Anna Seghers; to encouraging diverse receptions of GDR literature; to providing more information; and to suggesting new research orientations towards writers such as the Group 47, Thomas Mann and Heinrich Böll. For example, in *Lauter schwierige Patieten* [*Very Difficult Patients*], translated by Thế Dũng and Trương Thiện as *Những con bệnh khó chiều* [*Difficult Patients*], the German literary critic Marchel Reich Ranicki converses with the German journalist Peter Voss about 12 German-language writers of the twentieth century. The essay, speech and interview collections *Reden im Herbst* and *Im Dialog* by Christa Wolf were translated and merged into one book, entitled *Sống hay là bị sống* [*To Live or to Be Lived*]. Marcel Reich Ranicki's autobiography *Mein Leben* [*My Life*], translated by Lê Chu Cầu as *Đời tôi* [*My Life*], provides a brief sketch of 40 years of the GDR. These works offer great insights, particularly because scholars on opposing political sides might have originally articulated dogmatic or otherwise biased evaluations about writers with different ideologies. It was hard to detach political influence from literature in the highly charged time periods in which they were published. Translated into Vietnamese, such books by German intellectuals about German literature, culture and politics provide Vietnamese readers with insights to help them better analyse German literature from the viewpoints of those who lived on each side of the Elbe River. Through engagement with these texts, Vietnamese readers may achieve more profound understandings of the social context and literary activities in Germany and, later, the two Germanys during the Second World War and the Cold War.

The two works by Christa Wolf that were translated into Vietnamese in 1985 and 2010 belong to different genres, but they have the same theme: divided Germany. The differences in development between West and East Germany caused young people to flee, largely from East to West Germany, to seek a better life. *Der geteilte Himmel* was written, set and published in the early 1960s. Dr. Manfred Herfurth leaves the GDR and his beloved Rita Seidel for the Federal Republic of Germany (FRG). This intellectual and scientist had contemplated long and hard before choosing to cross the border, like many other young people of his time. Wolf depicts Rita as a young woman growing up with emotional pain, disappointment and loss. She survives hard experiences in life without changing her good nature and complete faith in her country. Rita embodies an ideal young citizen in the early years of the GDR, with great love for and faith in her nation, which helps young people make the right choices.

Wolf mentions young people again in *Reden im Herbst* and *Im Dialog*, which narrate the discussions happening between 1987 and 1989, when the GDR was struggling and coming to its end. More than 20 years after *Der geteilte Himmel*, public demonstrations and hot debates between the state and the people were challenging the nation. Wolf's sense of responsibility was expressed through the characters in her novels as well as in these interviews and essays. In her discussion with Gerhard Rein about the devastating weeks in October 1989, she recalls having felt 'shocked, sad, and agonized' upon seeing 'the television repeatedly broadcast images of young people leaving their country, feeling free and laughing happily'. She wondered: 'How could they take their leave that easily? Why did they find it difficult to voice their concerns about problems in GDR and choose to stay silent?'[2] Wolf poses many questions and repeats the words 'leave easily' many times during the dialogue. Her thinking and feeling about this issue had changed over time. In *Der geteilte Himmel*, she contrasted Manfred and Rita, evoking negative feelings about Manfred's decision to leave. More than 20 years later, instead of thinking negatively about those who left, she placed heavier emphasis on the urgent need for renovation of the GDR. She wrote: 'A

---

2 Christa Wolf, 'Yêu cầu đối thoại. Christa Wolf trò chuyện với Gerhard Rein' ['Aufforderung zum Dialog. Gespräch mit Gerhard Rein'], *Sống hay là bị sống* [*Leben oder gelebt werden*], trans. by Thế Dũng and Trương Thiện (Berlin: VIPEN, 2010), pp. 77–93 (p. 77).

crisis is not always negative; it even produces positive effects. A crisis pushes people forward by activating their inner mental strength and evoking their powerful emotion'.[3] Broadly speaking, *Der geteilte Himmel* demonstrates Wolf's strong belief in the existence and development of the GDR state, while *Reden im Herbst* and *Im Dialog* show a trust in socialism in general, rather than in a specific political system.

Decades later, her statements in 'Chúng tôi không học được điều đó' ['We Have Not Learned That'] (21 October 1989), also published in *Sống hay là bị sống*, express similar ideas. She worries that:

> We can see the result on the Western televisions. Waves of young people eager and happy to leave the country. They are all well-trained technological workers, secretaries, nurses, doctors, sellers, scientists, engineers, waiters, electric-locomotive drivers, etc. I have heard musings from older people, who had not had a chance to enjoy their youthful days. They wondered what those young departers wanted when they have already been given everything.[4]

Vietnam was politically divided for 21 years, a situation similar to Germany during its 40 years of separation. North and South Vietnam, East and West Germany, carried out their processes of national development according to different orientations. To many Vietnamese, North and South Vietnam – despite their opposite political systems – were two parts of a whole country, unlike the normalized states of East and West Germany, but the feeling of worry and uncertainty that the situation evoked was still the same. In *Im Dialog*, Wolf no longer expresses her belief in the longevity of the socialist state, as she does in *Der geteilte Himmel*, but instead expresses concern about migration and hopes that the younger generation will better understand the situation of their country. Wolf hoped that the GDR government would soon recognize that the social conditions no longer suited many of the younger generation and would make the 'necessary changes, which would be inevitable'.[5] From 1975 to 1991, more than one million Vietnamese people left their country – most of them illegally, on boats. The migration peak was in 1979, when about 200,000 people left for refugee camps in Southeast Asian countries, waiting for entrance into countries such as the US and various European countries. The policies of Đổi Mới created a better social environment, encouraging people to stay with their country and build up their lives there.

---

3 Wolf, 'Yêu cầu đối thoại. Christa Wolf trò chuyện với Gerhard Rein', p. 77.
4 Christa Wolf, 'Chúng tôi không học được điều đó' ['Das haben wir nicht gelernt'], in *Sống hay là bị sống*, trans. by Thế Dũng and Trương Thiện (Berlin: VIPEN, 2010), pp. 104–110 (p. 106).
5 Wolf, 'Yêu cầu đối thoại. Christa Wolf trò chuyện với Gerhard Rein, p. 78.

No full study has evaluated the influences of Wolf's books on Vietnamese readers or their reception of her works; this contribution only gestures in that direction. Vietnamese readers came to Wolf's novel and essays based solely on the introductions of translators. The selection of these works for translation indicates the friendship, trust and hope that socialist Vietnam felt towards the GDR; the socialist political and cultural context had been prepared over decades. Wolf's political beliefs and political personality have impressed Vietnamese readers for many decades. A 2010 commentary on Christa Wolf by the Eastern German visual artist Nuria Quevedo, cited and translated in Trần Đương's 'Văn học Đức. đôi nét phác thảo', affirms Wolf's political and literary confidence, which resonates with many Vietnamese readers:

> In serious moments that may choke her breath and destroy her inspiration, she remains tough and works vigorously, proving her desirable stability in the middle of the chaos thanks to her undefeatable nature. She silently walks towards the future and the development with neither a mask nor a lie.[6]

Literary translation in particular always aims to transfer literary values and aesthetic qualities between countries and cultures. At the same time, political similarities and differences, as well as the relationships between the source and the destination countries, seriously affect translation choices with regard to both how these different language versions express the original and which texts are translated. The translator stands in-between, transferring the writer's ideas to readers, which other contributions in this volume that study translation as a cultural practice explore in more depth. *Der geteilte Himmel* was translated and published in 1985, which was the final pre-Renovation year in Vietnam. Therefore, it was necessary to be cautious in choosing books for translation. Among those chosen to be translated in this period, Christa Wolf, Anna Seghers and Bertolt Brecht were most well received by Vietnamese readers.

Scholarly Literary Reception in Vietnam

Vietnamese researchers have paid attention to literary reception since the 1970s. Nguyễn Văn Hạnh initiated the trend with his articles published in *Tạp chí Văn học* [*Literature Journal*], 'Ý kiến của Lê-nin về mối quan hệ giữa văn học và đời sống' ['Opinions of Lenin about the Relations between Literature and Life'] (1971) and 'Một số điểm cần nói rõ thêm về vấn đề nghiên cứu tác phẩm văn học' ['A

---

6 Trần, 'Văn học Đức – Đôi nét phác thảo', p. 21.

Few Issues Needing Clarification in Studying Literary Works'] (1972). *Tạp chí Văn học* also published the majority of other articles about reception. In his two articles, Nguyễn Văn Hạnh's focuses on the 'reception' stage that produces new criteria with which to evaluate books. Hoàng Trinh's 'Văn học so sánh và vấn đề tiếp nhận văn học' ['Comparative Literature and Literary Reception'] (1980) studies literary reception in comparative perspective. Vương Anh Tuấn's important articles, 'Vị trí và vai trò tích cực của người đọc trong đời sống văn học' ['The Position and Positive Role of Readers in Literary Living'] (1982) and 'Xung quanh việc tiếp nhận văn học hiện nay' ['About the Current Literary Reception'] (1990), treat readers and their characteristics, with special attention to the notion of readers-critics.[7]

The Konstanz school of reception aesthetics was introduced to Vietnam through articles by Nguyễn Văn Dân in 1985 and 1986. He and his co-workers published the book *Văn học nghệ thuật và sự tiếp nhận* [*Literature, Arts and Reception*] in 1991, in which basic terms and general issues of literary reception – such as the 'horizon of expectation', 'aesthetic distance' and 'readers' – are discussed. In recent decades, many other researchers – such as Huỳnh Vân, Trương Đăng Dung, Huỳnh Như Phương and Trần Đình Sử – have studied literary reception and literary history. The essay 'Literaturgeschichte als Provokation der Literaturwissenschaft' ['Literary History as a Provocation to Literary Studies'] by Hans Robert Jauss has been translated into Vietnamese twice, first by Trương Đăng Dung in 2002 under the title 'Lịch sử văn học như là sự khiêu khích đối với khoa học văn học' ['Literary History as a Challenge to Literary Studies'][8], and then by Huỳnh Vân in 2015–2016 under the title 'Lịch sử văn học như là sự thách thức đối với khoa học văn học' ['Literary History as a Provocation to Literary Studies'][9].

---

7 Nguyễn Văn Hạnh, 'Ý kiến của Lê-nin về mối quan hệ giữa văn học và đời sống' ['Opinions of Lenin about the Relations between Literature and Life'], *Tạp chí Văn học* [*Literature Journal*], 4 (1971), 91–99; Nguyễn Văn Hạnh, 'Một số vấn đề cần nói rõ thêm về việc nghiên cứu tác phẩm văn học' ['A Few Issues Needing Clarification in Studying Literary Works], *Tạp chí Văn học*, 6 (1972), 117–126. Hoàng Trinh, 'Văn học so sánh và vấn đề tiếp nhận văn học' ['Comparative Literature and Literary Reception'], *Tạp chí Văn học*, 4 (1980), 88–93. Vương Anh Tuấn, 'Vị trí và vai trò tích cực của người đọc trong đời sống văn học' ['Position and Positive Role of Readers in Literary Living'], *Tạp chí Văn học*, 3 (1982), 18–25; Vương Anh Tuấn, 'Xung quanh việc tiếp nhận văn học hiện nay' ['About the Current Literary Reception'], *Tạp chí Văn học*, 6 (1990), 10–15.
8 Trương Đăng Dung, 'Lịch sử văn học như là sự khiêu khích đối với khoa học văn học' ['Literary History as a Challenge to Literary Studies'], *Văn học nước ngoài* [*Foreign Literature*], 1 (2002), pp. 71–112.
9 Nguyễn Văn Dân, *Văn học, nghệ thuật và sự tiếp nhận* [*Literature, Arts, and Reception*] (Hanoi: Viện Thông tin Khoa học xã hội, 1991). Huỳnh Vân, 'Lịch sử văn học như là sự thách thức đối với

Huỳnh Vân is an important researcher of literary reception in Vietnam who specializes in the Konstanz school. In 1990, he published the article 'Quan hệ văn học – hiện thực và vấn đề tác động, tiếp nhận và giao tiếp thẩm mĩ' ['The Literature-Reality Relation and Aesthetic Impact, Reception and Communication'], in which he presented two directions of literary study: one from reality to writer to work, and the other from writer to work to reality. In another article 'Nhà văn, bạn đọc và hàng hóa sách hay văn học là sự dị trị' ['Writers, Readers and Books as Goods, or Literature as a Different Control'] (1990), Huỳnh Vân discusses the book as a special kind of commodity and highlights the market economy as an intermediary subject between writers and readers and its strong impact on literature. Huỳnh continued his study with 'Vấn đề tầm đón đợi và xác định tính nghệ thuật trong mỹ học tiếp nhận của Hans Robert Jauss' ['About the Horizon of Expectation and the Determination of Aesthetic Properties in Aesthetic Reception by Hans Robert Jauss'] (2009) and 'Hans Robert Jauss. lịch sử văn học là lịch sử tiếp nhận' ['Hans Robert Jauss. Literary History and Reception History'] (2010).[10] In recent years, he has also translated and studied works by the reception theorists Wolfgang Iser and Manfred Naumann.

The theories on literary perception that have been translated into Vietnamese are mostly those of the Konstanz school, and they have made important contributions to changing how literary works are received and interpreted. As understood in Vietnam, the Konstanz school foregrounds the experience of readers and analyses literary works in relation to their specific cultural, political and social contexts, with the aim of extricating complex meanings from the works. Political affinities can be easily identified in Vietnamese reviews of works by authors such as Anna Seghers, Bertolt Brecht, Erwin Strittmatter and Eduard Claudius. For example, Trần Đương, a writer and translator who worked in the

khoa học văn học' ['Literary History as a Provocation to Literary Studies'], *Tạp chí Khoa học Trường Đại học Văn Hiến* [*Scientific Journal of Van Hien University*], 9 (2015), 92–98; 10 (2016), 85–93; 11 (2016), 116–126.

10 Huỳnh Vân, 'Quan hệ văn học-hiện thực và vấn đề tác động, tiếp nhận và giao tiếp thẩm mĩ' ['The Literature-Reality Relation and Aesthetic Impact, Reception and Communication'], in *Văn học và hiện thực* [*Literature and Reality*] (Hanoi: Khoa học Xã hội), pp. 200–228; Huỳnh Vân, 'Nhà văn, bạn đọc và hàng hóa sách hay văn học là sự dị trị' ['Writers, Readers and Books as Goods, or Literature as a Different Control'], *Tạp chí Văn học*, 6 (1990), pp. 19–21; Huỳnh Vân, 'Vấn đề tầm đón đợi và xác định tính nghệ thuật trong mỹ học tiếp nhận của Hans Robert Jauss' ['About the Horizon of Expectation and the Determination of Aesthetic Properties in Aesthetic Reception by Hans Robert Jauss'], *Nghiên cứu văn học* [*Literary Studies*], 3 (2009), 55–71; Huỳnh Vân, 'Hans Robert Jauss. lịch sử văn học là lịch sử tiếp nhận' ['Hans Robert Jauss. Literary History and Reception History'], *Nghiên cứu văn học*, 3 (2010), 36–58.

Vietnam News Agency in Berlin for 10 years, wrote in his 1985 foreword to *Bầu trời chia cắt*:

> The novel *Bầu trời chia cắt* has brought the eminent female writer of the GDR, Christa Wolf, to Vietnamese readers. Let us give a warm welcome to this novel as a beautiful flower in the blossoming literary garden of our brother country. The novel helps us to shape a firm attitude concerning 'which direction we choose to pursue and for which ideal we fight'. The magnificent development of the GDR today has richly rewarded people who have stayed faithful to their honourable ideal, which is to devote their lives to the mutual prosperity and happiness of the working class. This reality of the GDR also confirms our belief in a glorious future for our beloved Vietnam.[11]

Every political system works to develop society according to its own doctrines, expressed in its ideological and cultural propaganda. Translations of Christa Wolf in Vietnam express this purpose well, as Trần's words from 1985 clearly show. Due in part to its particular history – based in colonialism, war and resistance – Vietnam's context for literary reception is unique. At the same time, the example of Vietnam offers a case study that illuminates the imbrication of translation and politics in the nation from which the text originates, the nation into which it is translated and even the global context – here, the Cold War and its official end.

In this investigation of the reception of GDR literature – particularly that of Christa Wolf – in Vietnam, we have so far been concerned with international exchange and the similarities between the two political systems and their literatures, as well as explicit and implicit challenges for researchers in literary reception and their motivations for seeking new layers of meanings in literary works. Now we turn to two translations of Christa Wolf's works and consider their reception in Vietnam in more detail.

About the Novel *Bầu trời chia cắt*

As mentioned above, *Der geteilte Himmel* was the first of Wolf's works to be translated into Vietnamese – by Vũ Hương Giang, from the original German. Upon its publication in 1985, *Bầu trời chia cắt* resonated in Vietnamese society, which shared the same political system with the GDR and which had just experienced 10 years of unification – 10 years that were not sufficient to heal the deep wounds caused by the 21-year separation between North and South. The political

---

11 Trần Đương, 'Lời giới thiệu' ['Introduction'], in Christa Wolf, *Bầu trời chia cắt*, trans. by Vũ Hương Giang (Hanoi: New Works, 1985), pp. 14–15.

separation in Vietnam was different from that in Germany. Germany was separated without significant bloodshed during the Cold War, as was typical of how Allied-Soviet tensions played out in the global North. In contrast, there was a 'hot' war between North and South Vietnam during their separation. Despite this difference, after national unification Vietnamese readers still found their work towards the future of their socialist state similar to what was reflected in *Bầu trời chia cắt,* including the characters, settings and ways of thinking.

The manner in which Vietnamese readers perceived Christa Wolf and *Bầu trời chia cắt* indicates what they valued in their own lives. The protagonist, Rita Seidel, shared many characteristics with Vietnamese readers at the end of the 1980s, while Manfred Herfurth, who represented waves of German young people running from the GDR to the FRG, had little influence in Vietnam. While writing this investigation, I was reminded of the waves of Vietnamese people moving from North to South Vietnam between 1954 and 1956, during the regime of Prime Minister Ngô Đình Diệm, after the Geneva Accords. People left for South Vietnam mostly for religious reasons, although some also left for economic and political reasons. From the late 1970s to the early 1980s, as mentioned above, people once again left southern Vietnam. Two-thirds of these 'boat people' were Vietnamese of Chinese origin, who were strongly affected by the border wars between Vietnam and China in those days. The rest were those who could not cope with the new regime and wished to change their lives. This was the greatest migration in the history of Vietnam.[12]

During these two migrations, many people chose to leave for their imagined wonderland – as did Manfred Herfurth. It is hard to argue that this character explicitly influenced those who left, because Wolf was introduced to Vietnamese readers after the peak time of migration had passed, and German literature was no longer as robustly translated and received as it had been in the period between 1954 and 1975. Furthermore, mass migration certainly results from a specific historical and political situation, more than from the influence of literary characters. Rita was loved by readers who stayed with their country not because they followed her choice, but because she made the same choice they did. Western readers may be more interested in Manfred and his journey in search of a potential ideal life, but Vietnamese readers seem to love Rita and her ideal characteristics. I believe that even the Vietnamese people who were not in favour of the socialist system rarely identified themselves with Manfred, while Rita was

---

12 There are neither specific statistics of successful migrants nor of unsuccessful migrants who lost their lives at sea, nor are there specific studies of the reasons for migration. Many international humanitarian organizations gave a helping hand to the Vietnamese boat people during their time of need.

read as being very similar to those who chose to stay and who believed in the future of socialism.

For many Vietnamese readers, the identificatory protagonist Rita Seidel's developing socialist personality conveyed the author's sincere belief in the GRD. Trần Đương states that 'the story narrates Rita's awareness process, from confused and disoriented to determined and capable of clearly evaluating her own life'.[13] He emphasizes her 'self-awareness' through incidents and experiences. Trần Đương praises Rita and decries Manfred, whom he considers a 'selfish, self-centred and opportunistic'[14] capitalist intellectual. This type of black-and-white evaluation was common in North Vietnam from 1945 to 1975, as well as to some extent in the following period, as seen in this 1985 text. The literature at that time sharply contrasted 'right' and 'wrong' with regard to political issues, which encouraged readers to perceive literature accordingly.

Trần Đương has reviewed many German writers in Vietnam and has consistently introduced Vietnamese literature to German readers. He worked with the translator Vũ Hương Giang to bring *Bầu trời chia cắt* to Vietnamese readers when the GDR and Vietnam shared the same political system. In his review, Trần also provided information about other contemporary writers of the GDR, such as Erwin Strittmatter, Erik Neutsch and Hermann Kant, whose works remained unfamiliar to Vietnamese readers until the early 1980s. This information and evaluation by Trần Đương aimed to orient readers towards a specific type of literature and to strengthen their political beliefs, which was necessary for a young political system that needed protection and development.

About the Literary Dialogue *Sống hay là bị sống*

Christa Wolf makes an interesting case for studying the perception of East/ern German literature in Vietnam. Those of her early and late works that are available in translation evince shifts in her long relationship to the GDR. As I will sketch below, they also resonate with shifts in the work of some Vietnamese writers. Wolf's early considerations and concerns were expressed in fiction through the characters, atmosphere and setting of *Bầu trời chia cắt*. The non-fiction dialogues in *Sống hay là bị sống*, the second Vietnamese translation of Christa Wolf's work, presented her political mind and literary heart through treatments of national changes in the GDR, including the non-violent resistance in October

---

13 Trần, 'Lời giới thiệu', p. 16.
14 Ibid., pp. 8–9.

1989 and the demonstration by intellectuals and artists on 4 November 1989. Wolf experienced every change in the GDR, from its earliest to its final days. As mentioned above, *Sống hay là bị sống* was published in Germany in 2010 and translated from the two collections *Reden im Herbst* and *Im Dialog*. While the original titles carry neutral connotations, the Vietnamese title was taken from 'Leben oder gelebt werden' [To Live or to Be Lived], the title of the dialogue between Wolf and Alfried Nehring that took place on 30 October 1989. This was a challenging period for the GDR. In using this discussion as the title for the book, the translators wanted to convey Christa Wolf's inner turmoil to Vietnamese readers. The issue of actively living or simply existing, a great concern for twentieth century European writers, was once again at the forefront in literature and public debate in Germany and Vietnam.

Sống hay là bị sống has not been available on the Vietnamese market, nor has it been widely read in Vietnam, except among researchers and a few interested readers. They find copies of the book on the Internet or seek help from German libraries. This special case of a book translated into Vietnamese and published in Germany is quite uncommon. During the Cold War and even after the unification of Germany, many Vietnamese people came to Germany for refuge, family reunion, business or study, and they find their memories reflected in *Sống hay là bị sống*. Although its potential readers in Germany number much fewer than those in Vietnam, *Sống hay là bị sống* is very meaningful to this type of reader, with its literary dialogues awakening long-ago memories for these migrants.

On the face of it, the left-leaning political elements in Christa Wolf's writings seem to adequately explain why Vũ Hương Giang chose to introduce her to Vietnamese readers. However, the matter does not end here. In *Sống hay là bị sống*, the German intellectual expressed many concerns about life and her career upon facing the last days of the GDR, from late October 1989 to January 1990. Furthermore, in her 'Bài phát biểu tạm thời' ['Provisional Speech'], presented on the occasion of receiving her honorary doctorate at the University of Hildesheim on 31 January 1990, Wolf states:

> Literature must achieve what it has achieved elsewhere. It must discover dark spots in our history and bring people to new relationships. Any attempt at self-negating will destroy the root of creativity. I beg you to give us your sympathy with criticism and attention. They may help us to know each other better, enabling us to erase old misunderstandings and prevent potential misunderstandings in the future.[15]

---

15 Christa Wolf, 'Bài phát biểu tạm thời' ['Zwischenrede'], *Sống hay là bị sống* [*Leben oder gelebt werden*], trans. by Thế Dũng and Trương Thiện (Berlin: VIPEN, 2010), pp. 194–200 (p. 200).

In articulating those concerns, Christa Wolf expressed not only her own heart, but also the hearts of many other GDR writers after German unification.

Sống hay là bị sống also contains articles and dialogues that were of significant interest to audiences in Vietnam, although many were from earlier decades, and Wolf considered some of them out-of-date when the translation was published. Gender dynamics was an important theme expressed – for instance, in the short story 'Tự thí nghiệm' ['Selbstversuch'], originally published in 1972 and adapted into a movie in 1989. Envisioning the future capabilities of medical sciences, the story describes a female scientist's sex change and considers the lives of people after changing their sex. When asked by Alfried Nehring during their dialogue whether the movie would attract more attention if it were presented internationally, Wolf replied that the eponymous movie adaptation 'strongly highlights the original theme presented in the short story, which is to criticize the entire scientific system controlled by male thinking'.[16] The GDR public received both the short story and the movie enthusiastically, which was unexpected, because GDR writers had been quite reluctant to treat similar issues in the early 1970s. Other dialogues in *Sống hay là bị sống* treat various issues related to gender as well, particularly women's rights, roles and confidence in different spheres of life. Christa Wolf also indicates her debt to Anna Seghers, the canonical GDR female writer who helped Wolf orient her literary career and the other female GDR author who was introduced to Vietnamese readers. Belonging to two different periods of GDR history, these public intellectuals nevertheless shared a special connection and impressed readers in socialist Vietnam. Due to the lack of extensive study on Christa Wolf in Vietnam, many issues in her work – such as medical sciences and feminism and her relationships to writers such as Anna Seghers – have hardly been explored; they offer a rich field of potential research topics for researchers today.

In a manner similar to that in Germany just before and after unification, Vietnam from the late 1970s to the 1980s witnessed the emergence of writers whose literary works heralded the Renovation that officially began in 1986. After the collapse of communism in the Soviet Union and other Eastern European countries around 1989, Đổi Mới escalated, and writers and researchers quickly imported and adapted Western theories into their literary production and research. This entire literary period was 'rightfully entitled the Renovation, evoking fresh inspiration about reality, fresh opinions about life, and complex and diversified think-

---

16 Christa Wolf, 'Sống hay là bị sống?' [*Leben oder gelebt werden?*], *Sống hay là bị sống* [*Leben oder gelebt werden*], trans. by Thế Dũng and Trương Thiện (Berlin: VIPEN, 2010), pp. 115–138 (p. 120).

ing about the arts'.[17] The Renovation promoted many writers who then became famous, such as Nguyễn Minh Châu, Lê Lựu, and Nguyễn Huy Thiệp,[18] whose works stir up the public, evoke endless discussion and receive repeated praise to this day. They initiated a long-term journey of discovering, changing and developing socialist literature and have never stopped their meditations about life and literature. Readers can find similarities between the shifts in perspectives in the works of these committed Vietnamese writers and the shifts in perspective in the works of Christa Wolf, as seen in *Bầu trời chia cắt* and *Sống hay là bị sống*. Values once praised and considered orthodox were re-evaluated and re-examined from different perspectives. The entire political system, which had to renovate itself, encouraged writers to contemplate topics such as individual needs, conflicting perspectives, uncertainty and choices.

During the early years of the Renovation, Nguyễn Huy Thiệp attracted public attention throughout the country with discussions of his short stories. The researcher Nguyễn Hữu Sơn, in his article 'Đọc những cách đọc và thử đọc Nguyễn Huy Thiệp' ['Methods of Reading, and Reading Nguyễn Huy Thiệp'], stated: 'It seems that the Renovation encourages readers to incline towards new things, to consider new things, the expressions of growing up in a literary mindset'.[19] During the Renovation, many Vietnamese writers turned their backs on earlier popular topics and themes, such as praising heroic deeds and collective purposes and values, and wrote more about the development of the country in the new period, with new opportunities and challenges. Literature was given the guiding slogans 'Văn học nhìn thẳng vào sự thật' ['Looking straight into the truth'] and 'Lấy dân làm gốc' ['Taking the people as the root of the country']. Writings from this period contributed greatly to Vietnamese literature as a whole, with many important topics related to life in the countryside, war and post-war experience, love and family, written from different viewpoints than those of earlier periods.

Social and economic changes before and during the Renovation, in conjunction with literary scholars' and translators' work of preparing readers' intellect

---

17 Phong Lê, *Phác thảo văn học Việt Nam hiện đại thế kỷ XX* [*Brief sketch of Vietnamese contemporary literature in the 20th century*] (Hanoi: Tri Thức, 2014), p. 317.

18 Nguyễn Minh Châu (1930–1989): novel *Những người đi từ trong rừng ra* [*People from the Forest*] (1982); short-story collection *Người đàn bà trên chuyến tàu tốc hành* [*The Woman on an Express Train*] (1983); see also the controversial essay 'Hãy đọc lời ai điếu cho một giai đoạn văn nghệ minh hoạ' ['Let Us Read a Funeral Oration to Illustrative Literature'] (1987); Lê Lựu (1942–): novels *Thời xa vắng* [*A Time Far Past*] (1986), *Sóng ở đáy sông* [*Waves in the Riverbed*] (1994), and some short stories; Nguyễn Huy Thiệp (1950–): short-story collections *Tướng về hưu* [*Retired General*] (1987), *Con gái thuỷ thần* [*Daughter of Saint Water*] (1993).

19 Nguyễn Hữu Sơn, *Luận bình văn chương* (Tiểu luận – Phê bình) [*Literary commentary (Essay-Criticism)*] (Hanoi: Văn học, 2012), p. 196.

and emotion, decreased the aesthetic distance between these readers and foreign literature. At the same time, this literature did not seem completely foreign. For instance, the description of country life, industrial activities, factory production, education and medicine in *Der geteilte Himmel* are similar to those described and narrated in 1980s novels by Nguyễn Khắc Trường, Nguyễn Mạnh Tuấn and Nguyễn Huy Thiệp[20]. Wolf challenged herself to discover new values in literature and life, even those which she did not expect to be very successful, as with the short story 'Tự thí nghiệm'. Similarly, Vietnamese writers sought to discover new values for literature around the Renovation. They immersed themselves in new topics, discovering new ways to present reality, sometimes pushing to the farthest boundaries of discovery, reconsidering and challenging many values.

In conclusion, Vietnamese readers know Christa Wolf through two translations – *Bầu trời chia cắt*, published in Vietnam in 1985, when East Germany and Vietnam shared the same political system; and *Sống hay là bị sống*, published in Germany in 2010, when the two countries had changed radically. This latter translation of Christa Wolf's thoughts about the end of the GDR and the beginning of the larger Germany was published 20 years after unification and the arrival of Vietnamese boat people in Germany; their wounds had closed enough for them to look back at those days. The two countries had similar social and political contexts, both having suffered separation, having oriented towards and against socialism and having carried out extensive renovations after national unification. After its unification, Germany followed capitalism, unlike the GDR, while after its unification, Vietnam followed socialism and later developed a market economy. In such a shifting context – and perhaps due to it – Vietnamese readers perceived Christa Wolf with the affection of brotherhood. This investigation presents the perspective of younger Wolf researchers; we have diverse readers, of course, and – as is the case with studies of reception more generally – its conclusions remain speculative. Historically speaking, Vietnamese readers have been very interested in and had much respect for German anti-fascist literature and East German literature throughout our many years of constructing socialism; Christa Wolf's contributions are key examples of such work.

---

20 Nguyễn Mạnh Tuấn (1945–): novels *Những khoảng cách còn lại* [*Remaining Distance*] (1980), *Đứng trước biển* [*Stand before the Sea*] (1982), *Cù lao tràm* [*Tea-tree Island*] (1985); Nguyễn Khắc Trường (1946–): novel *Mảnh đất lắm người nhiều ma* [*Land full of People and Ghosts*] (1990).

Collated by Sonja E. Klocke

Christa Wolf: A Select Bibliography

Primary Works

Collected Works

Wolf, Christa, *Werkausgabe in 12 Bänden*, ed. by Sonja Hilzinger (Munich: Luchterhand, 1999–2001):
Volume 1: *Der geteilte Himmel*, Erzählung (1999).
Volume 2: *Nachdenken über Christa T.* (1999).
Volume 3: *Erzählungen 1960–1980* (1999).
Volume 4: *Essays, Gespräche, Reden, Briefe 1959–1974* (1999).
Volume 5: *Kindheitsmuster* (2000).
Volume 6: *Kein Ort. Nirgends. / Der Schatten eines Traums. Karoline von Günderode – ein Entwurf. / Nun ja! Das nächste Leben geht aber heute an. Ein Brief über die Bettine* (2000).
Volume 7: *Kassandra. Voraussetzungen einer Erzählung* (2001).
Volume 8: *Essays, Gespräch, Reden, Briefe 1975–1986* (2000).
Volume 9: *Störfall. Nachrichten eines Tages / Verblendung. Disput über einen Störfall* (2001).
Volume 10: *Sommerstück / Was bleibt* (2001).
Volume 11: *Medea. Stimmen – Roman / Voraussetzungen zu einem Text* (2001).
Volume 12: *Essays, Gespräche, Reden, Briefe 1987–2000* (2001).

Works Outside of Collected Works

Prose

Wolf, Christa, *Moskauer Novelle* (Halle: Mitteldeutscher Verlag, 1961); reprinted in *Christa Wolf. Die Lust gekannt zu sein.* Wolf, Christa, *Erzählungen, 1960–1980* (Frankfurt a. M.: Suhrkamp, 2008), pp. 9–95.
Wolf, Christa, *Der geteilte Himmel* (Halle: Mitteldeutscher Verlag, 1963).
Wolf, Christa, *Juninachmittag* (Berlin: Aufbau, 1967).
Wolf, Christa, *Nachdenken über Christa T.* (Halle: Mitteldeutscher Verlag, 1968).
Wolf, Christa, 'Selbstversuch' (1973), reprinted in *Gesammelte Erzählungen* (Darmstadt: Luchterhand, 1981), pp. 158–185.
Wolf, Christa, *Unter den Linden. Drei unwahrscheinliche Geschichten* (Berlin: Aufbau, 1974).
Wolf, Christa, *Gesammelte Erzählungen* (Darmstadt/Neuwied: Luchterhand, 1974).
Wolf, Christa, 'Unter den Linden', in *Gesammelte Erzählungen* (Darmstadt/Neuwied: Luchterhand, 1974), pp. 65–117.
Wolf, Christa, *Kindheitsmuster* (Berlin: Aufbau, 1976).
Wolf, Christa, *Kein Ort. Nirgends* (Berlin: Aufbau, 1979).

https://doi.org/10.1515/9783110496000-017

Wolf, Christa, *Kassandra. Vier Vorlesungen – Eine Erzählung* (Berlin: Aufbau, 1983).

Wolf, Christa, *Kassandra. Erzählung* (Darmstadt: Luchterhand, 1983).

Wolf, Christa, *Voraussetzungen einer Erzählung. Kassandra – Frankfurter Poetik- Vorlesungen*, 2nd edn (Darmstadt: Luchterhand, 1983).

Wolf, Christa, 'The White Circle', in *Save Life on Earth*, ed. by Nyna Brael Polumbaum (Berlin: Elefanten Press, 1986), pp. 104–105.

Wolf, Christa, *Störfall. Nachrichten eines Tages* (Berlin: Aufbau, 1987; Berlin: Sammlung Luchterhand, 1987).

Wolf, Christa, *Sommerstück* (Berlin: Aufbau, 1989).

Wolf, Christa, *Was bleibt. Erzählung* (Berlin/Weimar: Aufbau, 1990; Frankfurt a. M.: Luchterhand, 1990).

Wolf, Christa, *Verblendung. Disput über einen Störfall*, (Berlin/Weimar: Aufbau, 1991).

Wolf, Christa, *Medea. Stimmen* (Munich: Luchterhand, 1996).

Wolf, Christa, *Im Stein. Mit Radierungen und Steindruck von Helge Leiberg* (Rudolfstadt: Burgart Presse, 1998).

Wolf, Christa, *Leibhaftig* (Munich: Luchterhand, 2002).

Wolf, Christa, *Ein Tag im Jahr. 1960–2000* (Munich: Luchterhand, 2003).

Wolf, Christa, *Mit anderem Blick. Erzählungen* (Frankfurt a. M.: Suhrkamp, 2005).

Wolf, Christa, *Die Lust, gekannt zu sein. Erzählungen 1960–1980* (Frankfurt a. M.: Suhrkamp, 2008).

Wolf, Christa, *Stadt der Engel oder The Overcoat of Dr. Freud* (Berlin: Suhrkamp, 2010).

Wolf, Christa, *August* (Berlin: Suhrkamp, 2012).

Wolf, Christa, *Ein Tag im Jahr im neuen Jahrhundert. 2001–2011*, ed. by Gerhard Wolf (Berlin: Suhrkamp, 2013).

Essays, Talks, Interviews and Letters

Wolf, Christa, *Lesen und Schreiben. Aufsätze und Betrachtungen* (Berlin: Aufbau, 1972).

Wolf, Christa, *Fortgesetzter Versuch. Aufsätze, Gespräche, Essays* (Leipzig: Reclam, 1979).

Wolf, Christa, *Lesen und Schreiben. Neue Sammlung* (Darmstadt: Luchterhand, 1980).

Wolf, Christa, 'Die Dimension des Autors. Gespräch mit Hans Kaufmann', in *Lesen und Schreiben. Neue Sammlung* (Darmstadt: Luchterhand, 1980), pp. 68–99.

Wolf, Christa, 'Der Schatten eines Traumes. Karoline von Günderrode – ein Entwurf', in *Lesen und Schreiben. Neue Sammlung* (Darmstadt: Luchterhand, 1980), pp. 225–283.

Wolf, Christa, *Die Dimension des Autors. Essays und Aufsätze, Reden und Gespräche 1959–1985* (Berlin: Aufbau, 1986; Darmstadt: Luchterhand, 1987).

Wolf, Christa, 'Berührung. Maxie Wander', in *Die Dimension des Autors. Essays und Aufsätze, Reden und Gespräche 1959–1985* (Darmstadt: Luchterhand, 1987) pp. 196–209.

Wolf, Christa, 'Von Büchner sprechen', in *Die Dimension des Autors. Essays und Aufsätze, Reden und Gespräche 1959–1985* (Darmstadt: Luchterhand, 1987), pp. 611–625.

Wolf, Christa, 'Zum Erscheinen des Buchs *Kassandra*. Gespräch mit Brigitte Zimmermann und Ursula Fröhlich', in *Die Dimension des Autors. Essays und Aufsätze, Reden und Gespräche 1959–1985* (Darmstadt: Luchterhand, 1987), pp. 929–940.

Wolf, Christa, *Im Dialog. Aktuelle Texte* (Frankfurt a. M.: Luchterhand, 1990).

Wolf, Christa, 'Für unser Land', in *Im Dialog. Aktuelle Texte* (Frankfurt a. M.: Luchterhand, 1990), pp. 170–171.

Wolf, Christa, *Reden im Herbst* (Berlin/Weimar: Aufbau, 1990).

Wolf, Christa, 'Unerledigte Widersprüche. Gespräch mit Therese Hörnigk' (1987/1988), in *Reden im Herbst* (Berlin/Weimar: Aufbau, 1990), pp. 24–68; and in *Christa Wolf. Werke in 13 Bänden* (1999–2003), ed. by Hilzinger, Sonja (Munich: Luchterhand, 2002) Volume 12, pp. 53–102.

Wolf, Christa, and Brigitte Reimann, *Sei gegrüßt und lebe. Eine Freundschaft in Briefen und Tagebüchern 1964–1973*, ed. by Angela Drescher (Berlin: Aufbau, 1993).

Wolf, Christa, *Auf dem Weg nach Tabou. Texte 1990–1994* (Cologne: Kiepenheuer and Witsch, 1994).

Wolf, Christa, 'Santa Monica, Sonntag, den 27. September 1992', in *Auf dem Weg nach Tabou. Texte 1990–1994* (Cologne: Kiepenheuer and Witsch, 1994), pp. 232–247.

Wolf, Christa, and Franz Fühmann, *Monsieur – wir finden uns wieder. Briefe 1968–1984*, ed. by Angela Drescher (Berlin: Aufbau, 1995).

Wolf, Christa, 'Gang durch Martin Hoffmanns Räume', in Martin Hoffmann, *Reflexe aus Papier und Schatten* (Berlin: Janus Press, 1996), pp. 103–105.

Wolf, Christa, and Gerhard Wolf, *Unsere Freunde, die Maler. Bilder Essays, Dokumente*, ed. by Peter Böthig (Berlin: Janus Press, 1996).

Wolf, Christa, and Petra Kammann, 'Warum Medea? Christa Wolf im Gespräch mit Petra Kammann am 25.1. 1996', in *Christa Wolfs Medea. Voraussetzungen zu einem Text. Mythos und Bild*, ed. by Marianne Hochgeschurz (Berlin: Janus, 1998), pp. 49–57.

Wolf, Christa, *Hierzulande. Andernorts. Erzählungen und andere Texte 1994–1998* (Munich: Luchterhand, 1999).

Wolf, Christa, 'Begegnungen Third Street', in *Hierzulande. Andernorts. Erzählungen und andere Texte 1994–1998* (Munich: Luchterhand, 1999), pp. 7–41.

Wolf, Christa, 'Von Kassandra zu Medea', in *Hierzulande. Andernorts. Erzählungen und andere Texte 1994–1998* (Munich: Luchterhand, 1999), pp. 158–168.

Wolf, Christa, and Anna Seghers, *Das dicht besetzte Leben. Briefe, Gespräche und Essays*, ed. by Angela Drescher (Berlin: Aufbau, 2003).

Wolf, Christa, and Charlotte Wolff, *Ja, unsere Kreise berühren sich. Briefe* (Munich: Luchterhand, 2004).

Wolf, Christa, *Der Worte Adernetz. Essays und Reden* (Frankfurt a. M.: Suhrkamp, 2006).

Wolf, Christa, and Hartwig Hamer, *Sommerstück/Landschaften* (Halle: Projekte-Verlag Cornelius, 2011).

Wolf, Christa, *Rede, dass ich dich sehe* (Berlin: Luchterhand, 2012).

Wolf, Christa, *Moskauer Tagebücher. Wer wir sind und wer wir waren. Reisetagebücher, Texte, Briefe, Dokumente 1957–1989*, ed. by Gerhard Wolf with Tanja Walenski (Suhrkamp: Berlin, 2014).

Wolf, Christa, *Nachruf auf Lebende. Die Flucht*, ed. by Gerhard Wolf (Berlin: Suhrkamp, 2014).

Wolf, Christa, *Man steht sehr bequem zwischen allen Fronten. Briefe 1952–2011* ed. by Sabine Wolf (Berlin: Suhrkamp, 2016).

Film Scripts

Wolf, Christa, and Konrad Wolf, *Moskauer Novelle* (film was not realized, 1961).
Wolf, Christa, and Gerhard Wolf, *Der geteilte Himmel* (director: Konrad Wolf), 1964.
Wolf, Christa, Gerhard Wolf, and Kurt Barthels, *Fräulein Schmetterling* (director: Kurt Barthels, no public viewings), 1966.
Wolf, Christa, *Die Toten bleiben jung* (based on Anna Segher's homonymous novel; director: Joachim Kunert), 1968.
Wolf, Christa, and Gerhard Wolf. *Till Eulenspiegel. Erzählung für den Film* (1972). Film based on this script (director: Rainer Simon), 1975.
Wolf, Christa, *Selbstversuch* (director: Peter Vogel), 1989.

Radio Plays

Wolf, Christa, and Gerhard Wolf, *Kein Ort. Nirgends* (director: Ernst Wendt), 1982.
Wolf, Christa, *Kassandra* (director: Ernst Wendt), 1985 and 1987.
Wolf, Christa, *Störfall* (director: Götz Fritsch), 1988.
Wolf, Christa, *Medea. Stimmen* (director: Jörg Jannings), 1997.
Wolf, Christa, *Im Stein* (director: Jörg Jannings), 1999.

English Translations

Prose

Wolf, Christa, *Divided Heaven*, trans. by Joan Becker (Berlin: Seven Seas Books, 1965; New York: Adler's Foreign Books, 1983).
Wolf, Christa, *The Quest for Christa T.*, trans. by Christopher Middleton (London: Hutchinson, 1971; New York: Farrar, Straus and Giroux, 1970).
Wolf, Christa, *A Model Childhood*, trans. by Ursule Molinaro and Hedwig Rappolt (New York: Farrar, Straus and Giroux, 1980). Later published as *Patterns of Childhood*.
Wolf, Christa, *No Place On Earth*, trans. by Jan von Heurck (New York: Farrar, Straus and Giroux, 1982).
Wolf, Christa, *Cassandra. A Novel and Four Essays*, trans. by Jan Van Heurck (New York: Farrar, Straus and Giroux, 1984).
Wolf, Christa, *Accident. A Day's News*, trans. by Heike Schwarzbauer and Rick Takvorian (Chicago: Chicago University Press, 1989; New York: Farrar, Straus, and Giroux, 1990; New York: Noonday Press, 1991).
Wolf, Christa, *What Remains and other Stories*, trans. by Heike Schwarzbauer and Rick Takvorkian (New York: Farrar, Straus and Giroux, 1993).
Wolf, Christa, 'Unter den Linden', trans. by Heike Schwarzbauer and Rick Takvorkian, in *What Remains and other Stories* (New York: Farrar, Straus and Giroux, 1993), pp. 69–120.

Wolf, Christa, 'The New Life and Opinions of a Tomcat', trans. by Heike Schwarzbauer and Rick Takvorkian, in *What Remains and other Stories* (New York: Farrar, Straus and Giroux, 1993), pp. 121–151.

Wolf, Christa, 'Self-Experiment', in *What Remains and other Stories* (Chicago: Chicago University Press, 1993), pp. 197–228.

Wolf, Christa, *Medea. A Modern Retelling*, trans. by John Cullen (New York: Doubleday, 1998).

Wolf, Christa, *In the Flesh*, trans. by John S. Barrett (Boston: David R. Godine, 2005).

Wolf, Christa, *One Day a Year. 1960–2000*, trans. by Lowell Bangerter (New York: Europa Editions, 2007).

Wolf, Christa, *City of Angels. Or, The Overcoat of Dr. Freud*, trans. by Damion Searls (New York: Farrar, Straus and Giroux, 2013).

Wolf, Christa, *August*, trans. by Katy Derbyshire (Calcutta: Seagull Books, 2014).

Wolf, Christa, *27 September. One Day A Year*, trans. by Katy Derbyshire (Chicago: Chicago University Press, 2017).

Essays, Talks, Interviews and Letters

Wolf, Christa, *The Reader and the Writer*, trans. by Joan Becker (Berlin: Seven Seas Books, 1977).

Wolf, Christa, *The Author's Dimension. Selected Essays*, trans. by Jan van Heurck (Chicago: University of Chicago Press, 1993).

Wolf, Christa, 'A Conversation with Grace Paley', in Christa Wolf, *The Author's Dimension. Selected Essays*, trans. by Jan van Heurck (Chicago: University of Chicago Press, 1993), pp. 271–282.

Wolf, Christa, *Parting from Phantoms. Selected Writings, 1990–1994*, trans. by Jan van Heurck (Chicago: University of Chicago Press, 1997).

Chinese Translations

Wolf, Christa, 分裂的天空 [*Der geteilte Himmel* (The Divided Heaven)], trans. by Zhang Rongchang, *Foreign Literature Quarterly*, 1 (1982), 3–106.

Wolf, Christa, 分裂的天空 [*Der geteilte Himmel* (The Divided Heaven)], trans. by Diao Chengjun (Chongqing: Chongqing Press, 1987).

Wolf, Christa, 分裂的天空, [*Der geteilte Himmel* (The Divided Heaven)], trans. by Zhao Dan (Beijing: Dongfang Publishing House, 2012).

Vietnamese Translations

Wolf, Christa, *Bầu trời chia cắt* [*Der Geteilte Himmel*] trans. by Vũ Hương Giang (Hanoi: New Works, 1985).

Wolf, Christa, 'Yêu cầu đối thoại. Christa Wolf trò chuyện với Gerhard Rein' ['Aufforderung zum Dialog. Gespräch mit Gerhard Rein'], in *Sống hay là bị sống* [*To Live or to Be Lived*

('Leben oder gelebt werden' – contains *Reden im Herbst* und *Im Dialog*)], trans. by Thế Dũng and Trương Thiện (Berlin: VIPEN: 2010), pp. 77–93.

Wolf, Christa, 'Chúng tôi không học được điều đó' ['Das haben wir nicht gelernt'], in *Sống hay là bị sống* [*To Live or to Be Lived*], trans. by Thế Dũng and Trương Thiện (Berlin: VIPEN, 2010), pp. 104–110.

Wolf, Christa, 'Bài phát biểu tạm thời' ['Zwischenrede'], in *Sống hay là bị sống* [*To Live or to Be Lived*], trans. by Thế Dũng and Trương Thiện (Berlin: VIPEN: 2010), pp. 194–200.

Wolf, Christa, 'Sống hay là bị sống?' ['To Live or to Be Lived'], in *Sống hay là bị sống* [*To Live or to be Lived*], trans. by Thế Dũng and Trương Thiện (Berlin: VIPEN: 2010), pp. 115–138.

Secondary Literature

Agde, Günter, ed., *Kahlschlag. Das 11. Plenum des ZK der SED 1965* (Berlin: Aufbau, 1991).

Alaimo, Stacy, *Bodily Natures. Science, Environment, and the Material Self* (Bloomington: Indiana University Press, 2010).

Ammons, Elizabeth, and Modhumita Roy, eds., *Sharing the Earth. An International Environmental Justice Reader* (Athens: University of Georgia Press, 2012).

Ankum, Katharina von, 'The Difficulty of Saying "I". Translation and Censorship of Christa Wolf's *Der geteilte Himmel*', *Studies in Twentieth Century Literature*, 17 (1993), 223–241.

Anz, Thomas, ed., *Es geht nicht um Christa Wolf. Der Literaturstreit im vereinten Deutschland* (Frankfurt a. M.: Fischer, 1991).

Bammer, Angela, 'The American Feminist Reception of GDR Literature (With a Glance at West Germany)', *GDR Bulletin*, 16.2 (Fall 1990), 18–24.

Bao, Zhixing, 'The Contemporary German Woman Writer Christa Wolf and Her Works', *World Literature Recent Developments*, 3 (1981), 47–60.

Bate, Jonathan, *Romantic Ecology. Wordsworth and the Environmental Tradition* (London/New York: Routledge, 1991).

Bathrick, David, 'Productive Mis-Reading. GDR Literature in the USA', *GDR Bulletin*, 16.2 (Fall 1990), 1–6.

Bathrick, David, *The Powers of Speech. The Politics of Culture in the GDR* (Lincoln: University of Nebraska Press, 1995).

Beebee, Thomas O., and Beverly M. Weber, 'A Literature of Theory. Christa Wolf's *Kassandra* Lectures as Feminist Anti-Poetics', *German Quarterly*, 74 (2001), 259–279.

Berkéwicz, Ulla, in *Wohin sind wir unterwegs? Zum Gedenken an Christa Wolf* (Berlin: Suhrkamp, 2012), pp. 35–38.

Boa, Elizabeth, 'Labyrinths, Mazes, and Mosaics. Fiction by Christa Wolf, Ingo Schulze, Antje Ravic Strubel, and Jens Sparschuh', in *Debating German Cultural*

Böthig, Peter, ed., *Christa Wolf. Eine Biographie in Bildern und Texten* (Munich: Luchterhand, 2004).

Bomski, Franziska, '"Moskauer Adreßbuch". Erinnerung und Engagement in Christa Wolfs *Stadt der Engel oder The Overcoat of Dr. Freud*', in *Christa Wolf. Im Strom der Erinnerung*, ed. by Carsten Gansel with Sonja Klocke (Göttingen. Vandenhoeck and Ruprecht, 2014), pp. 257–282.

Bridge, Helen, 'Christa Wolf's *Kassandra* and *Medea*. Continuity and Change', *German Life and Letters*, 57 (2004), 33–43.

Brylla, Wolfgang, 'Zur Christa-Wolf-Rezeption in Polen nach 1989,' *Studia Niemcoznawcze*, 53 (2014), 379–395.

Buehler, George, *The Death of Socialist Realism in the Novels of Christa Wolf* (Frankfurt a. M.: Peter Lang, 1984).

Caspari, Martina, 'Im Kern die Krisis. Schuld, Trauer und Neuanfang in Christa Wolfs Erzählung "Leibhaftig"', *Weimarer Beiträge*, 49.1 (2003), 135–138.

Chiarloni, Anna, 'Rezeption in Italien', in *Christa Wolf-Handbuch. Leben – Werk – Wirkung*, ed. by Carola Hilmes and Ilse Nagelschmidt (Stuttgart: Metzler, 2016), pp. 350–354.

Cirker, Willkie K., 'The Socialist Education of Rita Seidel. The Dialectics of Humanism and Authoritarianism in Christa Wolf's *Der geteilte Himmel*', *University of Dayton Review*, 13.2 (Winter 1978), 105–111.

Colombo, Daniela, '"Die Zeitgeschichten, durch die ich gegangen bin". Christa Wolf in ihren autobiografischen Texten *Kindheitsmuster* und *Stadt der Engel oder The Overcoat of Dr. Freud*', in *"Die Mauer wurde nebenbei eingerissen". Zur Literatur in Deutschland und Mittelosteuropa nach 1989/90*, ed. by Stephan Krause and Friederike Partzsch (Berlin: Frank and Timme, 2012), pp. 195–202.

Cosentino, Christine, '"Aus Teufels Küche". Gedanken zur Teufelsfigur in der Literatur nach 2000 – Christoph Heins *Willenbrock*, Christa Wolfs *Leibhaftig* und Monika Marons *Endmoränen*', *Germanic Notes and Reviews*, 35.2 (2004): 121–127.

Costabile-Heming, Carol Anne, 'Illness as Metaphor. Christa Wolf, the GDR, and Beyond', *Symposium*, 64.3 (2010): 202–219.

Costabile-Heming, Carol Anne, 'Rereading Christa Wolf's *Störfall* following the 2011 Fukushima Catastrophe', in *Catastrophe and Catharsis. Perspectives on Disaster and Redemption in German Culture and Beyond*, ed. by Katharina Gerstenberger and Tanja Nusser (London: Camden House, 2015), pp. 90–105.

d'Eaubonne, François, *Le Féminisme ou la mort* (Paris: Femmes en Mouvement, 1974).

Dahn, Daniela, in *Wohin sind wir unterwegs? Zum Gedenken an Christa Wolf* (Berlin: Suhrkamp, 2012), pp. 43–47.

Dautel, Katrin, 'Rezeption in Film und Fernsehen, im Hörspiel und auf der Bühne', in *Christa Wolf-Handbuch. Leben – Werk – Wirkung*, ed. by Carola Hilmes and Ilse Nagelschmidt (Stuttgart: Metzler, 2016), pp. 370–376.

Deiritz, Karl, and Hannes Krauss, eds., *Der deutsch-deutsche Literaturstreit oder 'Freunde, es spricht sich schlecht mit gebundener Zunge'* (Hamburg: Luchterhand, 1991).

Diamond, Irene, and Gloria Feman Orenstein, eds., *Reweaving the World. The Emergence of Ecofeminism* (San Francisco: Sierra Club, 1990).

Diao, Chengjun, 'The Divided Heaven of Christa Wolf ', in *Appreciation of One Hundred Foreign Novels from the 20th Century*, ed. by De Dezhen, Tao and Zhang Zhaoke (Shenyang: Liaoning University, 2000), pp. 333–341.

Drescher, Angela, *Dokumentation zu Christa Wolf 'Nachdenken über Christa T.'* (Hamburg: Luchterhand, 1991).

Eigler, Friederike, 'Rereading Christa Wolf's "Selbstversuch". Cyborgs and Feminist Critiques of Scientific Discourse', *The German Quarterly*, 73.4 (2000), 401–415.

Eisler, Riane, *The Chalice and the Blade. Our History, Our Future* (San Francisco: Harper, 1988).

Emmerich, Wolfgang, *Kleine Literaturgeschichte der DDR* (Berlin: Aufbau, 2000).
Eysel, Karin, 'History, Fiction, Gender. The Politics of Narrative Intervention in Christa Wolf's "Störfall"', *Monatshefte*, 84:3 (1992), 284–298.
Finney, Gail, *Christa Wolf* (New York: Twayne, 1999).
Flotow, Luise von, 'Another Time, Another Text. From Divided Heaven to They Divided the Sky', in *They Divided the Sky. A Novel by Christa Wolf* (Ottawa: University of Ottawa Press, 2013), pp. v–xxiv.
Flotow, Luise von, 'Creatively Re-transposing Christa Wolf. They Divided the Sky', in *In Translation. Honouring Sheila Fischman*, ed. by Sherry Simon (Montreal: McGill-Queen's University Press, 2013), pp. 65–82.
Fox, Thomas C., 'Feminist Revisions. Christa Wolf's *Störfall*', *German Quarterly*, 63.3–4 (1990), 471–477.
French, Marilyn, 'Trojan Woman', *The Women's Review of Books*, 2.3 (Dec. 1984), 13–14.
Fries, Marilyn Sibley, 'Christa Wolf's "Ort" in Amerika', in *Zwischen gestern und morgen. Schriftstellerinnen der DDR aus amerikanischer Sicht*, ed. by Ute Brandes (Berlin: Peter Lang, 1992), pp. 169–182.
Fuchs, Anne, Kathleen James-Chakraborty, and Linda Short, eds., *Identity Since 1989*, (Rochester: Camden House, 2011), pp. 131–155.
Gallagher, Kaleen, 'The Problem of Shame in Christa Wolf's *Stadt der Engel Oder The Overcoat of Dr. Freud*', *German Life and Letters*, 65.3 (2012), 378–397.
Gansel, Carsten, ed., with Sonja Klocke, *Christa Wolf im Strom der Erinnerung*, (Göttingen: V&R unipress, 2014).
Gansel, Carsten 'Erinnerung, Aufstörung und "blinde Flecken" im Werk von Christa Wolf', in *Christa Wolf. Im Strom der Erinnerung*, ed. by Carsten Gansel with Sonja Klocke (Göttingen: Vandenhoeck and Ruprecht, 2014), pp. 15–41.
Gansel, Carsten, and Christa Wolf, 'Zum Schreiben haben mich Konflikte getrieben. Ein Gespräch', in *Christa Wolf. Im Strom der Erinnerung*, ed. by Carsten Gansel with Sonja Klocke (Göttingen: Vandenhoeck and Ruprecht, 2014), pp. 353–366.
Gansel, Carsten, and Therese Hörnigk, eds., *Zwischen Moskauer Novelle und Stadt der Engel. Neue Perspektiven auf das Lebenswerk von Christa Wolf* (Berlin: vbb, 2015).
Gansel, Carsten, and Monika Wolting, eds., *Deutschland- und Polenbilder in der Literatur nach 1989* (Göttingen: V&R unipress, 2015).
Garrard, Greg, *Ecocriticism* (London: Routledge, 2004).
Gerstenberger, Katharina, 'Störfälle. Literary Accounts from Chernobyl to Fukushima', *German Studies Review*, 37.1 (2014), 131–148.
Gimbutas, Marija, *The Language of the Goddess. Unearthing the Hidden Symbols of Western Civilization* (New York: Harper and Row, 1989).
Glotfelty, Cheryll, 'Introduction. Literary Studies in an Age of Environmental Crisis', in *The Ecocriticism Reader. Landmarks in Literary Ecology*, ed. by Cheryll Glotfelty and Harold Fromm (Athens: University of Georgia Press, 1996), pp. xv–xxxvii.
Goodbody, Axel, and Kate Rigby, eds., *Ecocritical Theory. New European Approaches* (Charlottesville: University of Virginia Press, 2011).
Grass, Günter, 'Was bleibt. Trauerrede von Günter Grass', *Frankfurter Rundschau*, 14 December 2011.
Graves, Peter, 'The Treachery of St. Joan. Christa Wolf and the *Stasi*', *German Monitor*, 30 (1994), 1–12.

Greiner, Ulrich, 'Die deutsche Gesinnungsästhetik', *Die Zeit* 45, 2 November 1990, 63.

Güntner, Joachim, 'Weich abgefederte Selbstbefragung. *Stadt der Engel oder The Overcoat of Dr. Freud* – Christa Wolfs kalifornisches Räsonnement', *Neue Zürcher Zeitung*, 22 June 2010 (http://www.nzz.ch/weich-abgefederte-selbstbefragung-1.6201888).

Haase, Horst, 'Nachdenken über ein Buch', *Neue deutsche Literatur*, 17 (1969), 174–185.

Haase, Michael, 'Christa Wolfs letzter Selbstversuch. Zum Konzept der subjektiven Authentizität in *Stadt der Engel oder The Overcoat of Dr. Freud*', in *Christa Wolf. Im Strom der Erinnerung*, ed. by Carsten Gansel with Sonja Klocke (Göttingen: Vandenhoeck and Ruprecht, 2014), pp. 215–231.

Hage, Volker, and Susanne Beyer, 'Wir haben dieses Land geliebt. Interview mit Christa Wolf', *Der Spiegel*, 14 June 2010, pp. 134–138 (http://www.spiegel.de/spiegel/print/d-70940417.html).

Halina Ludorowska, 'Rezeption in Polen', in *Christa Wolf-Handbuch. Leben – Werk – Wirkung*, ed. by Carola Hilmes and Ilse Nagelschmidt (Stuttgart: Metzler, 2016), pp. 360–363.

Hammerstein, Katharina von, 'Warum nicht Christian T.? Christa Wolf zur Frauenfrage untersucht an einem frühen Beispiel. *Nachdenken über Christa T.*', *New German Review*, 3 (1987), 17–29.

Haraway, Donna, 'Situated Knowledges. The Science Question in Feminism and the Privilege of Partial Perspective', *Feminist Studies*, 14 (1988), 575–599.

Hell, Julia, *Post-Fascist Fantasies. Psychoanalysis, History, and the Literature of East Germany* (Durham, NC: Duke University Press, 1997).

Herrmann, Elisabeth, 'Weltbürgertum und nationale Verstrickung in Christa Wolf's *Stadt der Engel oder The Overcoat of Dr. Freud*', *Triangulum. Germanistisches Jahrbuch 2015 für Estland, Lettland und Litauen*, 21 (2016), 459–468.

Hilmes, Carola, and Ilse Nagelschmidt, eds., *Christa Wolf-Handbuch. Leben – Werk – Wirkung*, (Stuttgart: Metzler, 2016).

Hochgeschurz, Marianne, ed., *Christa Wolfs Medea. Voraussetzungen zu einem Text – Mythos und Bild*, (Berlin: Janus, 1998).

Hörnigk, Therese, *Christa Wolf* (Göttingen: Steidl, 1989).

Huyssen, Andreas, 'Traces of Ernst Bloch. Reflections on Christa Wolf', in *Responses to Christa Wolf*, ed. by Marilyn Sibley Fries (Detroit: Wayne State Press, 1989), pp. 233–247.

Iovino, Serenella, and Serpil Oppermann, 'Introduction. Stories Come to Matter', in *Material Ecocriticism*, ed. by Serenella Iovino and Serpil Oppermann (Bloomington: Indiana University Press, 2014), pp. 1–17.

Jaccaud, Silvia, 'Urban Memory in Germany. The City as a Trace of History in Christa Wolf's Kindheitsmuster and Wim Wender's Der Himmel über Berlin', in *The City in Central Europe. Culture and Society from 1800 to the Present*, ed. by Malcom Gee, Tim Kirk and Jill Steward. (Aldershot/Brookfield: Ashgate, 1999), pp. 65–82.

Jacobs, Karen, 'Speaking "Chrissandra". Christa Wolf, Bakhtin, and the Politics of the Polyvocal Text', *Narrative*, 9.3 (2001), 283–304.

Jin, Xiuli, 'Oblivion and Memory. On *City of Angels or the Overcoat of Dr. Freud*', in *German Literature and Literary Criticism*, 7 vols., ed. by Wei Yuqing (Beijing: People's Literature Publishing House, 2013), pp. 155–171.

Kähler, Hermann, 'Christa Wolfs Elegie', *Sinn und Form*, 1 (1969), 2251–2261.

Kaufmann, Hans, 'Gespräch mit Christa Wolf', *Weimarer Beiträge*, 6 (1974), 90–112.

Klocke, Sonja E., '(Anti-)faschistische Familien und (post-)faschistische Körper – Christa Wolfs *Der geteilte Himmel*', in *Christa Wolf im Strom der Erinnerung*, ed. by Carsten Gansel with Sonja Klocke (Göttingen: V&R unipress, 2014), pp. 69–87.

Klocke, Sonja E., 'The Triumph of the Obituary. Constructing Christa Wolf for the Berlin Republic', *German Studies Review*, 37.2 (2014), 317–336.

Klocke, Sonja E., *Inscription and Rebellion. Illness and the Symptomatic Body in East German Literature* (Rochester, NY: Camden House, 2015).

Klocke, Sonja E., 'Patientin unter Palmen. Symptomatische Körper, Leiden und Heilung in Christa Wolfs Stadt der Engel oder The Overcoat of Dr. Freud', *Triangulum. Germanistisches Jahrbuch 2015 für Estland, Lettland und Litauen*, 21 (2016), 469–480.

Koch, Lennart, *Ästhetik der Moral bei Christa Wolf und Monika Maron. Der Literaturstreit von der Wende bis zum Ende der neunziger Jahre* (Frankfurt a. M.: Peter Lang, 2000).

Koerner, Charlotte, 'Divided Heaven. By Christa Wolf? A Sacrifice of Message and Meaning in Translation', *The German Quarterly*, 57 (1984), 213–230.

Kuhn, Anna K., *Christa Wolf's Utopian Vision. From Marxism to Feminism* (Cambridge: Cambridge University Press, 1988).

Kuhn, Anna K., 'Rewriting GDR History. The Christa Wolf Controversy', *GDR Bulletin*, 17 (1991), 7–11.

Kuhn, Anna K., '"Eine Königin köpfen ist effektiver als einen König köpfen". The Gender Politics of the Christa Wolf Controversy', in *Women and the Wende. Social Effects and Cultural Reflections of the German Unification Process*, ed. by Elizabeth Boa and Janet Wharton (Amsterdam: Rodopi, 1994), pp. 200–215.

Kuhn, Anna K., '"Zweige vom selben Stamm"? Christa Wolf's *Was bleibt*, *Kein Ort. Nirgends*, and *Sommerstück*', in *Christa Wolf in Perspective*, ed. by Ian Wallace (Amsterdam/Atlanta: Rodopi, 1994), pp. 187–205.

Kuhn, Anna K., *Christa Wolf's Utopian Vision. From Marxism to Feminism*, 2nd edn (Cambridge/New York: Cambridge University Press, 2008).

Kuhn, Anna K., 'World Literature Today', *World Literature Today*, 85.2 (2011), 69–70.

Kuhn, Anna K., 'Of Trauma, Angels and Healing. Christa Wolf's *Stadt der Engel oder The Overcoat of Dr. Freud*', *Gegenwartsliteratur*, 10 (2011), 164–185.

Kuhn, Anna K., 'Christa Wolf. Literature as an Aesthetic of Resistance', in *Literature and the Development of Feminist Theory*, ed. by Robin Goodman (New York: Cambridge University Press, 2015), pp. 155–171.

Lance, Alain, 'Rezeption in Frankreich', in *Christa Wolf-Handbuch. Leben – Werk – Wirkung*, ed. by Carola Hilmes and Ilse Nagelschmidt (Stuttgart: Metzler, 2016), pp. 354–360.

Lefkowitz, Mary, 'Can't Fool Her', *New York Times Book Review*, 9 September 1984.

Lewis, Alison, 'Reading and Writing the Stasi File. On the Use and Abuses of the File as (Auto)Biography,' *German Life and Letters*, 54.4 (2004), 377–397.

Li, Changke, 'Arrival Literature', in *History of German Literature*, 5 vols., ed. by Fan Dacan and others (Nanjing: Yilin, 2008), pp. 365–370.

Lionnet, Françoise, and Shu-mei Shih, *Minor Transnationalism* (Durham: Duke University Press, 2005).

Love, Myra N., '"To render the blind spot of this culture visible". Christa Wolf and the Citadel of Reason', in *Responses to Christa Wolf*, ed. by Marilyn Sibley Fries (Detroit: Wayne State University Press, 1989), pp. 186–195.

Love, Myra N., 'Christa Wolf and Feminism. Breaking the Patriarchal Connection', *New German Critique*, 16 (Winter 1979), 31–53.

Ludorowska, Halina, 'Rezeption in Polen', in *Christa Wolf-Handbuch. Leben – Werk – Wirkung*, ed. by Carola Hilmes and Ilse Nagelschmidt (Stuttgart: Metzler, 2016), pp. 360–363.

Magenau, Jörg, *Christa Wolf. Eine Biographie* (Berlin: Kindler, 2002).

Maliszewska, Margaret Elzbieta, 'Reise an den "Gedächtnisort" Polen in Romanen zeitgenössischer deutscher Autorinnen' (PhD diss., Queen's University, 2009).

Mayer-Iswandy, Claudia, 'Between Resistance and Affirmation. Christa Wolf and German Unification', *Canadian Review of Comparative Literature*, 22 (1995), 813–835.

Michelis, Angelica, '"To Learn to Live without Alternatives". Forgetting as Remembering in Christa Wolf's *The City of Angels; or, The Overcoat of Dr. Freud*', *Journal of Literature and Trauma Studies*, 3 (2014), 63–80.

Minden, Michael, 'Social Hope and the Nightmare of History. Christa Wolf's *Kindheitsmuster* and *Stadt der Engel*', *Publications of the English Goethe Society*, 80 (2011), 196–203.

Mohr, Heinrich, 'Produktive Sehnsucht. Struktur, Thematik und politische Relevanz von Christa Wolfs *Nachdenken über Christa T.*', in *Basis. Jahrbuch für deutsche Gegenwartsliteratur*, vol. 2, ed. by Reinhold Grimm and Jost Hermand (Frankfurt a. M.: Athenäum, 1971), pp. 191–233.

Murphy, Patrick D., 'Dialoguing with Bakhtin over Our Ethical Responsibility to Anothers', in *Ecocritical Theory. New European Approaches*, ed. by Axel Goodbody and Kate Rigby (Charlottesville: University of Virginia Press, 2011), pp. 155–167.

Nagelschmidt, Ilse, 'Von der Zeitgenossenschaft zur Zeitzeugenschaft. Christa Wolf in Zeit- und Generationszusammenhängen', in *Christa Wolf-Handbuch. Leben – Werk – Wirkung*, ed. by Carola Hilmes and Ilse Nagelschmidt (Stuttgart: Metzler, 2016), pp. 1–62.

Ning Ying, 'On the Contemporary East German Literature in the 1960s and 1970s', *World Literature Recent Developments*, 3 (1980), 2–19.

Ning, Ying, 'Persistent Pursuit. On Christa Wolf's Literary Quest', *Foreign Literature Studies*, 1 (1987), 16–22.

'Nötige Kritik oder Hinrichtung? SPIEGEL-Gespräch mit Günter Grass über die Debatte um Christa Wolf und die DDR-Literatur', *Der Spiegel*, 29 (1990), 130–143.

Oppermann, Serpil, 'From Ecological Postmodernism to Material Ecocriticism. Creative Materiality and Narrative Agency', in *Material Ecocriticism*, ed. by Serenella Iovino and Serpil Oppermann (Bloomington: Indiana University Press, 2014), pp. 21–36.

Paul, Georgina, '"aber erzählen läßt sich nichts ohne Zeit". Time and Atemporality in Christa Wolf's Subjectively Authentic Narratives', in *The Self in Transition. East German Autobiographical Writing Before and After Unification – Essays in Honour of Dennis Tate*, ed. by David Clarke and Axel Goodbody (Amsterdam/New York: Rodopi, 2012), pp. 109–121.

Paul, Georgina, 'Feminism in the German Democratic Republic. The Discreet Charm of the Bourgeois Literary Tradition', *Oxford German Studies*, 45 (2016), 62–82.

Pinkert, Anke, 'Pleasure of Fear. Antifascist Myth, Holocaust, and Soft Dissidence in Christa Wolf's 'Kindheitsmuster', *The German Quarterly*, 76.1 (2003), 25–37.

Pinkert, Anke, 'Toward A Critical Reparative Practice in Post-1989 German Literature. Christa Wolf's *City of Angels or The Overcoat of Dr. Freud* (2010)', in *Memory and Postwar*

Memorials. Confronting the Violence of the Past, ed. by Marc Silberman and Florence Vatan (New York: Palgrave Macmillan, 2013), pp. 177–196.

Preußer, Heinz-Peter, 'Medea-Kassandra/Kassandra-Medea. Apokalyptik und Identitätssuche bei Christa Wolf', *Literatur für Leser*, 28 (2005), 241–262.

Preußer, Heinz-Peter, *Mythos als Sinnkonstruktion. Die Antikenprojekte von Christa Wolf, Heiner Müller, Stefan Schütz und Volker Braun* (Cologne: Böhlau, 2000).

Qi, Kuaige, 'Polyphony and Dialogue. Research on Christa Wolf's *Medea*', *Contemporary Foreign Literature*, 3 (2002), 89–94.

Rechtien, Renate, 'From Vergangenheitsbewältigung to Living with Ghosts. Christa Wolf's *Kindheitsmuster* and *Leibhaftig*', in *The Self in Transition. East German Autobiographical Writing Before and After Unification – Essays in Honour of Dennis Tate*, ed. by David Clarke and Axel Goodbody (Amsterdam: Rodopi, 2012), pp. 123–143.

Rechtien, Renate, 'The Topography of the Self in Christa Wolf's *Der geteilte Himmel*', *German Life and Letters*, 63.4 (2010), 475–489.

Rechtien, Renate, 'Cityscapes of the German Democratic Republic: An Interdisciplinary Approach – Introduction', *German Life and Letters*, 63.4 (2010), 369–374.

Resch, Margit, *Understanding Christa Wolf. Returning Home to a Foreign Land* (Columbia: University of South Carolina Press, 1997).

Reso, Martin, ed., *Der geteilte Himmel und seine Kritiker. Dokumentation* (Halle: Mitteldeutscher Verlag, 1965).Rigby, Kate, 'Confronting Catastrophe. Ecocriticism in a Warming World', in *The Cambridge Companion to Literature and the Environment*, ed. by Louise Westling (Cambridge: Cambridge University Press, 2013), pp. 212–225.

Rigby, Kate, 'Gernot Böhme's Ecological Aesthetics of Atmosphere', in *Ecocritical Theory. New European Approaches*, ed. by Axel Goodbody and Kate Rigby (Charlottesville: University of Virginia Press, 2011), pp. 139–152.

Rigby, Kate, 'Tragedy, Modernity, and Terra Mater. Christa Wolf Recounts the Fall', *New German Critique*, 101 (2007), 115–141.

Rossbacher, Brigitte, *Illusions of Progress. Christa Wolf and the Critique of Science in GDR Women's Literature* (New York: Peter Lang, 2000).

Rzezniczak, Damian, *DDR-Staatsdichterin oder Autorin von gesamtdeutschem Rang. Christa Wolf im Rampenlicht des kulturpolitischen Lebens der DDR* (Hamburg: Diplomica, 2005).

Sakova-Merivee, Aija, 'Die Ausgrabung der Vergangenheit in *Stadt der Engel oder The Overcoat of Dr. Freud*', in *Christa Wolf. Im Strom der Erinnerung*, ed. by Carsten Gansel with Sonja Klocke (Göttingen: Vandenhoeck and Ruprecht, 2014), pp. 245–256.

Samson, Gunhild, 'Die "neue Sprache" bei Christa Wolf. Utopie und Wirklichkeit', *Germanica* 25 (1999) (http://germanica.revues.org/2342).

Sawko-von Massow, Anna, 'Katastrophenbilder. Ein Störfall und seine Folgen in der deutschen Literatur', in *Sprache und Literatur im Spannungsfeld von Politik und Ästhetik. Christa Wolf zum 80. Geburtstag*, ed. by Sabine Fischer-Kania and Daniel Schäf (Munich: Iudicium, 2011), pp. 98–111.

Schenk, Ralf, 'Ein Gespräch mit dem Regisseur Kurt Barthel', in *'Fräulein Schmetterling', 1966–2005. Geschichte und Hintergründe* (Berlin: DEFA Stiftung and Bundesarchiv-Filmarchiv, 2005), pp. 19–27.

Schenk, Ralf, 'Informationsblatt zu Fräulein Schmetterling (DEFA 1965/2005). Zur Erstaufführung der dokumentierten Szenenfolge, Juni 2005' (Berlin: DEFA-Stiftung, 2005).

Schirrmacher, Frank, '"Dem Druck des härteren strengeren Lebens standhalten". Auch eine Studie über den autoritären Charakter – Christa Wolfs Aufsätze, Reden und ihre jüngste Erzählung *Was bleibt*', *Frankfurter Allgemeine Zeitung*, 2 June 1990.

Schoefer, Christiane, 'The Attack on Christa Wolf', *The Nation*, 251 (October 1990), 448.

Scholz, Hannelore, 'Projektionsraum Romantik', in *Christa Wolf-Handbuch. Leben – Werk – Wirkung*, ed. by Carola Hilmes and Ilse Nagelschmidt (Stuttgart: Metzler, 2016), pp. 143–163.

Schwarz, Peter Paul, and Sebastian Wilde, '"Und doch und doch…". Transformationen des Utopischen in Christa Wolfs *Stadt der Engel oder The Overcoat of Dr. Freud*', in *Christa Wolf. Im Strom der Erinnerung*, ed. by Carsten Gansel with Sonja Klocke (Göttingen: Vandenhoeck and Ruprecht, 2014), pp. 231–244.

Scribner, Charity, 'Von "Leibhaftig" aus zurückblicken. Verleugnung als Trope in Christa Wolfs Schreiben', *Weimarer Beiträge*, 50.2 (2004): 212–226.

Sevin, Dieter, *Christa Wolf. Der geteilte Himmel / Nachdenken über Christa T.*, Oldenbourg Interpetation 28 (Munich: R. Oldenbourg, 1982).

Silberman, Marc, *The Literature of the Working World* (Berlin/Frankfurt a. M.: H. Lang, 1976).

Simon, Jana, '"Weder hier noch dort gut". Interview mit Christa Wolf', *Die Zeit*, 'Kultur', 23 April 2015 (http://www.zeit.de/2015/17/christa-wolff-flucht-ddr).

Simon, Jana, *Sei dennoch unverzagt. Gespräche mit meinen Großeltern Christa und Gerhard Wolf* (Berlin: Ullstein, 2013).

Skare, Roswitha, 'Unsere Freunde, die Maler. Zum Verhältnis von Text und Bild in Christa Wolfs *Sommerstück*', in *Neulektüren – New Readings. Festschrift für Gerd Labroisse zum 80. Geburtstag*, ed. by Norbert Otto Eke and Gerhard P. Knapp (Amsterdam/New York: Rodopi, 2009), pp. 273–291.

Skare, Roswitha, 'Was bleibt, sind Bilder. Bilder als paratextuelle Elemente in Christa Wolfs "Sommerstück" und "Was bleibt"', in *Text + Kritik 46. Christa Wolf*, ed. by Nadine J. Schmidt (Munich: edition text + kritik, 2012), pp. 97–106.

Skare, Roswitha, *Christa Wolfs 'Was bleibt'. Kontext – Paratext – Text* (Münster: LIT, 2008).

Smith, Colin E., *Tradition, Art and Society. Christa Wolf's Prose* (Essen: Blaue Eule, 1987).

Starhawk, *The Fifth Sacred Thing* (New York: Bantam Books, 1993).

Stephan, Alexander, 'The Emancipation of Man. Christa Wolf as a Woman Writer', *GDR Monitor*, 2 (1979/80), 23–31.

Stephan, Alexander, *Christa Wolf*, 4th edn (Munich: Beck'sche Reihe, 1991).

Summers, Caroline, 'Patterns of Authorship. The Translation of Christa Wolf's *Kindheitsmuster*', *German Life and Letters*, 67 (2014), 378–398.

Summers, Caroline, 'World Authorship as a Struggle for Consecration. Christa Wolf and *Der geteilte Himmel* in the English-speaking world', *Seminar*, 51 (2015), 148–172.

Summers, Caroline, *Examining Text and Authorship in Translation. What Remains of Christa Wolf?* (London: Palgrave Macmillan, 2017).

Sun, Yue, 'The Divided Heaven', in *Dictionary of Foreign Literature Appreciation*, ed. by Zhang Hong (Shanghai: Lexicographical Publishing House, 2009), pp. 186–198.

Taberner, Stuart, 'Memory, Cosmopolitanism and Nation. Christa Wolf's *Stadt der Engel* (2010) and JM Coetzee's *Disgrace* (1999)', *Comparative Critical Studies*, 11.1 (2014), 49–67.

Taberner, Stuart, *Aging and Old Age Style in Günter Grass, Ruth Klüger, Christa Wolf and Martin Walser* (Rochester, NY: Camden House, 2013).

Tate, Dennis, *Shifting Perspectives. East German Autobiographical Narratives Before and After the End of the GDR* (Rochester, NY: Camden House, 2007).

Viergutz, Corinna, and Heiko Holweg: *'Kassandra' und 'Medea' von Christa Wolf. Utopische Mythen im Vergleich* (Würzburg: Königshausen and Neumann 2007).

Vincke, Hermann, ed., *Akteneinsicht Christa Wolf. Zerrspiegel und Dialog – Eine Dokumentation* (Darmstadt/Neuwied: Luchterhand, 1993).

Wang, Shidan, 'The Subject Awareness of Christa Wolf's Creation', *Foreign Literature Review*, 4 (1988), 71–77.

Warren, Karen, 'The Power and Promise of Ecological Feminism', *Environmental Ethics*, 12.2 (1990), 125–160.

Warren, Karen, and Jim Cheney, 'Ecological Feminism and Ecosystem Ecology', in *Ecological Feminist Philosophies*, ed. by Karen Warren (Bloomington: Indiana University Press, 1996), pp. 244–262.

Wilke, Sabine, '"Dieser fatale Hang der Geschichte zu Wiederholungen". Geschichtskonstruktionen in Christa Wolfs *Kindheitsmuster*', *German Studies Review*, 13.3 (1990), 499–512.

Wilke, Sabine, 'Between Female Dialogics and Traces of Essentialism. Gender and Warfare in Christa Wolf's Major Writings', *Studies in 20th & 21st Century Literature*, 17.2 (1993), 243–262.

Wilke, Sabine, 'Die Konstruktion der wilden Frau. Christa Wolfs Roman *Medea. Stimmen* als postkolonialer Text', *German Quarterly*, 76 (2003), 11–24.

Wilke, Sabine, *Ausgraben und Erinnern. Zur Funktion der Geschichte, Subjekt und geschlechtlicher Identität in den Texten Christa Wolfs* (Würzburg: Königshausen and Neumann, 1993).

Winkler, Markus, '"Kassandra", "Medea", "Leibhaftig". Tendenzen von Christa Wolfs mythologischem Erzählen vor und nach der "Wende"', in *Wende des Erinnerns? Geschichtskonstruktionen in der deutschen Literatur nach 1989*, ed. by Barbara Beßlich and others (Berlin: Schmidt, 2006), pp. 259–274.

Wittek, Bernd, *Der Literaturstreit im sich vereinigenden Deutschland* (Marburg: Tectum, 1997).

Wohin sind wir unterwegs? Zum Gedenken an Christa Wolf (Berlin: Suhrkamp, 2012).

Wolting, Monika, '"Zukunft? Das ist das gründlich Andere". Zu Aspekten der Rezeptionsgeschichte von Christa Wolf in Polen', in *Zwischen Moskauer Novelle und Stadt der Engel. Neue Perspektiven auf das Lebenswerk von Christa Wolf*, ed. by Carsten Gansel and Therese Hörnigk (Berlin: vbb, 2015), pp. 151–170.

Yin, Zhihong, 'Collective Memories in *The Divided Heaven* and *The Wall* and *The Property*', *Contemporary Foreign Literature*, 4 (2011), 128–137.

Yin, Zhihong, 'The Pursuit of Subjectivity in *Cassandra* in Light of Eastern Philosophy', *Contemporary Foreign Literature*, 3 (2002), 95–102.

Zapf, Hubert, *Literature as Cultural Ecology. Sustainable Texts.* (London: Bloomsbury, 2016).

Zehl Romero, Christiane, 'Rezeption in den USA', in *Christa Wolf-Handbuch. Leben – Werk – Wirkung*, ed. by Carola Hilmes and Ilse Nagelschmidt (Stuttgart: Metzler, 2016), pp. 363–369.

Zehl Romero, Christiane, 'Was war? Was bleibt? Was wird? Christa Wolf Then and Now', *Michigan Germanic Studies*, 21.1/2 (1995), 103–138.

Zhang, Fan, 'Women Illness as Metaphors of Epochal and Social Symptoms. On the Illness Imageries in Christa Wolfs Works', *Yilin*, 4 (2009), 208–211.

Contributors

Yutian Chen is a Ph.D. candidate of German literature at Shanghai International Studies University, PRC, China.

Regine Criser is an Assistant Professor of German at the University of North Carolina at Asheville, USA.

Birgit Dahlke is a Professor of German Literature, leading the research institute for Christa and Gerhard Wolf's private library at Humboldt University Berlin, Germany.

Anna Horakova is Harvard College Fellow in the Department of Germanic Languages and Literatures at Harvard University, USA.

Jennifer Ruth Hosek is an Associate Professor in Languages, Literatures and Cultures at Queen's University in Ontario, Canada.

Deborah Janson is an Associate Professor of German at West Virginia University, USA.

Sonja Klocke is an Associate Professor of German and Gender and Women's Studies at the University of Wisconsin – Madison, USA.

Anna K. Kuhn is Professor Emerita of Gender, Sexuality, and Women's Studies (GSWS) at the University of California – Davis, USA.

Sabine von Mering is a Professor of German and Women's, Gender, and Sexuality Studies at Brandeis University, USA.

John Pizer is Professor of German and Comparative Literature at Louisiana State University, USA.

Roswitha Skare is a Professor in Documentation Studies at the University of Tromsö – The Arctic University of Norway, Norway.

Catherine Smale is a Lecturer in German at King's College London, UK.

Caroline Summers is a Lecturer in Comparative Literary Translation at the University of Leeds, UK.

Curtis Swope is an Associate Professor in the Department of Modern Languages at Trinity University in San Antonio, USA.

Huynh Mai Trinh is a lecturer at Vanhien University – Hochiminh City, Vietnam.

https://doi.org/10.1515/9783110496000-018

Beverly Weber is an Associate Professor of German at the University of Colorado – Boulder, USA.

Fan Zhang is a literary critic, translator, and Professor of German at Shanghai International Studies University, PRC, China.

Index